DISNEY'S
WORLD

"Veteran biographer Leonard Mosley shows us the Disney that was airbrushed out of the official, authorized histories. Though he was an entrepreneurial wizard, and one of the giants of American film, the private Disney was a driven, insecure and often tyrannical human being." – *Newsday*

"We see a man driven by dreams. Recommended."
– *Providence (Rhode Island) Journal*

"Eminently satisfying. An excellent, informative, readable book."
– *Best Sellers*

"Watching a Mickey Mouse cartoon will never be the same. Mosley does an admirable job of presenting a balanced view of Disney."
– *Wilson Library Bulletin*

"Walt Disney could have made quite a movie from this book. It reads with all the page-turning fascination of a good novel. Disney has been the subject of at least three other biographies. Mosley's book is the best of the lot."
– *The Tulsa Tribune*

"A fitting epitaph for a true American genius." – *Detroit Free Press*

ALSO BY LEONARD MOSLEY

NONFICTION
Zanuck: The Last of the Hollywood Tycoons
Marshall: Hero for Our Times
The Druid
Blood Relations: The Rise and Fall of the du Ponts of Delaware
Dulles: A Biography of Eleanor, Allen and John Foster Dulles
Lindbergh: A Biography
The Reichsmarshal: A Biography of Hermann Goering
Power Play: Oil in the Middle East
Backs to the Wall: London in World War II
On Borrowed Time: How World War II Began
Hirohito: Emperor of Japan
The Battle of Britain
Haile Selassie: The Conquering Lion
Faces for the Fire: A Biography of Sir Archibald McIndoe
The Glorious Fault: The Life of Lord Curzon
The Last Days of the British Raj
The Cat and the Mice: A German Spy in Cairo
Duel for Kilimanjaro
Castlerosse: The Life of a Bon Vivant
Gideon Goes to War: A Biography of Orde Wingate
Report from Germany: 1945
Downstream, 1939
So Far So Good: A Fragment of Autobiography

FICTION
The Seductive Mirror
Each Had a Song
War Lord
No More Remains
So I Killed Her

DISNEY'S WORLD

A biography by

LEONARD MOSLEY

Scarborough House/*Publishers*

Scarborough House/Publishers
Chelsea, MI 48118

FIRST SCARBOROUGH HOUSE
PAPERBACK EDITION 1990

Disney's World was originally published in hardcover by
Stein and Day/Publishers.

Library of Congress Cataloging-in-Publication Data

Mosley, Leonard, 1913-
  Disney's world: a biography / by Leonard Mosley. -- 1st
Scarborough House pbk. ed.
     p.   cm.
  Reprint, with rev. epilogue. Originally published: New York :
Stein and Day, 1985.
  Includes index.
  ISBN 0-8128-8514-7
  1. Disney, Walt, 1901-1966.   2. Animators--United States-
-Biography.   I. Title.
[NC1766.U52D553   1990]
791.43'092--dc20
[B]   90-41402
                                                                CIP

CONTENTS

LIST OF ILLUSTRATIONS

ACKNOWLEDGMENTS

NO ONE WITH long and happy memories of a legend wants to have them too woefully disturbed, and this biography is not intended to upset or destroy the image so many people cherish of that remarkable American Walt Disney.

Since Disney is regarded by millions of people, particularly in the United States, as perhaps this century's most brilliantly successful creator of screen animation, I think I should make one thing clear right away. I share the general admiration of a man whose cinematic achievements were always so happily inspired and inspiriting. But—and this is where I differ from uncritical idolators—I have to know all the facts, no matter how unpalatable, as well as all the romantic myths about any great man or woman I admire. Many of the myths that have been created by his publicists about Walt Disney are unpalatable, unbelievable, and unsatisfactory because so much of the real Walt Disney has been deliberately concealed.

As I have tried to show in most of my previous biographies, particularly the one I wrote about my own special childhood hero, Charles Augustus Lindbergh, I am suspicious of a legend whose image is so artificially polished that it shows no lines or warts on the face, no faults in the interior makeup, no flaws or weaknesses in the character. In some ways I sympathize with George Kaufman, who once remarked about Lindbergh that "the trouble is all heroes are horses' asses." By that he meant that Lindbergh was often his own worst enemy and many of the most painful episodes in his life were due to faults of arrogance and pride.

Walt Disney, though totally unlike Lindbergh, also had grave flaws in his character—and in some ways I find that comforting. I do not believe in perfect people, especially perfect heroes. I have to know all the facts about what they were really like, convinced as I am that they, too, must have had their imperfections, their weaknesses, just like all of us, and are therefore measurable men and women capable of being not only admired but emulated, too, even if not equaled.

I first became aware that Walt Disney was, thank God, a human being—with all the faults as well as virtues that such a state entails—when I went to see him at his studio in Burbank in the fifties. I was then film critic for the London *Daily Express* on one of my biannual visits to Hollywood. The studio publicity machines in the film colony had, as usual, gone out of their way to try to persuade me, as a writer for a powerfully influential British newspaper, that this was a city of flawless gods and goddesses, full of clean-living, sanitized stars. No one ever got drunk (not even Ava Gardner), no one ever beat her children (not even Joan Crawford), no one ever cheated on his wife (not even Jack Warner or Clark Gable or Darryl Zanuck).

It was even more of a deodorized world at the Walt Disney Studio where the publicity men insisted their boss was faultless—never drank too much, never used a swearword, never lost his temper, never quarreled with his wife or family, never let down a friend. And woe betide anyone who tried to suggest otherwise. Members of the resident foreign and local press risked their jobs if they dared to write stories inferring that Walt Disney could be domineering, implacable, and unforgiving (as was the case, for instance, before, during, and after the 1941 studio strike). The Disney flacks were capable of exerting heavy pressure on editors and proprietors or, through the advertising pages, against anyone who inferred Walt Disney was not the epitome of well-scrubbed and benevolent perfection.

A few days spent talking to Disney's family, directors, technicians, animators, and artists soon revealed a very different version of the great man. I even encountered one of his most gifted collaborators, whose later comments figure largely in these pages, who maintained he was writing Walt's biography and calling it A GREAT MAN BUT—THE TRUTH ABOUT WALT DISNEY. (What happened to that project I never discovered from our later conversations. Certainly, it never saw the light of day. Pressure? Censorship?) The extracts he read me and the accounts he gave me of what life was like working with Disney, when added to the rueful anecdotes of his associates, helped, even that long ago, to reassure me. Walt Disney was not, after all, the whiter-than-white sepulcher the studio propagandists made him out to be, but a remarkably talented and mortal human being who did regrettable things, too; he was, in fact, a far from perfect and therefore much more fascinating man—one not to be worshiped or drooled over but written about with all his blemishes showing.

While not neglecting his virtues or his genius, this biography has included most of those blemishes. I hope and believe his image has been enlarged rather than diminished because of that.

THIS BOOK PROBABLY would never have been written had it not been for the encouraging insistence over the years of one very good friend, the well-known screenwriter and novelist Jack Davies, who has written scripts for most of the famous producers in the world, with the exception of Walt Disney. But he knew him well and met him frequently during his long and distinguished career and always sensed that there was much more to learn about this unique American phenomenon than has been revealed in the many books about him. Jack pushed me into continuing my researches, even during moments of great difficulty and setbacks, and I thank him for his amiable persistence.

As I have already indicated, so far as the facts in this book are concerned, they are based on research going back to the fifties; more recently this culminated in several long stays in Hollywood and Burbank as well as sessions with Disney alumni in all parts of the world. I cannot, for space and other reasons, name all of the Disney associates and veterans to whom I have talked; some of them, for instance, have insisted on anonymity because, they point out, they still rely on the goodwill of the Disney organization for pensions and medical insurance. But wherever they are quoted in this book, they have read the remarks they made to me and have had the opportunity of checking, cutting (or expanding) what they told me in the course of their tape-recorded conversations.

In the case of the Disney organization, they have *not* seen anything of the text. However, I think I should stress that I am nevertheless extremely grateful to them for the help they gave me in allowing me access to their records. This is unusual, for this is a nonauthorized book as far as they are concerned. In such cases, they normally decline all cooperation and, in particular, refuse to allow the use of their copyright photographs to "outside" authors unless they promise to let the Disney organization see what they are writing. After initial opposition, however, they did decide to make a special exception in my case and gave me unsupervised access over several months to the extensive archives in their Burbank studio. I have quoted from these records and oral histories with permission, but my interpretations are, of course, strictly my own and have been made without Disney censorship of any kind. I have also been allowed to draw from Disney's unique collection of copyright photographs though, in this case, Disney officials have seen and corrected the captions to their own pictures.

But I can honestly stress that all opinions about Walt Disney expressed by me are strictly my own, and this is an entirely independent and unsponsored book.

The chief Disney archivist, David R. Smith, who has an encyclopedic knowledge of Disney facts and figures, and his amiable staff were indefatigable in helping me track down obscure documents and early photographs of Disney's pioneering days. I also owe heartfelt thanks to Wayne Morris, manager of Disney's merchandising and publication division, for allowing me to use these and other illustrations (the Disney copyright to which are acknowledged elsewhere). I may say that I have been asked not to mention the above two officials by name, but in view of their assistance, I feel I should override their modest request for anonymity and name them just the same with my thanks.

Not only from David Smith and Wayne Morris, of course, did I receive precious help from inside the Disney organization. For instance, little of this material could ever have been uncovered had it not been for the friendship, advice, and influence of Disney's most sage and successful alumnus, Vincent Jefferds, whose genius as the exploiter of Disney's immortal characters and spin-offs from the studio's most famous films was earning the company $50 million a year in royalties when he retired a short time ago. A talented artist himself and a genius in the arts of corporate publicity, Jefferds had some enthralling stories to tell about Walt and Roy Disney and of the making (as well as the exploitation) of such famous projects as *Peter Pan, Davy Crockett,* Disneyland, and Walt Disney World. I am also grateful to the help and encouragement of his charming assistant, Queenie Osinoff. In addition, my fellow researcher and I will long savor the fascinating evenings we spent listening to Jefferds and his amusing, intelligent, and beautiful wife, Jean, at their lovely home in Tigertail Road, Westwood.

Perhaps the frankest and most educative of all my encounters with Walt Disney's former associates was with the artist/animator who came closest to him during their long professional life together. This was the brilliant and salty-tongued Ward Kimball, whose many imaginative cartoons and short films for Disney won world-wide fame in addition to being awarded well-deserved Hollywood Oscars. Kimball's passion for locomotives and railroad lore was (and is) such that he still has two full-size working locomotives and other impedimenta in his garden, a former citrus grove in the San Gabriel Valley of California; it also contains tracks along which the locomotives (one wood-burning, the other coal-fired) can run, a fullscale model of a Western railroad station, and one of the world's most comprehensive collections of model trains. Kimball's enthusiasm for his hobby fired Walt Disney with the same passion, and they traveled the United States together tracking down rare specimens of ancient railroad memorabilia, until finally Disney built his own train and track in the garden of his house in Holmby Hills.

I found Kimball a good example of someone who loved and admired

Walt Disney while being well aware of his boss's faults and weaknesses, and he gave me a wonderfully rounded picture of one of the greatest, and yet most fallible, men he had encountered in his lifetime.

I had been given an introduction by an old friend, the famous plant and orchid expert, Russell Seibert, to the California landscape gardener, Bill Morgan-Evans. Now living in Malibu, Morgan-Evans laid out Disneyland in California and Walt Disney World and EPCOT in Florida. In doing so he created gardens and spectacular landscapes out of what before had been citrus groves and virgin swamps, and they are among the greatest transformations of raw countryside since Capability Brown "made the desert smile" in eighteenth-century England.

Traveling north to Santa Barbara, I spent some time with the former English matte painter Peter Ellenshaw and his American wife, Bobbie. Ellenshaw, who worked on some of Disney's most successful films *(Treasure Island, 20,000 Leagues Under the Sea, Mary Poppins)*, is now a famous painter. He took time out from preparing a big new exhibition of his work to talk about his long association and deep affection for Walt Disney, whose equal as man, filmmaker, and boss he believes he will never meet again.

David Swift (maker of many box office hits for Disney, including *Pollyanna)* is still as handsome and as boyishly active in films as ever and still a successful Hollywood director. Like his close friend, Ward Kimball, he went through all the departments at Disney in the course of his early career, and he retains a shrewd, realistic, and affectionate memory of his former boss's reactions at some of the most critical moments of his lifetime.

One of the reasons that Swift's *Pollyanna* was so successful was the heartwarming performance of its English child star, Hayley Mills, now a gracious and lovely grown-up actress. She came to see me from her home beside the River Thames in Surrey and soon made it clear that, so far as she was concerned, Walt Disney was an adorable memory, thoughtful, protective, sensitive to her childhood worries and apprehensions. So far as Hayley was concerned, he had no blemishes whatsoever, and joy still throbs in her voice as she talks about her first encounters with him.

Peter Ustinov, a tennis buff whom I saw in London between rounds of the Wimbledon championships, was, on the other hand, somewhat cooler in his enthusiasm. He found Walt Disney a remote and almost unapproachable figure, and though he made several successful films at Burbank, never really got to know him though he did have a disturbing final meeting with him just before Disney's death.

Ustinov was much more forthcoming and much more admiring of Walt Disney's favorite producer, the late Bill Walsh, with whom he worked on several Disney films. I have made extensive use of the oral histories that

Walsh left behind; they are now in the Disney archives and are quoted here with permission. I also talked at some length with the lovely ex-dancer Nola Fishman, now the wife of a well-known California TV anchorman, about her earlier marriage to Walsh and her stormy fight to save it from the pressures of Walt Disney.

Two other old friends, the director Ken Annakin and his wife, Pauline, talked in great detail, at their home in Malibu, in England, and at my home in Florida, about their long and close collaboration with Walt Disney. Annakin made five films for Disney (four in Britain and Europe, one on this side of the Atlantic) and often mixed socially with Walt and his wife, Lillian, at their former home in London and at the Disney winter home in Palm Springs.

Annakin arranged a meeting for me with his producer, Bill Anderson, who took over the running of the Disney studio when feature film production resumed after World War II. During our session at Newport Beach, his wife, Virginia (Ginny) Anderson, described in colorful detail how she and Pauline Annakin "discovered" Hayley Mills in London and recommended her for stardom in *Pollyanna*.

In Florida Julia C. Wilson, associate managing editor of the Orlando Sentinel, was kind enough to give me the run of the reference library of her newspaper. Its librarian, Judy Grimsley, and her staff helped me track down every clipping I wanted. It was one of the Sentinel's reporters, Emily Bavar (now Emily Kelly) who first broke the story that Disney was building a great theme park in central Florida, and she gave me a vivid account of how she stumbled on the story while talking to Walt and Roy Disney in California.

It was my agent, John Cushman, whose sudden and tragic death sadly interrupted work on this biography, who introduced me to his cousin, John Nesbit, a Disney executive in Florida; and it was my neighbor on Captiva Island, Dewitt Jones, who revealed that he too had worked for Disney for many years and gave a lively account of what it was like to be at Burbank in the great days of the company after the end of World War II.

Other present and former employees (many of whom are, alas, no longer with us) talked to me over the years. Others left behind memories, either spoken or written, that have been of enormous help to me in recalling life as it was lived at the Burbank studio. They include: John Lounsbery, Gordon Legg, Dick Lundy, Don Lusk, Ham Luske, Hazel George, Kay Nielsen, Ken O'Brien, Bill Peet, Rico Lebrun, Milton Kahl, Glen Keane, Richmond Kelsey, Eric Larson, Josh Meador, Martin Provensen, Art Riley, Joe Rinaldi, Retta Scott, Mel Shaw, Gustaf Tenggren, Bill Tytla, James Algar, Art Babbitt, Mary Blair, Claude Coats, Norm Ferguson, Hugh Fraser, Don Griffith, T. Hee, John Hench.

In addition, I have relied for a great deal of my information about animation on that splendidly illustrated monster tome by Frank Thomas and Ollie Johnston (two of Walt's most brilliant ex-animators) *Disney Animation: The Illusion of Life*, from which, alas, I have been refused permission to quote. I have also been helped in my research by two books that Peter Ellenshaw gave me: a hard cover volume of his collected works (1929-1983) (New York: Hammer, 1983), which includes some of his work for Disney; and *Walt Disney's Fantasia* by John Culhane (New York: Abrams, 1983). Other books that have proved to be invaluable guides are *The Art of Walt Disney* by Robert D. Feild (London and Glasgow: Collins, 1945), *The Art of Walt Disney* by Christopher Finch (New York: Abrams, 1975), and Richard Schickel's *The Disney Version* (1968), a realistic look at Disney's character.

Also extremely helpful were two other biographies of Walt Disney in which I have found nuggets of interesting and invaluable information. One is *The Story of Walt Disney*, by his daughter, Diane Disney Miller, based on long conversations with her father and written in collaboration with Pete Martin (New York: Henry Holt, 1957). In a conversation with me while this acknowledgment was being written, Mrs. Miller stressed to me how she had loved and admired her father, and it shows in this book—as, I hope, it will in mine. The other is the splendidly written and researched *Walt Disney* by Bob Thomas, the veteran Associated Press correspondent in Hollywood (New York: Simon & Schuster, 1976).

Finally, I would like to express my thanks and admiration to my distinguished editor, Patricia Day, for her acuity and patience in dealing with the necessary difficulties associated with the production of this book.

And once more, my gratitude to my fellow researcher, beloved fellow traveler, and wife, Deirdre, for her constant encouragement and help.

PART 1

The Men from Isigny

1
Roots

HALF A DOZEN times a year, even this long after his death, newspaper organizations telephone, or researchers visit, the archives at the Walt Disney Studio in Burbank, California, to confirm stories they have been given of where, and under what conditions, Walt Disney was born. Some are convinced that they have discovered a skeleton in the Disney cupboard and that Walt Disney was in fact Spanish—and born out of wedlock, too.

Perhaps it is inevitable. Given the measure of international fame and the universal affection in which he was held, both during his life and after his death, millions of non-Americans refuse to believe that the United States could have produced such a phenomenon. Spain, for instance, claims Walt Disney as its own.

Stories about his Spanish birth have, in fact, now become so established that a small town in the mountains behind Almería, in southern Spain, until recently, actually carried a plaque on the road leading to the town square announcing:

MOJACCA
Birthplace of Walt Disney

Jane Wyatt, the Hollywood star, saw it some years ago during a trip in the mountains, while she was making a film in Almería, and she still regales her dinner guests in Malibu with revelations of the "truth" about Walt Disney's birth.

The story in Mojacca itself is that one of the village maidens, Consuela Suarez, became engaged at the turn of the century to a local boy who was killed in Morocco before they could be married. She was already pregnant when news of his death reached her. Thanks to the efforts of the local priest, the baby son Consuela subsequently bore was seen by an American couple who took him off to the United States, and Consuela presently followed. There she signed the papers that enabled her son to be formally adopted and made a U.S. citizen. Only when she came home to Mojacca to die did she reveal that her secret son was now named Walt Disney, the famous father of Mickey Mouse.

However, the facts are as proved by the Walt Disney Archives, one of whose functions is to prevent any word of untruth or scandal from being attached to the Disney name and reputation: that Walter Elias Disney was indubitably a native American and that Chicago was where he first saw the light of day. His birth certificate, a copy of which can be obtained in Chicago, will testify to that.

On the other hand, like many Englishmen who boast that their ancestors "came over with William the Conqueror," Walt Disney could legitimately claim he had Norman forebears, too. Generations ago, his ancestors were French peasants who originally came from the Norman cheese-making town of Isigny, through whose winding streets GIs of the U.S. Army fought during World War II. His family was named after their place of residence.

In 1066, a date known to every English schoolboy as the year his country was conquered by the French, several members of the d'Isigny family swarmed across the English Channel as part of the invading army of William of Normandy. When William ascended the English throne, his mercenaries, including Jean-Christophe d'Isigny and several others of the same clan, were encouraged to settle in the conquered territories, and they were given title to the English lands and properties. They married English women, and, anglicizing their name from d'Isigny to Disney, they became rich and prosperous English gentry, although one of them ended up as a disreputable, corrupt, and womanizing lord high sheriff of London. In the seventeenth century, the family made the mistake of supporting the Duke of Monmouth's rebellion against King James II. The heads of the family were ordered arrested and incarcerated in the Tower of London, and their lands were confiscated by the crown.

The Disneys scrambled for cover, however, and made their way to the safety of Ireland. There they settled in County Kilkenny, where, to give themselves a cloak of respectability, they again took up Roman Catholicism, which they had allowed to lapse in Protestant England, and became regular worshipers at the local church.

But the land they rented was poor, taxes were high, and the pickings meager. They soon began looking around for opportunities outside Ireland to restore their shattered fortunes. For this reason, in 1834, the Disneys began moving again, first to the United States and then, a year later, to Canada, where they had heard there were fortunes to be made out of the new land developments around Lake Huron. They joined an immigrant community consisting mostly of Scottish, German, and Dutch families;

and it is typical of the easygoing attitude of the Disneys that they quickly reconverted to Protestantism once they realized their nonconformist neighbors were hostile and suspicious of Catholicism.

It was in Huron County that Elias, the father-to-be of Walt Disney, was born in 1859.

THE EARLY RECORDS of the Disney family confirm that they were, on the whole, an amoral and easygoing lot, much given to dancing, drinking, and periodical hell-raising.

Elias Disney seems to have been the exception. He was the one member of the clan who had picked up stern religious (and later political) beliefs along the way, and by the time he was sixteen years old he could spout whole passages from the Bible, had resolved to adopt a God-fearing way of life, and looked down on self-indulgence in any form as sinful. In 1878, his father, Kepple Disney, announced that he was leaving with two of his older brothers to seek a fortune in the California goldfields. Elias was to go with them.

To his father and his brothers, the journey was a joyful excuse to relax after the hard labors of Lake Huron farming, and they binged their way westward in a succession of drunken celebrations. Elias was shocked at their rowdy, blasphemous behavior, which reached its climax in a bordello in Ellis, Kansas, where his brothers hired one of the girls to initiate Elias into the secrets of sex, while they watched through peepholes.

Horrified at the girl's shamelessness, outraged at the obscene laughter of his drunken brothers (who had hidden themselves inside a closet) Elias first drove the weeping whore out of his room and then informed his sheepish father that he was dropping out of the party. Kepple Disney was so ashamed of his family that he agreed to allow Elias to stay on in Ellis and gave him half his money as a stake to tide him over until he came back to collect him.

Then he and the others traveled on to California, where they spent several weeks panning (in vain) for gold. On his way back, broke and disillusioned, Kepple expected to find his youngest son in similar straits. On the contrary, Elias had not only found himself a job but he had also used the money his father had given him to buy a tract of Kansas land. It was good land, too, suitable for a small farm. Kepple, to whom Kansas seemed to have a much kindlier climate than Canada, especially in winter, decided to stay in Ellis and telegraphed his wife, Maria, to sell their Lake Huron property and join him and his family in the United States.

It was in Ellis, Kansas, that Kepple and Maria subsequently swore fidelity to the flag and, thus, became American citizens.

Although he differed from his kin in being so straitlaced, Elias Disney had inherited the family inability to stay put. "Pa always had ants in his pants," said his third son, Roy, later. "He could never stay in one place long enough to warm a seat."

Elias quickly tired of Ellis, Kansas, and got himself a job helping build the railroad across Kansas and Colorado; he was finally paid off in Denver at the end of two years. Home again in Ellis, he fell in love with Flora Call, a neighbor's daughter, but he was too shy to court her. It was four years before he realized how much she meant to him. By that time, she and her family had moved to Florida. Her departure left such a gap in his life that he resolved to go after her and propose; but he felt so shy and uncertain about his prospects that he was willing to make the journey only if his parents agreed to accompany him to Florida and support his suit. They needed a break from farm chores and consented to go with him, even briefly considering selling everything and moving south. But once they got there, they quickly discovered they hated Florida and soon got tired of hanging around in the humid heat waiting for their son to pluck up enough courage to ask Flora to marry him. Only when Kepple told his son that they were going back to Kansas was Elias finally emboldened to propose.

Flora had been in love with him since she was fourteen and thought he would never get around to asking. Now she was nineteen and he was twenty-eight. The wedding took place in Akron, Florida, in January 1888, after which Kepple and Maria took the train back to Kansas, and Elias and his bride went off for their honeymoon at Daytona Beach.

While on their honeymoon Elias, who had started out sharing his parents' antipathy to Florida, told Flora that he had changed his mind; and shortly afterward he bought some land near Kissimmee, where he proposed to raise cattle. Unfortunately, unused as he was to the problems of hot-weather farming, his cattle became diseased and died, forcing him to put the farm up for sale.

To get money to pay his debts, he persuaded the owner of the Halifax Hotel, Daytona Beach, to let them move in and manage it; and so they took over for the season. But when the last guest moved out to go north for the summer, the hotel closed. The proprietor told them to find other work and accommodations until the next season. By this time Flora was pregnant, so Elias gladly accepted an offer from the postmaster in Kissimmee to take over one of the rural mail routes.

At the end of 1888, just prior to her twentieth birthday, Flora gave birth to their first son, Herbert Disney. She hoped the fact that they had now started a family would persuade Elias to settle down. Suspecting that he was unhappy in his mail job and looking around for something else to do, she drew her savings out of the bank, appealed for financial help from her parents, and bought them a citrus grove outside Kissimmee.

Unfortunately, Elias had already made other plans for himself. The newspapers were full of rumors of the approaching war against Spain, and he came home one day to tell his wife that he had volunteered for the militia and, though war was still years away, said he expected to be fighting overseas soon. When she told him about the orange grove, he swore that it was too late to back out now and added that he refused to let down his country if it was going to be involved in a war. Instead of the action he craved, however, he found himself undergoing basic training in the sticky heat of a boot camp outside Tampa, and he hated it.

Weeks went by. Flora, unable to look after her young baby and take care of the citrus grove at the same time, was soon writing Elias desperate letters telling him that he had to come home. So one day he walked out of camp and took the train back to Kissimmee. He was in the orchard spraying his orange trees when the military police arrived to arrest him for desertion.

An angry and indignant Elias summoned a local lawyer who pointed out to the MPs that since his client had freely volunteered for the militia, he could just as freely elect to resign from it. It was such a simple and plausible-sounding argument that the astonished police said they would have to go back and consult with the military authorities and, in the meantime, demanded that Elias hand over his uniform. This he refused to do on the grounds that he had bought it himself. Baffled, they finally retreated, promising to return. But they never did.

Elias's defiance did not do him much good as far as orange growing was concerned. That winter a record frost hit central Florida; the crop was ruined and so were they. The good Lord would provide, Elias told his wife.

He had heard things were booming in Chicago, so they moved there in the spring of 1889. Flora Disney was by this time pregnant with their second child, but her husband refused to be rushed into taking any old job. Instead, he enrolled in a local night school for a course in carpentry and discovered that he had a natural gift for furniture making. While still studying, he began taking commissions, and his flair soon attracted many orders. With the money he earned from making chairs, tables, and wardrobes, and from selling his designs to local stores, he saved enough to buy a plot of land on Tripp Avenue in the area called Northwest Town, a Chicago suburb. Flora drew up the plans for the house, and Elias built it, single-handedly. It was admired so much that they bought land next door, built two more houses, sold them, and made a considerable profit.

It seemed as if Elias had found his niche at last, and Flora began to think the house on Tripp Avenue could become their permanent home. Her second son, Raymond, was born there at the end of 1890, and a third son arrived in 1893.

There was a brief family struggle over the third son's name. He was born in the year of the World Columbian Exhibition in Chicago. Elias had received several commissions to make furniture and provide designs for the fair, and he made so much money from the exhibition that when his third son was born, he considered naming him Columbus, as a gesture of gratitude. But Flora would not hear of saddling her son with such an outlandish name, and finally they christened the new arrival Roy Oliver Disney.

Three sons. That, both Elias and Flora decided, was enough. They settled down into solid, comfortable, middle-class respectability in suburban Chicago and became regular worshipers and valued parishioners of St. Paul's Congregational Church in Northwest Town and close friends of its minister, Reverend Walter Parr.

Reverend Parr launched an appeal to build a new church in 1898, and Elias not only dug into his savings to help find the funds but put on his coveralls and helped build the edifice. The new St. Paul's was consecrated in 1900 with an elaborate double celebration since the arrival of the twentieth century was being hailed at the same time. Reverend Parr informed the congregation that he had appointed Elias Disney deacon of the new church and smilingly indicated the loft where Flora Disney, a passable pianist, was installed as the new organist. It was an emotional and stimulating occasion for everyone, and Flora came home to the house on Tripp Avenue with her eyes shining.

It had been nine years since her last child had been born; but when, in the spring of 1901, she shyly announced that she was pregnant again, Reverend Parr revealed that his wife was also with child. He gleefully pointed out that it looked as if the births might happen at the same time and added to Elias, "If your wife has another son, you must call him Walter, after me. And if my wife has a son, I will christen him Elias, after you." And that was how it worked out.

The fourth Disney son was born on December 5, 1901, in the family bedroom at 1249 Tripp Avenue, Chicago. A short distance away, the minister's wife was also in labor and delivered a baby boy the following day. They were known locally as the "Consecration Babies," and presents for them poured in from the congregation.

There was a joint christening ceremony just before Christmas 1901. True to his word, Reverend Parr dubbed his new son Elias; and then, over the other mewling infant, he intoned, "I baptize this child Walter Elias Disney in the name of the Lord God Almighty."

IT TOOK ANOTHER five years before Walt Disney's father, Elias, succumbed to the itch to start traveling once more, and by that time the first and only girl in the Disney family had arrived. The daughter, Ruth Flora Disney, was born in 1903, and it was she who caused the next family upheaval.

When the Disneys first arrived, Northwest Town had been a quiet suburb of law-abiding, middle-class citizens, but as the Middle West grew and prospered, immigrants from Italy, Ireland, and central Europe swarmed into the city. Soon they began to take over the inner suburbs, transforming the once-quiet streets into gaudy, raucous bazaars that sometimes looked, especially on weekends, like areas of Naples, Ennis, or Bratislava. Criminals moved in, too, and the police, well bribed to look the other way, preferred to ignore their sometimes violent lawlessness.

A state law forbade the opening of saloons within half a mile of a church, which protected St. Paul's, but there were plenty of rowdy establishments just beyond the boundary lines. Their drunken patrons rolled home along Tripp Avenue and often brawled beneath the Disney windows until the early hours.

Elias galvanized his fellow parishioners to accompany him as a delegation of protest to the police, but they scoffed at his demand that the saloons be shut down or cleaned up and that the streets be patrolled for drunks. Angry and frustrated, Elias told Flora that the only way to preserve the sanctity of his family was for them to move out of Chicago before this cesspool of sin and licentiousness corrupted their sons and endangered the virtue of their daughter.

Elias Disney still thought of himself as a man of the soil and dreamed of having a viable farm of his own. He and Flora finally found what they wanted in Marceline, a quiet community of three thousand people 120 miles northeast of Kansas City. It was a mixed fruit and stock farm of forty-eight acres, and they bought it for thirty-five dollars an acre.

They signed the purchase papers on March 5, 1906. They moved to Missouri in the spring of the same year.

It was there, in Marceline, that Walt Disney spent the happiest and most influential years of his childhood.

Walt Disney was five years old when he first saw the farm. Elias had arranged for his two older sons, Herbert and Raymond, to help him with the final packing in Chicago, so he sent Flora on ahead to their new home. She took with her the three younger children—Roy, now thirteen; Ruth, three; and Walt—and one of the new neighbors met their train and gave them a lift from the railroad station to the farm. All three children were immediately enchanted with their first sight of their new home. "It was set in green rolling countryside," Walt said later, "and the apple and plum orchards were just starting to blossom. I thought it was a beautiful place."*

---

*These early impressions made such an impact on Walt Disney that he often used to recall them in later life. This and other quotations are reconstructed from later conversations—with the author during several interviews and with directors and animators (like Ken Annakin and Ward Kimball) with whom he frequently reminisced.

Coffman, their farmer neighbor, had indicated the jackrabbits gamboling in the fields when they arrived, and warned them that they were pests.

"Kill 'em off," he advised. "Otherwise, they'll gobble up everything in sight. Besides," he added, with a smack of his lips, "jackrabbits is good eating."

Crawling through the fields, Roy and Walt were able to observe the animals at their spring mating games—the females provocatively waving their scuts in the spring air, the males standing on hind legs to signal them. Walt was thrilled and excited at the rituals he and his brother observed; and in the next few days, scribbling in crayon on a square of packing paper, he made his first drawings—of a whiskered rabbit waving frantically to another concealed in the grass. He was appalled at the idea of harming such delightful creatures.

Roy was more practical. On their way to Marceline, they had stopped with their mother at Fort Madison to visit with Flora's married sister, and just before leaving, Roy had been presented by his uncle with an air gun "to keep down those thieving grackles you're going to find around the farm." Now Roy put the gun to his shoulder, fired, and brought down a magnificent jackrabbit as he was posturing above the scrub and signaling to a potential mate. The beautiful creature was still alive and squirming when the boys reached it, and Walt burst into tears as his older brother reached down and casually broke its neck.

He refused to eat the rabbit stew that Flora subsequently made for supper.

It was a week before Elias arrived, and Walt enjoyed every moment of it. Like his brothers and sisters, he was afraid of his father, who never laughed, never played with them, and scared them with his permanent expression of frigid disapproval. It was a relief not to have his icy presence around for a while. Even Flora was much calmer and relaxed and laughed and played with the children much more.

The farmhouse was roomy, with a parlor, living rooms, a good kitchen, a pantry and lots of storerooms, and three bedrooms. A tall elm grew just outside the front door and its leafy branches threw a welcome shade over the shingle roof and the porch. While waiting for Elias and the two older boys to arrive with the furniture, Flora and the youngsters camped in the house.

"It was no hardship at all sleeping on the hard floor of that empty house," Walt said later. "Mom read us to sleep by candlelight and reassured us when we shuddered at the eerie hooting of the owls outside. She made us feel like pioneers and it was a great adventure. I remember we laughed a lot and were sorry when father and my brothers eventually arrived."

Elias, Herbert, and Raymond had traveled rough from Chicago in a boxcar containing not only the furniture but two workhorses that Elias had bought just before his departure. It was on one of them, called Charley, that Roy later learned to ride. The horse was too big for Walt's tiny legs to straddle, so Walt stayed a nonrider until the day Elias came back from Marceline with a herd of hogs and a load of ducks, hens, and pigeons. Walt later boasted that, at the age of five, he became the youngest hogherd and the smallest poultry keeper in Marceline County.

One day, after enviously watching Roy ride majestically by on Charley, he decided to mount a charger of his own and picked Porker, the biggest sow in the herd. Leaping on her back, he grabbed the frightened and snorting animal by the ears and was carried on a wild and noisy ride across the farmyard.

Two minutes later, the indignant sow ploughed into the duck pond and tossed him contemptuously into the mud.

"I never did learn to stay on Porker's back," Walt said, "and I always ended up the same way, covered in duck feathers and mud. I think Porker got as much of a kick out of it as I did. She used to stand there in the pond after she'd tossed me in the slime, her curly tail whirling away like a watch spring and her piggy eyes streaming with water and what looked like tears—tears of laughter, I always used to think. She just loved throwing me off into the mud. Once when I got chicken pox and had to stay in bed for a few days, she came up to the porch and honked the house down. 'What's Porker want?' I asked Mom. 'You,' she said. She did, too. Later, when I recovered, Porker practically invited me to climb on her back and stayed as peaceful as pie while I crawled aboard—no tantrums, no protests. She was as proper as a show horse as she cantered me across the farmyard. I was convinced I had tamed her, and she was really glad to see me back. But I should have known better and guessed she was only biding her time. We ended up in the same way. She waded me into the pond, stood quite still for a few seconds, and suddenly tossed me like a tadpole into the deepest and slimiest part of the pond. Then she splashed back to her sty, snorting and snickering in triumph. For the rest of the evening, I could hear her honking away between snores—with smug satisfaction, I suspect."

Paper was scarce around the Disney household, and when Walt discovered he wanted to draw the domestic animals with which he was now surrounded, he resorted to toilet paper. He later gave that as the reason why his earliest drawings were never preserved.

"You can guess what I did with them, especially as I ate a lot of green apples in those days," he said. "Anyway, that's all those drawings were really good for—and that's where they went, down the can. Childish scribbles, that's all. The only interesting thing is I did them at all. I suppose I did them because just about everything around me at Marceline excited me. Even the chores with the birds. Feeding them every day,

I got familiar with the shapes and the habits of ducks, chickens, and pigeons. I can't remember I ever made a real pet of any of them, though I did learn their language, and I think they learned to understand me. What I mean is they'd come when I called them, even individually, when I summoned them by name. There was one pullet I called Martha, who used to come over when I shouted her name and lay an egg right in my hand."

On the other hand, none of the birds meant as much to him as Porker, who became both a challenge and a close friend. "I used to horse around with her a lot," he said. "I guess I really loved that pig. She had an acute sense of fun and mischief, and when she wanted to be, she could be as naughty as a puppy and nimble as a ballet dancer. She liked to creep up, nudge me up the rear, and then sashay off, squealing with delight, especially if she'd tipped me over. Do you remember the Foolish Pig in *Three Little Pigs?* Porker was the model for him. I did the preliminary sketch from remembering Porker, and I was practically weeping with nostalgia by the time I had finished."

In many ways, the animals around the farm—young, noisy, and playful as they were—gave him more companionship than he found in his father and brothers. Elias was too forbidding and had absolutely no sense of fun. His brothers were all so much older than he was, and his sister Ruth was too young. On the other hand, the barnyard stock, in all their different moods, fed his need for affection; and he gave them names, carried on conversations with them, and made up stories about them. His brothers jeered at him and scoffed when he walked through the farmyard raising his hand and saying, "Hi, Effie!" or "Hello, Elmer!" or "How're the old feet this morning, Mortimer—frozen?" to a pullet or a cockerel or a duck. He felt the birds would have been hurt if he had failed to say hello.

The only human being with whom he had a real rapport and with whom he shared his fantasies in those days was his father's brother, Uncle Ed, who often came to visit them on the farm. In appearance Ed was small and slightly hunched, with a lined, tanned face that made him look, Walt said later, like a cross between a leprechaun and a prune. He usually sported a battered derby and someone's cut-down suit; and he would turn up unexpectedly with his few belongings in his carpetbag, brightly announcing to his brother and sister-in-law; "Well, now, here I am again. Could you take me in for a few days?"

Uncle Ed could always be sure of a welcome. Even Elias seemed sunnier at the sight of him. As for Walt, he would greet Uncle Ed with such pure pleasure that it was as if Santa Claus had suddenly arrived. Not inappropriately, he always referred to him not as Uncle Ed but Uncle Elf—he looked and behaved like an elf. He would park his bag in the spare room and then scamper down the stairs to join Walt on an expedition into the fields. He adored the boy and was inordinately proud of the fact that Walt obviously looked up to him and admired him.

Ed was so much at home in the fields that all the birds and animals and insects seemed to know instinctively that he would never harm them. He was expert at catching grasshoppers and frogs. Field mice liked to creep up his arm and snuggle in his pockets, where he always kept bits of cheese. He could do uncanny imitations of birds, which came down, flew around his head, and perched on his shoulder. He taught Walt how to tickle fish and unhook catfish from his line without being injured by the spines. He liked nothing better than squatting in a field, munching muddy turnips, or leading a raid on a neighboring farmer's orchard.

Remembering Elias's stern prohibitions—he not only disapproved of liquor and cigarettes for grown-ups but candy for small boys, too—Uncle Ed always brought bags of hard candy with him to satisfy the cravings of Walt's sweet tooth. Once he even produced a particularly forbidden luxury in the shape of a packet of chewing gum, sticks of which his nephew munched delightedly for hours and then parked under the railing of the front porch, for use on the morrow.

Uncle Ed never overstayed his welcome. One day he would creep out of the house before dawn and tramp off down the dusty road, on his way to visit yet another of Elias's relatives. He never left behind a note of thanks or warned anybody he was leaving, but had always made his bed and tidied up the room before he crept away.

Every few months or so, he came back, and the woods and meadows at Marceline once more echoed to Uncle Elf's whoops and whistles and bird calls and the happy laughter of his six-year-old friend.

Then one black day, Walt came home from school to learn that Ed had been "taken bad" while staying with another relative and had to be sent to a home for the retarded near Chicago. Elias and Flora sometimes went to visit him but, as if sensing it would be too distressing, did not take Walt with them.

He never saw him again. It was years later that a message was received that Ed Disney was dead, and by that time, Walt retained only a fading memory of him. But, of course, he never really forgot him. Many years later, Ward Kimball came up with some spritely sketches of a top-hatted and half-humanized grasshopper. Everybody liked it, even Walt Disney who pored over Kimball's drawings, half frowning, half smiling. Then he took a brush and pen and played with the facial features until someone remarked that he now "looked like a prune." And like Uncle Elf, Walt might have added.

If Walt Disney was happy at Marceline, his father, mother, and two older brothers were not. Elias was soon having trouble making the farm viable, and the weather was no help to him. The hogs got swine fever, and there came the terrible day when even Porker had to be shipped off and destroyed. Two years in a row the crops failed, and Elias was forced to mortgage the farm. Bad times made him short-tempered and even more tyrannical than usual, and he railed at his sons when they failed to turn up at breakfast for early morning prayers or when, at night, he caught them reading "frivolous books" instead of the Bible. In return for their labor, he had promised Herbert and Raymond that in lieu of pay he would turn over several arable acres of his land to them so that they could begin farming on their own. They took it badly when he was forced to explain to them that, because of the mortgage, he could no longer carry out his pledge. There was a bitter quarrel, and in the early hours of the next morning, the two older boys ran away from home.

Herbert was nineteen years old and Raymond seventeen, and they left a note for Flora saying they were tired of being treated like wicked children by their father. They wrote her a weekly letter and reported to her that Herbert had found himself a job at Sears, Roebuck and Company in Kansas City, while Raymond had a job with a local bank. Shortly afterward, they began sending parcels of their old clothes home to Marceline so that they could be cut down and adapted for Roy and Walt.

Considering their youth and their rebellious mood, they both stayed remarkably free from the temptations of the big city. But they still smarted at the treatment they had received from their father and could not resist pretending to that stern and unforgiving man that they had gone to the dogs. For instance, they would fill the pockets in the old clothes that they shipped with the odd stub of a cheroot or cigarette or with torn scraps of newspapers and magazines showing scantily clad women, knowing how deeply he abhorred smoking or the images of licentious women.

Elias never did realize it was all a joke and was convinced his two older sons had sold their souls to the Devil. He told Flora he would never allow them to set their sinful feet inside his house again.

SHORTLY AFTER THE departure of Herbert and Raymond, genuine disaster struck the rest of the Disney household. The family and the livestock got their water from a well on the farm, which, they had been assured by the previous owners, was one of the purest in the county. But after swine fever hit the hog herd, Elias came down with a bad case of typhoid. Authorities who came to analyze the well announced it was questionable whether it was suitable for animals and definitely unfit for human consumption. Luckily, Flora, Roy, and Walt all remained untouched by the tainted water, but Elias had to be sent to a hospital, where he hovered between life and death for several weeks.

Meanwhile, Roy, as the eldest male left in the household, took over the farm chores and the remaining livestock and labored manfully to keep things going. But it was soon obvious to Flora that even with her help and that of Walt, he could not manage and still keep up his schooling. Elias returned from the hospital in need of a long convalescence. He was unfit to undertake any strenuous work on the farm, so Flora persuaded him that there was only one thing to do—sell the farm and return to the city. It was midwinter, 1908-9, and the Midwestern plains were subjected to an even more bitter winter than usual. While the frail and sickly Elias Disney huddled in his chair near the stove, his two sons, Roy and Walt, trudged through the snow nailing signs to trees and fences, announcing the forthcoming auction of their farm.

Sometimes the local physician Dr. Caleb Sherwood, who made his rounds in a beautiful cutter drawn through the snow by a magnificent stallion called Rupert, would pick them up and give them a lift into Marceline. Walt, who hated the cold, always remembered the joy of snuggling under the thick fur rugs draped across the front seat of the sleigh and peeping out at the round rump of Rupert steaming in the frozen air.

Walt was almost eight years old at the time, and Flora had now managed to buy him a book for his drawings. Doc Sherwood liked what he had seen of Walt's sketches of the lamented Porker and Martha, the hen, and he encouraged him to continue. When Walt tearfully told him that Porker was dead and Martha had now been put into the family pot, he took the boy home and down to the barn in his yard where Rupert was stabled when his day's work was over. Handing him cardboard and crayons, he told Walt to make him a picture of the horse.

After he had inspected the finished drawing, Doc Sherwood announced himself satisfied. He handed the boy a whole fifty-cent piece and said he would buy it. It was Walt Disney's first commission, the first time in his life he was ever paid for a picture. It is one more drawing by the young Walt Disney that has since disappeared.

THEY GOT A good price for the farm at the auction, enough, at any rate, to pay off their mortgage and their debts and have something left over with which to start again.

Elias started making plans to move his family to Kansas City, but Flora would not hear of leaving right away. Now that they had a little money in the bank, she said, she was determined to see that the two boys finished the school year in Marceline. (She didn't worry too much about Ruth since girls' education did not get the same consideration in those days.) She maintained that taking them out of a small-town school and plunging them into a big-city educational establishment without careful preparation might well prove too much of a psychological wrench.

So, although the family farm was sold in 1909, it was not until the summer of 1910 that they rented a house on East 31st Street in Kansas City, and a few months later moved again to 3028 Bellefontaine Avenue.

2
Roy Runs Away

ELIAS DISNEY PASSED his fifty-first birthday shortly after they all arrived in Kansas City, but his family did not celebrate the occasion, knowing how much the head of the household disapproved of such frivolities. In any case, Elias was not in the mood to salute another milestone in his life. To be over fifty could be the beginning of old age in those days, and Elias was already behaving like an old man.

The years and his recent illness had sapped his strength, and his outlook on life had soured. In earlier days he had been interested in left-wing politics and had always closely related his religious with his ideological beliefs. Though he still professed faith in the same religious and political standards—attended church and spoke at left-wing meetings and regularly continued to vote for the Socialist leader, Eugene Debs—his glowing vision that a brighter new world would soon be dawning seemed to have dissipated and bitter pessimism had taken its place.

Walt had always been too afraid of his father to realize he had now got worse. It was his brother, Roy, who made Walt aware of the change in him and of how deeply he resented it. Roy complained to Walt that their father had become a hypocrite. Back in Chicago, he pointed out, while it was true Elias had seen no contradiction in being a Christian Socialist while running a prosperous capitalist enterprise at the same time, he had at least given some of his money to worthy causes. But now all he seemed to think of was making money for himself and doing it by exploiting everyone around him.

His father had become a fraudulent windbag, Roy told his brother. He was nothing but a ruthless capitalist exploiter, just like all the others, especially where his own sons were concerned.

And, in one way, it was true. Too physically frail to do manual work anymore, Elias put his sons to work for him—and, in Roy's view, cheated them. After looking around Kansas City for a way of making money, Elias had decided his best bet was obtaining a franchise from the circulation people of the local newspapers, the morning Kansas City *Times*, and the *Evening* and *Sunday Star* group. The circulation manager of the *Star* group was not too eager to turn the franchise over to Elias since he thought he looked too old and ill. Elias, however, swore he would prove a better delivery contractor than any he had already franchised if only he were given a chance to prove himself.

Roy was out of school by now and was immediately recruited as a delivery boy. Soon afterward so was Walt, though he was only ten years old. When the boys asked about pay, Elias told them they would receive no actual wages, but he swore he would reward them by investing a regular sum for each of them for every week's work they did for him.

It was midwinter when the boys' chores began. Elias, of course, was too frail to do the rounds regularly with them; however, he did accompany them occasionally but only to keep a hawklike eye on them to see that they were obeying the rules he had laid down.

Roy and Walt had to crawl painfully out of their warm beds at 3:15 every morning; slog their way through the dark, frigid, snowbound suburban streets, loaded down with papers; and slip and stumble as they mounted the icy steps to the customers' houses. Almost invariably double storm doors confronted them, one of which had to be pried open and the newspaper securely anchored inside. It was dreadfully hard work, especially for a ten-year-old boy, and Walt had a terrible time trying to remember which customers took the *Times* and didn't take the *Star*, or vice versa. Sometimes he had to retrace his steps and rescue a paper he had delivered to the wrong house, wasting precious time and missing his breakfast, and he was often punished for arriving late at school. When school was over for the day, Walt had to rush back to the newspaper office to collect the afternoon *Star* and once more make the delivery rounds.

Sundays brought no respite. In fact both boys found it a particularly hard day because the Sunday edition of the *Star* bulged with advertisements and was heavy and awkward to lug around. But when the boys grumbled about it, Elias gave them a solemn lecture, saying they should give thanks for being so usefully occupied on the Lord's day and should be glad that they had only one newspaper to deliver and only church services and Sunday school classes to attend afterward.

Walt Disney remembered that he was always so tired that he sometimes fell asleep while making the rounds, napping in doorways or outhouses. So anxious was Elias to prove to the *Star* people and to the customers that he was well up to the demands of the franchise, he refused to let his sons deliver in the manner American newsboys have made famous—by riding down the street on their bikes and hurling the rolled-up papers onto the porch or the garden paths of the customers' houses. Elias insisted the papers be kept impeccably flat and delivered, unrolled, on the customers' doorsteps. In addition, they must be anchored down by a brick or stone to prevent them from blowing away.

Elias recruited a team of newsboys to help them. It was impossible for Elias to hold back the pay of his newsboy team—he had to give them the going rate of $2.50 a week—but he still kept his purse shut tight when it came to his own sons. He kept reminding them that he was investing their wages—in what he said was a thriving jelly factory run by a friend of his in Chicago—and that, one day, they would thank him for providing each of them with a nest egg.

Roy finally insisted on being given at least some of his back pay, and there was a showdown. Elias explained to the boys that he couldn't give them anything because the factory was having "a little money trouble," and though their nest eggs were safe, they couldn't be touched for the moment. Roy refused to believe his father and insisted they were being "cheated."

Walt wanted pocket money. Without telling his parents, he got a job working in the candy store during lunch recess at school. At least this enabled him to satisfy his sweet tooth and earn a quarter or so a week from the proprietor.

Then one morning someone not on his list of regular newspaper customers stopped him and mentioned he would like to become a subscriber, so Walt went down to the *Star* offices and ordered extra papers. Other new customers followed.

He now had a spare newspaper route of his own going, the existence of which he concealed from Elias. It meant getting up at 3 A.M. instead of 3:15 A.M.; he was even more frequently late for school and so exhausted when he got there that he dozed through the lessons. But, as he said later, "I had inexhaustible energy in those days, and I didn't mind being scolded by my parents for bad marks and beaten by my teachers for inattention. In any case, I needed the money. I ate candy like a mad fool."

IT WAS JUST about this time that Walt's older brother finally decided he had had enough. He confided one night to Walt that he was getting out and was gone by morning. Flora Disney wanted to report her son missing to the police, but Elias forbade it and told his wife and Walt he never wanted to hear Roy's name mentioned in the house again. A letter came a week later from Elias's brother, Will Disney, to say Roy had turned up at his farm in Ellis, Kansas, and was helping with the harvest.

"I told you I never wanted to hear his name again," Elias thundered. "He has turned his back on us—and on God."

Roy Disney never did go back home to his parents. In 1913, he took a job as a clerk in a bank in Kansas City at nineteen dollars a week. And in 1917, when rumors of American involvement in World War I began to sweep the country, he volunteered for the navy and was sent to the Great Lakes Training Camp nineteen miles north of Chicago.

At about the same time, Herbert Disney, the oldest Disney son, who had run away from home with his brother Raymond some years earlier, turned up again. He brought with him a wife and daughter and asked for help because he was out of a job. After he had humbly apologized to Elias for his previous transgressions, he was grudgingly given accommodations in the family home on Bellefontaine Avenue.

But Elias was restless again, and Herbert's arrival seemed to catalyze a sudden itch to get moving. He announced to his family that he was selling off the newspaper franchise and turning the Bellefontaine house over to Herbert and that they were moving back to Chicago. This, he explained to Walt, would give him a chance to keep a closer watch on "our investment." He had been offered a job in the Chicago jelly factory run by his friend. In addition to making jelly, it seemed, it was about to expand and would soon begin turning out a new soft drink called Ozell, which was going to make their fortune. In return for investing a further sixteen thousand dollars in the factory ("Part of it was the money he'd squeezed out of Walt and me," Roy would say later), Elias would run the operation and wait for the profits to roll in.

Once more Flora Disney put her foot down. Walt and his sister, Ruth, were still in school in Kansas City, and she was determined Walt should not be taken out of school until the end of the term. Elias was adamant in refusing to let her stay behind with her son, so it was finally arranged that Walt should lodge with Herbert and his family in the Bellefontaine house until school was over.

Walt was delighted. It enabled him to carry on with his bootleg newspaper route until the summer term at school came to an end; then, he sold it to the man who had bought his father's franchise and took a summer job as a news butcher on the Pacific Railroad running between Kansas City and Jefferson, Missouri.

"What more could a young boy want?" he asked later. "I was seeing the world and earning money while doing it! In addition, I didn't have my father always hovering over me, badgering me. I don't want anyone to think my father was a tyrant, but he did have a terrible temper, and he was always trying to make you do things for which you weren't suitable. For instance, I was only fifteen then but I already knew I wanted to draw. But when I told my father, he just scoffed at me and said if I was foolish enough to want to become an artist, I should learn the violin; and then I could always get a job in a band if I was in need of money. He tore up my drawings, brought out his own violin, and forced me to saw and scrape at it for hours every day, although he must have known from the squawks I was making I was tone-deaf and would never be any good at music."

"It was good to get away from him—and from that fiddle," he added. "Even I hated the sounds I was making."

It was not until the end of the summer of 1917 that he finally moved to Chicago. His family was now living at 1523 Ogden Street and he enrolled for his final year in school at McKinley High School on Adam Street. The main attraction of McKinley for Walt was that it had a school newspaper called *The Voice,* and it printed drawings. He persuaded the editorial committee to let him be junior art editor.

His illustrations were crude attempts at imitating local cartoonists and humorous drawings he saw in *Judge* and *Life,* and the jokes he appended to them were poor; but at least he was aware of his lack of expertise and was not afraid to work at the job of conquering his amateurishness.

While still in school, he enrolled as a night student at the Chicago Academy of Fine Arts, though he did not tell his father and paid the fees out of his savings from Kansas City.

The academy was a private institution, run by a dedicated teacher named Carl Wertz. What differentiated Wertz from the other art teachers in the city was that he encouraged his pupils to draw from live models—hens, cats, chickens, dogs, even human beings. It made all the difference to Walt in improving his technique, and Wertz particularly liked the comic, almost satirical, line he put into his caricatures of the birds and animals, though he didn't do so well with the human models.

Walt didn't tell Wertz, but it was almost like being back on the farm again. "All I needed was Porker," he said later.

Some of the teachers at the academy worked as cartoonists on Chicago newspapers, and it was because of one of them, Leroy Gossett of the *Chicago Herald,* that he became interested in learning cartooning techniques.

Under Gossett, Walt improved a lot and began to concentrate on his ideas and put flair and humor into his work. On one occasion the most famous Chicago cartoonist of the day, Carey Orr of the *Tribune,* took the class. Orr was impressed with Walt's work, so much so that he invited Walt to visit him at the *Tribune* office and introduced him to the rewrite editors and the reporters. Walt came away filled with the ambition to be a newspaper cartoonist like Carey Orr.

DESPITE THE GAP in their ages, Walt missed his brother, Roy, whose practical view on life he had grown to admire and respect. But except that they knew that he was now fighting in the war, it was hard to get news of him because all letters from him were burned in the stove by the unforgiving Elias. It was not until Walt celebrated his sixteenth birthday that his mother revealed what Roy was doing. News had secretly reached her—by way of her brother-in-law, Will Disney, in Kansas—that Roy was now on active duty with the U.S. Navy. He was serving on a destroyer convoying merchant ships between America and Europe.

How Walt envied him! He was suddenly desperately eager to see his brother again and also longed to emulate him and serve with U.S. forces in the war. For the moment this ambition drove all thought of a cartooning career out of the boy's head, and he began haunting army and navy recruiting offices in an attempt to enlist. He was always turned away for being underage and underweight.

But like many another patriotic American in those days, he was determined to get into the war somehow. So he added a year to his age and persuaded a Red Cross recruiter in Chicago to let him join up with one of the units due to be shipped to France.

After persuading the recruiter, he had to go home and argue his parents into letting him go. Flora was reluctant, but once she was convinced of his determination, she went to work on Elias. He didn't approve of this war in any shape or form and withheld his consent for weeks. There were many fierce arguments before Flora won the day.

But by the time Elias had grudgingly agreed and the Red Cross induction formalities were completed, it was 1918 and World War I was all but over. Walt sailed for France aboard the SS *Vaubin* in November 1918, with the last batch of fifty Red Cross volunteers to be shipped to the war.

He would miss Roy, who was being invalided out of the service at that very moment. And he would miss the fighting. But he would at least see the devastated lands over which the so-called "War to End All Wars" had been fought. Moreover, he would be fulfilling a long-cherished ambition to see something of the world beyond Missouri and Chicago.

3
Yankee Doodle Kid

A GIRL NAMED Su Pitowski had been in Walt Disney's class during his year at McKinley High, and he thought she was the most beautiful, but also the most unattainable, girl he had ever seen. Bright eyed, glowing with energy, vocal, and intelligent—she had so many beaux hanging around her after school that he could never get near enough to catch her eye and decided she would never notice him even if he did. Nevertheless, he tried everything to attract her attention and win her esteem. He took up tennis because she played the game, but since the sexes were segregated on the courts, he never did succeed in playing with her. As he said later, however, "The thought that she might be watching me did improve my backhand enormously."

Then he discovered Su had a brother who was in the army and fighting in France, and this explained why she was so madly patriotic. She took part in school plays in which she wrapped herself in an American flag and declaimed passionate verses about the gallantry of our boys "over there." She also wrote pieces in the McKinley High newspaper, *The Voice*, exhorting readers to do more for the war effort.

The fact that she was involved with *The Voice* and so many other school activities had been an incentive for Walt to volunteer for the job of junior art editor; and it had spurred his ambition to do a good job of it when he realized that she would be looking at the drawings that went into its pages. To catch her interest, he had started a section called "*The Tiny Voice* (McKinley's Smallest Paper)," which he filled with a series of cartoons, almost all of which he drew himself.

He may well have sensed that what would stir her interest most in his drawings would be their patriotic content because most of his cartoons exhorted his readers to rally around and help win the war. There were caricatures of Uncle Sam with a sickle in his hand surveying a vast farm

and saying, "I have the land. You furnish the help." There was a marksman winning a prize for shooting the steel helmet off the Kaiser, with a
caption declaring, "Volunteer! You may hit the bull's eye, too!" There
was a cartoon of a plump citizen saying complacently, "I am too fat to
fight, and I guess there is nothing I can do to help win this war." At which
a small figure pipes out from the side of the drawing, "Why don't you stop
eating so much and save food for the boys over there! *And* you will reduce
so that you can fight." The fat man looks surprised. "I never thought of
that," he says. At the bottom of the cartoon page was a strapline saying:
"Buy savings stamps and help win the war!" followed by a credit line:
"Walter Disney, Editor" and then "With apologies to Orr." Orr was, of
course, Carey Orr, the *Tribune* cartoonist to whom he owed the inspiration for many of his cartoons.

They certainly weren't strikingly original cartoons, but what they
lacked in expertise was compensated for by flair and panache; and, in any
case, Su thought they were wonderful. She began to take an increasing
interest in this shy, solemn, fair-haired kid who shared so much of her
fervor for "our boys." When Walt told her he wanted to improve his
technique as a draftsman and had signed up for night classes at the
academy, she did likewise, mainly to stay close to him. Soon they were
sharing class rings and going to patriotic meetings together. She was
tremendously proud of him when she heard that he had volunteered for
the Red Cross, and she greeted the news of his acceptance with an
impulsive kiss. Emotion burning in her bright brown eyes, she faithfully
promised to write to him "at least twice a week" while he was serving his
country overseas.

She was true to her word, too, and once he reached France, the letters
began to arrive regularly and were even more frequently answered. He
kept her picture under his pillow while in camp in France and dreamed of
the bliss awaiting both of them when he returned at last from doing his
bit for his country. All he worried about was whether he was good
enough for her.

ALCOHOLIC DRINK HAD always been regarded as the Devil's brew in the
Disney household, so he didn't dare tell his parents in his letters home
that he had spent his seventeenth birthday buying hard liquor for his
Red Cross comrades and even drinking a drop or two of it himself.

The fifty-strong intake of new Red Cross personnel was shipped first
of all to a camp behind the headquarters of the famous French military
school, St. Cyr, and it was there, on December 5, 1918, that one of his
comrades enticed Walt into a bar, promising to buy him an innocuous
drink called a grenadine. But once he was inside, the rest of the unit

suddenly appeared and began singing "Happy Birthday" to hail the fact that he was now 17 years old. Some of them even drank their toasts in grenadine, too, and others in white and red wine; but then the real drinkers among them began changing to pastis and cognac, and at the end of a raucous session Walt found himself stuck with a whopping bill, which he didn't have the money to pay. His first paycheck from the Red Cross was overdue.

Someone suggested that he sell his spare pair of service boots to a local Frenchman, pointing out that what with leather and other shortages, footwear was scarce and he shouldn't have much trouble making a sale. He came back with a sheaf of francs and paid off his debts.

He realized he had been conned by his comrades, and while he didn't resent them taking advantage of his youthful naïveté, he had already spelled out a rule for himself: never repeat a mistake, and never let anyone con you twice. He didn't intend to be caught without money again, and pending the arrival of his first paycheck (he was due $40 a month, later raised to $52), he looked around for ways of raising cash.

For 15 francs a week, paid out of unit funds, he agreed to make some signs around the camp to show personnel where things were. With the aid of his crayons and drawing paper, he plastered the camp with posters pointing the way to the canteen (an arrow over a huge steaming mug), the bathhouse (a knobbled and mud-spattered foot dipping a grimy toe into a steaming tub), and the toilets (a pair of hairy legs, pants around the ankles, dangling from a giant water closet, with a line underneath saying: "And DON'T Steal the Toilet Paper!").

Even at St. Cyr, far away from the trenches and the fighting, they had, when they first arrived, heard the thud of the big guns thundering over the western front. But by the time the unit was transferred closer to the actual battlefields, the war was over and the armistice signed, and everything was strangely quiet. Their new location was the small town of Neufchâteau, which was on the railroad connecting the rear areas with what had been the main battlefronts of the Marne only a few weeks before. Already the first troops were coming back down the line from the trenches on their way to the demob centers, and new shipments of draftees, although too late for the fighting, were still being sent up to the front as temporary replacements. Since every train that came through stopped at Neufchâteau, the unit's job was to meet the weary veteran troops and see that they were greeted as returning heroes and given plentiful food, candy, and hot coffee.

But it was from the influx of new recruits that money was to be made. Walt formed a friendship, and then a partnership, with a Red Cross comrade who was, because of his Southern accent, known to everyone as "the Cracker." He was in fact a streetwise kid from New Orleans, and there was nothing he hadn't learned about how to make easy money from dealing with the tourists in his native city back home.

To the Cracker, the recruits now arriving on the Western Front were just the same sucker breed as the tourists disembarking from the buses in the French Quarter. He saw in their eager eyes the same willingness to hand over their surplus cash in return for souvenirs. The moment they smelled the acrid reek of the battlefields, growing stale though it now was, they began clamoring for war mementos. The Cracker set out to give them what they wanted, and more.

Whenever he and Walt had a day off, they would borrow a Red Cross ambulance, drive up to the front line, and scour the trenches for the flotsam of the fighting. Mostly they would load up the ambulance with German steel helmets, which they would then sell as genuine souvenirs of the fighting.

The most popular items among the troops were what the Cracker termed KSDs, or "Kraut Sniper Derbies," which usually meant steel helmets with bullet holes in them. These were so eagerly sought that the doughboys fought among themselves to get hold of them and didn't mind what they paid. Not unnaturally, genuine KSDs were few and far between since there had been only a limited number of German snipers in the front lines and, of them, quite a few had survived and got away. So it was difficult to keep up with the demand.

Then Walt had an idea. He would take a limited number out of each load of helmets and set to work adapting them, firing bullets into them, treating the holes so the burn marks stayed but didn't appear too new, and generally doing a job on the helmets themselves until they looked as if they had just fallen into the mud straight out of a sniper's nest.

As both demand and prices soared, he grew more skillful at dressing up his souvenirs, coating the inside of the bullet holes with grease, hair, and even stains of dried blood, to make them appear as if they had been ripped from the heads of the dead or wounded snipers.

"Some of the boys would hand over every cent they had to get them. And the gorier they looked, the more they'd pay," Walt said later.

WHEN YOU ARE only 17, money and success rapidly go to your head, and Walt Disney was soon the cockiest kid in the unit. He hardly touched his Red Cross pay and sent home over half of it each month for his mother to bank for him. He learned how to drink and smoke and got himself a girlfriend, a sympathetic American auxiliary who helped out at the Red Cross. He took her out with him to the local *estaminets,* and she taught him how to dance the tango and the bunny hug. They sometimes sneaked into the station waiting room and "canoodled," as they called it, after their evening out. But that, he confessed later, was as far as his youthful love life went. He hadn't the courage to snatch anything more than a fumbling embrace from the American girl.

There were plenty of French girls available, of course, but he didn't speak their language; and he was, quite frankly, scared of "catching something" from them. He was very conscious of one of the posters he had drawn after arriving at Neufchateau to warn the personnel of the dangers of venereal disease. It had turned out to be one of his most graphic and effective efforts since he had crammed all his own fears into it. Done in bold red and black, it showed a half-undressed doughboy staring down in horror at a loathsome bug crawling up his leg, while a shapely female limb decorated with a red garter was visible behind. The caption warned: "Beware the BUG!! Don't Let It Bite You! Keep CLEAN! Keep PURE!! Beware VD!!!"

Venereal disease was rife in that part of France and not even the professional prostitutes in the bordellos were said to be immune. His comrades were all too willing to risk the disease, but Walt was so scared that he never did dare accompany them when they went off for a night in the brothels of Neufchâteau and Nancy.

He did spend a lot of time in camp drinking and gambling. The Cracker taught him how to play a smart game of poker, and in one all-night session he won two thousand francs. He went to the bank the next day, had half of it converted into dollars and wired it home to his mother.

With part of the remainder he bought himself a young collie pup. He called it Carey, after the *Tribune* cartoonist, and until the dog grew too big, he carried him around in his musette bag wherever he went. Carey barked to waken him at reveille every morning and learned to dig out his spare underwear and shirt and hand it to him in his teeth.

Walt liked to draw him in his more playful moods and sent a number of the drawings back to Flora. The one she liked best was a sketch of Carey as a puppy peeking saucily out of her son's musette bag. She kept it in her kitchen drawer and liked to take it out and look at it.

Carey adored his master. Sleeping at the foot of his bunk, ever watchful to defend him from enemies or intruders, he liked wearing Walt's forage cap and showing off the many tricks he learned to perform. He could even stand on his hind legs and salute with his right paw whenever "The Stars and Stripes" or the "Marseillaise" were played.

Back in Chicago, Walt had made friends with a young man, and they joined the Red Cross together. He also had a pet dog. His name was Russell Maas, and he lived in Waukegan, Illinois. Chiefly because of the dogs and because they came from the same state, they struck up a friendship. Soon they were planning to spend part of their demobilization leave together. Walt always knew he would go back to Chicago and renew his association with Su Pitowski, with whom he was still keeping up a warm and, on his part, increasingly passionate correspondence. But before settling down to life with Su and the job he hoped to get in the cartoon department of the *Chicago Tribune*, he thought it would be exciting to see a little more of the world.

Both boys dreamed of adventures of the kind they had read about in books, their favorite being *The Adventures of Huckleberry Finn*. They decided it would be a great adventure to build a raft and float down the Mississippi to New Orleans, and when they mentioned their project to the Cracker, he enthusiastically invited them to visit and stay with him at the end of their journey. They would take the dogs with them, of course, to ward off any suspicious characters who might try to board their raft enroute.

It never worked out, and Walt Disney always regretted it didn't—and never really forgot about it, either. Instead, Russell got bad news from Waukegan—his mother was ill—which made him apply for compassionate leave, and he was told he was being shipped home and discharged instead. Since he had to go through the formalities of shipping home his own dog, he arranged to take Carey with him, too, and said he would look after the collie until Walt came back for him.

He tried to persuade Walt to ship home, too; after all, he pointed out, the war was over and there was no reason to stay on. But by that time Walt was thinking of volunteering for a Red Cross unit going to Albania, where forces were still fighting, and casualties were dying for lack of medical help. Volunteers were being sought by the Red Cross and offered $150 a month, and Walt was tempted by the money.

So he said an aching good-bye to Carey and watched his beloved pet and his best friend leaving to go home. He was lonely and miserable after they had gone. So much so that, after hesitating for a few weeks, home-sickness became too much to bear, and he decided to apply for a discharge, too. Once his mind was made up and the formalities completed, he happily sent a cable telling Su Pitowski the good news that they would soon be together again.

Suddenly, everything around him in France seemed strange and foreign, and he could hardly wait to get back home. He pictured the glorious moment when he and Su saw each other again and locked in a fond and emotional embrace, and then imagined the two of them journeying to Waukegan together for his reunion and Su's introduction to the dog he was so painfully missing.

He could hardly wait for the sailing date to arrive and was racked with agonies of impatience and delicious anticipation.

WHEN HE STAGGERED out of the train in Chicago, loaded down with bottles of perfume, boxes of delicate underwear, yards of lace, and other expensive presents for Su (including a "genuine" pair of German sniper's binoculars, which he had bought from the Cracker after being assured his comrade had personally taken them from the neck of a fallen German marksman), he made his first discovery of the perfidy and the deviousness of women. Su had married someone else three months earlier—and had gone on writing while neglecting to tell him of her wedding. He was so angry at first that he was tempted to throw his gifts away but was finally persuaded by his frugal-minded mother to pass them on to some of her friends.

Even harder to bear was the news that he got when he journeyed alone to Waukegan that weekend. Russell took him on a street-by-street tour of the city in his brand-new Model T Ford, proudly showing off both his skill as a chauffeur and his new fiancée, a brassy blond who shared the front seat and giggled loudly at every remark her boyfriend made.

When, after more than an hour, Walt finally managed to interrupt his friend's boasts and the girl's raucous laughter long enough to ask when he was going to be reunited with Carey, the girl burst into more fits of giggles. Then Russell, almost casually, informed him that the dog had died of distemper shortly after his return to Waukegan.

"I'd have written you about it," Russell said, "but I'm not much good at letters. And anyway, what did you care what happened to that scruffy little mutt? As Ellie here says, you can always buy another dog."

At which she sputtered with renewed giggles, and Russell went on to talk about something else, as if the death of Carey was the most unimportant thing in the world.

"If we hadn't been in a car with a girl," Walt said later, "I'd have punched him in the nose."

The news about his dog's death hit him harder than the betrayal by his girl. In a way, he was relieved that Su had let him down. It was as if he had never been emotionally involved with her. He didn't care if he never saw her again, and he didn't hate her either—she just turned him off females, and the only woman he would trust for the next few years was his mother.

On the other hand, he felt bitter and sad over the death of Carey. He had really loved that dog and he realized now that Carey had been the only real friend he had made during his service in France. He would never forgive Russell Maas for letting Carey die.

He asked his mother to let him have one of the drawings of Carey he had made during his sojourn at Neufchâteau, but she had thrown all of them away with the exception of the one of the puppy in the musette bag, and she refused to part with that. It so happened that he had plenty of pictures of Su Pitowski, but that was no compensation. When he took them out of his wallet they no longer meant a thing to him, and he tore them up without a qualm.

4

K. C. Blues

ONE OF THE ambitions Walt Disney had carried with him to France was to become a newspaper cartoonist when he got back home.

"Let me know when you get back from France, kid," Carey Orr had told Walt just before he sailed. "I like the way you draw. You've got a good line and flair. All you lack at the moment is bite, but that should come when you get a little more disillusioned with people. Just keep on drawing while you're away and contact me when you get back. Then we'll see how you've developed and what we can do."

So a couple of weeks after his return from France, he went to the *Tribune* office to show his latest work to Carey Orr. But if he expected to come away with a job, he was to be disappointed. Orr received him hospitably enough and made it plain that he was glad to see him back. He listened with grins of appreciation to the tale of his adventures in France and nodded in sympathy at the woes that had greeted him on his return.

Then he reached out for the young man's portfolio and began to leaf through his drawings. But he was disappointed with what he saw. The drawings were good, there was no doubt about that, and his technique had improved beyond measure since he had last looked at Walt's work. He laughed at most of the sketches and thought most of them were funny and remarkably cute.

But that was the trouble with this kid—he was definitely too nice. You could tell that, unlike most cartoonists, he didn't really hate anybody. He had seen the carnage and stupidity of war in France, he had been betrayed by his girl, his best friend had let him down over his favorite dog, he was unhappy at home. But did this kid let his anger show in his attitude or his drawings? On the contrary, he was still the most amiable and forgiving of young men; there wasn't an ounce of bitterness or ill feeling in him, and his way of getting back at the world was to draw something that made you laugh.

The way Carey Orr saw it, that attitude might well turn Walt Disney into a splendid artist one of these days, but it sure as hell wasn't going to make him into a cartoonist.

It was fortunate there were genuinely no vacancies at that moment in the *Tribune* cartoon department, or else Orr might have been forced to tell Walt Disney why this really was no place for him and why it might be better to forget his ambition to be a newspaper cartoonist. Instead, he told him to take another job until conditions were more propitious.

FLORA DISNEY WAS secretly pleased at her son's rejection since she figured it would persuade him to forget his artistic aspirations and settle down to something more practical. Besides, it would keep him at home.

Elias Disney reminded his son that there was a twenty-five dollar a week job waiting for him at the jelly-making factory, and asked why he was dragging his feet. There was a blazing row when Walt contemptuously spurned the proffered job and insisted that he was going to be an artist, no matter what the setbacks.* His father, scoffing at such lofty ambitions, angrily told him that he had grown swollen headed over his experiences in France and that it was time for him to face facts. The result was that both father and son used words Walt, at least, later regretted, and it ended with the last of the four Disney boys walking out of the family home.

Flora pleaded with him not to leave.

"I have to, Mom," Walt said. "I only wish I could take you with me. But you wouldn't do it, would you?"

She shook her head. "No," she said, but he knew she was tempted.

Fortunately, Walt had somewhere to go now that he, too, had walked out on his parents. Roy would help him.

He had always had a distant, almost hostile relationship with his two older brothers, but Roy was different. It was true that there was an eight-year gap between their ages and that temperamentally they were completely opposite. But if he had sometimes found him dull and unresponsive to his whims and unimaginative over his sudden enthusiasms, at least Roy had tried to understand them—which was more than could be said for Elias. In many ways he had come to regard Roy as a substitute father who would respond when he needed him. And he did not fail him now.

Roy, in fact, was far from well, having been discharged with a disabil-

---

*It was just as well that he rejected the job offer. Not long afterward, the jelly factory went into bankruptcy; its principal owner was charged with embezzlement and sent to prison, and Elias lost his investment in the enterprise.

ity pension from the U.S. Navy. For the moment he was back in his prewar job in the Kansas City bank and living with Herbert Disney and his wife and children in the old family home on Bellefontaine, where he paid rent for a parlor and bedroom in the back of the house. He persuaded Herbert to let Walt sleep on the parlor settee for an extra three dollars, and he told his kid brother that he would be glad to share his living quarters with him—and temporarily pay his rent. They had an affecting reunion because the brothers had not seen each other since Roy himself had walked out of the family home, and they had many gaps to fill in.

Roy Disney was a much more businesslike, practical person than Walt, and less commonplace and unimaginative than most people, including Walt, suspected. He was not just fond of his youngest brother. He sensed something special in him, surmising that he was the most gifted, brainiest—and most vulnerable—member of the family. He felt protective toward him.

As Walt spilled out the sorry story of all that had happened to him since he had come back from France, Roy put the events commonsensibly in place as he guessed they had affected his brother. He was not in the least worried over what Su Pitowsky had done to him. He rightly guessed that females played no important part in Walt's scheme of things—for the moment, anyway—and he would soon forget all about the girl's rejection of him. The death of his dog, though more important, was one of those hurts only life and experience would teach him to absorb and accept, and there was nothing Roy could do about that.

On the other hand, he had been disturbed to hear of the rejection Walt had suffered in his ambition to be a cartoonist. He had always been a keen admirer of his brother's artistic talent and he was irritated that it should have been spurned by Walt's own idol, Carey Orr.

Gently, he set out to probe what was going on in Walt's mind now. What did he most want to do now that he was in Kansas City? Did he still want to work as a cartoonist? He did? Then Roy was all for helping him achieve his ambition.

He took time off to accompany him to the office of the *Kansas City Star,* where they had both once worked as delivery boys, and they hung around the city room for several days trying to persuade the art editor to give Walt a job. Walt brought along his portfolio of wartime drawings, and each day, before arriving, he would do a sketch to illustrate one of the main stories on the *Star*'s front page, to show how he might be used as a news sketch artist. But it did no good. There was no job available.

There was very little money, either. It was true Flora Disney was still holding on to the hoard of dollars Walt had sent her from his Red Cross pay (and poker winnings) but he hated to admit failure by wiring home for funds.

It is a measure of the rapport between the two brothers that Roy, though aware of the situation, did not complain and went on staking Walt with free board and lodging. But there were some irksome moments. Roy had a girlfriend named Edna Francis, who also worked in the bank. A willing and accommodating woman, Edna stoically put up with the fact that whenever she met Roy, his brother was sure to be there, too. There were times when she longed to have Roy to herself, but it was never possible. Walt didn't seem to go out like other boys but stayed home to read books about drawing or sit in a corner making sketches, all the time saying: "Don't mind me."

But, of course, they did. And even when he was not there physically, he reminded them of him by leaving notes around saying: "No canoodling!" Or he would draw pictures of two soppy-looking love birds cradled in a nest, beak to beak; and once he shocked Edna by having her actually laying an egg. She finally lost her temper when he slipped under the sofa a toy duck, which he had specially designed so that it squeaked only under the weight of two bodies. Edna was deeply embarrassed and annoyed when she was pressed down on the sofa by Roy's passionate embrace and the duck set up a violent squawking—at which Walt peeked around the door and, grinning broadly, wagged a reproving finger at them.

All this increased Roy's determination to find his kid brother something that would get him out of the house, bring in a paycheck, and satisfy his artistic aspirations. It so happened that two of his clients at the bank were in advertising, and Roy plucked up courage to ask if there were any jobs going for a young and promising artist. He was lucky. The two clients ran the small Pesmen-Rubin Agency, which provided illustrations for the advertisements and catalogs put out for its customers by the bigger Gray Agency, and it turned out that they were looking for an apprentice.

Roy told Walt to apply, and he was hired on the strength of his wartime caricatures. He was so delighted at getting a job that he not only began paying Roy five dollars a week for his bed and board but also splurged on a long-distance phone call to his mother and told her the good news. He had to confess it was a temporary job but did not add that the pay was only twelve dollars a week. This was just as well since Elias reacted skeptically to the news, refused to congratulate him on his good fortune, and prophesied he would soon be out of a job again.

He worked for the agency for nearly two months and said later that he picked up more technical skills in that period than he had learned at the academy in Chicago in a year. The two illustrators, Louis Pesmen and Bill Rubin, thought up the layouts and did the principal drawings for the Gray Agency, which chiefly did advertisements for farm equipment manufacturers. After making rough sketches they passed them over to Walt and another apprentice for them to add the final touches.

The other apprentice, Ubbe Iwwerks, a shy and tongue-tied son of a

Dutch immigrant family, was already a quick, smooth, and efficient draftsman; he had picked up all the tricks of the trade and was generous in showing Walt the professional shortcuts he had learned in drawing technique. He taught him how to spruce up and enliven a drawing by the deft use of razor-blade marks on white paint and by the practical uses of a pantograph to increase his output.

Iwwerks was also full of ideas for brightening up Pesmen-Rubin's often mundane sketches for their clients, adding crowing cocks, barn-yard animals, and cloud-flecked skies as background to the sketches of the ploughs and hoes and carts they were advertising. Walt respected his talent and was grateful for his help, but found it difficult to resist the temptation to play tricks and make fun of his fellow apprentice, who was an intensely shy and naive young man.

Walt Disney at nineteen had a sunny disposition, and when things were going well, a tendency to boast about himself. There was nothing he liked better than to tell tall tales that he did not mean to be taken seriously. Few people did, in fact.

"Pull the other one, Walt!" they would shout, when he started a particularly outrageous story.

Unfortunately, Iwwerks was so credulous that he believed everything Walt told him, and brooded, in resentful disillusion, when he realized his fellow apprentice had been taking advantage of his gullibility. Though he never gave any signs of anger or irritation, he hated being made fun of, and was deeply mortified when he found himself taken in by Walt's tall tales or made the butt of Walt's often crude and juvenile practical jokes.

WALT DISNEY HAD been hired as an apprentice by Pesmen-Rubin in October 1919 because it was the busy season, what with all the Christmas catalogs to prepare as well as the brochures for the January sales. After that business sagged, the new apprentice was let go at the end of November. Walt was not too downcast about that; he was confident that he could now make a living as a commercial artist.

In the meantime, to build up his funds, he did what he had done before when he was short of cash—he went to the central post office in Kansas City and got a temporary job sorting and delivering the Christmas mail. It was after one session of tramping the Kansas City streets with his heavy load that he came home and found the forlorn figure of Ubbe Iwwerks awaiting him on the outside steps.

Iwwerks too had been let go, and for him it was a catastrophe. It took Walt some time to get the truth out of him, but he finally extracted from the reluctant Iwwerks the fact that his father was a hopeless inebriate, his mother was an invalid, and there were several younger children in the family. They had relied on the fifteen dollars a week Iwwerks earned to pay the rent and keep them clothed and fed. Without his weekly stipend they were in danger of being thrown out onto the streets to starve. What was he to do?

Walt took him inside, gave him a meal, and, after some thought, decided the only solution was for them both to go into business together as free-lance illustrators. He tucked a ten-dollar bill into Iwwerks's pocket and sent him back home to pick up samples of his work. Combining them with his own, he went to see a man named Jake Carter, who ran a fly-by-night publication called *Restaurant News.* It was one of those newspapers distributed free in cafés and restaurants that advertised in its twelve flimsy pages.

Carter ran his throwaway paper on a shoestring and had no money to spare to buy illustrations. But even at eighteen, Walt Disney had a line of talk capable of charming even the stoniest man, and it did not take him long to persuade the reluctant editor that he and his partner would be good for business.

He showed Carter a picture that he had drawn of the most glamorous film star of the day, Gloria Swanson, seated at a table sipping champagne and seductively smoking a cigarette in a long, long holder. Walt had actually adapted the drawing from a publicity still of the big film then showing in town, Cecil B. de Mille's *Male and Female,* but he had added some familiar potted palms and roman urns featured at a well-known local restaurant, and the caption underneath had Swanson saying, "I always dine at Alfredo's when I'm in Kansas City."

He promised that if they were given the chance, he and his partner could provide similarly attractive come-ons for every eating place in town, and Carter could sell advertising space on their illustrations alone.

The editor was won over to the extent that he promised to pay the partners ten dollars a week, and also provide them, rent free, with a workroom in his small suite of offices. Actually, it turned out to be the spare office bathroom, with absolutely nothing in it but a sink and a toilet. But Walt was not in the least abashed. He decided at long last to send home for the money Flora Disney was guarding for him, and asked her to wire him five hundred dollars at once.

Unfortunately, all messages arriving at the Disney household in Chicago, no matter to whom they were addressed, were still opened by Elias if he was at home when they were delivered. He read Walt's wire to Flora and sternly forbade her to send any money at all until she had first learned exactly what he proposed to do with it.

"What business is that of father's?" Walt asked, indignantly. "It's my money, isn't it?"

But then, anxious not to make trouble for his mother, he explained he needed to pay for furnishing the new office he was setting up with a partner in Kansas City. His mother, on Elias's instructions, wired him $250 only and it was with this sum, less than half of what he had sent home from France, that he bought desks, easels, drawing boards, and airbrushes.

He also arranged for a sign to be posted on the door with the name of the new firm. He had already persuaded Iwwerks to drop the superfluous letters from his name so that he would henceforward be known as Ub Iwerks, and, at Ub's suggestion, he had shortened his own name from Walter Disney to Walt Disney. But what would the new partnership call itself?

At first he had instructed the sign painter to give his young partner top billing and put IWERKS-DISNEY on the door, but then Carter came past and jibed that it looked like a dentist's sign. Finally, they decided on:

IWERKS & DISNEY
Commercial Artists

They were in business.

IN NO WAY could they live on the ten dollars a week Jake Carter was paying them, not even with free office space; and it was urgent that they find other clients without delay. Iwerks was no help in this at all. He was struck dumb by the presence of other people, and his talents as a salesman were nil.

So it was left to Walt, a born promoter, to drum up prospects likely to pay them money. He decided his best plan was to seek business from all the printers in town. He designed and produced a flashy-looking contract, which pledged Disney & Iwerks would become the "official art department" of any printer who signed an agreement to pay them thirty dollars a month, in return for which they would produce all the artwork the printers needed on demand.

Most of them were shrewd enough to know a bargain when one was offered. After looking over his samples, they signed up. By the end of their first month in business, the partners were making twice what their combined earnings at Pesmen-Rubin had been.

Their first client was a printing firm that sent them a promotional prospectus from an oil company and asked them to illustrate it. The oil company wanted investors' money. Walt, always the inspired visualizer, designed, and Iwerks drew, an oil well from which gushers of twenty-dollar bills were seen to be raining down. It was startling and effective. Both printer and promoter were delighted.

The partners soon had enough in the bank to move out of Carter's bathroom and rent an outside office near the railroad station. One day, Ub confessed to Walt that as a result of his new-found prosperity, his father had gone on the wagon, his mother had been seen by a doctor, and all members of the family were eating as much as they wanted.

He would like to have added how deeply grateful he was to Walt for what he had done for him, but he was tongue-tied when it came to showing his emotions. Then, too, each time he made a special effort and summoned up sufficient courage to express his heartfelt thanks, Walt would spoil everything by playing a practical joke on him or making fun of him in front of other people. The words would freeze in his throat, and he would find himself feeling resentful again toward his benefactor.

In the spring of 1920, Iwerks read an advertisement in the *Star* for a cartoonist for the Kansas City Film Ad Company. For some time now, the partners had been fascinated with the cartoon features that were now being frequently shown in the local movie houses, and Walt had begun experimenting with comic strips, which he dreamed one day of animating for films.

Iwerks, who had some lively ideas of his own, saw the ad in the *Star* as a great opportunity to fulfill their ambitions. Well aware of his own inarticulateness, he urged Walt to answer it for both of them and try to sell their joint services for the job, which they could easily do in addition to their ordinary work for the local printers.

Walt was offered the job by the film advertising agency as soon as he showed his portfolio, but the moment he mentioned doing it part time in collaboration with his partner, he was crisply informed this was a full-time position for one person only. Moreover, though the advertising man apologized for offering only forty dollars a week for the job, he did add that there were good prospects for advancement.

Forty dollars a week! It was more money than Walt had ever dreamed of making. . . . Why, he would be rich!

But what was he going to say to Ub?

He took his time walking back to the office, his pace getting slower and slower as he drew near. Ub would be devastated if he told him he was going to take the job and break up the partnership.

On the other hand, how could he possibly turn down the offer? Now that he had seen the kind of work the film ad company was doing, he knew this would be the fulfillment of a dream. He realized that this was the kind of artwork he had always wanted to do—animating cartoon characters on a screen. Those were the kind of images that blazed through his head when he dreamed at night. He had to take the job.

But what about Ub?

Just before he opened the door of Iwerks & Disney on his way back from the interview, he finally made up his mind and knew what he was going to do—even if still not sure of what he was going to say.

But for once Iwerks took the words out of his mouth. Seeing the expression of suppressed excitement on his partner's face, he hastily interjected, "I know. They offered *you* the job and not the partnership. How much are they paying?"

"Forty dollars a week!" Walt said, trying to keep the wonder out of his voice.

"Why, it's a fortune!" Iwerks exclaimed. He was silent for long moments while he struggled with his emotions, and then he burst out, "You just have to take it, Walt. There will never be another opportunity like it!"

"But what about you—about *us?*" Walt said, doubtfully.

"Don't worry about me! I'll manage," Iwerks said, falsely cheerful. Then he drooped, as if the implication of what was happening was just beginning to sink in. He looked so forlorn that he reminded Walt of a sparrow that has just been caught in a downpour of icy rain.

But then a thought occurred to him, and he cheered up again. "Why, I can always go on running Iwerks & Disney on my own," he said. He looked anxiously at Walt. "Provided you'll turn the assets over to me, of course, and let me carry on with the firm—and the name."

It was what Walt had been going to suggest as the solution, and he was relieved that it was his partner who had proposed it. "I'll turn everything over to you—all our contracts, assets, everything."

So it was arranged that all the goodwill and assets of Iwerks & Disney would be transferred from their joint names to that of Ub Iwerks alone. Only the airbrushing equipment, which Walt had purchased personally and still owed money on, was sold to Iwerks on an installment basis.

They shook hands on the deal. Then the partners, not looking at each other, wished each other luck in their future ventures.

ANY FEELINGS OF guilt Walt Disney might have had over his desertion of Ub Iwerks were soon dissipated. He was conscious of a lift in his spirits, and he knew it had as much to do with the break in the partnership as with excitement over his new job. Responsibility for his erstwhile partner's welfare had been a troublesome burden from which he was now free.

"Don't think I won't miss Ub, worry about him, feel I have to keep an eye on the guy and make sure he isn't in trouble," he later confessed to his brother Roy. "But for the moment, I'm darned glad to be rid of him. And frankly, I don't care if I never work with him or worry about him again."

5

An Animated Life

WALT DISNEY WAS always in fine physical condition and was usually so tired at the end of his day's work that he slept like a baby from the moment he climbed into bed at eleven each evening. Nevertheless, there were moments during the night when he heard, through the thick mists of sleep, the sounds of painful bouts of coughing and of pacing up and down from the adjacent bedroom. He began slowly to realize that something was very wrong with Roy.

Sometimes he was shocked by his appearance in the morning. Roy's gaunt, sweating, haggard face; his deep-set eyes; and his long, sharp, pasty-colored nose seemed to Walt to belong more to the head of a sick eagle than to a human being. When he emerged from his bedroom, his puny body was often racked by convulsions that brought up gobs of phlegm, which he hurriedly concealed in his handkerchief and then surreptitiously examined for signs of blood.

In the spring of 1920, Roy came down with a bout of influenza and was so seriously ill that it was decided to transfer him to a hospital. His recovery was slow and painful, and the doctors confessed they were worried about him. He went back to work in the bank, but it was obvious that he was not getting any better. When he and Edna were in Roy's quarters, Walt could hear his brother and his fiancée muttering together urgently, as if they had something other than "canoodling" on their minds.

Frequently, he caught his own name being mentioned, and once, he detected Edna whispering fiercely, "But he'll be a grown man! You can't look after him all his life!"

At which his brother whispered back, "But he's family! I feel responsible."

As indeed he did, and the knowledge of it did nothing to help his physical recovery.

One day, in 1920, the reason for all that groaning, heaving, coughing, and midnight pacing from the bedroom next to his was revealed to Walt. At first his doctor had blamed the condition of Roy's tonsils for the continual bouts of influenza that had afflicted him that winter. But when he went to a local surgeon for a cut-rate tonsillectomy, he collapsed on the way home and had to be rushed to the veterans hospital where the hemorrhage was stopped, but a spot was discovered on his lungs. He was told that he had a serious case of tuberculosis and advised to leave Kansas City right away for a drier, warmer climate.

It is a measure of Roy Disney's regard for his brother that, although he worried about what effect the news of his medical condition would have on his fiancée, he was almost equally concerned about what it could do to Walt. How would the kid manage if left to fend for himself?

It was true that he wouldn't be leaving him entirely alone. Herbert Disney would still be around with his family; but Herbert was too wrapped up in his own affairs to keep a benevolent eye on Walt. Besides, Roy knew both Herb and his wife objected to the boy's breezy manner and rather patronizing attitude toward them, and if they sensed that he had any special qualities, they resented rather than appreciated them. What he had to do, Roy decided, was make sure Walt was safely settled in a good job before his own physical crisis came to a head.

The result was that in his spare hours, during a period when he was only too aware that his condition was deteriorating, he spent much of his time working on his younger brother's future security. Roy had sworn to himself that, no matter what it took, he was somehow going to get Walt a job on the staff of the *Star* so that he could leave Kansas City with a clear conscience, knowing that Walt was safe and settled.

So while Walt, toiling in the cramped bathroom of the *Restaurant News,* was drawing pictures of glamorous film stars to drum up ads for local bistros, and while he was slogging around the city's printers in search of contracts for himself and Ub Iwerks, the ailing Roy was doing some canvassing himself. He had gone through the lists of the bank's customers and set his sights on any of them who worked for the *Star* group. One by one he cultivated them in order to show off his brother's drawings and sing his praises as a potential newspaper illustrator.

Early in 1920, his efforts were rewarded and a call came from one of the editors of the *Star*'s morning paper, the *Times,* to say a cartoonist was leaving, and if Walt was ready to start the following week, there was a job for him as an assistant. But this happened about a month after Walt had begun working at the film ad company, and his outlook had changed radically.

Absorbed as he was in his new work, Walt was hardly aware of what a tremendous effort his brother had been making on his behalf. So he had no compunction in saying flatly that he was no longer interested in a newspaper job because he had found work he was enjoying very much more.

"Of course I'm not going to take it!" said Walt, bluntly. "It's too late. They had their chance months ago when we offered my services, and they kicked us out."

The strength of Roy Disney's affection was such that he showed not the slightest resentment at Walt's rough rejection of what his brother considered a tremendous opportunity. Roy did not try to argue with Walt. His brother's tone of voice was enough to convince Roy that he really needn't have worried, after all. His kid brother had found his niche.

WALT DISNEY WENT to the movies at least five times a week, and unlike most young men of his age, it was not simply to drool over the sight of undraped sirens like Mae Murray or Betty Blythe or Nazimova but to study the short films that were always an integral part of the programs in those days.

He was, of course, an admirer of the Hollywood comics who figured regularly in the short-feature programs. He not only was a fan of Charlie Chaplin, Buster Keaton, Ben Turpin, and the antics of the Keystone Cops but closely watched their techniques, too; in the dark of the theater, he scrawled down notes about their facial expressions, body language, and the methods they used in the construction of their gags.

He had another particular interest when he went to the movies, and that was to watch the animated cartoon shorts that were beginning to be a popular feature of movie programs at the time. He was both fascinated and dissatisfied with them and was already convinced that he could do better himself.

Thanks to Ub Iwerks, who had lent him books about art and the cinema, he had taken to patronizing the Kansas City Public Library, where he read every book and magazine article about cartooning and cinematic animation he could lay his hands on. Not that there was all that much material available at the time. But he did discover that the idea of putting animated drawings on the cinema screen had attracted artists and illustrators from the earliest days of the movies, and names like Georges Melies and Winsor McCay began to figure largely in his consciousness and his conversation.

Melies was a French magician and illusionist who, in 1902, had made a short film, using live actors and sketched backgrounds, called *Trip to the Moon*. McCay had been one of the great newspaper cartoonists of his day, working for the *New York Herald* as its principal cartoonist. He had fallen in love with the movies when he saw an early work of Thomas

Edison, starring D. W. Griffith, called *Rescued from an Eagle's Nest*, and felt that many of its amateurish flying sequences could have been vastly improved by graphic animation.

McCay had begun experimenting by making his own animated cartoon films, using animal characters, and they were remarkably lifelike in appearance—so much so that, after their first public showing, critics accused him of tracing his cartoon characters from photographs. To demonstrate how wrong they were, he invented a character called "Gertie the Dinosaur," which could not possibly have been copied from any photograph.

Quite fortuitously, McCay did something else to Gertie that had been missing from his previous cartoon animals and from other animated films. To stress Gertie's originality, both as a drawing and a personality, he gave her a character of her own—she smiled seraphically when she sniffed (and then ate) spring flowers on a hillside; she writhed, danced, and opened her great mouth to sing; she cringed when she accidentally trod on a friendly mouse and wept, tears rolling down her pendulous cheeks, when she surveyed the tiny animal's broken body.

It was the first time anyone had ever given personality to a cartoon character, and if Gertie had been anything but a great mountain of an animal, she might have caught on with the public. But no one was interested in the antics of a dinosaur, even one with feelings, and Gertie died at the box office.

McCay labored on for the next ten years but, by 1921, found himself no longer able to afford his animated cartoons, nor could he persuade anyone in the film world to finance his work. Out of sheer hunger, he went back to salaried cartooning with the *New York Herald*. His early work was forgotten until movie researchers discovered it and marveled at his technique fifty years later. Ub Iwerks had caught one of the "Gertie the Dinosaur" films in a small downtown movie house and raved about it to his associate when he and Walt were still working together at the *Restaurant News*.

But when he dragged Walt back to the theater to see it, the cartoon had already been taken off, and one of the popular "Felix the Cat" series had been substituted. "Felix the Cat" was the invention of an illustrator-animator named Otto Messmer, and as Iwerks pointed out, it had no personality of its own but relied entirely on action, situation, and fast-moving gags to give it character.

The two young men often spent hours in those days dreaming up characters for animated cartoons of their own. What they envisioned was a cartoon animal who would become as real to anyone watching it on the screen as humans like Chaplin, Turpin, or Larry Semon.

After all, Walt pointed out, human or not, these comedians were only celluloid characters, too. Why couldn't he and Ub create an animated cartoon animal whose appearance and foibles would be appreciated in the same way as Chaplin's mustache, winsome smile, battered bowler, cane, and funny walk—remembered not simply for its gags and unlikely situations, but for its personality.

Convinced that this was the way to go for any newcomer to animated cartooning, Walt openly scoffed at the creations featured on the local screens. One of the particular objects of his contempt was the most popular animation series of the day, Max Fleischer's "Out of the Inkwell." Walt maintained that the "Inkwell" characters, no matter how ingeniously they were drawn, were forgotten moments after they spilled onto the screen because Fleischer never thought of them as anything but quaint creatures involved in comic situations. He was confident that he could invent a cartoon character that movie audiences would learn to love and remember not for its comic gags but for itself.

For the moment, involved as he was in his new job at the Kansas City Film Ad Company, Walt did not have time to do much creating. In any case, he was too busy completing his education in the basic skills and techniques of animated cartooning.

The film ad company made most of its income from publicity shorts for local shops and businesses. The clips lasted from thirty seconds to two minutes and were shown in local movie houses between the short subjects and the main feature. Most of them used animated characters, but the technique was old-fashioned even for the 1920s.

Walt and the other artists (there was a staff of sixteen) drew animal and human characters that were then pasted to cardboard and painstakingly cut out and fixed to a drawing board, with their arms, legs, and bodies separated and pinned so that they could be moved. A cameraman photographed the cutouts in stop-motion, then moved the limbs and body and photographed them again and again so that when projected, the series of pictures gave the impression of motion.

Even a beginner like Walt Disney knew that in New York and other big moviemaking centers, they had already gone beyond these techniques and were using drawings instead of cutouts. In the Kansas City Public Library he had found two books that now became his learning manuals. One was a volume by Carl Lutz on the art of animation. The other was a book of stop-and-go photographs taken by Eadweard Muybridge of animal and human motion. After poring over the text and the illustrations, Walt abandoned the painstaking cutout techniques used by the film ad company as too excruciatingly jerky and unrealistic. He began making a succession of drawings in which the characters fractionally changed (or "moved") in each different frame and could be photographed in stop-motion without being cut out and clumsily maneuvered on the drawing board.

When projected on the screen the movements appeared much smoother and more realistic and would be even more so, Walt decided, if he increased the quality of the technique and the number of drawings.

Walt was always realistic and honest with himself about his own talents, and he was aware that his drawings had more flair than polish. So far as draftsmanship was concerned, he knew there were many others—Ub Iwerks, for instance—who could surpass him in quality. So though his employers were impressed with the results of his experiments, he was dissatisfied with his own achievements. He knew he did not have the patience to complete sufficient drawings to eliminate all jerkiness from the projected images, nor did he have the expertise to make the movements of the characters in each frame blend smoothly with the next. He badly missed the technical help that had always been at hand when he and Ub had worked together, so he was pleased, if hardly surprised, when he came back to his rooms one night in 1920 and found Iwerks forlornly waiting for him on the doorstep.

With shamed apologies, Ub confessed that the firm of Iwerks & Disney was on the verge of bankruptcy. Since he had assumed sole direction of the company, Ub's lack of ideas and salesmanship and his timidity and ignorance of business know-how had brought the company to a standstill. A once-thriving enterprise was on the verge of disaster; and once more, he had come to Walt, the man he both loved and resented, to plead with him to save him from ruin.

Walt made a few inquiries and quickly came to the conclusion that Iwerks & Disney was beyond saving. He advised Ub to start bankruptcy proceedings without delay. When Ub asked miserably, "But what about me? What am I going to do?" his friend told him not to worry.

Walt had by this time achieved enough prestige with his new employers to be able to ask them to hire his erstwhile partner, and so Ub Iwerks came into his life again, at a crucial moment in his professional career.

Henceforward, it was Walt Disney who provided the rough drawings and brilliant ideas at the film ad company and Ub Iwerks who took them in hand and smoothly executed them.

Nothing had changed in the relationship between the two young men except that Ub Iwerks was, if anything, more sensitive than ever to slights, more vulnerable to assaults on his *amour propre*. This was unfortunate, for at the same time, Walt Disney, now twenty years old, had grown into a bouncy and self-confident young man. Though never deliberately cruel, he could be thoughtless and never did understand the weaknesses and hidden resentments of his friend.

His employers had by now upped Walt's salary to sixty dollars a week, which was enough in the Kansas City of those days to finance a life-style of some affluence for an unattached young man. He patronized the best tailors in town and became a flashy dresser, with sharp suits and bright how ties. He began to be seen in the best restaurants, and his name figured in the society columns among those who went to charity fancy-dress balls. He was even photographed at one such party doing rope tricks while dressed in a cowboy costume complete with a ten-gallon hat.

At the same time, he treated everyone, including Ub Iwerks, with breezy insouciance and seemed sublimely uncaring (or unaware) that some men are tender plants who must be handled with special care. He was very much a practical joker. He was never vindictive about it, as some famous practical jokers of the time—the name of Alfred Hitchcock comes to mind—could be. He did not get a kick out of making his fellow mortals feel humiliated or inferior, as Charles Lindbergh, for instance, used to do. It was just that he was always unable to resist an easy mark; and Ub was an easy mark.

Fortunately, most of the tricks he played on him were harmless enough and were easily forgotten. Knowing that he was acutely shy and that he hated to draw attention to himself, Walt would lock Ub in the office toilet until he was forced to hammer on the door to be freed—by one of the girls that Walt had let in on the joke. He sent him saucy postcards at the office signed "Lulu" or "Fifi" because he knew he was terribly embarrassed about girls.

But sometimes he caused pain.

Ub was hopeless with girls. There was a pretty girl in the office named Margaret Metzinger whom he adored, but she was hardly aware of his existence; and he was, in any case, far too shy to ask her for a date. Actually, Margaret had a "crush" on Walt, which he did not reciprocate. One night, he persuaded her to meet him in a downtown restaurant—and then sent Ub instead. Ub was the last person Margaret wanted to see. That might have caused them only temporary embarrassment had not Walt also persuaded one of the staff cameramen to make a secret film of the rendezvous, with close-ups of their expressions when they realized that they had been tricked. Walt screened the film the next day in front of the rest of the office. Amid the jeers and laughter, Margaret Metzinger threw a pot of ink over Walt and ruined his jacket. But Ub walked out of the projection room without saying a word, and Walt realized that perhaps he might have gone too far.

INEVITABLY, WALT'S SUCCESS and self-confident manner aroused a certain amount of jealousy in other quarters at the Kansas City Film Ad Company, and one of those who openly resented him was the head of the art department. He was heard to remark on one occasion, after Walt had been praised for some of his work, "Young Disney's head is getting so swollen he won't be able to get his hat on soon."

One of the weaknesses of Walt's draftmanship was his inability to draw lifelike human faces. The art director, aware of this and determined to draw his boss's attention to it, ordered him to execute a series of ads for a local hat merchant, insisting each hat in the illustration be drawn with a face beneath it. Walt realized the art director was setting him up so he turned in a series of drawings in which each hat was perched on an electric light bulb or an egg, with eyes, nose, and mouth crudely but comically sketched in underneath the brim. The art director triumphantly marched into the boss's office to demonstrate Walt's incompetence and was mortified when the boss laughed out loud and praised the young man's ingenuity.

Meanwhile, after only a short pang of conscience over his friend's discomfiture, Walt was back at his old habit of teasing Ub Iwerks. He put mice in his pockets, guinea pigs in his desk, and, once found an African macaw in a downtown pet shop that talked in Afrikaans, the nearest he could get to Dutch. He smuggled it into Ub's locker, and, when he opened it, the bird came out squawking, "Dod, waar is de prickel? Scrabble op de beestjes!" He continued to be unaware of how much Ub resented his jibes and crude schoolboy tricks.

AT TWENTY WALT was a cauldron bubbling and seething with energy, ambition, and ideas. He spent every waking hour working out characters and situations for animated cartoons, and the jealous art director began complaining that Walt was using too much office time and space on his own preoccupations. Walt's reply was to march into his boss's office and persuade him to lend him one of the agency's cameras so that he could continue his experiments at home.

His brother Roy, who was getting paler, thinner, and sicker every day, insisted on helping Walt and Ub rig up a makeshift studio in the garage of Herbert's house on Bellefontaine; and there Walt began making a series of animated shorts. They were slickly made and smartly drawn, and they were funny; but they certainly didn't incorporate any of the new ideas Walt had been discussing with Ub.

Ub would have preferred him doing something more original, but for the moment Walt needed money and a reputation, and he decided the only way to get them was by playing safe. So in imitation of Max Fleischer's "Out of the Inkwell" series, he drew a picture of his own hand on the screen seeming to sketch comic gags about local situations. The first featured an open automobile filled with a family out for a Sunday picnic. As the car proceeded down Kansas City's main streets, which were full of potholes, it started to shake itself to pieces. The false teeth of the father and mother flew out and did a dance together on the pavement. Kids bounced in the air and fenders, hubcaps, and finally rear wheels came off and created havoc all around them.

The condition of Kansas City's streets was notorious, and the cartoon graphically drew attention to it. In 1920, Walt had no difficulty selling it to Milton Feld, who ran a chain of movie houses in the city known as Newman Theaters. It was such a success and caused so much talk, the city actually got around to voting money for road repairs.

Feld decided Walt's cartoons would work best as advertising films and contracted for twelve more, which he named Newman's Laugh-O-Grams. His audiences liked them. So did local merchants, who lined up to have Walt do Laugh-O-Grams about their products.

By 1921, Walt felt confident enough to begin introducing some of his new ideas into the cartoons. They were effective and demonstrated that his wit and ingenuity more than made up for any shortcomings he might have as a draftsman. For instance, in subsequent Laugh-O-Grams he never showed the telephone number of a client simply as a set of letters and figures but gave each letter and number legs and arms and had them scurrying around and jostling each other for a place until he got them in the right order. He did an ad for an auto company that fitted new tops on open cars and had a proud purchaser being asked, as he drove a slick-looking car out of the garage, "New car, old top?" to which he smugly replies, "No, new top, old car."

For another cartoon, Walt's hand on the screen drew a huge and elaborate birthday cake from which, in a burst of fireworks and flames, the images of Gloria Swanson and Mae Murray spilled out, plus all the other stars of the new films coming to the Newman Theaters.

The bane of a moviegoer's life in those days was the sound of other members of the audience reading out loud the subtitles of the silent films. To curb this disturbing habit, Walt invented a crazy professor who was seen on the screen stalking through the audience flattening with a huge mallet anyone caught reading the subtitles out loud.

Soon everyone was talking about Newman's Laugh-O-Grams, and Walt Disney's success was such that he resigned his job with the Kansas City Film Ad Company and formed his own production company, called, inevitably, Laugh-O-Gram Films, Inc.

This was 1922. He was not destined to make his fortune, though. Not yet. Sheer lack of business experience on Walt's part prevented his cartoons—even the Laugh-O-Grams he had already finished—from making the profits they deserved.

When Milton Feld first asked him to name a price for his shorts, Walt had asked for thirty cents a foot of film, which was exactly what the cartoons cost him to make. He was given a contract for the amount he named. So he gained nothing at all, except a local reputation; and he had no capital to spare when he incorporated his production company and branched out into new ventures.

Fortunately, he had already acquired a reputation in Kansas City for his skills and resourcefulness, and a number of local citizens clubbed together to contribute a capital of $15,000 in $250 shares. With this Walt was able to put new films into production.

He made two seven-minute films, both based on well-known fairy tales, one called *Puss in Boots* and the other *Red Riding Hood.*

The two cartoon shorts did sufficiently well locally to persuade Walt to hire salesmen to sell them nationwide, and both *Puss in Boots* and *Red Riding Hood* and other shorts were soon being seen on movie screens in New York, Chicago, and Philadelphia. But none of the salesmen ever turned over the receipts from these showings, and by the end of 1922, Laugh-o-Gram Films, Inc. was desperately short of money. The shareholders in Laugh-O-Gram shied away when they were asked to provide further capital while the situation was straightened out.

All might have gone well had Walt had the help of Roy in managing his business affairs, but Roy was no longer available. Toward the end of 1920, army doctors had sent him West to convalesce at a veterans hospital in Arizona, and they said they were going to keep him there for at least a year.

As a farewell gift to his kid brother, Roy paid Herbert a year's rent in advance for lodging and use of the garage-studio at Bellefontaine, and he gave Walt one hundred dollars to tide him over any emergencies that might come up. Walt saw him off, and only the presence of Edna Francis, who was weeping bitterly at her fiancé's departure (Roy's illness had interrupted their marriage plans, and she would have to wait another five years until they were reunited), prevented him from bursting into tears himself as his brother's train pulled out. "Keep in touch, kid," Roy said. "I'll always be ready when you need any help."

HE HAD CHARGED his fiancée with keeping an eye on Walt, and she faithfully discharged her responsibilities. Edna Francis, in fact, proved to be both tactful and understanding. She often slipped around to Walt's lodgings to do his laundry and to make sure that his bed sheets were changed regularly and that he had food in his cupboard. But motherly and attentive though she proved to be, he still missed Roy badly. His brother had come to mean much more to him than Elias. He couldn't bear to think that Roy might succumb to his illness. From the moment he departed for Arizona, he began bombarding him with "get well" cards, and Roy wrote back to him almost every day.

But, of course, he missed Roy for practical reasons, too. Roy could have handled the affairs of Laugh-O-Gram Films, Inc. and made sure the receipts came in, the bills were paid, and the profits accumulated. Without his economic skills to look after the affairs of the corporation, Walt realized that he was on the road to bankruptcy, despite the promising quality of his films.

By 1923 Walt was desperate. He felt his only chance to restore his fortunes was to risk everything. So he pooled all his resources and managed to raise enough cash to tackle his most ambitious venture so far. It was a film called *Alice's Wonderland* and was based on the Lewis Carroll character. It used a real-life Alice—a six-year-old moppet with blond corkscrew curls—whom he surrounded with animated cartoon animals, drawn with the help of Ub Iwerks and a small band of student animators.

Walt was convinced that the successful launch of Alice would save him from disaster, and he put all the skill and know-how he had picked up so far into its production, plus his own considerable ingenuity and inspiration.

But worthy though the production proved to be, it came too late to save Laugh-O-Gram Films, Inc. from ruin. Only one of the original shareholders still had faith in him and continued to send a weekly check for a modest sum. It helped to keep some of the creditors at bay.

Roy Disney did what he could, too. From his convalescent hospital, first in Arizona, then in West Los Angeles, he kept mailing blank checks to his young brother telling him to "fill them out for any sum you like up to thirty dollars." They were welcome, but they were not enough to pay off the debts nor enough to keep Walt in lodgings and food.

Trouble, in fact, was now coming at him from all directions. Herbert Disney, who still worked for the post office, had been transferred to Portland, Oregon, and departed with his family. Elias and Flora Disney then arrived to take up residence at the Bellefontaine house. The jelly factory in Chicago in which Elias had invested all his money had collapsed and Elias was now looking for a carpentry job. When he failed to find one, he put the Bellefontaine house on the market, told his son he would have to find other accommodations, and left for Oregon to join his eldest son.

It was a bad time. Walt had found himself a small downtown office in which he crammed his camera and equipment, and he slept in a chair or on the floor at night. Once a week he went to Union Station where, for a dime, he got a towel, soap, and the use of the depot's bathing facilities.

Along with all his other ventures, his cartoon school had collapsed, and the students had departed. Ub Iwerks, who had worked without salary when business turned sour, had used up his savings and reluctantly gone back to work at the Kansas City Film Ad Company. He sometimes lent Walt a couch at his own lodgings when his erstwhile associate could no longer bear the unrelenting hardness of the office floor. But Ub, who was owed one thousand dollars in back wages by Laugh-O-Gram, needed every dime he could lay his hands on. He was still taking care of his family and had no money to spare for Walt.

"It was probably the blackest time of my life," Walt said later. "I really knew what hardship and hunger were like. I remember a couple of Greeks who ran a restaurant below my office gave me credit to run up food bills for a time, but even they grew hard-hearted in the end, and though they never really let me starve, they always made sure I got the cheapest food in the house and fed me on leftovers. It was a pretty lonely and miserable time of my life."

A memory of what it was like was later provided by a local dentist, Dr. Thomas McCrum, who had seen some of the Laugh-O-Grams in the Newman movie houses and thought Walt could make a cartoon film for the Kansas City Dental Institute, teaching young people how to take care of their teeth. He went to see Walt and was surprised at the seediness of his office. There was a half-eaten can of corned beef with a jackknife in it on the desk and no staff visible.

Walt told the dentist an animated cartoon could be made for around five hundred dollars, and Dr. McCrum said he would consult his colleagues at the institute. A few nights later he telephoned to tell Walt that the project had been approved and said that if he would come to the dentist's office, he could sign the contract and be handed the money.

There was a long pause before Walt said, "I can't come. I haven't any shoes. They were falling apart, and I left them with the shoemaker around the corner, and I don't have the dollar and a half to collect them."

"Stay where you are," Dr. McCrum said, "I'll be right over." He went to pick up Walt's shoes, paid the $1.50, and arrived with them thirty minutes later. Then they drove back to the dentist's office together, where they signed the deal for the film.*

BUT OBVIOUSLY, IT would not be long before Laugh-O-Gram—or Walt—collapsed entirely.

Roy Disney wrote him from Los Angeles, "Call it quits, kid. You can't do anything more than you've already done."

The company filed for bankruptcy in the spring of 1923 and Walt persuaded the creditors to allow him to hold on to his camera and to a copy of the Alice film, which he intended to use as a sample for soliciting

---

*It was subsequently made single-handedly by Walt and called *Tommy Tucker's Tooth.* In McCrum's words it was "a little comic gem. The kids loved it." He added, "Later on, when I met Walt again in Hollywood, I said that must have been the worst moment of his life, having to eat corned beef out of a can. Walt vigorously shook his head. 'Oh, no,' he said. 'I'm nuts about corned beef.'"

future work. All his other equipment and the few tangible assets he possessed were seized.

He wrote his brother that a local Kansas City moviemaker had offered him a job making animated cartoons for him, but he had decided to make a completely fresh start and planned to leave for either New York or Hollywood. Roy wired him to come out West.

First he had to pay off his personal debts and raise the money for his railroad fare. To that end he got himself a job as a stringer for the Universal and Pathé Newsreel companies, and he found it an exhilarating experience. Using the camera his creditors had allowed him to keep, his cap rakishly worn backward, and his camera perched on the back of a rented open Ford auto, he soon became a well-known figure in the city as he cruised the streets looking for stories.

Pathé paid him a bonus for his work, which was enough to enable him to leave Kansas City at last. Tired of skimping, desperate for a little luxury, he bought himself a first-class one-way ticket to California. For the trip he wore a checkered jacket, blue pants, a bright red bow tie, and he carried a small suitcase with two spare shirts and a spare set of underwear.

Ub Iwerks and Edna Francis came to see him off, and they all wept, Walt included, as his train pulled out. He was convinced that he was going out of their lives forever, and for the moment, at least, it seemed a devastating thought. Ub, in particular, looked so lonely and forlorn that, for a moment, Walt was tempted to get off the train and stay with him.

But then he cheered up. It was July 1923. He was twenty-one years old and had fifty dollars in his pocket, plus his camera. By the time the train got up speed and began to fly across the flat Kansas plain, his spirits had risen, and life seemed full of promise again.

6
New World

FORTUNATELY FOR WALT. his uncle, Robert Disney, had retired to Los Angeles after a successful career in mining. He lived with his second wife, Charlotte, in a house on Kingswell Avenue, in Edendale, and since he had always been close to Elias, he felt an obligation to do what he could for his brother's sons. He and Charlotte regularly visited Roy Disney in the Sawtelle Veterans Hospital in West Los Angeles, where he was still convalescing; and when Walt turned up with his shabby suitcase on Kingswell Street one morning in July 1923, he was taken in without question and given a room.

When Robert asked Walt what he intended to do for a living now that he was in California, the young man loftily replied, "I'm going to direct films."

As he explained to Roy when they celebrated their reunion at Sawtelle the following day, he had decided to abandon his career as a maker of animated cartoons. For one thing, he had no staff and had lost his equipment. Besides, all the newest techniques in cartoon films were being developed in New York, which was the heart of the industry. Hollywood had neither experts nor interest in animation.

In any case, Walt had developed new interests. Working as a newsreel cameraman in Kansas City had given him a taste for making pictures about human beings. Roy, always the prudent older brother, warned Walt that directing jobs in Hollywood were not all that easy to come by, even for bright kids, and counseled him not to throw away the experience as an animator he had so painfully accumulated in Kansas City. But after a time he accepted the fact that Walt had made up his mind.

The government was paying Roy a pension of eighty-five dollars a month, over half of which he was saving, and promised to be good for a loan when the rest of Walt's fifty dollars ran out.

THE EARLY TWENTIES were good days in Hollywood. The movie industry was booming and bustling with new stars and talent, and the film city was still small and parochial enough for its most famous personalities to be unafraid of mixing with ordinary people. A star-struck newcomer who strolled along Hollywood Boulevard on a Sunday morning could be sure of catching a glimpse of celebrities such as Ramon Novarro, Adolphe Menjou, Mae Murray, or Clara Bow on their way to a rendezvous at one of the nearby restaurants. Everyone from Lionel Barrymore to Zasu Pitts and Slim Summerville came out on their free weekends to show themselves off.

But for Walt Disney, who seemed impervious to the beauty and sex appeal of famous female stars—or of beefy male stars either—the magnet that drew him into Hollywood on the weekends was never one of the glamorous movie idols of the day, but the possibility that he might sight one of the film colony's great comedians.

He had hovered in vain outside Charlie Chaplin's studio, hoping to catch him as he came out at the end of the day, only to be taken by his uncle and aunt to Musso's Restaurant on Hollywood Boulevard for Sunday brunch, where he found himself sitting at a table next to the great man himself. He was overawed and did not dare ask for an autograph, but it was an experience he continued to savor for years after the event.

His ambition was to direct comedy films, perhaps starring one of these revered masters of the comic arts, and one of the first things he did was to go to the studios where the Keystone Cops reigned, after which he went to the lots where Mack Sennett produced and Harold Lloyd operated, hoping to get inside to watch them at work and then, perhaps, cajole someone into giving him a job. But at every studio he was refused admittance and told to apply at the employment office, where he was curtly informed that there were no jobs available.

He still held on to the press card Universal had given him when he had worked as a newsreel stringer in Kansas City, and he used this one day to bluff his way onto the Universal lot and the set where Lon Chaney was starring in *The Hunchback of Notre Dame*. But then another observer, arrogantly surveying the scene from the sidelines, put a monocle to his eye to examine the youngster at his side and decided he didn't belong. Haughtily calling on a couple of crew members, he demanded Walt's instant removal, and it gave the young man no comfort at all when he discovered later that he had been thrown off the set by none other than the great Erich von Stroheim. The rest of his fifty dollar hoard lasted over a month, and he supported himself for another two weeks by exploiting his riding skills, for which he earned eight dollars as a cowboy extra at Warner Brothers.

But that was the only money he made, and even his Uncle Robert began to hint that he was wearing out his welcome and that it was time for him to find a place to live and a job. In the meantime, he asked Walt to start paying five dollars a week toward his room and board. That was the moment Walt decided he had been wasting his time, and it would perhaps be wise, despite his qualms, to begin exploiting his know-how as an animator.

He informed both Roy and his uncle, much to their relief, that he was going back to making cartoon films and, if necessary, financing himself through making the Laugh-O-Gram type of advertising film he had pioneered in Kansas City.

In that case, his uncle said, he could have the use of his garage as a workshop for an extra dollar a week. Roy lent him ten dollars to get himself some letterheads announcing that "Walt Disney, Cartoonist" was back in business. And with the new sense of realism hunger always induced in him, he began the familiar task of peddling his wares and ideas. He didn't have much luck.

In the meantime, he had contacted a well-known New York film booker, Margaret Winkler, whom he had met when she visited Kansas City, to let her know that he was still in business. She had always been an admirer of Walt Disney's work and had recently written to point out that he had never, as he had once promised, let her see a copy of his last animated short, *Alice's Wonderland*.

The film was, in fact, one of the principal assets that had been seized by his creditors in Kansas City when he went bankrupt, though they had allowed him to retain a print of the movie. Now he wrote Mrs. Winkler a letter disingenuously designed to conceal the extent of the disaster he had suffered and to exploit what he had managed to salvage from the wreckage.

> Dear Mrs. Winkler,
>
> This is to inform you that I am no longer connected with the Laugh-O-Gram Films, Inc. of Kansas City, Mo., and that I am establishing a studio in Los Angeles for the purpose of producing the new and novel series of cartoons I have previously written you about [a series based on the adventures of the Alice of *Alice's Wonderland*].
>
> The making of these new cartoons necessitates being located in a production center that I may engage trained talent for my casts, and be within reach of the right facilities for producing. I am taking with me a select number of my former staff and will in a very short time be producing at regular intervals. It is my intention of securing working space with one of the studios, that I may better study technical detail and comedy situations, and combine these with my cartoons. . . .

He had written Mrs. Winkler about *Alice* in the past, but she never did see a copy of the film. He sent one now, explaining that it remained the property of Laugh-O-Gram Films, Inc., but that he had permission of his successors to let her see it "to give you an idea of the characters and situations I propose to use in the new series."

It seems unlikely that Mrs. Winkler was ignorant of the fact that Laugh-O-Gram Films, Inc. had gone bankrupt and that Walt Disney was not being entirely frank about his professional situation. But, in the film industry, that could scarcely have surprised her.

She had *Alice* screened and liked what she saw. She already knew Disney's previous work with *Puss in Boots* and *Red Riding Hood* and recognized that here was someone who might lack expertise but was certainly rich in talent. She sent back a telegram dated October 15, 1923, saying:

> BELIEVE SERIES CAN BE PUT OVER BUT PHOTOGRAPHY OF ALICE SHOULD SHOW MORE DETAIL AND BE STEADIER. THIS BEING NEW PRODUCT MUST SPEND LARGE AMOUNT ON EXPLOITATION AND ADVERTISING, THEREFORE NEED YOUR COOPERATION. WILL PAY FIFTEEN HUNDRED DOLLARS EACH NEGATIVE FOR SIX,* AND TO SHOW MY GOOD FAITH WILL PAY FULL AMOUNT ON EACH OF THESE SIX ON DELIVERY OF NEGATIVE. THIS PROVIDING SAME ALICE AND CAST BE USED. LETTER AND CONTRACT FOLLOW. WINKLER.

Walt opened the telegram in front of his uncle and aunt, let out a whoop of triumph, and dashed from the house without informing them of its contents. He rushed down to the trolley car and began the long journey to the Sawtelle Veterans Hospital to let his brother Roy in on the good news.

He badly needed his brother's advice. What should he do now? In his search around Hollywood for openings, he had had an offer from Alexander Pantages, who owned a cinema chain in Southwest California, for a series of one-minute reels. Should he take it? Or should he accept Mrs. Winkler's offer and plunge into big-time animation with the Alice project?

Roy Disney was fast asleep in the hospital ward when Walt burst in on him, with the result that the discussion of Walt's future had to take place in whispers, amid the complaints and snores of half a dozen other convalescents.

But Roy did not let his brother down. Calmly they discussed the pros and cons of the situation. What Roy wanted to know was whether Walt could deliver the Alice films for the price Mrs. Winkler was offering.

---

*She later made that twelve.

"For half of that," Walt said, confidently. "We'll make seven hundred fifty dollars profit on every one of the series!"

"*We?*" Roy asked.

"Yes, *we*," Walt repeated. "I can't possibly do it unless you come in with me. I need your help, Roy. You've just got to get out of here and join me. Please say you'll do it."

There was a long pause while Roy wrestled with his problem, tossing and turning in his bed as he went over the pros and cons of the situation. He was unable to make up his mind until, according to Walt's later account of that evening, the patient in the next bed to Roy rolled over and growled in exasperation, "Say yes, for Christ's sake, and then we can all get back to sleep!"

Next morning, Roy Disney discharged himself from Sawtelle and went to Los Angeles, where Walt had already found a cheap apartment. Roy's doctors had warned him that his tuberculosis was far from cured and that he must take special care of himself, spend most of his time in bed, and sleep at least every afternoon. But from then on he would be too busy working with Walt Disney as a partner to worry about trivialities such as spots on his lungs. He was never troubled by his illness again and lived and worked to a lively old age.

There was one big problem. In the contract that presently arrived from Mrs. Winkler, what had been suggested in the telegram of acceptance became a stipulation. In the film, the part of Alice was played by a lively six-year-old schoolgirl named Virginia Davis. Mrs. Winkler thought she was marvelous and insisted that the same girl be used in the series. Unfortunately, Walt Disney was now in Los Angeles, and the little girl lived with her parents in Kansas City.

How on earth could he get her to California, and what would her father and mother say if he proposed it?

"Leave it to me," Roy said, now filled with enthusiasm, and promptly got in touch with Edna Francis. His patient fiancée still worked in a Kansas City bank and waited faithfully for Roy to send for her. Edna was charged with the task of visiting the little girl's parents and persuading them to allow their daughter to go to California and star in the series at a salary of one hundred dollars a month.

Walt feared Mr. and Mrs. Davis would turn the proposition down flat. To his amazement and delight, Edna's depiction of the glamour of California and the potential of Hollywood stardom for their daughter so dazzled Mr. and Mrs. Davis that they decided to accept and to accompany Virginia. They drove with her to Los Angeles in the family car and personally delivered their daughter to Walt at the makeshift studio he had established two doors up from Uncle Robert's house on Kingswell Street.

Meanwhile, Robert Disney had been approached by his nephew for a loan to help set them up in business. He demurred at first but, in the end, gave the two brothers five hundred dollars and wished them well. With Roy's savings, which amounted to some three hundred dollars, this was enough to rent equipment, hire extras, and start rolling.

Their first cartoon, entitled *Alice's Day at Sea*, starred Virginia Davis and a dog that performed cute tricks; and with the embellishment of some animated cartoon characters and backgrounds, it came out looking fresh and funny. Walt had done the direction and all the animation himself, aided only by two girls who inked and painted the celluloids for fifteen dollars a week. It had cost exactly seven hundred fifty dollars to make.

Walt shipped it to New York, and Mrs. Winkler was so pleased with it she sent a telegram saying:

DAY AT SEA RECEIVED TODAY. SATISFACTORY. MAILING TODAY DRAFT ON LOS ANGELES BANK WITH DETAILED LETTER.

A few days later fifteen hundred dollars arrived together with a contract for a further series of six films. Mrs. Winkler's only criticism of the first effort was "unsteady camera work" and the jerkiness of some of the animation.

Walt was only too well aware of these faults and the reasons for them. To save money, he had used the camera he had brought with him from Kansas City, and it was really not suitable for studio work. In addition, he had brought in Roy to work the camera, and Roy could not crank it with the even rhythm of a professional operator, so the pictures were jumpy and sometimes out of synch.

He rented a studio camera for five dollars a day, which Roy found easier to use. But then, as rumors swept around the makeshift studio of Walt's initial success, those involved in the series—who had accepted fifty cents a day for their services—began to feel that they might have sold their services too cheaply. The parents of the child extras used in the film demanded prevailing Hollywood rates for future productions. Expenses rose. The performing dog Walt had used in the first film was Uncle Robert's German shepherd, Peggy; but Peggy got sick, and a professional pet had to be employed—and paid for. Moreover, the father of the star, Virginia Davis, who had hoped to find a job in Los Angeles, failed to do so. He decided to leave Virginia behind with her mother and go back to Kansas City in the family car. Meanwhile, he demanded, and got, accommodation expenses for his daughter and Mrs. Davis plus the doubling of her monthly salary. All this drained the company's resources, and quickly exhausted any funds that they had built up.

Once more they needed money, desperately. But who could they tap this time? Walt tentatively suggested that Roy approach his fiancée, Edna Francis, since she must have started accumulating a little nest egg over the years in anticipation of her marriage. Indignantly, Roy refused to do any such thing, but Walt wrote to her secretly, anyway, beseeching her to help and pledging her not to say anything to Roy about it. She sent back a check for twenty-five dollars, which was all she could afford, and it arrived just in time to pay off creditors who were beginning to besiege the studio.

This time they weathered the storm and more help began to come in. Carl Stalling, organist at the Isis Theater in Kansas City, sent $275. Walt had once made a cartoon film for one of Stallings' sing-alongs and charged a special low rate; now he had written reminding the organist of the favor he had done him and asked for a gesture in return.

The $275 could not have arrived at a better moment, for it enabled Walt and Roy to finish film number 6 of their contract. They had barely wrapped up their project when in walked Mrs. Winkler; she had come from New York with bad news.

She announced that though there had, as yet, been no public showings, sales of the first series of *Alice* films to the renters had been very disappointing; she attributed it to the fact that Walt had seemed to lose the fun and fresh quality that had been such a feature of his first film. Mrs. Winkler said she was doing so badly on the rentals that she had decided she did not need the next series, and she wanted the contract for the next six films canceled right then and there.

Roy seemed resigned and ready to accept this disastrous news without protest. But not Walt. "Oh, no you don't!" he said to Mrs. Winkler. "We have a contract with you for six more films, and we're sticking with it."

When Mrs. Winkler started to get angry, he went on, "Okay, I know about some of those earlier films. They missed out. We played safe with them—because we were too worried about money to take risks—and I agree that some of them might have been dull and boring. But just you have a look at film number 7, which we've just finished. I've changed my style and said to hell with playing safe. Because we're now in such a bad way, we don't have anything to lose. Just let me set up the projector and look at the new film. It's a whole new ball game."

And, indeed, it was. Although it still lacked "flow" in some of its sequences, number 7 of the *Alice* series *(Alice's Spooky Adventure)* had all the old originality and sense of fun that Walt had pumped into *Alice's Day at Sea.* In addition, it had expensive production values not usually seen in shorts in those days—and these, Mrs. Winkler surmised, were probably the reason why the Disneys had used up the last of their monies. But she recognized that they made all the difference in the film.

She was so delighted that she was more than willing to keep to her contract, and even improve on it a little if this is what Walt was going to give her. She wrote out a check for two thousand and departed with the canisters of film under her arm.

Back in New York, after receiving number 8 of the *Alice* series, she expressed her satisfaction in an even more tangible way, by offering Walt a contract for a new series of twelve Alice films, after the present series was finished.

"I am very optimistic about the future and believe we have something here of which we will all be proud," she wrote, adding that the very first film, *Alice's Day at Sea,* would open in New Jersey, Pennsylvania, and Washington, D.C., in March 1924, to be followed by *Alice's Spooky Adventure.* In another letter she wrote, "But do try to get a livelier quality into your cartoon characters. Everyone around here agrees the ideas are brilliant, but your execution lacks something."

Walt Disney knew exactly what she meant. Always aware of his own inadequacies as a draftsman and of his tendency to skimp, he had hired the services of a professional animator to help him get out the right number of drawings, and the right quality of drawing. But first-class animators were still scarce in the cartoon business, and the one he had hired lacked the requisite flair. Walt had the answer to his problem but felt uncomfortable even thinking about it. Back in Kansas City was the only animator who was worth a damn, who could make all the difference to Walt's cartoon ideas, as he had done in the past: Ub Iwerks.

More than ever, Walt needed the sensitive genius with the patience, the persistence, and the magic sense of line. Ub was still slogging away for the Kansas City Film Advertising Company, his salary there having now risen to fifty dollars a week. If only he were in Los Angeles, most of Walt's troubles would be over. Ub could make all the difference to his films, give punch and impact to his bubbling ideas.

But Walt felt guilty about Ub. When Laugh-O-Gram Films, Inc. had collapsed, Ub had been owed one thousand dollars in salary. Although sales of Laugh-O-Gram's assets had since realized enough to reimburse him in part (four hundred dollars), he still had many out-of-pocket expenses and needed every dime he could earn to keep his family from starvation.

How could he possibly appeal to Ub to help him now, when he couldn't even afford to pay Ub's fare from Kansas City? How could he guarantee Ub, whose only interest was job security, that disaster would never confront them again? What if things went wrong, as they surely might, and he had to let him down once again?

Roy Disney knew all about the situation between Walt and Ub, and he urged his brother to forget his scruples and write Ub about his difficulties. When Walt was still reluctant, Roy wrote the letter in Walt's name. He went so far as to suggest that if Ub would make the move to Los Angeles, there was the prospect that he would be offered a partnership in the new company.

Walt would subsequently deny such an offer was ever made, and cited the letter (dated June 1, 1924) he wrote back once Ub had expressed interest in making the move: "Everything is going fine with us and I am glad you made up your mind to come out. Boy, you will never regret it—this is the place for you—a real country to work and play in." He added: "I can give you a job as artist-cartoonist and etc with Disney Productions. Most of the work would be cartooning. Answer at once and let me know when you want to start. The salary is forty dollars a week. At the present time I have one fellow helping me on the animation and three girls that do the inking, etc. while Roy handles the business end."

On the other hand, Frank Thomas and Ollie Johnston, two veteran Disney animators who wrote the authorized history of Disney's cartoons operations, flatly state that while "[Ub Iwerks] had been lured from Kansas City on the promise of a partnership . . . 'They were partners but Walt was the boss.'"*

Ub Iwerks and Walt Disney settled on the $40 a week salary, and Disney Productions (as they were now officially known) did not even have to pay Ub's expenses from Kansas City since Mr. Davis was coming to see his wife and his daughter, Virginia, and gave him a lift in his car.

Ub Iwerks's arrival had a revolutionary effect on the operations of Disney Productions.

Other Disney animators have pointed out that Ub was not a great draftsman, but he had a special feel for animation. True, the work in those days was crude, but his facility was amazing. He could produce 600 drawings a day, think up gags, organize the layout and the plot, train his assistants, and, in his spare time, repair the company car and keep it going! But his greatest gift was to sense what Walt was aiming for and produce it for him in a dynamic series of drawings. It was an amazing gift for which he had had no formal training. He had just picked up his flair as he went along, and in many ways it had the quality of genius.

Walt was delighted to see his old collaborator back with him, for he was genuinely fond of him. But he still did not understand the nature of

---

Disney Animation: The Illusion of Life by Frank Thomas and Ollie Johnston (New York: Abbeville Press, 1981).

his friend and associate, nor did he realize how sensitive and vulnerable he was.

Nobody guessed how much Ub hated the way he was pushed around by everybody, particularly by Walt. To everyone else in the studio he always seemed the most gentle and helpful man, ever willing to be interrupted, to halt his own work in order to encourage others. And when Walt thumped him on the back, or tripped him up, or directed him to open a cupboard door out of which a pail of water spilled over him, he never complained even as everyone else roared with laughter at his discomfiture. He just sighed, sucked in his gut, and went away in silence. "What a good sport he is!" everyone said and failed to divine how much he hated the way his boss treated him.

THERE WERE MORE ups and downs for Disney Productions, even after Ub rode in to the rescue. For one thing, Mrs. Winkler suddenly remarried, retired from business, and let her new husband take charge of the distributing company. And, like the death of a close adviser, that made a change for the worse.

The new head of the agency, named Charles Mintz, had never met or been charged by the bright and cheerful Walt Disney as Mrs. Winkler had. She had seemed to understand instinctively that the more money Walt could lay his hands on, the more he would pour into his films, for he was a perfectionist who would never cease trying to do better. So she had always made sure he was paid promptly for his productions, knowing she and her clients would reap the benefit eventually from better-quality productions. Her new husband, on the other hand, was a renter of the old school who never paid up until he was all but sued for what he owed. Walt was soon calling him "Mister Minge," because he dodged sending the full fee when a film arrived and tried to fob off the brothers with a half payment.

The Disney files at Burbank are filled with letters to "Mister Minge" from Walt complaining about the late delivery of money they were due. "We need money," he wrote, in August 1924. "We have been spending as much as you have been paying us . . . in order to improve them and make them as good as possible, and now that we are receiving only $900.00 from you [in partial payment] it puts us 'in a 'ell of a 'ole.' I am not kicking about that, however, I am perfectly willing to sacrifice a profit on this series, in order to put out something good, but I do expect you to show your appreciation by helping us out. As you know, if we haven't the money to spend on them, we will have to skimp. And at this time, it would not be best to do that. So please, for our sake as well as your own, give this more consideration and instead of sending us $900.00, make it the full amount excepting a fair discount which will enable us to pull through this period."

"Mister Minge" replied, pleading poverty because of delay in his own rental receipts and, perhaps deciding the best defense was offense, launched into a sharp criticism of the latest Alice films because of their lack of comic gags. Back came a hot reply from Walt, announcing the delivery of a new film that was, he acidly pointed out, "nothing but gags, and the whole story is one gag after another."

Fortunately, at this juncture, the film-trade press began reviewing the *Alice* films and hailed them for their wealth of "imagination and cleverness." They described the last one, *Alice Cans the Cannibals*, as "a corker." Either those notices or the backstairs influence of Mintz's wife (to whom Walt had, in desperation, written secretly) produced a change in the renter's attitude. At the end of the series he offered a contract for eighteen more *Alice* films at eighteen hundred a piece plus a share of the profits.

In the next three years, Walt later told his daughter, they averaged a profit of two thousand a film and, at last, began accumulating capital. But they were so afraid of new disaster that solvency made no difference to their way of life. They continued to live very frugally in their one-room apartment and drew out only thirty-five dollars a week for rent and food. Most of the time, in obedience to medical advice, Roy went home early from the studio for his afternoon nap, after which he got up and prepared the evening meal for when Walt came home.

He was a poor cook, and Walt was always complaining about the quality of the food. One night, when Walt yet again disgustedly pushed his plate to one side and remarked that he couldn't possibly eat "this mush," Roy grabbed the plate of stew and poured it over his head. "That does it," he cried. "I'm finished! No more cooking. No more of your goddamned complaints." He slammed out of the room and went down the hall to the bathroom and did not reappear until Walt was in bed and asleep, traces of stew still clinging to his hair.

The next day, Roy sent a telegram to Edna Francis:

WHAT ARE WE WAITING FOR STOP WHY DON'T YOU COME OUT HERE AND TIE THE KNOT STOP

Edna Francis arrived in Los Angeles with her mother on April 7, 1925, and she and Roy were married on April 11. The ceremony took place at the home of Uncle Robert Disney.

Elias and Flora Disney came from Oregon for the wedding, and Herbert Disney accompanied them. Walt, who had long since made up with his brother, was best man. And at Walt's request, there was one maid of honor. She was a pretty girl named Lillian Bounds, who had recently come to work for Disney Productions as an inker.

7
Rabbit Trick

WALT DISNEY'S DAUGHTER once described her father as "a low-pressure swain," and it is an accurate assessment of his attitude toward women. Even in his early twenties, when the sap should have been running strong, he never allowed himself to get passionately involved with the opposite sex—or, for that matter, with sex in any shape or form.

Two attractive young women, one of whom was Margaret Metzinger, fell in love with him while he was still working for the Kansas City Film Advertising Company. Both found him funny, bright, charming, and attractive and made it plain they would have welcomed any amorous approach he might have been inclined to make toward them. They always accepted organized weekend outings (to Swope Park, for instance—a favorite picnic rendezvous for the film ad company employees) in the hope that he would be there. He usually was because Walt was a gregarious young man who liked company; but though they repeatedly tried, neither ever succeeded in cutting him off from the others, even temporarily, so that they could make time with him alone. He deftly evaded all their ploys and stayed with "the gang" and carefully refrained from indicating a preference for one over the other.

Occasionally, they must have found him an infuriating young man. Even when he went to a charity ball, he usually invited both young women to go as his partners, and though they always accepted, it must have been a frustrating experience for both of them.

What they can hardly have failed to realize, in the end, was that his deliberately innocent attitude toward them was quite disingenuous. For instance, that he knew exactly how Margaret Metzinger felt about him was shown by the trick he had played on her with Ub Iwerks.

But neither she nor any other girl who fell for him during this period seemed able to accept the truth about Walt Disney—that sexually he just wasn't interested and that all he really wanted from the female sex was what he wanted from the male sex, too: friendliness and companionship.

"Quite frankly," he once said to Ward Kimball, "I prefer animals to people."

In later years he was to indicate that the great crush of his life had been on Su Pitowski in Chicago in his teens and that the way she had let him down had practically broken his heart. But this wasn't true.

Actually, Su had hurt his pride. It was the death of his beloved dog, Carey, that had broken his heart. What Su's defection seems to have done was turn him off women because they couldn't be relied on. After that, he seemed wary and afraid to trust them—especially with his feelings.

It was in the wake of his shattering experience with Su Pitowski that he began to proclaim his view that a young man was a fool if he married before he was twenty-five years old and then only if he had at least ten thousand dollars in the bank. It seems likely that if Roy had not suddenly decided to wed Edna Francis, he might have happily continued to share bachelor quarters with his brother for years to come. Not that he hated women. The more beautiful they were, the more pleasure he got out of admiring them. In California he liked nothing better than to take a pretty girl to a movie or to invite her back to the apartment he shared with his brother until Roy's marriage (where, it must be admitted, he and Roy usually inveigled her into cooking the meal). He was proud and pleased when he was congratulated on the charm and beauty of his female companions.

But, he insisted, the female of the species was someone you lived with only when you had achieved financial independence and the wisdom of maturity and only after your chosen companion knew her place, was willing to cherish and obey you, look after your home, see to your creature comforts, and be a good mother to your children. As far as he was concerned, passion or love did not really enter into it.

So it is to be doubted whether he would ever have considered Lillian Bounds as a potential wife had not Roy Disney's sudden decision to marry Edna acted as the catalyst. Roy's departure from their shared apartment after his marriage had a profoundly disturbing effect upon Walt. He was the most undomesticated of young men—he did not cook, could not make a bed, and was completely unaware that dust and dirt accumulated in an untended household. He found the consequent upheaval of bachelor life acutely uncomfortable.

For purely practical reasons, he was for a time seriously tempted to move in with Ub Iwerks. Only the prospect of having to face that moody and lugubrious young man at breakfast every day restrained him. Life with Lillian Bounds—who was pretty, intelligent, and cheerful—was certainly preferable to him.

LILLIAN BOUNDS ORIGINALLY came from Lewiston, Idaho. She had arrived in Los Angeles to visit her married sister, who lived in Edendale. While there she met a neighbor who had worked for some time for Disney Productions as what the animators called an "ink and paint girl." She had the tricky job of copying the animators' drawings with ink and paint.

Lillian, who liked California and wanted to stay, asked her if there were any jobs available and was told to apply in the "ink" department at Disney, where there was a vacancy. She was taken on at the prevailing wage of fifteen dollars a week and quickly learned the painstaking routine.

But she soon grew to like the work and was beguiled by the atmosphere of the Disney studio, the friendliness of the animators, the willingness of everyone to work hard and stay late, and particularly, the lack of stiffness and protocol in the attitude of the Disney brothers, who never made anyone feel like an employee.

Her sponsor had warned her not to try to marry herself off to either of them since they were confirmed and determined bachelors. But after Roy confounded everyone by his sudden decision to at last marry Edna, Lillian found herself regarding Walt with new speculation.

To her he was an immensely attractive and personable young man, even if she thought the mustache he was growing at the time, in an attempt to make himself look older, highly unsuitable and the stained and shabby clothes he invariably wore hardly the proper attire for the head of a film studio. Except for a friendly wave of the hand, he never seemed to take much notice of the girls in the ink department, but sometimes on late or rainy nights, he would give Kathleen and her a lift home in his old Ford jalopy. Once, during one of these rides, she plucked up the courage to ask him what he looked like in a tie and suit, and he laughed and replied that he didn't have either—what he was wearing were the only clothes he possessed.

Shortly after that, he came into the ink department one night when Lillian was the only girl working late and said he would wait for her and give her a lift home. She became acutely aware that he was hanging around the office, staring thoughtfully at her; and presently she felt him coming up behind her. Suddenly he leaned over and kissed her on the back of her neck. She was startled and pretended not to notice, though she was blushing furiously.

When he left her on her doorstep a little later, he suddenly blurted out: "If I went out and bought myself a suit, would you invite me inside to meet your sister?"

"You can come in now, if you like," Lillian said. "My sister won't mind." But he refused and, as if nothing unusual had happened between them, got back in his car, waved his hand, and drove away.

The next day, he went to Roy and asked him for forty dollars out of the money reserves his brother guarded for both of them and for the studio. Roy was always reluctant to part with any of their savings, even now that they were beginning to be in the money. "What do you want forty dollars for?" he asked, suspiciously.

"I want it to buy a suit," Walt said.

"A suit! For God's sake, what do you want a suit for?"

Walt took a deep breath. "To get married in," he said.

Not that he had proposed to Lillian yet. Somehow he did not seem to be able to make up his mind about her, even though, correctly besuited, he frequently went to supper at the home of Lillian's sister.

Lillian thought he looked so smart in his new light blue outfit that he made his old Ford seem even shabbier than when he had driven around in it, wearing his old clothes; and on one occasion she told him so. He was silent for the rest of the outing and seemed preoccupied with his own thoughts when he finally kissed her a chaste goodnight.

Next night, he took her to the movies in Riverside, and when they were on their way home, he burst out impulsively, "You're right about this car, and I know it's time I bought a new one. But I know you're a practical girl, Lilly. So tell me, which would you rather have me buy—a new car for both of us or an engagement ring for you?"

"An engagement ring," Lillian said, without hesitation.

"Oh," he said.

Lillian told her daughter many years later, "He seemed quite disappointed I didn't let him buy the car."

However, she was more than satisfied with the ring he eventually bought and still cherishes it. It is a three-quarter-carat diamond in a basket, surrounded by blue sapphires, and it was Roy Disney who found it for his brother. He knew a jeweler in downtown Los Angeles who was reputed to specialize in bargain jewelry. He took Walt to see him.

The jeweler drew the two young men conspiratorially into the back of his shop and brought out of a drawer a ring with a stone in it "which looked like a locomotive headlight to me," Walt said later. He thought it was "so fancy" that he was attracted to it at once and asked its price.

"Seventy-five dollars," the jeweler said.

Roy Disney pretended to faint. "Who do you think he is?" he asked, pointing to his brother. "Rockefeller? He's not buying the crown jewels. It's just a little token for his girlfriend. Come on, show us some of your bargains for *poor* people!"

Reluctantly, the jeweler drew out a tray of smaller stones for $35, and Roy pretended to drool over them. But to Walt they seemed cheap and mean and he couldn't bear to look at them, nor could he take his eyes off the "locomotive headlight still lying around on the table." Its glorious size and sparkle fascinated him. He was determined to have it. Dragging Roy to one side he vehemently whispered to his brother that he had to have the ring because it was a bargain, insisting no one would ever be able to buy such a marvelous ring for less. At which point the jeweler spoke up and told them he would give them a real break—they could have it for seventy dollars.

"It's a deal!" Roy cried, unable to resist a bargain. While Roy was peeling off dollar bills from the roll in his pocket, Walt clutched the ring in its box as if it were the Koh-i-noor diamond itself.

LILLIAN'S BROTHER WAS the fire chief of Lewiston, Idaho. It was in his home, in the presence of her widowed mother, that Lillian and Walt were married on July 13, 1925.

They had made arrangements to spend their honeymoon sailing aboard the coastal steamer, *H. E. Alexander,* from Seattle to Long Beach, California; and their wedding night was spent on the Lewiston-Seattle express. It was not quite what Lilly had expected, for Walt was suddenly stricken with a violent toothache and passed the night not with his new bride but helping the Pullman porter to polish the passengers' shoes. He explained to her that it helped him forget his pain.

He had the infected tooth pulled in Seattle, but spent the next few days, including a trip to Mount Rainier, with a scarf wrapped around his face, "looking like a bear and just as grumpy as one," as Lilly later said. But once they were aboard ship, the sun and sea breezes seemed to cure everything, and Lillian was soon writing home to her mother that Walt was "sweet" and she was "divinely happy."

Just before leaving for Idaho to marry Lilly, Walt had made what then seemed to him an even bigger decision. He and Roy had withdrawn four hundred dollars out of their joint bank account and put it down as part payment on a new studio they planned to build at 2719 Hyperion Avenue, in the Silver Lake district of Los Angeles. Lilly had her eye on a house in the same area the moment they could afford the down payment, but for the moment, the newly wedded couple arranged to rent a one-room apartment with kitchen facilities for forty dollars a month. Roy agreed that now that Walt was a married man he should increase his weekly stipend to forty dollars a week.

Out of this modest salary Lilly received ten dollars a week as a housekeeping allowance, and another thirty dollars a month went for paying the installments on furniture for the apartment plus a new car—Lilly, remembering Walt's disappointment, had persuaded her new husband that he needed a replacement after all.

MARRIAGE SEEMED TO make a change in Walt Disney's relations with his brother. From the moment he came back from his honeymoon, he began relying less and less upon Roy's advice and judgment about production matters, though he still left his brother in complete charge of the company's finances.

One evidence of his new-found independence was his decision, once they moved into the new Hyperion Avenue studio, to change the name of the operation from Disney Brothers Studio to the Walt Disney Studio, and he made it plain to everyone, including Roy, that from now on, he was in charge of the show.

Even in his dealings with the distributor, Charles Mintz, the note of subservience disappeared from his correspondence and an often-impatient acerbity crept in. This was principally because of Mintz's increasing dilatoriness in making payments for the *Alice* films Walt went on delivering. Mintz had altered the method of payment and now had the money delivered personally to the studio by his brother-in-law, George Winkler, whom he had appointed his Hollywood representative.

Winkler was almost always late in arriving with the badly needed cash and sometimes did not turn up at all. At the beginning of October 1925, Walt made his exasperation plain in a letter to Mintz: "It is my intention to live up to my contract and I expect you to do the same," he wrote. "I intend to continue shipping pictures to you as fast as completed, which is about every sixteen days. I will expect you to take them as delivered and remit immediately. Your failure to do so will constitute a breach of contract and will force me to seek other distributors."

A few days later Walt wrote to Mintz: "Haven't you a single spark of appreciation in your whole soul? . . . You should be wholeheartedly ashamed of yourself."

Mintz replied by criticizing the appeal of recent *Alice* films and claimed their popularity was decreasing with both renters and paying public. Walt was honest enough to realize that he might have a point, even though, for the moment, he believed the improved quality of the animation and production values more than made up for their lack of freshness and humor.

But he was aware that the *Alice* series had suffered a blow, principally because of the loss of winsome and attractive Virginia Davis's performance in the starring role. Virginia's parents, tempted by offers from other Hollywood movie producers, had decided that their daughter had a big future as a child star with the major studios and had refused to sign a new contract with Disney.

Both sides lost from this decision. Virginia's new career quickly petered out. Margie Gay, the simpering little girl Walt enrolled as a substitute, lacked her warm, innocent appeal and forced him more and more to rely upon the cartoon characters with which he surrounded her, particularly an eccentric animal he called Julius the Cat.

However the *Alice* series was lagging, there was no doubt about that. And when the question of a new contract came up, Mintz's offer was considerably below what he had been paying in the past. "This may seem a little hard on you" Mintz wrote, "but before making any definite decision I would advise you to digest this letter thoroughly, talk it over with Roy and your uncle or whomever you wish, and don't make any hasty decisions."

Walt talked it over with no one. He hastily sent back a counterproposal asking for more money "in view of increased production values," to which Mintz replied, "If you think this is a fair offer, you have another think coming."

Upon receipt of this communication, Walt sent an angry telegram:

MY OFFER IS THE LIMIT I CAN GO. YOUR OFFERS ARE ALL UNAC-CEPTABLE TO ME. THEREFORE UPON THE DELIVERY OF THE NEXT SUBJECT THE FINAL OF THE 1925 SERIES I WILL CONSIDER ALL MY CONTRACTUAL OBLIGATIONS FULFILLED.

The quarrel was patched up eventually and a new agreement signed, but everyone sensed Alice's appeal was slipping. Even Walt, who remained stubbornly convinced the series had not yet worn out its welcome, was stunned when Mintz's wife, who had always been the young man's most sympathetic supporter, secretly wrote to advise him to look for a new subject for a series.

She was tactful enough not to make it plain what she thought about the talents of the new Alice, but she did suggest that it was time that he begin thinking of an all-cartoon film since the public was growing tired of "live" actresses "who have so much less animation than the creatures of your marvelous imagination."

In the fall of 1926 Mintz came to Hollywood, bringing his wife with him. A few days later Margaret Mintz turned up at the Hyperion Avenue studio. Walt was delighted to see her, and they spent a pleasant afternoon together. He showed her the new studio, a neat and spacious one-story complex; and she was amused to find him so boyishly proud of the fact that for the first time in his life he had his very own office and bathroom facilities. She looked around and said the office was missing only one thing, and that was a desk, at which he said he didn't like desks and pointed to a low table by the window. "That's what I use," he said. "It puts me on the same level with kids when they come in to see me, and adults with a grievance find themselves looking down at me, and it makes them feel better at once. Desks seem to intimidate people and give those who sit behind them a false sense of grandeur."

He took her all around to say hello to Roy Disney and Ub Iwerks and introduced her to his team of animators (who now had a spacious studio to themselves). She then suggested they go back to his office for a talk and revealed the real purpose of her visit. She told him that she and her husband had spent the morning out at Universal conferring with Carl Laemmle, the head of Universal Pictures. Laemmle had informed them that he was in the market for a new cartoon series, which he wanted to distribute through his theater chain, and had asked the Mintzes for suggestions.

When Charlie Mintz mentioned that he was thinking about a new series of *Alice* films from Walt Disney, Laemmle had dismissed them with the savage comment, "Out-of-date crap."

The novelty of live actors with cartoon characters had worn off, Laemmle said, and what movie audiences wanted now was some sort of series starring a zany animated animal who got into all kinds of crazy and comic situations.

"What sort of animal?" Margaret Mintz had asked.

"How about a rabbit?" Laemmle asked. "A lovable ball of fluff—but with brains, guile, and mischief."

Margaret Mintz then confided to Walt that she had talked the situation over with her husband and had persuaded him that a cartoon rabbit was just the sort of character Walt Disney would be able to develop. Looking Walt straight in the face, she asked him whether he would be prepared to phase out the *Alice* series and substitute one starring a zany rabbit? But it must be something fresh and completely different from Alice, she emphasized.

"And with no live humans at all," she warned. "Laemmle just hates that new girl in Alice. And," she added, in a rush, "so do I!" Of all the women in the world, Walt considered Margaret Winkler Mintz his friend and felt he could trust her. She was lively, intelligent, and he admired her judgment. For her he was ready to try anything.

In a sudden rush of enthusiasm, he went across to his low table, grabbed some paper and began to draw a series of sketches. A few minutes later, he had already roughed out a half dozen drawings of a long-eared, pointy-nosed animal with a twitchy white tail and a saucy, knowing grin, dodging dogs and ferrets, diving down rabbit holes, sailing over hedgerows, stealing rides from birds.

Margaret was delighted with the conception and bore off the sketches in triumph to her husband, who said he would take them along for Carl Laemmle's inspection the following morning. "But you can't show him this cute thing without giving him a name," said Margaret. "What do we call him?"

Mintz woke up in the early hours of the morning and shook his wife awake. "I have it," he said, triumphantly. "Oswald! Oswald the Lucky Rabbit! He *always* gets out of trouble!"

The next day, Carl Laemmle gave his approval of Walt's sketches and offered a contract, backed by a two thousand–dollar advance; and the Walt Disney Studio settled down to make its first all-cartoon film. Universal wanted the initial film in the series in a hurry, so Ub Iwerks was called in and told to get working on the sketched outline of a story. He did a masterly job of turning Oswald into a plump, eccentric country cousin of a rabbit, dressed in ill-fitting pants held up by suspenders, with a stupid and innocent look belied by his native shrewdness and cunning.

Oswald was made to look so simple and vulnerable that all the animals and birds in the cartoon thought he was an easy victim—until, painfully, they learned otherwise. When he saw the outline sketches, Roy Disney expressed the opinion that Ub had created Oswald as a mirror image of himself.

"It's the way Iwerks sees himself, and I can't say that I think it works," Roy said.

Universal Pictures agreed and didn't like the conception one bit. Walt delivered the first of the *Oswald the Lucky Rabbit* series, called *Poor Papa*, to Mintz in New York in April 1927; and a showing was arranged for the New York booking agents. They came back with a scathing report in which they listed several problems.

1. Approximately 100 feet of the opening is jerky in action, due to poor animation.
2. There is too much repetition of action. Scenes are dragged out to such an extent that the cartoon is seriously slowed down.
3. The Oswald shown in this picture is far from being a funny character. Sometimes, there are hints that something is going on underneath, but it is buried too deep to bother about. He's just flat. He has no outstanding trait. Nothing would eventually become characteristic insofar as Oswald is concerned.
4. The picture is merely a succession of unrelated gags, there being not even the thread of a story throughout its length.
5. Why is Oswald so old, sloppy, and fat? Audiences like their characters young, trim, and smart. This one is practically decrepit.

For all these reasons, they concluded, they were unprepared to accept *Poor Papa* and could not recommend it for public showing under the Universal banner.

Walt was stunned. Angrily, he leaped to the defense of Ub Iwerks's labors, maintaining that he was "now without question, the most talented animator in the business," but he did admit the first Oswald film had been made in a hurry, that they had "taken shortcuts to meet deadlines," and insisted the purchase of a new automatic camera would correct the "wobbles." He went on to reassure the Universal distributors that he was now working with his animators on the task of transforming Oswald into "a younger character—peppy, alert, saucy, and venturesome, keeping him also trim and snappy."

Then he and Ub got down to the task of recreating Oswald. They smartened him up, took off his old-fashioned overalls and suspenders, and made him a faster-moving, altogether younger and more virile animal; but still there were grumbles from the New York office. It was not until Oswald's third adventure, into which Walt poured his best ideas and his most painstaking and expensive production values, that Mintz and the Universal renters were satisfied.

THE CRISIS PRODUCED by Universal's disapproval could not have come at a more appropriate moment. It forced Walt Disney to face up to his own faults as a cartoon filmmaker just when a reassessment of himself was necessary. He had forgotten how, in Kansas City, he had once criticized his predecessors for their easy gags and sloppy characterizations. He had hardly noticed that since moving to California and getting himself accepted by the bookers, he had fallen into lazy habits himself.

The panic-causing news that Universal was turning him down had galvanized him into looking at himself anew and made him realize that he had become slipshod, had lost his dynamic as a new kind of cartoon filmmaker. If he was to save the situation (and the future of the Walt Disney Studio), he had to rethink his whole outlook and transform his methods of presentation.

He resolved to never take it easy as a creator again and to make sure that his cartoon characters were never allowed to become mere drawings, brought to life only by the gags and situations in which they were involved. Oswald the Lucky Rabbit must always be more than a run-of-the-mill stick figure. He must be seen, and received by the public, as a real character with a personality you could love or hate or despise but never ignore.

The first *Oswald the Lucky Rabbit* film to be shown publicly, *Trolley Troubles,* was the second made at the Disney studio—the first, *Poor*

Papa, was held back by Walt for some time, but it was finally released as part of the series. *Trolley Troubles,* with Oswald as the conductor of a Toonerville-type trolley, was hailed by the trade press and public alike. New York was still the center of the animated cartoon industry, and among the cognoscenti Walt Disney's deft (albeit costly) presentation of the rabbit was noted and admiringly commented upon. *Trolley Troubles* became something of a classic in the trade. The experts were made aware, as they had not been before, that here was a newcomer who was revolutionizing the nature of their craft and would be a force to be recognized in the days to come.

The film made its impact on audiences, too. The public showing of this and others in the *Oswald the Lucky Rabbit* series led to an interesting development, although no one except Walt and Ub Iwerks grasped its significance at the time.

Letters began to come in to the distributors asking not for Walt's autograph, as had happened in the past, but for Oswald's. As his popularity grew, merchants approached Universal Pictures for the right to use Oswald's name or image on their products. His likeness was printed on boxes of candies, and schoolkids could buy Oswald the Rabbit badges and wear them in the lapels of their jackets. (These were the days before logos on T-shirts.) If Universal and Mintz received any royalties for these gimmicks (and Carl Laemmle was surely too smart to miss out on any means of making a profit), they did not pass any of them on to Walt, who had to be content with the free publicity.

But otherwise, the Walt Disney Studio did well with Oswald, and everyone felt the benefit of it. Even Charlie Mintz started paying on time, and a check for $2,000 arrived (still by the hand of Mintz's brother-in-law, George Winkler) within days of the delivery a new film in the series. Other checks for the same sum began coming in at regular intervals from then on. Walt and Roy were so glad to get the money, they did not question the amounts they were receiving or wonder why they were always the same (the sums were supposed to vary according to their share of the rental fees).

Walt was only too happy to have more money for his studio budget. It enabled him to raise the salaries of his overworked animators, who were lucky if they were making more than twenty-five dollars a week, and to bring in more of them for the studio. As a result, the work went more easily, and the quality of the product improved; it also became possible to deliver a new film in the series every ten days to two weeks.

He was able to eliminate "timesavers," too. There have always been shortcuts for saving money in animation work—so-called "cycles," for example, which, by using repeat action sequences, enable the animators to duplicate earlier frames and so eliminate hours of work at the drawing board. But from now on, Walt could afford to ban such tricks in his studio. Each sequence had to be newly and painstakingly drawn.

With money in the bank, Roy persuaded his brother that both of them now had enough to provide decent homes for their wives and, maybe, he added, for the children both their wives so patiently yearned for. They found plots of land side by side on Lyric Avenue, around the corner from the studio, and erected houses for themselves at a cost of $7,000 apiece. Lillian and Edna were delighted.

Walt made one other gesture as a result of his new affluence. He knew Ub Iwerks had been badly bruised by the criticism of his early animation work on Oswald the Lucky Rabbit. Now he called Ub into his office and told him he was raising his salary to $120 a week (which was a very good wage at the time) and was also, with Roy's agreement, giving him a block of shares in the studio, thus cutting him into the annual profits, if any.

He could not have chosen a more fortuitous moment to make the gesture to his touchy associate because a conspiracy against the Disneys was developing, and Ub was involved in it. A few days earlier, Ub had been secretly approached by George Winkler, who was still Mintz's Hollywood representative, and had received an interesting offer: If he would join a new operation that the Mintz organization was about to set up, he would be offered a long-term contract at double his present salary.

Winkler had assured Ub that the new organization would do absolutely no harm to Walt Disney's operations and added that the Disney brothers would eventually be invited to join it on such favorable terms that they would undoubtedly accept. At the same time, Winkler had emphasized that all this was extremely confidential but had gone on to reveal to Ub that several of Walt's animators had already accepted offers to transfer to the new operation.

Ub had certainly been tempted since he was always strapped for money. Besides, harboring the secret resentments that he did against Walt, he could not help relishing the prospect of seeing him humiliated. He had told George Winkler he would think the matter over and let him know.

Now Walt's generous gesture toward him had intervened and it was so unexpected and sincerely offered that it persuaded Ub to stick with the Disney organization. One of the first things he did after gratefully accepting Walt's offer was to telephone George Winkler and turn him down.

But that was far from being the end of it.

In the spring of 1928, Walt's contract with Charles Mintz for the Oswald series was due for renewal, and the success of the sprightly rabbit was such that, at the time, both Walt and Roy were convinced that they could renew on much more lucrative terms. So confident was Walt, in fact, of a more favorable contract that he told everyone he and Lilly would be going to New York, where he would personally conduct the negotiations with Charlie Mintz.

When Ub Iwerks heard about the trip, and its purpose, he had an attack of conscience, and after much soul-searching, he went to Walt and warned him about George Winkler's poaching trips to the studio, without mentioning the offer that he himself had received. To his astonishment, Walt curtly dismissed his charges. What, George Winkler trying to steal away his animators? Ridiculous! They were far too loyal, far too dedicated to the Walt Disney Studio, and neither Winkler nor Charlie Mintz had a hope in hell of tempting them away. Anyway, why should they want to leave, when things were going so well and he had treated them so fairly?

Ub Iwerks was both appalled and enraged by Disney's naïveté. It had taken a great deal of courage on Ub's part to break his unspoken pledge to George Winkler and snitch on his colleagues, and it was particularly humiliating not to be believed. And what arrogance on Walt Disney's part to be so confident of his employees' loyalty. It irked Ub that Walt should feel so comfortably immune to the normal jealousies, envies, and resentments of the people around him. How could he be so sure of himself—and of other people?

WALT AND LILLIAN arrived in New York on February 6, 1928. Charlie Mintz had booked them into a suite at the Astor Hotel, a favorite haunt of film people, and the day after their arrival, they lunched with him in the hotel restaurant. Walt was pleased when Charlie brought his wife, Margaret, along with him, and the meal was a happy occasion, frequently interrupted by film people coming over to say hello. Mintz introduced his guests and always mentioned that Walt Disney was the talented young man from Hollywood who produced the *Oswald the Lucky Rabbit* series, which did not fail to make a good impression.

Later that afternoon, however, the warmth of that first encounter quickly cooled after Mintz took Walt back to his office off Times Square to begin negotiations over the new contract. Walt had already talked over the situation with Roy, and they had mutually decided that they would ask for twenty-five hundred dollars per cartoon (instead of $2,250) plus a percentage of the gross, which would, they thought, be a modest enough financial demand in view of the success of their recent efforts.

But when he presented this proposal to Mintz he was, to his astonishment, turned down flat. "I'm only prepared to offer eighteen hundred dollars a film, and no percentage," Mintz said bluntly.

"But that's less than the films are costing to make," Walt protested, accurately enough. "We'd be losing money on every film."

Mintz shrugged his shoulders. "Take it or leave it," he said, and as Walt flushed and prepared to protest once more, he added, "Look, Walt, don't be a fool. I have to remind you that I and Universal own Oswald. We thought him up and he's our rabbit, and we have documents to prove it. You'd better face up to the situation, kid. If we want to carry on production without you, we can do it. I can take your organization away from you just like *that*," he said, with a flick of his fingers. "Why, you don't even have a production organization left if I decide otherwise. Don't you know what's been going on in your own studio?"

Mintz picked up the telephone and offered it to Walt. "Here. Call up your studio and find out what's really taken place out there.... Ask your animators who they're really working for. Kid, you don't even have a production staff anymore. They belong to me. I have all your animators already signed up."

Angrily, Walt refused to believe it and stormed out of the office, spurning the use of Mintz's telephone. However, when he got back to his hotel, he called up Roy and repeated what Mintz had told him. Roy telephoned back a few hours later to say it was true—all the animators in the studio, with the exception of Ub Iwerks and two others, had contracted to go with the Mintz organization.

"Yes, I know it's terrible," Roy said. "But hold on, kid. Don't do anything foolish. Go back to Charlie Mintz and be polite with him. Don't, for God's sake, make any definite break with him. Maybe it's true what he says, and he's working in our own best interests. But meantime, contact the Universal organization in New York and find out what they think about Mintz's position. And find out how they feel about Oswald." Then he added, "Whatever you do, kid, keep calm. Hold on to everything and don't offend *anyone*. Otherwise, we could have a disaster on our hands."

Meanwhile, Margaret Winkler Mintz had heard what had happened and immediately intervened in the situation. She telephoned the Astor Hotel to offer her advice and sympathy to Walt and beseeched the young man not to be too hasty but to talk to her husband. "He really likes your cartoons and wants to go on working with you," she said. "He has a plan for avoiding any break between you, and I think you ought to listen to it."

He had indeed. Mintz offered a new contract under which he and Universal Pictures would, in the future, pay all the expenses for films in the *Oswald the Lucky Rabbit* series, take over the salaries of the animators in California, put one of their supervisors in the Walt Disney Studio and, henceforth, work in full partnership with Walt. Universal and he would guarantee all expenditures and would, in return, receive 50 percent of all profits. In an apparent afterthought he added that, as part of the deal, copyright of the Oswald character must be recognized by the

Disneys as belonging to the Mintz Agency, which would have full control of all the rabbit's activities, on screen or off.

It was only too obvious to Walt that what both Charlie Mintz and Universal wanted to do was not just take the *Oswald* series but get their hands on his whole operation. He still believed Mintz was the chief villain behind the whole thing and was convinced Universal would never consent to such an outrageous rip-off. At first he refused to accept the claim that Oswald the Rabbit did not legally belong to the Disney organization—although, in fact, Mintz had a good case to prove otherwise—and made an emotional appeal to the heads of Universal's New York office, stressing the work his studio had done on Oswald and beseeching them to recognize his success instead of penalizing it.

On March 7, 1928, he wrote to Roy:

> Well, we are still hanging around this Hellhole waiting for something to happen. Before you get this letter, I hope you will have had a wire containing good news. I can't rush things any faster—just have to do the best I can. *But I will fight it out on this line if it takes all summer.* It sure looks like a fight to the finish. Charlie is very determined to get control of everything and will do all in his power to gain his end. But unknown to him, we have a stronger power on our side."*

In fact they had none.

Universal Pictures soon demonstrated that they were fully and completely in cahoots with Charlie Mintz and were convinced that eventually the Disneys would give in to his demands. They were confident that there was no other way out for the Disneys and that a promising little studio full of bright young men would soon be falling into their hands.

They didn't know Walt.

Outraged by the perfidy and double-dealing of the distributors, heartbroken by the disloyalty of the animators with whom he had worked so hard and so long, he eventually made up his mind. One day toward the end of March 1928, without informing Roy, he marched into Charlie Mintz's office, flung an Oswald the Lucky Rabbit badge onto the renter's desk, and said, "Here, you can have the little bastard! He's all yours."

When Mintz started to reason with him, he shouted back, "Can't you understand what I'm saying? I renounce my rights to Oswald the Lucky Rabbit! I don't want him any more! Just trying to draw him after all this would make me sick to my stomach! You can have him—and good luck to you!"

---

*Disney Archives, Burbank.

"But you can't do that!" cried Mintz. "You still have three Oswald films to go on your contract. Sick or not, you'll have to stay with him."

"Not me," said Walt. "All those animators you stole—they can work out their notices finishing up the lousy series."

Once more Mintz attempted a soft-spoken approach. "Come on, kid, be reasonable," he said. "You know we need each other. We want to keep Oswald going, and so do you. I know your situation. You need the money. What's going to happen to you if you walk out now? How are you going to get by without Oswald?"

"Don't worry," Walt said. "There are plenty more characters where he came from."

Roy Disney was appalled when he heard the news. "Do you realize what sort of a situation we are in?" he asked his brother. "We've lost all our animators and it looks like we're losing our studio. It's a desperate situation. All you think we have to do is hire new artists and get a new series going. But how? Where the hell is the money coming from—*and* the ideas? I can't sell a new series just on talk. I have to have it on film."

"Don't worry," Walt said, yet again. "We'll find new animators, and we'll soon get a new series going."

"You make it sound so easy," Roy said, bitterly. "It isn't easy. I am the one who has to find the money. And if we do get new animators and do start a new series," he added, "what do we use? What in the hell are we going to choose as a new character? A rabbit? Those bastards have stolen and copyrighted our rabbit. A cat? The public is goddamn sick of cats! Every cartoon film has one. A dog? Always pissing against the wall or a tree to get a cheap laugh? Ugh!"

"We won't use a cat," Walt said, "and no dog either. Relax, Roy. We'll think of something."

In fact, according to one legend, he already had. Two days earlier, as their westbound train was crossing the Mississippi on their melancholy journey back to California, Walt Disney had looked up from his drawing board, where he had been doodling since leaving New York, and said to Lillian. "How about a mouse? Someone like this, for instance."

He had passed a rough series of drawings of a big-eared mouse across to her.

"I think I'll call him Mortimer," he said.*

---

*This was one version of Mickey's creation. Ub Iwerks later maintained he was thought up at an animators' meeting in Hollywood.

8
And Brought Forth a Mouse

IT WAS THE last week in March 1928, when Walt Disney returned to the Hyperion Avenue studio—and it was rather like walking into a morgue.

By this time, most of the animators who had signed up with Mintz knew Walt had broken off negotiations with him and realized their days at the studio were numbered. Of the fourteen staff animators, only two, Les Clark and Johnny Cannon, had resisted George Winkler's blandishments and would therefore be staying on—plus, of course, Ub Iwerks.

Since the rest were still under contract to the Walt Disney Studio for another four weeks, they were informed by Roy that there would be no possibility of letting them go early. On the contrary, they should count on being busily engaged for every remaining hour of their time, finishing off the last three of the Oswald series for "your new boss, Charlie Mintz."

"And," Roy added, crisply, "in your own interests, you'd better make sure he likes 'em."

Clark and Cannon were instructed to oversee the final chores of the departing animators, and Walt instructed them to "keep the bastards' noses to the grindstone. I want those Oswalds all finished before it's time for them to quit. Don't even give them time to wipe their noses."

He had another reason for keeping the disloyal animators busy. He suspected they had been primed by Mintz to find out what he was up to, and he was determined not to have another of his cartoon characters stolen. So while they slaved sullenly over their drawing boards in the main animators' studio, Walt and Ub Iwerks worked in secret on the new series about a mouse.

Ub had been shown Walt's preliminary sketches, and his first comment was that the tiny rodent "looks exactly like you—same nose, same face, same whiskers, same gestures and expressions. All he needs now is your voice." Walt admitted that he had occasionally used his own face in the mirror as a model and that a lot of the expressions were his, though he swore the character was based on an actual mouse that had once prowled his tiny office in Kansas City.

"It used to crawl across my desk and I'd feed it bits of cheese," he said. "I got quite fond of it and looked forward to its visits. It was so tame—and cheeky, too, I guess—it would take cheese right out of my fingers and then curl up and go to sleep in the palm of my hand. It was a good thing I didn't have much work in those days because I couldn't do any drawing until it woke up and scampered away."

That was when he had run into real bad times in Kansas City, he would tell Ub and Roy, and there had come a period when he couldn't even afford cheese for the mouse any longer. "And that was when I got worried," he told them. "I was afraid I'd given it a taste for cheddar and it would get itself killed trying to steal the cheese the guys downstairs were using to bait their traps in their restaurant kitchen. So one day, I took it to the woods outside of town and let it go."

He added, "I hope he made it. I called him Mortimer. Don't you think that's a good name for him? Mortimer the Mouse."

But they agreed with Lilly that Mortimer was a sissy name for a mouse. They preferred the one she came up with: Mickey.

Mickey Mouse. They liked that much better.

Ub agreed with Walt that Mickey should be a brash, impudent little chap; kind to old ladies but mischievous with those who could look after themselves; and up to all sorts of tricks. Painstakingly, they built up a personality for him.

Mickey's main trouble was that he hated bullies, and his gallantry and courage were bigger than his muscles. He was always running into difficulty trying to rescue weaker people from oversized villains and getting creamed for his temerity. But it never stopped him, and his resourcefulness always won out in the end.

The concept was effective enough. But how were they going to introduce Mickey Mouse to the public? They were all aware of the need to give him a really splashy debut. As it happened, the newspapers at that time were still full of the exploits of Charles Augustus Lindbergh, who had been the first man to fly solo across the Atlantic and was being hailed as a national hero. Both Walt and Ub thought it might be a good idea to exploit the current passion for planes and pilots, and Walt had typed out a rough scenario called *Plane Crazy,* which Ub promptly took and turned into a vehicle for Mickey Mouse.

Both Walt and Ub still suspected that the departing animators were peeking over their shoulders, so Ub left his studio office during the day and worked in the garage under Walt's house on Lyric Avenue. He was always a prodigious worker, and he excelled himself on the first Mickey Mouse cartoon, knowing how urgently the new series was needed.

For a five hundred-foot cartoon film, over 14,400 pictures were required; Ub produced 600 drawings a day. To keep the secret operation in the family, Lillian Disney was brought back to work, and she and Roy's wife, Edna, who had also worked in the studio, daily went to the garage and spent hours inking and painting Ub's animation onto the "cels."

Then, when the studio closed for the day and the animators had departed, Walt took the cels back to Hyperion Avenue and spent the night putting them on camera, carefully cleaning up all traces of his work after his nocturnal labors were finished.

Plane Crazy, the first cartoon film in which Mickey Mouse ever appeared, had a sneak preview at a Hollywood movie house in May 1928 and was pleasantly if politely received by the audience. Mickey's impact on the public was, to begin with, negligible, and officials at the big Hollywood studios were not much more enthusiastic. Walt took *Plane Crazy* to Culver City and showed it to the bookers for MGM, who all seemed to enjoy it.

Nevertheless, Walt realized what he was up against when one of them leaned back and said, "Very nice. There's only one trouble. Nobody's ever heard of Mickey Mouse."

It was such a stupid remark that all that Walt could think of in reply was, "They will." But not, for the time being, through being shown in MGM movie houses.

Nevertheless, Walt Disney believed in his creation enough to risk putting a second Mickey Mouse film into production, called *Gallopin' Gaucho*. Since the disloyal animators had by this time departed, there was no longer any reason for secrecy, and Ub was able to move back to the studio to draw the master frames for this second film. Moreover, he had the help of several newly hired animators.

As usual, Walt sat in on the preparation and, with uncanny mimicry, acted out every scene in which Mickey appeared. Sometimes, to heighten the effect of the atmosphere he was trying to create, he ad-libbed dialogue for Mickey in a high-pitched voice that sent everyone who heard him into fits of laughter.

"If only we had sound," Ub said, "you'd bring the house down as the voice of Mickey."

SOUND IN FILMS was, in fact, very much in the news. Before Mickey Mouse made his debut, the sensational premiere of the first talking film, *The Jazz Singer*, had taken place in New York; and the whole nature of the movie business had radically changed. Overnight, exhibitors had begun to clamor for sound films, and every producer in Hollywood was desperately trying to give his latest epic music, sound effects, and dialogue.

Meanwhile, there were still no customers for the first two Mickey Mouse films. Although most exhibitors liked the new character, they hesitated over the price and conditions. Each Mickey was costing the studio twenty-five hundred dollars to make, so Walt and Roy had decided to ask for three thousand dollars per film plus an agreement to take a minimum of 24 in the series.

Walt blamed the lack of takers on the confusion caused by the advent of sound. In view of the revolution that was taking place in the industry, you could hardly fault exhibitors for wondering whether anyone would want to see a silent cartoon film a year from now. They needed to be reassured that Mickey Mouse, too, would be moving with the times.

Walt decided to give them that reassurance. Although the first two productions had put a serious dent in the studio budget, he declared that he was going ahead with a third Mickey Mouse film, to be called *Steamboat Willie*. Moreover, he announced, this one would have full sound, including music.

In the roughly written and illustrated draft scenario that he prepared, he inserted two main music sequences and stressed that the sound effects—the Mississippi steamboat's whistle, the noise of the ship's engines, the splash of paddle wheels—must be used in a novel and amusing fashion. He also emphasized that although Mickey would not be talking much in this particular cartoon, every effort must be made to delineate his character with, where necessary, the aid of sound. When he whistled or sighed, for instance, he would be heard doing so.

The original script of *Steamboat Willie* is still to be found in the archives of the Disney studio in Burbank, California, and the following extract gives an idea of the effect Walt was trying to achieve in rounding out the character of Mickey Mouse.

Scene #32.
Dolly-Mickey . . . Medium shot. . . . Mickey looking into open mouth of Captain with a frightened expression on his face . . . Little girl at right of scene with surprised expression as she watches them . . . doorway to kitchen between girl and captain . . . Mickey draws away from captain and stands with scared look on face . . . Captain closes mouth and gives him a mean look . . . Mickey tries to appear at ease . . . Does a silly forced grin at captain . . . this slowly dies away into scared expression . . . He puts hands in pocket and whistles a couple of measures of "Yankee Doodle" . . . Looks back to captain with a sickly forced grin . . . then does a sickly little laugh . . . which gradually dies off as his expression changes to scared look . . . turns to camera and gives a deep nervous sigh . . . The captain is very sore . . . He grabs Mickey by the tail and drags him into kitchen . . . girl watches with frightened bewildered expression . . .

However, there were problems. For instance, how were the sound effects to be added? And what method of recording were they going to use? For the moment, Walt Disney Studio possessed no sound equipment and no technicians who would have known how to use it, anyway. It was a time when even the major studios were still trying to work out which was the best method of sound synchronization to use, and there was widespread ignorance and confusion in Hollywood. Certainly, no one had yet given a thought to the peculiar problems of fitting sound to cartoon films, where the technique of synchronization was especially tricky.

All Walt Disney knew was that sound film ran through the projector at the rate of twenty-four frames every second, and from this it was easy to work out that if the musical accompaniment to the cartoon was two beats every second, they had to have a beat every twelve frames of the cartoon. But how did you make sure of the precise timing?

Luckily, a young man named Wilfred Jackson had recently come to work for the Walt Disney Studio, and he was fascinated to the point of obsession with the art of cartoon films. Eager to become an animator, but completely ignorant of the technique, he had turned up at the studio one day and offered to work for nothing until he had gained experience. Although he had graduated from the Otis Art Institute and was an efficient illustrator, he was put to work at the humblest and messiest job in the studio, washing the ink and paint off the cels so that they could be reused. One day, while he was wrestling with his synchronization problems, Walt wandered through the lab where the cel washing was done and heard the sound of someone playing the harmonica. The performance was highly professional, and the performer was Jackson.

Walt stopped and asked him if he knew anything about music, and Jackson said, "A little." Walt prided himself on knowing a little about music, too, thanks to those years when his father had forced him to saw away on the violin, and he thought that, between them, he and Jackson might find a way of solving the synchronization problem.

"Jackson went out and bought a metronome," he said later, "and we moved to the studio and began to work things out. I had a pad of bar music sheets, and I started the metronome and asked Jackson to play a tune on his harmonica. While it ticktocked away, he would play out our frames so we had exactly the right ratio of frames to each bar of music."

Next, Walt went on a shopping spree to the five and ten, buying up gadgets and noisemakers like cowbells and tin cans. "I bought a couple of plumber's friends* and some slide whistles and ocarinas," he said later. "We played around with these for a while to work out the sound effects.

---

*Rubber plungers for cleaning out blocked drains. When in action, they make a squishy sound.

When I say we, I mean Ub Iwerks, young Jackson, and myself. A few nights later, we asked our wives to come over and see something new. We had no projection room, and our sheet hung on a garage doorway. It was a warm night, so we put our wives in chairs facing the open garage doorway with the sheet hanging over it. Then Roy turned on the projector and began to run *Steamboat Willie*. Iwerks, I and Jackson got into the garage behind the sheet, where we could watch the picture from the rear and make our various noises." It must have been quite a spectacle, and Walt wondered later on what the neighbors thought of it.

"Jackson tootled music on his mouth-organ," he said. "The rest of us hit cowbells, ocarinas, and whistles and scrubbed away at the washboard. Iwerks had rigged up a microphone to an old radio speaker, so our wives would be able to hear the sound effects clearly."

Walt had scored the cartoon so that sound came out of everything Mickey looked at or touched. The steamboat whistle tootled a tune; cows, pigs, and kettles mooed, squealed, and fizzed to music.

"We beat our brains out synchronizing that cartoon," Walt recalled, "and when we were through we ran around the sheet, and Roy came running up from the projector, and we looked at our wives expectantly and said, 'How was it?' All they said was 'Nice' and went on gossiping, as they had done, Roy said bitterly afterward, all through the screening."

"What did they expect?" Lillie asked later. "We had absolutely no idea what was going on. And in any case, it sounded terrible." But the effort was not completely wasted. The al fresco performance had enabled Walt, Ub, and Jackson to mark off the film in exactly the right places for synchronization.

Now to get it professionally recorded. There was only one place, New York, where all the latest developments in sound recording were being perfected. With the canisters of *Steamboat Willie* under his arm, Walt set off for Manhattan, stopping off en route in Kansas City to persuade his old organist friend Carl Stalling to compose a score for the film exactly timed to the beats they had marked out.*

IN NEW YORK the movie industry was in chaos over the sound situation. In a letter to Lilly, which he wrote on September 9, 1928, Walt described it as "a madhouse." Everyone was scrambling to get his hands on record-

---

*These included the two big musical numbers that were incorporated into the film, "Turkey in the Straw" and "Steamboat Bill," and it was a complicated job of scoring under the special circumstances. But Stalling did it in seventy-two hours and agreed to be paid later. Walt never forgot his debt to Stalling—who had already, it will be remembered, come up with a loan of $275 when the Disneys badly needed it—and he made sure the organist was richly rewarded for his efforts when the Disneys were finally in the money.

ing equipment, and bootleg models of RCA sound recorders were the hottest items along Film Row.

So far only a few of the major companies had the right to use the sound-on-film method pioneered by RCA, who were desperately trying to keep it out of the hands of their rivals. As a result, Walt was advised to use the alternate (and cheaper) method. This meant putting his score on phonograph discs, as many companies were already doing. He went to see a movie using this sytem and walked out in disgust, determined to have no part of it. During one reel, the projectionist put the needle in the wrong groove, with the result that all the dialogue and sound effects were out of synch.

He figured that if something like that happened to *Steamboat Willie* it would ruin Mickey Mouse's debut. In any case, the idea of having canisters of *Steamboat Willie* going around the country with separate sound discs accompanying them, and the consequent danger of their being mislaid or damaged, was too awful to contemplate.

Walt was convinced that only the sound-on-film system would do for *Steamboat Willie*, and therefore only RCA could synchronize the film. He showed *Steamboat Willie* to the chief sound technician at RCA, who was extremely blasé about the film ("He didn't crack a smile once during the run-through," Walt said later) but said he could certainly add sound effects to it. He warned Walt that it might be expensive and that they would want cash on delivery. Did he have sufficient money for a deposit—say five hundred dollars?

Walt swallowed hard, said he was sure that he could find what it cost to do a good job, and went back to telephone Roy. Roy said if Walt was sure RCA could produce the goods, he would find the money somehow but beseeched his brother to drive a hard bargain and watch every penny he spent from now on.

"They sound awfully expensive to me," Roy said. "Are they gonna throw in a booking for the film, too?" Unfortunately, there was no chance of that. Not only did Walt agree that they did sound expensive, but he might have added—which for the moment he did not—that they also seemed excessively complacent and superior about their technical abilities. Initially, he had been overawed by the RCA engineer's patronizing manner, but gradually, he became increasingly suspicious of the whole set up and grew apprehensive about what terrible things they might be planning to do to his masterpiece.

By this time he had grown very attached to *Steamboat Willie*. Convinced that it was the best cartoon film he had ever made, he had a strong premonition that his future and those of his associates would stand or fall on what happened to it. The setup at RCA filled him with foreboding.

To find out how they operated, he asked for a demonstration of something they had already worked on, and they gave him a run-through of a Movietone cartoon of an Aesop fable. He was astonished and alarmed. So far as sound effects were concerned, all they seemed to have added were music and trap drum rolls to emphasize action.

"*My gosh—terrible*—A lot of racket and nothing else," he reported back to Roy. "I was terribly disappointed. I had expected to see something halfway decent. *But honestly*—it was nothing but one of the rottenest fables I ever saw. It merely had an orchestra playing and adding some noises. . . . The talking part does not mean a thing. It doesn't even match. . . ."

After the demonstration was through, he swung around to the expectant engineer. "Is that *all* you can do?" he asked. To him it looked and sounded just like a silent film, except it now had canned, instead of live, accompaniment and, in his view, had been ruined in the process.

"What more do you want?" the engineer asked.

"I expected *real* sound effects," Walt said. He pulled out the marked score Carl Stalling had written for *Steamboat Willie* and indicated the beat marks on the film's frames. "This is the method we have worked out for my film. See, every word and every sound effect has been meticulously timed, and these marks show you exactly when and how to get them right on the beat."

The engineer glanced casually at the score and scornfully threw it back at him. "Why, to do it that way would cost you a fortune," he said. "You'd have to hire an orchestra, pay royalties to a publisher, plus music tax and all the trimmings, not to mention our fee." He did some quick figuring with a pencil and paper. "Cost you around thirty-five hundred dollars at the very least. Have you got that kind of money?"

"No," Walt said, "but if you can do the job exactly the way I want it done, and if you can get the sound effects exactly right, I'll find the money somehow. The question is, are you capable of doing it—properly, I mean?"

"Here, what are you trying to do, teach us our job?" the engineer asked, suddenly angry. "Look, sonny, we know all about this sound business, and we've worked out how to do it cheaply and effectively. We have our own methods and our own music. You just give us your film and leave it to us. We'll put in the sound." His tone changed and he added, "You know the best thing for you to do, son? The best thing for you to do is go away and relax. Forget about your precious film, and put it in our hands. We know what's best for it. Come back in a couple of days, and we'll have it all blended in. Nice music, nice sound effects, and nobody'll notice whether it's synchronized or not."

"I'll notice," Walt said, firmly. Clutching the canisters of *Steamboat*

Willie under his arm, he walked out of the office. He was finished with RCA.

"I've dropped them from my mind entirely," he wrote to Roy.

But where was he to go now to get what he wanted? Surely, somewhere in New York, there must be someone who could understand why *Steamboat Willie* was special, and why it was so vital to give it the authentic sound effects its leading character, Mickey Mouse, needed to make the audience remember him and turn him into a star?

There was indeed someone. His name was Pat Powers. He had access to all the new sound equipment and knew just what Walt's new production required. Unfortunately, there was one thing wrong with Powers. He was a crook.

PATRICK A. POWERS was one of those professional Irishmen whose brogue made him sound as if he were just off the boat. He was, in fact, a second generation American from upstate New York whose easy smile and broth-of-a-boy charm concealed a heart of stone.

In a milieu never exactly notable for its honesty of purpose, most veterans of Film Row regarded him as one of the most unscrupulous and untrustworthy of their brethren and were full of tales of his genial rapacity. Pat Powers had been in the movie business from the early days when fur salesmen like Adolph Zukor came out of the Bowery and began making films. His capabilities as a con man can be measured by the fact that he even talked Carl Laemmle into making him a partner in Universal Pictures and then proceeded to rob that shrewd and hardheaded character blind.

When the truth finally dawned on Laemmle that he had been well and truly cheated, he challenged Powers to produce the financial records of Universal's transactions—records that Laemmle had foolishly allowed him to keep and manipulate. Passionately protesting his purity as a God-fearing son of the "Auld Sod," Powers angrily rejected what he termed Laemmle's outrageous impugnment of his honesty and melodramatically flung the records out of the window of Universal's New York office at 1600 Broadway. What he did not tell Laemmle was that he had an accomplice waiting on the sidewalk below, ready to catch the manipulated records and make sure the police and Universal's watchdogs never saw them again.

In 1928, he was still at his old tricks. The advent of sound in the movies was just the gimmick for which he had been waiting to make yet another fortune. Aware that RCA and Movietone had secured a monopoly of the sound-on-film system and that they were now worth their weight in gold, he had bribed and corrupted company engineers into providing him with the technical details and then persuaded them to build him a bootleg system, slightly modified, which he called Cinephone.

All he needed now was a movie to which he could add music and sound effects and launch it as the first Cinephone talking film; then he would be in business, and all those Hollywood companies that had been locked out of RCA would come flocking to his door.

So when Walt Disney walked into his office one morning in the fall of 1928, with the canisters of *Steamboat Willie* under his arm, Pat Powers listened to his story, put an affectionate arm around the young man's shoulders, and drew him, an unwitting fly, into his parlor.

9
Unseemly Powers

WALT DISNEY WAS twenty-six years old in 1928. In many ways he was still a naive kid from the sticks, longing for someone to hold his hand in the big city.

"This damn town is enough to give anybody the heebie jeebies," he wrote home in a letter to Ub Iwerks, after his bruising experiences with RCA.

For the moment he had lost his self-confidence and faith in his capacity to judge his own work. There were moments when he even began to have doubts about *Steamboat Willie*. Indicative of his mood just before his meeting with Pat Powers was a downhearted letter he wrote to Ub in which he did not bother to conceal his feelings.

> "Personally I am sick of this picture, *Steamboat Willie*," he wrote. "Every time I see it, the lousy print spoils everything. Maybe it will be different looking at the picture with sound. I sure hope so. I am very nervous and upset and I guess that has a lot to do with my attitude in the matter. . . . I sure wish I was home. I sure wouldn't make a good traveling salesman. I can't mix with strangers and enjoy myself like some people. This is not affecting my attitude toward the matter I came here for. That is the only thing that is on my mind. But I have so much time to kill at nights that I almost go nuts."*

In this mood, he was an easy mark for Pat Powers's hospitable Irish charms and persuasive manner. Powers did not just enthuse about the qualities of *Steamboat Willie* but also promised that, once it had been fitted with "the magical sound effects it truly deserves," he would see to

---

*Disney Archives, Burbank.

it that it was adequately publicized and sold to the biggest chain of movie theaters in the nation.

Walt was so taken with his powerful connections ("he seems to know everybody who is anybody in the film world and talks to them all the time on the telephone—uses their first names, too—it's all Adolph, Louie and Myron") that he agreed to pay Powers one thousand dollars plus a percentage of the fees, for handling the film and arranging the recording sessions. He wired Roy to make sure they had enough cash in the bank to cover the down payment he handed over.

Powers also produced a distinguished musician named Carl Edouarde, who ran the pit orchestra at the Strand Theater on Broadway and said he was the one to conduct the players needed for the dubbing sessions. Walt spent some worrying hours with Edouarde, going over Stalling's score for *Steamboat Willie*. He carefully pointed out the guideposts that had been inserted into the *Steamboat Willie* film to make sure every bar of music and every sound effect would be on the right beat.

"We had drawn a mark on our film every twelve frames in India ink," Walt said later, "and when projected it made a white flash on the screen. If you watched for the flash, it was a substitute for the ticktock of an old-fashioned metronome. Just by watching it, the conductor could stay on the beat and know just when to allow for a sound effect."

Unfortunately, Edouarde was sublimely contemptuous of such unmusical aids and kept interrupting Walt's lecture with a comment that Walt had already heard only too often during his pilgrimage along Film Row, "Why don't you just leave it to me?" Edouarde asked, loftily.

When Walt confided his doubts to Pat Powers, his new protector responded, soothingly, "Don't be impatient. Do like he says. Eddie's a good musician. If you have any doubts, just sit in on his sessions and make sure he gets in all your sound effects. But let Eddie handle the musical side. He knows what's what. In any case, if it doesn't work out right, don't worry. We'll do the recording over again—and it won't cost you a nickel. I'll stand the expense."

Walt needed such reassurances because the specter of a money shortage was beginning to gibber before his eyes again. Roy, who was alarmed, communicated regularly to warn him that their resources were being drained. He began to suspect that his hick brother was being taken for a ride by this glib city slicker in Manhattan.

BY NOW WALT seemed to have put his complete trust and confidence in the ability of Pat Powers to lead them to fame and fortune—so much so that he had telegraphed Ub Iwerks to put yet another Mickey Mouse film in the works. Though it would be the fourth in the series, not a single one so far had secured a booking or made any money for the Walt Disney

Studio. The new one, to be called *The Barn Dance*, would cost yet another twenty-five hundred dollars, and that was more money than they now had in the studio kitty.

Meanwhile, Maestro Edouarde, who had originally calculated that all he would need for the recording sessions on *Steamboat Willie* was a five-piece combination plus drummers, turned out, on the appointed day, to have called in a seventeen-member orchestra plus no less than three trap drummers and effects men.

Walt Disney never forgot that first dubbing session; everything went wrong. It was seven o'clock on a cool September morning in 1928 when he arrived at the downtown recording studio. His confidence was hardly bolstered when the first musician made his appearance. He was a double-bass player, who had come, pale, haggard, and unshaven, straight from an all-night recording session for Victor Records at their studio in Camden, New Jersey. "The first thing he did," remembered Walt later, "was open his double-bass case and take a swig from a bottle."

When the full orchestra was at last assembled, Maestro Edouarde proceeded to put them through a full rehearsal of the main musical numbers in the score, including "Turkey in the Straw," "Yankee Doodle" and "Steamboat Bill." Since it was costing him seven dollars an hour for the players plus ten dollars an hour for the sound-effects men and twenty dollars an hour for Edouarde, Walt felt a full rehearsal was hardly called for, especially as it was setting him back $270 before the dubbing had even begun.

And once it began, there was a succession of disasters. "Every time the bass player sawed into his instrument and went zoom," he said later, "the volume was such that he blew out a bulb in the recording mechanism. The first time it happened, the sound men moved the bass player further back. But it made no difference, and he promptly blew another bulb. Even when they moved him to a far corner of the studio, he still went on blowing bulbs each time he dug into his fiddle. Finally, he was told to go play outside the studio door, where even we couldn't hear him. At seven dollars an hour!"

Maestro Edouarde's arrogant self-confidence was beginning to seep away, too, as he began to realize that sound recording was not as simple as he had presumed it to be. Time and again, when *Steamboat Willie* was run through and came to an end, he found himself with pages of sound effects left over. But he kept reassuring Walt by saying, "Never mind, we'll get them all in next time."

By the end of the morning, everyone realized the recording session had gone catastrophically wrong. Walt, anxious to conceal from his brother just how disastrous it had really been, made haste to assure him that all was well. He sent him a telegram:

ALL CONCERNED DESIRE BEST RESULTS OBTAINABLE THERE-
FORE ARE REMAKING IT USING DIFFERENT EFFECTS MEN. I AM
VERY OPTIMISTIC ABOUT RESULTS AND OUR FUTURE LOOKS
BRIGHT. GAVE POWERS CHECK ONE THOUSAND. BE SURE IT IS OK.

In fact, the future looked anything but bright. After Edouarde had sent
his musicians off to lunch, he said thoughtfully to Walt, "Next time, I
think I'll try that idea you were telling me about—you know, using those
flashes as a visual metronome. It'll mean a whole new session."

"You mean, a complete rerecording?" Walt asked, thinking of the extra
cost that would involve.

"Oh yes," Edouarde said. "We just have to do it all over again."

Walt went to see Pat Powers and reminded him that if a rerecording
became necessary, Powers had promised he would pay for it. "That's
right," Powers said. "I said I'd pay for any rerecording, and I will."

"What about the orchestra?" Walt asked. "It's costing two hundred
seventy dollars an hour."

"I didn't say anything about the orchestra," Powers said.

With some trepidation, Walt telephoned Roy and said they would need
another twelve hundred dollars since he had run into some unexpected
charges. Roy immediately went to see Lillian and told her he wanted his
brother's automobile—it would have to be sold to meet the new expenses.

"It'll break his heart," Lillian said. "He just loves that car. Do you
really have to?"

"It's either the automobile or Mickey Mouse," Roy said. "From now
on, we can't afford both."

Walt was stunned when he heard the news. In some ways, that
beautiful new automobile—an open Moon four-seater—had been his
most treasured and pampered possession. The knowledge that it had
now passed into some philistine's uncaring hands was hard to bear. Its
loss galvanized him into demanding drastic economies at the recording
sessions. It was too late to save his automobile, but he slashed expenses
anyway by demanding that the size of the orchestra be cut down to
sixteen and that two sound-effects men be fired. This time he stayed
close to the conductor's podium to make sure Maestro Edouarde followed
the flashes on the screen. The result was that this time the orchestra
finished up simultaneously with the fade-out of *Steamboat Willie*, and all
the vital sound-effects were right on the beat. Late that night, at the end
of a nerve-frazzling and exhausting session, Steamboat Willie had been
wired for sound at last, and exactly the way he wanted it.

All his earlier doubts about *Steamboat Willie* as a production and about
Mickey Mouse as a brand-new star were dissipated when he saw the first
run-through of the completed film. It was funny, it was fresh, it was

entertaining. With pride and joy, he handed it over to Pat Powers and told him that now was the time to make good on his promise and get out and sell it. He did not tell him how badly he and his associates now needed the money.

Weeks passed and there were no sales. This was not entirely the fault of Pat Powers. He arranged special showings of *Steamboat Willie* all over town, and the bookers for the big movie chains all turned up to see it. Some of them even laughed in places and told the anxious Walt that they thought it might well have a future. But no one booked it.

Walt was so downcast that he confessed later, "I sometimes felt like shooting myself." It was now October, and he longed for the blue skies of California. He felt as if he had been in New York for years, and he had hated every moment of it.

"I have certainly learned a lot about this game already," he wrote to Lillian. "It is the damndest mixed-up affair I have ever heard of. It sure demands a shrewd and thoroughly trained mind to properly handle it. There are so damned many angles that continually come up that if a person hasn't the experience, etc. it would certainly lick one. They are all a bunch of schemers and full of tricks that would fool a greenhorn."

He still had implicit faith and trust in the benevolent interest of Pat Powers, and he went on, "I am sure glad I got someone to fall back on for advice. I would be like a sheep among a pack of wolves. I have utmost faith and confidence in Powers and believe that if we don't try to rush things too fast that we will get a good deal out of this. We will all just have to have patience and confidence. I am very optimistic about everything and want you all to feel the same way. I really think our big chance is here."*

One morning, after yet another trade showing of his film, he hung around in the lobby, listening in on the comments of the exhibitors as they came out, hoping to hear one of them say he was going to make a booking. He felt a touch on his arm, and a man named Harry Reichenbach introduced himself.

"Trying to find out what they think about your little number?" he asked, jerking a contemptuous thumb at the bookers. "I can tell you what they think. They like it. In fact, they like it a lot. But it doesn't mean they're going to book it," he added. "That's the trouble with all these guys. They're scared to make a decision. It's the same in Hollywood. It's the disease of the movie business. They're all scared of following their instincts and making up their minds. And Mister, as far as your film is concerned, you can hang around here until Hell freezes over, and you're not going to get a decision out of these clucks. They're afraid to take a

---

*Letter dated October 20, 1928. Disney Archives, Burbank.

chance—just in case they back the wrong horse. They're waiting for someone to tell them what to do. And do you know who's going to tell them? John Q. Public, that's who. The paying customers themselves."

"And how in hell are they going to do that?" Walt asked, helplessly, "when I can't even get a public showing?"

"Well, now, as far as that's concerned, I have an idea," Reichenbach said. He began leading Walt out of the movie house. "Look, let's you and me go and grab a bite to eat. I have a proposition I want to put to you."

Although Walt Disney didn't know it at the time, Harry Reichenbach had once been one of the most successful press agents in New York. He was the man who had been hired to promote the public showing of the famous painting *September Morn* and had drummed up a raging scandal over the exhibition of this modest display of female nudity. He had now moved on to the movie business and handled the films for Universal Pictures through its Manhattan outlet at the Colony Theater.

Reichenbach thought *Steamboat Willie* was terrific and would wow the general public once it had a chance to see it. And he proposed to Walt that he put it on at the Colony Theater for a two-week showing with his latest Hollywood feature.* Would Walt be prepared to let him have it for a rental of five hundred dollars a week?

"It's more than anyone has ever paid for a cartoon film before," Reichenbach informed him, "but I happen to think it's worth it. This little film is going to cause a sensation. And once it does, all the bookers are going to come knocking at your door. But I'd like to get in first."

Steamboat Willie opened at the Colony Theater on November 18, 1928, and the press as well as the general public had been invited to what was billed as "the first animated sound cartoon." It was a cold night but the reception could not have been warmer, and the next day many of the critics ignored the main movie and stage show to lavish praise on the cartoon film, which *Variety* called "a peach of a synchronization job all the way."

It was left to *The New York Times* to register the debut of "a new cartoon character henceforth to be known as 'Mickey Mouse.'" The newspaper saluted the production as "an ingenious piece of work with a good deal of fun," and in a reference to its sound track, added, "It growls, squeaks, and makes various other sounds that add to its mirthful quality."

At last. After all the pain and anguish, Walt Disney's work had been recognized.

And, as if to prove Reichenbach's cynical point, the bookers came beating a path to Walt Disney's room at the Algonquin Hotel. Almost

---

*Gang War, starring Jack Pickford.

without exception, every big movie theater chain in the United States sent around its representatives—the same ones who had previously held back—with offers of bankrolls and contracts. Suddenly, all the Hollywood studios were interested in a Mickey Mouse series. There was one unexpected touch to all this excitement. Reichenbach gave a celebratory luncheon at the Waldorf Hotel after the press showing of *Steamboat Willie*, and by happenstance or design, Margaret Winkler Mintz turned out to be one of the guests. In the few minutes that they managed to snatch alone, she asked Walt once more to listen to a proposition her husband was planning to make to him.

AT A MEETING in the boardroom of Universal Pictures at 1600 Broadway, at which Harry Reichenbach and Pat Powers were both present, Charlie Mintz said he was speaking on behalf of the Universal Board of Directors and offered Walt Disney and his partners a tempting deal to make future Mickey Mouse pictures for them.

It was an ironic occasion, in more ways than one. For instance, Carl Laemmle, the Universal chief, had once sworn that the arch enemy Pat Powers would never again contaminate his offices with his thieving presence, after the crimes he had committed against the company. And yet here he was once more, gazing fondly and proprietorially around the familiar Universal boardroom as if he were back in his ancestral home.

Then, too, for Walt, there was the monstrous irony of staring into the smiling faces of Charlie Mintz and the Universal directors, the same men who had once stolen Oswald the Rabbit and his artists away from him and who were now benevolently regarding him as if he were their long, lost son. "Join us," Charlie Mintz urged. "We'll give you studio space, all the backing you need, and a generous share of the profits if you'll only bring your superlative new cartoon character, Mickey Mouse, over to Universal."

He even had the nerve to add, with a roguish twinkle, "Furthermore, we can provide you with your own animators, if you still want them. They've been waiting all this time to get back to work with you."

Walt could not help remarking, "I wouldn't have them back if they came crawling on their knees."

In spite of the hypocrisy, the Universal offer was tempting because it would make him and his associates rich. Never again would he have to worry about money for dubbing, about whether there was enough in the bank to cover a check. Never again would Walt need to sacrifice his beloved automobile just to keep up with the bills.

But there was, of course, a catch. In return for the long-term contract they were offering—plus all the money—Universal wanted control of, and the copyright on, Mickey Mouse. Walt said no. Mickey Mouse was not for sale to anyone. Mickey Mouse was Walt Disney's baby and belonged to him and to him alone. No one was going to get his hands on him. Ever.

After the meeting, when they were back on Broadway again and strolling toward the Algonquin Hotel, Pat Powers said, "Nice going, Walt. I'm glad you turned them down—shows that you're independent. It's the only way to treat those bastards."

In the bar of the Algonquin, he took a long pull at his tumbler of Bushmill's and said, "Now I've got a proposition for you." He saw the expression on Walt's face and added, hastily, "Now don't get me wrong. You know me. I'm on your side. Besides, I'm not really interested in that crazy mouse of yours. All I'm interested in is the future of my sound apparatus, Cinephone. So here's what I'm going to do."

10
The Revenge of Ub

IF ONLY PAT Powers had been trustworthy, there would have been absolutely nothing wrong with his proposition. On the face of it, the deal he offered Walt Disney was an attractive one.

In 1928-29, if a producer made a film and could not or would not sign a distribution contract with one of the major Hollywood studios (who controlled their own chains of movie theaters at the time) he could sell the "states rights" of his film to the so-called "independents." These were the owners of movie houses—sometimes quite large chains of them—who operated in different states in competition with those controlled by the Hollywood companies.

They booked their own films. They made their own deals with the producers whose movies they rented and had exclusive rights to show them in the particular areas that they controlled. And depending on the part of the country in which they operated, they paid a percentage of what would have been a national rental for each film.*

Powers offered to advance to Walt Disney Studio the money to pay for future films in the Mickey Mouse series. At his own expense he would pay the salaries of the salesmen who would be sent out to sell the films to the independents. All he would ask in return was a modest 10 percent of the gross receipts.

For its part, the Walt Disney Studio would retain complete control of Mickey Mouse, and its only obligation would be an agreement to rent and use Powers's Cinephone sound equipment for all its animated films in the future.

As a pledge of his benign intentions, Powers pressed a check for three thousand into Walt's hand, and it was a gesture that Walt warmly and

---

*New York state rights were calculated at 12 percent of the agreed national rental: New England at 8 percent, California territory (which then included Arizona, Nevada and Hawaii) at 6 percent.

gratefully appreciated. Walt Disney was by no means accustomed, as yet, to the byzantine maneuverings of the film world, and the arduous and stressful negotiations of the past few weeks had disturbed and exhausted him. He had been profoundly shocked by the chicanery and venality he had encountered in his dealings with the movie men; and the affectionate goodwill and generosity with which Powers now so benevolently took charge of his future, he found all but overwhelming.

He signed the contract Powers offered him without a moment's hesitation and, reading it through later in the privacy of his hotel room, had absolutely no qualms about its conditions. He could not wait to show it to Roy. He had only one more chore left to perform before he went back in triumph to Hyperion Avenue. Ub Iwerks had done a marvelous job of animating the new Mickey Mouse cartoon, *The Barn Dance*, and delivering it on time, and now he called Carl Stalling and asked him to come to New York and write a score for it. He also asked him to do the same for the earlier Mickeys, *Plane Crazy* and *Gallopin' Gaucho*, to which sound would now be added.

This time it was Stalling who sat in on the recording sessions with Maestro Edouarde, and they went without a hitch. By the time the films were dubbed and ready, Pat Powers's salesmen had no less than four Mickey Mouse films to offer to the independent renters. On his last night in New York, Walt went to the Colony Theater to say good-bye to Harry Reichenbach and to watch the final performance of the local run of *Steamboat Willie*. As the ripples of happy laughter spread through the theater, Walt was so relieved that he felt tears rolling down his cheeks and, embarrassed, did his best to conceal them from his companion.

His experiences in New York had, indeed, been shaking. But he comforted himself with the thought that not all of the men had turned out to be villains. Two had proved to be different from the others and had been real friends in need and he would never forget what they had done for him. His feelings toward Harry Reichenbach and Pat Powers were such that he would willingly have trusted his life with them.

NOT EVEN ROY Disney's skepticism rocked his faith in Pat Powers. Roy went through the contract his brother had signed and strongly objected to some of its terms. What particularly irked him was a clause under which the Walt Disney Studio agreed to pay twenty-six thousand dollars a year for ten years for the use of Cinephone sound equipment. He considered that a real rip off. Were the rumors he had heard correct? Did Cinephone really belong to Powers or not? Or were they likely to be involved in a lawsuit over patent infringements?

Walt brushed his doubts aside. He grew particularly incensed when Roy mentioned Hollywood gossip that Powers was a con man and not to be trusted. His brother's snide remarks made him angry, and he insisted, "Pat Powers is one of the nicest and most honest men I've ever encountered."

He refused to listen to a word against him, and once the popularity of the Mickey Mouse films began their meteoric rise, it was he who insisted they change the agreement with Powers and begin paying him a regular distributors' fee of 35 percent of the gross receipts.

"He's earned it," Walt declared. "He's made Mickey Mouse into a household name."

And there was no doubt at all of Powers's success in building up the fame of the Disney cartoons. In less than a year, Mickey Mouse had made it as a national character—and an international one, too. Movie houses were even beginning to put his name and the title of his films on the marquee alongside the feature film, which had never happened before. He drew big crowds. Magazines did articles about him. Newspaper cartoonists picked him up and used him as a feisty symbol in their work. Each new Mickey Mouse film was an immediate hit, and feature writers flocked to Hyperion Avenue demanding interviews with the creator of what they now began calling the Mighty Mouse.

There was only one problem. Walt and Roy should now be rich as well as famous. True, more animators had been hired, and budgets for the cartoons had increased to at least five thousand dollars a segment. Still, *Variety* calculated that the Disneys were making forty thousand dollars in receipts from each cartoon, and the profits should have been rolling in.

Only they were not. Pat Powers was proving a little dilatory in his payments. To excuse him, Walt insisted to his brother that film people were always like that—they just couldn't maintain an efficient accounting system. But as the weeks went by without any checks from New York, the time came when Roy had to say to him, "Look, Walt, we have to face the situation. Here we are, owners of the most famous cartoon character in the United States—in the world, maybe—with crowds lining up to see him in movie houses from Anchorage to Buenos Aires, and we're flat broke! We don't have enough money in the bank to finance the next series, and I'm not sure whether they're going to let us have the credit. I think Pat Powers is screwing us."

Roy announced that he was leaving for New York and was going to get some money out of Powers "even if I have to squeeze the SOB like a lemon." He came back completely frustrated. Powers had smothered him in Hibernian charm but had skillfully avoided showing him the accounts, meanwhile maintaining that the expense of launching Mickey Mouse and the Disneys meant the series hadn't yet earned a dime. All the profits had been swallowed up in the cost of publicity.

Moreover, Powers had taken the wind out of Roy's sails by launching into a more-in-sorrow-than-in-anger attack on Walt Disney himself, accusing him of abandoning Mickey Mouse just when he was about to become a money-maker for all of them. "He wants to kill off the Mighty Mouse," Powers had announced, sententiously, "and begorra, he's going to kill all of us off in the process."

It was a wild exaggeration but at least partially true. Walt Disney, who was, by this time, in an extremely nervous and exhausted state, had begun to grow tired of sketching out plots for more and more Mickey Mouse films. There were moments when he was sickened by the thought of having to write another draft scenario about the mouse.

Furthermore, his relations with Ub Iwerks, who still took Walt's creations and turned them into actual cartoon films, had grown increasingly strained. Nowadays, Walt didn't just tease the timid Ub; he barked at him and criticized his work. Seemingly oblivious of the fact that Ub was tearing his guts out trying to keep up with the public's demands for more Mickey Mouse shorts, he would sometimes come into the studio late at night, lean over the desk where Ub was working overtime, and tear his sketches off the drawing board. Flinging them across the room, he would angrily complain that this wasn't the conception he wanted, that Ub was turning Mickey into a silly, simpering clown.

As usual, Ub never complained. Sometimes, Lilly Disney came to the studio with Walt, and, as time passed, would curl up on a couch and go to sleep while Walt mooned around the office, checking on the day's work. But then she would be awakened by the abrasive sound of her husband barking at the crushed and silent Ub.

"Really, Walt," she was often moved to remark, "you shouldn't be so rough on that poor little man. The way you treat him! The things you say to him! Sometimes you're so rough on him, he looks as if he could kill you."

"Nonsense," Walt said. "Ub doesn't mind criticism from me. He knows me too well to get mad with me. He's the most understanding character in the world. He'd do anything for me."

WALT, IN FACT, was sick and tired of Mickey Mouse and would have been critical no matter how Ub animated him. He was longing to create something new—and he had an idea. It is a measure of how much he still trusted Ub's judgment and understanding that it was to him that he first expounded it.

He described how Carl Stalling had played him a piano extract one night from Saint-Saëns's "Danse Macabre."

"It's all about skeletons coming out of their graves at midnight and doing an eerie dance," Stalling had said. "It would make a riveting cartoon if you used the right musical accompaniment." Walt asked Ub what he thought of the idea, and his associate was enthusiastic.

He went off to the library and looked up references. He came back in triumph with some reproductions of skeleton dances from the walls of ancient Etruscan tombs and of a graphic series of drawings of skeleton dances by Rowlandson, the great English cartoonist. Together, he and Walt got down to work. Walt, as usual, did the original drawings; Iwerks did the rough conception and handed it on to the animators; and between them they superintended the result.

In a couple of weeks they had sent a finished cartoon to New York for dubbing. Stalling and Edouarde dubbed it to the music of "The Hall of the Mountain King" and the main theme from Saint-Saëns's eerie and macabre piece.

Walt thought he and Ub had created a startlingly effective cartoon, both novel and amusing, and he told Lilly he was convinced "it will be a real hit when it is shown." At first he called it *The Spook Dance* but then changed the name to *The Skeleton Dance*. He planned to send it out as the first of a series that, he said, would probably be known as *Silly Symphonies*.

Pat Powers saw *The Skeleton Dance* just about the time that Roy came to see him in New York, and he hated it. So did all the exhibitors to whom he showed it.

"What's he trying to do, ruin us?" Pat asked Roy. "You go back and tell that brother of yours the renters don't want this gruesome crap. And as for calling a whole series of them *Silly Symphonies*, what sort of a crazy idea is that? Why, the name alone will keep the public away in droves. What they want is more Mickey Mouse. You go back and tell Walt. *More mice*, tell him, *More mice!*"

The fuss Pat made about *The Skeleton Dance* was one of the reasons that Roy never did get around to persuading him to show him the Mickey Mouse accounts. It was only when he returned to California that he realized he had been conned. "That man's a crook," Roy said to Walt when he got back. "I'm sure of it now. He's cheating us out of our money."

Still, Walt had faith. Not even Powers's devastating criticism of *The Skeleton Dance* could shake his trust in him. Anyway, he could be right. Maybe the new cartoon was too gruesome and *Silly Symphonies* was a ridiculous name for a new series. For the first time in his life, he began to have doubts about his own work. He kept calling in Ub, and they would sit in the tiny projection room running *The Skeleton Dance* over and over again.

"Tell me, Ub," Walt would ask desperately, "is it any good or not?"

"Don't you really know?" Ub asked.

"No," Walt confessed. "I can't seem to be able to tell anymore." Ub would glower at him in silent resentment. He did not believe his self-confident boss had suddenly developed doubts about his own judgment.

He was convinced that Walt was putting him on, that he was indulging in a new form of teasing. So he said nothing, and it widened the increasing gulf between the two men.

Walt's uncertainty about his new cartoon was hardly helped by the hesitations he encountered when he tried to hawk it around the bookers in Los Angeles. One of them visibly shivered after he had seen it and said it would give his customers goose bumps. Then, after some desperate maneuvering, he managed to persuade Fred Miller, owner of the Carthay Circle Theater, to have a look at it. Miller liked it so much that he put it alongside an upcoming feature film and announced its arrival on his marquee:

A WALT DISNEY SILLY SYMPHONY: THE SKELETON DANCE.

Not only was *The Skeleton Dance* a hit with the public, but all the critics praised it, too. Miller held it over for a couple of weeks and, when he heard of its failure to find a New York booker, alerted his friend, Sam Rothafel, who ran the big Roxy Theater in Manhattan.

By the time Walt had shipped the Los Angeles notices to Pat Powers, Rothafel had already been on the telephone demanding a viewing of *The Skeleton Dance*. The new cartoon went into the Roxy program a few days later and was such a success that Rothafel held it over an extra week. Then bookings began to come in from all over the country.

At the end of a few months, *The Skeleton Dance* was a smash hit and launched the *Silly Symphony* series on a successful career. Pat Powers, of course, hastened to claim all the credit. He insisted he had known all along that *The Skeleton Dance* was a potential winner. It had needed extra careful nurturing, that was all.

"If you believe that, you'll believe anything," Roy said scornfully to his brother. And for the first time, the seeds of doubt about Pat Powers's honesty and goodwill were planted in Walt's mind.

PAT POWERS WAS, in fact, on the horns of a dilemma. To begin with he had quite genuinely taken on *Steamboat Willie* as a vehicle for selling his bootleg Cinephone sound system, and the success of the Mickey Mouse series had surprised him. Suddenly, the money had come pouring in, and the temptation to hold on to most of it had been too strong to resist, especially since Walt Disney was so trusting and naive.

But now, he realized the bonanza might well be coming to an end. So negative a feeling had he had of Mickey Mouse to begin with, he hadn't even tried to pin Walt down to a long-term contract, except for the rent of the Cinephone equipment. He had signed up to act as Disney distributor for only a year—just long enough, he had thought, to give the public a chance to listen to Cinephone in action in the theaters. Only it was Mickey Mouse who had made the impact on them. And at any moment now, his participation in the success of the cartoons would be over. The year was almost up.

How could he persuade the Disneys to renew the contract, only, this time, for a really long period? The Disney boys were growing up, and it was now going to take more than Irish charm, he felt, to persuade them to renew. By the spring of 1929, when contracts for the future needed to be made, Pat Powers was prepared to use any method—blackmail, strong-arm methods, or guile—to hold on to the gold mine that Mickey Mouse, the *Silly Symphonies,* and the Disneys were proving to be.

Meanwhile, Roy Disney had heard rumors that Pat Powers was planning something, but exactly what he couldn't pin down. He still did not respond to Roy's repeated demands for an exact accounting of the Mickey Mouse rentals, but money did suddenly begin to arrive. Not nearly as much as the Disneys calculated they should be receiving, but they began to get checks from Powers for three thousand and once even for five thousand. It was not enough to pay the studio bills, but it was sufficient to whet Roy's appetite for what he was now convinced they were due.

He decided the time had come to consult a lawyer. It just so happened that an attorney had recently arrived in Los Angeles with some publicity fanfare. His name was Gunther Lessing and he had represented, of all people, the Mexican revolutionary leader, Pancho Villa, who had fought a war along the U.S.-Mexican border in 1916 against the American army under General Pershing.

Lessing had managed to sue successfully on behalf of Pancho Villa's widow and heirs. Roy Disney figured that if an attorney could get away with that, he could probably handle Pat Powers. Walt had already arranged to go to New York and have a showdown with Powers, and Roy persuaded him to take Lessing with him.

The first meeting took place on a cold January day in 1930 at Powers's office, and at Walt's insistence, he went alone. Powers received him as usual with fond affection and was full of flowery compliments about the wonderful entertainment value of Mickey Mouse.

Once more he insisted that all he was interested in was pushing the success of Cinephone and that the only reason he had acted as a distributor for Disney and the cartoons was out of the kindness of his heart. When the question of a contract renewal was eventually broached, Walt immediately said, as Roy had instructed him, that he was not going to sign any further agreement with Powers until he had seen the accounts and found out what monies were owed to the Disney organization.

Powers looked as if he had been struck by his own son. "After all I've done for you!" he said. "Are you suggesting that I've been cheating on you and your brother? After all the sleepless nights I've spent worrying about how I can make you some money, is this the way you repay me?" Walt retorted mildly that all they wanted was what was due them.

"And how much *is* due you?" Powers asked, a wicked gleam in his eyes. "Don't you think I know who is the real reason for your success? Who made the Mickey Mouse cartoons? Who was responsible for *The Skeleton Dance* and the *Silly Symphonies?* Well, you may have kept it a secret from everyone else, but I know who it is. His name is Ub Iwerks, and you can't do without him."

Walt Disney, startled at the sudden introduction of Ub's name, managed to stammer out that Iwerks was certainly a valuable associate of the Walt Disney Studio, but what did Powers mean by saying he couldn't do without him?

"Exactly that," Powers said. "If you lost Ub Iwerks, you'd lose everything. Your studio would come to a halt. Who's done all your animation? Who's made sure you've met all your deadlines? Ub Iwerks, that's who. I know he's indispensable to you, that losing him would be a disaster for your operation. And let me just make this clear to you, Walt. If you don't renew your contract with me, losing Ub Iwerks is just what you're going to do. Because I've got him—signed, sealed, and delivered!"

"I don't believe it," Walt said. "Ub would never do this to me."

"Read this," Powers said. He passed over a telegram from his representative on the West Coast. It confirmed that Ub Iwerks had signed a five-year personal contract with Powers the previous day. He would soon be heading a new animation operation and creating a new cartoon series—for a salary of $300 a week.

"I still don't believe it," Walt said.

Powers suggested he call Roy and find out exactly what was going on. When Walt demurred (he didn't want to talk to his brother with Powers listening in), Powers changed tack and became the charming Irishman again. "Listen, Walt," he said. "Don't be upset over Ub. You haven't really lost him. Not if you sign up with me. Look, I've been going over our association, and although my primary interest is Cinephone, I don't want to run out on you. I like you. Truly, I have the best interests of you and your brother at heart. And I'd like to make you a wonderful proposition. I know you and Roy need money, and I hate to see you worrying about it. Now I know how to handle these things. So let me take over your operation. I'll look after all the expenses in the future, and you'll never have to fret about bills ever again. What's more, I'll pay you and your brother fifteen hundred dollars a week. Just think of it! Fifteen hundred dollars a week! Each! Not only that, I'll give you back Ub Iwerks to work for you as long as you need him."

Walt said bitterly, "If Ub's done what you say he's done, I wouldn't ever want him to work with me again."

"Don't be like that," Powers said. "Just go back and talk to your brother."

LATER THAT NIGHT, Roy Disney confirmed that Ub Iwerks had been in to see him. Without mentioning the fact that he had signed up with Powers, he had said he had decided to quit the Disney studio. When asked the reason, he had cited increasing tensions between himself and Walt and said he couldn't stand the quarrels any longer. He wanted to leave at once and asked Roy to arrange for his interest in the Walt Disney Studio to be liquidated.*

Walt was so shocked over Ub's action that he could hardly bear to continue his discussions with Powers. He mentioned to Roy that he was seeing him the following day and taking the lawyer with him. This time, he added grimly, there would be a showdown. "Don't break with him finally until you've got some money out of him," Roy said. "Our situation is desperate. We need cash, and we need it badly."

The following day, Walt changed his mind and saw Powers alone again. He found him surprisingly conciliatory. When the question of a new contract came up, Walt said he had been told not to discuss it until he had some money. At which Powers pulled a checkbook out of his desk and wrote a check for five thousand dollars. "Will this be enough?" he asked.

Walt rushed the check back to Roy and, as soon as it had cleared the bank, sent in Gunther Lessing to deal with Powers. Lessing later confessed that handling the affairs of Pancho Villa had been much easier. Pat Powers was used to dealing with lawyers and was not one whit abashed by Lessing's demands that he open his accounts to him.

Of course he was willing to show the lawyer his books, he said. All Walt and Roy had to do was sign a new contract appointing him the sole representative of the Walt Disney Studio and he would be glad to open his records to any inspection the lawyer wished to make.

"We'll get a court order," Lessing said.

"You do that," Powers said. "And see how much time and money it will cost you."

By clandestine means, Roy had discovered Powers owed him and his brother a minimum of $150,000 in receipts from the Disney films. He was

---

*His contract was later terminated legally, and Iwerks's 20 percent interest in the company was bought out for less than three thousand dollars. It was all the Disneys could afford at the time. It was calculated that Ub's interest in Disney would have been worth much more had he waited another three years.

also unpleasantly aware that they would have to spend much more than that if they hoped to get a dime of it back through the courts. After much discussion, they decided to take their losses and walk away.

BUT WHOM WOULD they sign up with now to distribute their films?

MGM suddenly showed an interest but then shied away when Pat Powers sent them a writ and threatened to sue if they attempted to handle Disney's productions. Powers was no longer the charming stage Irishman. He was good and mad, and he let it be known along Film Row that he would take anyone to court who associated with the Disneys. Though it seems hard to believe, because it was all a bluff and he knew he didn't have a leg to stand on, he succeeded in scaring off the distribution companies. Suddenly no one would handle Mickey Mouse and the *Silly Symphonies*.

There was one exception. In Hollywood at that time there was an up-and-coming young director named Frank Capra, who subsequently made some classic movies, and he happened to be a Walt Disney fan. Every time he felt low or out of ideas, he slipped into a movie house and watched Mickey Mouse or a *Silly Symphony* and came out enlivened and refreshed.

Capra was working for Columbia PIctures at that time, and when he heard what had happened to the Disneys—and that it might mean no more cartoons from Walt—he stormed into the office of his boss, Harry Cohn, and told him he had to take over the distribution rights of Disney's cartoons.

Harry Cohn had the reputation of being one of the most ruthless and unsavory producers in Hollywood, but he knew a good movie proposition when it was put to him. Moreover, he had one virtue. No one could scare him—not even Pat Powers. He told his legal department to fight any attempt by Powers to stop Columbia from handling Disney productions in the future. Meanwhile, he offered the Disneys a contract under which Columbia would finance their future productions and pay them 65 percent of the gross receipts received, with books open to inspection by their legal representatives.

Cohn turned down only one request the Disneys made of him. He refused to have anything to do with the Mickey Mouse films and the first of the *Silly Symphonies, The Skeleton Dance*, which Pat Powers had previously handled. It would get them involved in too much legal wrangling, he said. Why not let Powers keep them and put someone in to keep an eye on his accounts?

But Walt, who would never forgive Powers for his perfidy, could not bear the thought of continuing an association with him in any shape or form. He was determined to get him out of his life. He instructed Gunther

Leaping to arrange a settlement with Powers under any sort of conditions that would sever his connection with the Disneys once and for all. It ended with Walt Disney Studio paying Powers fifty thousand dollars (which they borrowed from Columbia) to return the rights of all the cartoon films he had previously handled.

And though it was Powers who should have been compensating them—for he still owed them $150,000 —Walt made no complaint. He felt every penny of the $50,000 was worth it just to be rid of him.

On February 7, 1930, he telegraphed Roy from New York:

HAVE DEFINITELY BROKE[N] WITH POWERS. WILL DELIVER NO MORE PICTURES. PLAN TO TEMPORARILY SUSPEND PRODUCTION OF MICKEYS AND CONCENTRATE ON SYMPHONIES WHICH WE WILL DELIVER TO COLUMBIA.

The trauma was over.

OR WAS IT? A few months later, Lillian went into their bedroom and found her husband had collapsed. She called the family doctor, whose first instinct was to rush in a medical team and pump out the contents of his stomach. Eventually, they managed to bring him back to consciousness without resorting to such drastic measures, but Lilly confirmed to the doctor that Walt had been taking sleeping pills.

When he had recovered sufficiently, the doctor went to talk to Walt and afterward admitted to Lilly that he was deeply worried about her husband's state of mind. He said he believed Walt was on the verge of what was known in those days as a nervous breakdown. From the way Walt looked and talked, in fact, there seemed a strong possibility that he was in a deep emotional depression, and heaven knows what might happen next unless some drastic actions were taken.

Among the many telegrams that flooded in when news hit Hollywood of Walt Disney's illness was one that he kept and never destroyed. It came from Ub Iwerks. PLEASE GET WELL was all it said.

"That bastard," Roy said, when he heard about it. "I'm glad he's out of your life."

"He isn't," Walt said. "He'll be back."

11
Apotheosis

LOOKING BACK, WALT attributed his suicidal bouts of depression in 1931 to worry about the future of the Disney studio. And it was true that Disney's finances were giving him and his brother cause for concern. Even under the terms of their new distribution contract with Columbia, they were still not making enough money to meet their commitments. New animators had had to be brought in from New York (in part to take the place of Ub Iwerks, who had always done the work of at least three men), and as they were highly qualified, they were paid more than the normal rate. They needed to be because Walt had become a highly critical and demanding employer.

In the period between Ub's departure and his own breakdown, Walt's manner and attitude toward his staff changed radically. So did his temper. No longer was he the smiling, easygoing boss who joshed around with the animators and the inkers and then walked out of the room with a wave of his hand, telling them to "take it easy." The phrase became taboo now around the studio. He had once taken shortcuts with cartoons to save time and money, but now he became angry with anyone who took an easy way out with a drawing or tried to cut corners with a cartoon sequence.

He was constantly setting his artistic sights higher and demanding more from his animators. And it showed in the quality of the new productions. Disney cartoons noticeably improved during this period, even if studio morale deteriorated. But if the quality of the product went up, so did the cost of each new film. Certainly, the cartoons were more popular than ever, and Walt Disney's name was now, as one studio publicist put it at the time, "better known than Confucius in China,

Shakespeare in England, the Blarney stone in Ireland, Voltaire in France, and Tarzan of the Apes in Tanganyika. Walt Disney—a household name from Tel Aviv to Timbuktu!"

On the other hand, profits were not coming in quickly enough to meet the studio's bills, in particular the money the Disneys had borrowed and still owed to their distributors, Columbia Pictures. "Each [cartoon] we finished just about paid off for the next one," Walt said later. "I kept adding people to the staff but in spite of that I had to work overtime. I'd either go to a restaurant or I'd drive home for an early dinner, and then I'd say, 'If you don't mind, I'll go back and do a little work.' Lilly would go with me. I had a davenport in my office and Lilly would lie down and go to sleep."

He would then go on working until he would look at his watch and see that it was two-thirty in the morning. If "Mother," as he called Lilly, was still asleep he would sometimes continue at his drawing board until dawn.

"I guess I was working too hard and worrying too much," he said later. "In 1931 I had a nervous breakdown. Each picture we made cost more than we figured it would earn. First we began to panic. Then, I cracked up. I couldn't sleep. I reached the point when I couldn't even talk over the telephone without crying. I was in a highly emotional state."

But it was not really concern over the financial state of the studio that was shredding his nerves. Walt left money matters to his brother Roy, and it was he who did the worrying over them. Walt was uncaring, even a spendthrift, about money. True, he did not lavish it on himself or on Lilly or on luxury living. Any money he could lay his hands on, he spent on his cartoons. The more money they made, the more he would pour into his productions to improve their quality, to reshoot, to try out new ideas and techniques, and to introduce new characters. And if the profits weren't there, he went on spending anyway—until Roy cried halt. No, the real cause of Walt Disney's emotional breakdown in 1931 was not money at all, which would always be the least of his troubles. Nor was it simply the blow he had suffered over Ub Iwerks's defection. It was much more complicated than that. He was thirty years old in 1931, and his trouble was that he had suddenly lost faith in himself, not as an artist, not as a cartoonist and filmmaker, but as a man.

WALT DISNEY WAS a product of his time and his background. Like most white American males of his day, he had been brought up in a masculine-dominated society in which women were indulged, cherished, and protected—even worshiped when they became mothers of strong sons and healthy daughters. But it was with men that you made your friendships, men whom you respected and whose advice you took, men with whom you normally foregathered in your moments of leisure.

The America from which Walt Disney came was a man's country, with women very much the second, and inferior, sex. Women were regarded by their menfolk as adorable but fallible creatures, whose intentions might be good but likely to be unreliable. You loved them, and you married them. But it was men you trusted, and once you had won their friendship, they could be relied on. Your pals never let you down.

It was because these ideas were deeply ingrained that his disillusionment with Pat Powers had been so profound. He had counted Powers as a friend, and the fact that he had so shabbily deceived him had shaken both his self-confidence and his belief in his ability to judge the worth of his fellow man.

Coming on top of Pat Powers's deceitfulness, the defection of Ub had hurt him even more. He had always considered Ub his closest and most reliable friend.

What kind of a world was he living in where two men he had so implicitly relied upon could betray him? It shattered his faith not only in them but in his own judgment, and he blamed himself for not having seen through them, for having been so naive and vulnerable.

To add to these psychological wounds, Roy had unwittingly administered another, and this one was even more painful to bear. Roy had become the father of a son. His wife, Edna, had given birth to Roy Edward Disney in January 1930. And nothing had more poignantly brought home to Walt Disney the sense of his own inadequacy. He saw himself not only as a poor judge of men, a sucker for cheats, tricksters, and traitors, but also as a weakling who couldn't even match up to the ordinary American male and produce a child of his own.

He and Lilly had tried hard enough. Since their marriage over four years before, they had been longing for a child. They had consulted doctors and were told to go on trying. But it hadn't happened. And since their consultant had broadly hinted that it wasn't Lilly's fault, it had hardly helped the marriage run smoothly.

Each time Walt produced a new cartoon character—Julius the Cat, Oswald the Lucky Rabbit—it seemed like a form of sublimation. There were times, during their quarrels, when Lilly hinted as much. And, of course, after his triumphant creation of Mickey Mouse, there were those who suggested that the cheerful rodent was Walt's compensation/substitution for Lillian's empty womb.

It was this gap in his family life, plus his bitterness over the defection of his friends, that brought Walt Disney low in 1931. He went to the christening party for Roy Edward Disney, Jr., and found it hard to share Roy's pride in being the father of the infant in Edna's arms.

He felt hypocritical in congratulating his brother and his wife. He knew he would never learn to love his nephew—though he did not guess what trouble his antipathy would stir up in the future. He went home with Lilly after the christening party and felt so disgusted with himself that there was one moment when he seriously contemplated killing himself. What good was he to anyone?

It was the low point of his life, and Lilly was afraid for him.

WALT DISNEY HAD never forgotten the dream he had shared with his Red Cross buddy, Russell Maas, of a trip down the Mississippi on a raft with their two dogs.

Now, as he convalesced from his breakdown, Walt had an irresistible urge to do something about it. His doctor had advised him to take his wife on a trip, so he told Lilly to pack their bags and they boarded a train for St. Louis. From there he knew what they were going to do. They would take the next best thing to a raft, a paddle steamer down the Mississippi to New Orleans and perhaps sail on—to who knows where?

Unfortunately, reality rarely measures up to boyhood dreams. It turned out that passenger boats had for the time being ceased making the trip between St. Louis and New Orleans, and the disappointment did not improve Walt Disney's pessimistic mood. But Lilly, who loved traveling, was determined to enjoy herself and immediately proposed they go on a tour of Washington, D.C., instead. Her ebullience was catching and after three days spent sightseeing, Walt's spirits began to lift. She had been quietly patient, sympathetic, and understanding all through her husband's crisis, and now she felt the turning point had come.

Walt's fame as the creator of Mickey Mouse had preceded him to the nation's capital, and the publicity man at the Mayflower Hotel, where they were staying, put himself at the service of the Disneys, offering to open any doors for them. Walt, who had once chauffeured Pershing's son in France, asked if he could arrange a meeting with General John Pershing, who had commanded the U.S. armies on the western front in World War I and was one of his boyhood heroes. Crestfallen, the press agent came back and confessed that Pershing was too busy to see him, and both Walt and Lilly burst into laughter when he offered, instead, a private audience with President Hoover at the White House.

"It sure restores your sense of American values," Walt said.

The trip lasted nearly two months, took them via Key West to Cuba and back through the Panama Canal to California, and by the time they returned, Walt was his old resilient, optimistic self. And it made all the difference to his marriage. In the summer of 1932, some months after their return to California, Lilly happily told her husband that she was pregnant. As it happened, it turned out to be a false alarm, but at least it was an indication of the change in the nature of their relationship.

Just before Walt had left on his recuperative vacation, Roy had informed his brother that he was breaking their connection with Columbia and seeking a tie-up with a new studio. The burden of paying off the fifty thousand-dollar debt to Columbia had proved to be impossible as long as Harry Cohn would advance only seventy-five hundred dollars for the cost of each new cartoon; but when Roy had asked Cohn to increase his subvention to fifteen thousand dollars a cartoon, Cohn had turned him down flat.

As a result, Roy had searched for a new studio that would prove to be more generous and had found one at United Artists. Walt was pleased when he heard since UA was the home of his favorite comedian, Charlie Chaplin, who was known to be a Mickey Mouse fan.

United Artists had agreed to finance future Disney cartoons at fifteen thousand dollars each and signed up for a series of twelve *Silly Symphonies*. But UA wanted quick delivery and exhibition of their first brand-new Disney cartoon. So Roy had come to Walt and asked him to put a new *Silly Symphony* into production before he left with Lilly for their vacation.

It was a moment when he was in the depths of his depression and no sudden flash of inspiration had come as he sat down and sweated over the drawing board. In the end he had concocted a rough draft that he called *Flowers and Trees*. He left it to the animators to flesh it out with sequences of daisies dancing, oak trees swaying rhythmically in the wind, and birds twittering through the forest glades. In truth, he just didn't give a damn how it turned out.

By the time he came back with Lilly, *Flowers and Trees* was finished and ready to be delivered to the new distributors. And when he saw it, even in his new and buoyant mood, he thought it was terrible. He was ashamed of it—it lacked all those qualities that had made the earlier *Silly Symphonies* so special. His instinct was to trash it and start all over again—a prospect that appalled the budget-conscious Roy Disney—but when Lilly came to tell him that she was pregnant, he was so happy that he got a better (if even more expensive) idea.

Nathalie Kalmus, the head of Technicolor, had recently given him a private view of his lab's new three-color process, which he was preparing to launch on the Hollywood film world. Walt was entranced by the revelation of what the addition of color could do to a movie, and he came back seething with enthusiasm, convinced his future cartoon films must, whenever possible, be made using this spectacular new process.

And what better way to mark his joy over Lilly's good news that she was expecting than do something spectacular with *Flowers and Trees?* He would make it all over again, despite Roy's qualms; but what he would principally do was add color. *Flowers and Trees* would become an idyll of the forest with the flora and fauna coming together in one great splash of color. He would design it as a tribute to Lilly and all that she meant to him, and he would be celebrating not only the birth of his first child but also a new kind of Disney cartoon such as no one had ever seen before.

Roy Disney sourly pointed out that remaking *Flowers and Trees* in Technicolor would add two-thirds more to the budget of the film. He reminded Walt that they had already settled the price with UA for the twelve-film series, and it was now too late to go back on the agreement. If they added color, the increased cost would ruin them. When Walt took no notice of his warnings, Roy went back to his office to study his figures and brood about his brother's profligacy. Then he heard some news that galvanized him into making one more effort to curb Walt's extravagant ideas.

After Ub Iwerks had quit the Disneys, he had started a new Hollywood operation on his own (financed in part by Pat Powers), and the rumor was that the first of the productions from the Ub Iwerks Studio would soon be appearing and that it would be a *Silly Symphony*-type cartoon film. Moreover, the story was that Ub had been to Technicolor, too, and had let it be known that his first venture would also be in color. Roy hoped the news would goad his brother into halting his own plans with Technicolor. In fact, it had the opposite effect.

Walt was never a vindictive man, and in his present mood, warmed by Lilly's news of her pregnancy, he felt benevolent even toward his enemies. On the other hand, he knew this was a critical time for the Walt Disney Studio, and he would have been foolish not to see the threat presented by competition from Ub. He had never had any doubt about the quality of work produced by his erstwhile associate. If Ub was now proposing to add color to his cartoons, he could prove to be an embarrassment to them all.

So Walt went to see Kalmus and put Disney's prestige on the line. If Technicolor desired to exploit the Disney name as one of their customers, there had to be a quid pro quo. Kalmus immediately understood what Walt was suggesting. The result was that Technicolor gave the Walt Disney Studio a two-year exclusive right to use their new system in cartoon films, and Ub Iwerks—along with all other cartoon film-makers—was turned away.

At that time, Lilly let Walt know that she was not going to have a baby after all. By then *Flowers and Trees* was well into its new production, and he did not tell her that it had been intended as a special tribute to her. It would have been too late to stop it, anyway, even had he wished to do so.

But halfway through the remake, Walt brought Lilly to the studio to see the rough cut. She told him that she thought that it was wonderful. "I'm glad you think so," he said. "I made it for you and," patting her empty stomach, "for him."

"Don't worry," she said. "There's always a next time."

On the strength of Lilly's reaction to *Flowers and Trees,* Walt showed the rough cut to Sidney Grauman, who ran the famous Chinese Theater on Hollywood Boulevard. Grauman was so sure that it was going to be a winner that he booked it into his theater for his next world premiere, which would be a Hollywood version of Eugene O'Neill's *Strange Interlude,* with Norma Shearer and Clark Gable. In the end, *Flowers and Trees* got a much more enthusiastic welcome from the critics than did the main feature. But Roy was not so euphoric as Walt over the audience's enthusiastic preference for the cartoon. "They'll never be satisfied with black and white again," he grumbled. "And just think of how much extra that's going to cost us!"

He was quite right, of course. The difference in the impact between this and the earlier *Silly Symphonies* was so striking that it was obvious that they would all have to be made in color in the future. And that would greatly inflate the size of Roy's budget. But the Walt Disney Studio gained rather than lost because of the transformation. So entranced were audiences by the dramatic effects color added to them that the *Silly Symphonies* rarely ran for just one week, as the black-and-white ones had done, but were held over, sometimes for more than a month. The rentals doubled, trebled, and quadrupled as a consequence, and the extra profits more than compensated for the added cost.

Flowers and Trees was not exactly financially harmed, either, by becoming the first Disney cartoon to win Walt an Oscar. As if to mark their awareness that there was now a new cinema phenomenon in their midst, Walt's fellow workers in the film industry voted, in November 1932, to recognize his special qualities. Later that same evening his contemporaries added a special award for his creation of Mickey Mouse.

Among the thousands of congratulatory notes he received the next day was one that surprised him—from Ub Iwerks. Walt threw all the others away, but this one he kept.

IN THE EARLY summer of 1933, Lilly informed him that she was pregnant again and assured him that this time it was no false alarm. She had seen her doctor, had been through all the tests, and her condition was confirmed.

Walt celebrated the coming event by moving his wife into a new house that he had built in the Los Feliz area of Los Angeles, and, since the money was now beginning to flow in, he encouraged Lilly to furnish it in any way that she wished and damn the expense. It was a much more spacious and handsome home than either had ever had before, with a large swimming pool, and it had a spectacular view over the southern California hills. Lilly loved it. But that, he decided, was not enough.

As the weeks passed and Lilly grew big with child, Walt knew he had to make a film for her. It had to be something special, of course. But what?

Talking it over with his friend, Carl Stalling, he was reminded of the case of Richard Wagner, who had celebrated the birth of his son by giving his wife, Cosima, the first performance of the *Siegfried-Idyll*. Walt did not particularly like Wagner's music, which he found a little too rich for his taste, but he liked the nature of the gesture.

What could he produce for Lilly that would move her to laughter instead of Wagnerian tears? *Pigs!* Pigs made her laugh. He remembered telling her about how as a boy he had herded hogs on the farm in Marceline and the way she had laughed over his story of riding the big sow home each evening and being tipped into the duck pond.

The story of the *Three Little Pigs* had been on his desk for a long time as a possible subject for a cartoon, and he and Ub Iwerks had played around with the idea before Ub's abrupt departure. Somehow, it hadn't worked out; they failed to solve the problems it presented. As a black-and-white cartoon, the confrontation between the hungry wolf and the innocent pigs had seemed too grim. The wolf had looked too menacing, the pigs too much like porkers ready for the butcher. Both of them had felt audiences would be turned off by the sinister aspects of the story.

Would the addition of color lighten it up? Walt did a color sketch from memory of Porker, the old sow from Marceline, and circulated it through the studio along with an outline script and asked for ideas and conceptions. The response surpassed all his hopes and expectations.

One of the newly arrived animators from New York, Norm Ferguson, came into Walt's office shortly afterward and produced a series of brilliant drawings of the Big Bad Wolf. He had slavering fangs and an evil look; but with extraordinary humor, adroitness, and dexterity, Ferguson had somehow turned him into a kind of raffish stage villain more likely to move audiences to chuckles than to send shivers down their spines. It was the youngest member of the Walt Disney staff, an eighteen-year-old named Fred Moore, who did the drawings of the three little pigs. Moore was a self-taught artist, who liked doodling around on a drawing board; the only art classes he had ever attended had been in high school. His favorite doodles were saucy pictures of sexy girls who seldom wore clothes but always looked innocent. But as it turned out, he also had a deft line with pigs.

He had grasped what Walt Disney was seeking in the characters of the *Three Little Pigs* without being told about it and had humanized them so that an audience could laugh with them; share fear, joy, and panic with them—and identify with them, too. Shrewdly, as if suspecting Walt's fond memories were more than sentimental, he had kept his boss's original sketch of Porker but added a mannish and roguish look. "Know who he is?" he asked Walt.

"*She* used to be an old sow I knew in Missouri," Walt said, "but you've changed her sex. Now—well, let's see." He studied Moore's drawing more closely. "Yes, I know! This is the Foolish Pig character, isn't he?

Couldn't be anyone else." Fred Moore nodded and grinned. He knew his boss was already sold on his drawings.

By this time they had a scenario, which Ted Sears had fleshed out from Walt's outline. Ferguson and Moore, on the strength of their sketches, were assigned the film and had a feeling from the start that they were on to a winner.

When someone suggested that they give it music and songs, Walt enthusiastically agreed. But who would do the music? He was now fizzing with enthusiasm over the *Three Little Pigs* and was determined to spare no expense to get the best talent available. Agents were alerted to approach famous composers like Gershwin, Rodgers and Hammerstein, and Irving Berlin to come up with tunes and themes. Then someone mentioned the name of Frank Churchill.

Churchill was a humble piano player in the Disney music department who helped put sound tracks on the cartoons. He had read Walt Disney's memo and inquired whether there would be any songs in the film. When told that there would be, he turned up with a sheaf of catchy jingles. To one batch Ted Sears added words and played and sang them for the animators. Norm Ferguson and Fred Moore were both hooked and rushed over to tell Walt. He didn't have much faith in his own musical judgment, but the enthusiasm of Norm and Fred was such that they won him over. With a warning that they still might have to fall back on Gershwin or Berlin, he told them to go ahead.

One of the ideas they came up with a few days later was a song for the little pigs to sing. It became one of the great moments of the cartoon and a world hit under the title "Who's Afraid of the Big Bad Wolf?"

Three Little Pigs opened at Radio City Music Hall in May 1933 and, much to Walt Disney's disappointment, was received with only luke-warm enthusiasm. He had hoped to take Lilly along for the first performance since it was "her" film, but she was not in fit condition to travel. It was just as well. Roy Disney went to the New York opening instead, and believing as he did that *Three Little Pigs* was the best thing the Walt Disney Studio had ever done, he fumed with frustration at the wooden public response and the lackluster reception by New York critics.

"We all know they can't recognize a masterpiece when they see one," he told Walt, of the critics' reception. "But it's depressing when the masterpiece happens to be ours." Maybe it was the sheer size of the music hall and the vastness of the screen that inhibited audience reaction to *Three Little Pigs*. At any rate, the moment it moved out of the gigantic showplace to upper East Side movie houses in New York, the film seemed to catch fire. By word of mouth, the high spirits of the cartoon spread through the city, and the lines began to form.

Suddenly radio stations around town all began clamoring for permission to play "Who's Afraid of the Big Bad Wolf?" Since the United States was still in the depths of a depression, the Big Bad Wolf became a symbol of hard times and the survival of the little pigs a message of hope. Soon everybody was singing "Who's Afraid of the Big Bad Wolf?" as a sort of chant of defiance against the threat of economic disaster.

So unexpected was the impact of *Three Little Pigs* and its music, in fact, that the Disney organization hadn't even issued sheet copies of the music for the "Big Bad Wolf," and one of the familiar sights at the showings from now on were arrangers scribbling away by flashlight in the audience, frantically copying down the words and music from the screen so that their band-leader bosses—like Paul Whiteman and Guy Lombardo and the Dorsey Brothers—could respond to hundreds of requests to play the increasingly popular song. Publishing houses rushed to buy up the rights, and Roy made a deal with Irving Berlin's own music company.

Three Little Pigs eventually became one of the most popular and profitable cartoon Disney film of the 1930s. It rarely ran for just a week but was held over with different feature films, sometimes for months. It had given three young members of Walt Disney's staff the opportunity of showing what they could do. The two animators became famous inside Hollywood as masters of their craft, though they did not figure in the credits for the film and remained unknown to the public.

Norman (Fergie) Ferguson went on to draw Pluto, Disney's imperishable dog star, and the Witch in Snow White. Fred Moore became a key animator of Mickey Mouse.

Their success could not have come at a more crucial moment for the future of the studio. The doomsayers in Hollywood were still prophesying disaster for Disney after the loss of Ub Iwerks and forecasting that Walt would lose his dynamic. Ferguson and Moore proved that they could more than fill the gap and that Walt Disney had lost none of his talents for inspiring and galvanizing people.

On December 18, 1933, Lillian Disney gave birth to a baby daughter. She was christened Diane Marie. A week later, on Christmas Day, Walt rigged up a screen in the nursery of the Los Feliz home and gave Lilly her very own showing of *Three Little Pigs*.

"It's the best thing you've ever done," she said, when it was over. And then she went on, "But you know, I somehow feel I ought to have given you . . ." For a moment it seemed as if she were about to say "a son," but then she added quickly, with a laughing nod at the screen, "Triplets!"

PART 2

Branching Out

12

Voices

1933 WAS THE year the sun shone upon the Disneys. The highly profitable success of *Three Little Pigs* made any kind of Disney cartoon a necessary item in movie programs, and the scramble to book the *Silly Symphony* and Mickey Mouse series was such that it was hard for the studios to keep up with the demand. All over the nation (and all over the world, in fact) film distributors were stridently crying out for "More mice!" or "More pigs!"

Both Walt and Roy Disney sensed that the nature of their operation was changing, if not their personal functions. Walt would go on being the brains, the inspiration, and the catalyst in the organization; and Roy would always be the moneyman. But of necessity, their day-to-day roles were being transformed and so were the pressures under which they worked. Had they been tillers of the soil, 1933 would have been the year when they ceased being family farmers and became directors of a vast and still-expanding agribusiness.

What they had to learn now was how to cope with the problems of success instead of the possibilities of failure; and in learning, Walt showed a new side to his nature—and it was a tough one. As an expanding enterprise, the Walt Disney Studio was already bulging at the seams, despite the fact that an extra administration building had been erected on Hyperion Avenue. The number of personnel now employed by the studio passed the one hundred mark early in 1933 and doubled that number in the next twelve months. More animators were desperately sought to keep up with the demand for more Disney cartoons. The studios of rival companies in New York were combed for bright, restive, and ambitious illustrators; and scores were tempted with good contracts and brought to the West Coast.

But the supply of real talent was limited, and more sources needed to be tapped, not only because the size of Disney was changing but to cope with Walt's own ideas for improving the nature and quality of his cartoons.

1933 was the year when Walt Disney showed his new side. One morning in the fall of that year, he called a meeting of his artistic staff in the main studio of the production building on Hyperion Avenue and announced that he had something important to tell them. He had worked out a revolutionary new policy for future productions and planned to commit the studio's growing capital to improving the all-around quality of Disney cartoons. By spending large amounts of money on training new talent, implementing new techniques, and adopting new processes, Walt believed he could give his output a kind of *fluidity* and *realism* such as had never been achieved in animated cartoons before.

The day of "stick figure" cartooning had long since passed, he told his animators, but many of the cartoon characters still moved as if they had rubber hoses for arms and legs. The motions they went through, as seen on the screen, were jerky and abrupt. The figures did not look real, and the audiences did not accept them as such.

He was about to change all that. From now on he intended to see that new methods were adopted to give his cartoons the appearance of smoothness and conviction. Not only would there be no more shortcuts to save production expenses, but there would be no more tricks-of-the-trade on the part of his animators to save themselves time and trouble.

To an increasingly apprehensive audience, Walt warned that much of the expertise they had acquired at the studios over the years was now unnecessary, out of date, and would have to be unlearned. There were a lot of veterans around, who had come up through the "stick figure" era, had never really lost their old habits, and were not likely to do so now. He knew how much the Disney Studio owed them for their loyalty and dedication over the years; and they must not think that Disney was about to let them go, just because he did not expect old dogs to learn new tricks. They could rest assured that the studio would find other jobs for them somewhere, and their loyal service would always be remembered; but Disney had to move on, and new talent was needed. To fill the gaps in the animation department, recruiters were being sent to art schools all over the country to sign up promising young students to come West and train as animators at the studio.

It was a chilling outline of things to come, and it was a very sober bunch of animators who went back to their desks. No one raised any vocal objections at the meeting, mainly because everyone was suddenly frightened for his job. The prospect of an influx of young and eager new artists swarming into the studios was scary. The animators were jolted and shocked not so much by Walt's action as by the abrupt way in which he had announced it. Is this what success did for a man?

THERE WAS STILL a depression in the United States, and jobs were scarce. The Walt Disney Studio did not have much trouble persuading young artists to join the organization, even though the salaries Roy Disney proposed to offer were extremely modest. Why should they be paid full salaries, he argued, when they were amateurs learning on the job, when work elsewhere was nonexistent, and when there was the additional prestige of being associated with Disney?

Walt made a deal with Mrs. Nelbert Chouinard, of the Chouinard Art Institute of Los Angeles, to teach apprentice Disney animators in her night classes. Because many of them did not have transportation, he ferried them in his own car to the classes and paid for their tuition at night classes. When the numbers grew too large, he hired one of the Chouinard teachers to give lectures on classical art and biology at the studio.

Don Graham, who taught the life classes, ran into criticism and derision from his students. They had all done this kind of work in art school, and they accused him of being too rigid about the living forms he asked his classes to reproduce. What possible connection could this have with new ideas in animated cartooning? Walt was increasingly demanding that his young animators make their cartoon characters "flow," and how could that be achieved if they were expected to do as Graham demanded, by meticulously sketching the models he brought to the studio? It was true that the models changed poses, but the poses were always static. And didn't static sketches produce jerky cartoons?

After some sarcastic comments had been scrawled on the studio bulletin board by skeptical students, Walt consulted Graham. They changed the routine and now had the models move around the studio during the sketching sessions, doing handstands and acrobatics; they never stood still. Then they would slip away and leave the students to sketch all their different poses from memory, in the hope that they would recapture the flow of their movements.

It worked so well that even some of the old hands in the animation department started attending the sessions. At the same time, Walt started a small private zoo at the studio and filled it with deer, rats and mice, rabbits, parrots, cougars, and ostriches, whose movements the students were expected to study and sketch.

To induce his animators to get more liquidity into the movement of their characters and more drama into their backgrounds, he established a laboratory where drops of water were dripped from heights and filmed close up with macrocameras. Balls were bounced and shot in slow motion to show in detail how they changed in shape as they hit the ground or a wall or a baseball bat.

The search for new effects worked well. The new recruits proved to be bright, fresh, willing, and innovative; and though they were resented and cold-shouldered to begin with, after a time their enthusiasm stimulated their older, professional rivals. Connoisseurs of Disney films have noted that the cartoons made at this period show a dramatic improvement, the characters seeming suddenly to become living and breathing and all but three-dimensional images instead of mere animated drawings.

It was a fecund period in another way, too. New characters were being born, some of them spinoffs from the Mickey Mouse and *Silly Symphony* series.

Norm Ferguson, who had created such sly and comic malevolence in the character of the Big Bad Wolf, had been experimenting and achieving some notable comic effects with a dog, a bloodhound, that had made its first appearance in a cartoon short called *Chain Gang.* The comic characteristics of the animal were such that he stood out from the others in the cartoon and made audiences remember him.

Ben Sharpsteen (later head of the animation department) remembered it later, "Fergy was successful in getting a looseness into the bloodhound that exaggerated its ability to sniff (a wrinkling of the nose) and to think (facial expressions, such as a quizzical look or a sudden smile directed at the audience). Fergy succeeded in getting a feeling of flesh into his animation. No one realized what Fergy had done, however, until after the preview."

After the preview everybody wanted to see the bloodhound again, and Walt Disney decided he had distinct possibilities. He called Ferguson into his office and suggested he play around with the bloodhound and develop his potential. Walt didn't exactly request Fergy to change the dog. Veteran animators remember that he never at any time suggested in words how the dog should appear—that was not his method. But he did act out the character, scratching, sniffing around, until everyone was laughing at his antics.

As far as the bloodhound's development was concerned, the animators remembered that Walt called a staff meeting and started reminiscing about an old dog he remembered from his boyhood on the farm at Marceline, and he began describing the animal's antics.

It became funnier and funnier. He would clown the dog's expressions, lifting one eyebrow and then the other, using those penetrating eyes of his to reinforce his comic expressions. And all the time, Fergy was watching him.

The first tests of the bloodhound that Fergy showed at the studio were so effective that everyone was enthusiastic, and he was encouraged to do more. He went on to sketch a famous comic sequence in which the bloodhound accidentally sits down on a roll of sticky flypaper, and his contortions and facial expressions as he attempts to free himself are excruciatingly comic. No one who saw these preliminary sketches had any doubt about the bloodhound's future. He was so delightfully funny in Fergy's conception that he was bound to end up as a star of future cartoons, perhaps even in a series of his own.

But what would they call him? He had been just an anonymous pooch in *Chain Gang*, with a resonant bass bark. Finally, someone said that since this was a hound whose voice came from the depths, why not call him Pluto? The suggestion took Walt Disney's fancy, and Pluto went on to be one of the most durable and likeable of Disney's stars.

RESPONSIBILITY FOR PLUTO'S invention and development was to cause some unhappiness at the Walt Disney Studio in the months to come. Most of Walt's veteran animators had learned early to accept the rule that their boss took the principal credit for everything achieved in the studio, and their contributions to a film or a sequence or a character were expected to remain anonymous.

Most of Disney's employees had loyally accepted this fact of life until the new apprentice animators began arriving and veterans who had been with the studio for years suddenly realized that they were expendable. What if they were suddenly thrown out to make way for a talented tyro? Shouldn't they be able to take their credits with them? Shouldn't they be able to boast they had invented Pluto or the Foolish Pig or Donald Duck?

One of the animators who had been particularly shocked by the change in Walt Disney's attitude toward his loyal veterans had been Norm Ferguson. He now made it plain that he wanted recognition as Pluto's creator and did not like sharing credit for his invention with Walt. He admitted that his boss had partly inspired Pluto and that no one watching the way he had drawn the character could have any doubt about where he had found the model for his creation. The way the bloodhound's eyebrows moved and his excruciating facial contortions could only have been copied from Walt Disney's own facial mannerisms.

But did that make Walt responsible—or even partly responsible—for Pluto? Norm Ferguson did not think so. However, not all of his fellow animators agreed with him. Two old hands, Frank Thomas and Ollie Johnston, have since written about Pluto's invention and have no doubt that Walt Disney should have equal share of the credit; they seem to chide Fergy for insisting otherwise, maintaining that without Walt there would have been no Pluto, since Fergy on his own could never have conceived him, that he was Walt's inspiration from the start—and that it was Walt who turned him into a world-famous cartoon character.

Norman Ferguson certainly did not agree with them. His dissatisfaction at being given what he considered less than his due over Pluto's creation was to have an unhappy sequel later.

Unaware of this gnawing bitterness among his veterans, Walt Disney was worrying about something else. What would Pluto sound like, and who would be his voice? Walt appreciated only too well the importance of making his cartoon characters sound authentic. The sound had to be just right or the effect of the image on the screen could be ruined.

It was hardly surprising, and not simply by accident, that Walt had found his own voice ideally suited to become that of Mickey Mouse. The squeaky, high-pitched notes that he had used when acting out Mickey's character in front of his animators made the mouse so funny and, yet, so believable that the sound just had to be incorporated onto the sound track.

In any case, everybody around the studio had by this time accepted that Mickey Mouse was really the cartoon version of Walt Disney himself, his screen alter ego. Mickey even resembled his creator both in appearance and character. He had the same habits, the same outlook, the same mischievous sense of fun, and the same tendency to take foolish risks and bite off more than he could safely chew. The addition of Walt's own voice to the cartoon character logically completed the conception. Having heard Mickey speak for the first time, it was thereafter impossible to imagine any other vocal chords repeating the dialogue—which is why Mickey sounded so strange and unreal speaking in French or German or Italian versions, in which he was dubbed by native speakers.

As the new characters spilled onto the drawing boards of Disney's animators in the 1930s, Walt found himself eagerly seeking to match their appearance and mannerisms with their voices. It was obvious how Pluto must sound. How could a bloodhound have anything but a deep and commanding bass or baritone intonation? He tried out opera singers and the bass voices of the Mormon Tabernacle Choir. Finally for Pluto (and eventually for one of his spinoffs, Goofy), he found the ideal vocal chords right inside the studio.

Pinto Colvig was yet another worker in the Disney music department. He played the clarinet and ocarina. When Frank Churchill, composer of "Who's Afraid of the Big Bad Wolf?" in *Three Little Pigs,* had searched around for an effective way to end his song, it had been Pinto who had found the ideal envoi in a five-note musical flourish on the ocarina.

No one seemed to have noticed that this narrow-framed little man also had a deeply mellifluous baritone voice until one day Walt came into the music studio and found him doing a vocal imitation of Pluto. He was quickly put to work dubbing first the bark for Pluto and then the voice of

Goofy; and he gave them that extra dimension that brought them to life on the screen.*

This was the period when yet another of Disney's most memorable characters was in the process of conception. A duck had caused a lot of laughter and attention in a *Silly Symphony* in 1934 called *The Wise Little Hen,* and he became the egotistic and short-fused bird afterward known as Donald Duck. But all of Donald's peculiarly feisty characteristics remained two-dimensional so long as his termagant nature could not be wedded to the right kind of voice. And the suitable voice was just what they were unable to find. Then one day, Walt listened to an amateur radio show and heard a contestant named Clarence Nash doing bird imitations. "That's Donald Duck!" he cried, as Nash launched into a particularly raucous birdcall.

Clarence Nash, who had been a California school teacher until then, joined the Disney staff as the voice of Donald Duck and was still doing it as abrasively as ever on Donald's fiftieth anniversary in 1984.† In Donald Duck's case, Nash did the foreign voices and, as he later said, he learned to quack in French, Spanish, Portuguese, Italian, Japanese, Chinese, and German.

IT IS DOUBTFUL that the public was conscious of the new technical changes Walt was making, but it was certain that Disney cartoons were outdistancing the competition everywhere. Statesmen and politicians mentioned Mickey Mouse in their speeches. It was leaked from the White House that *Three Little Pigs* was President Roosevelt's favorite screen entertainment.

Walt and Roy were now not only celebrated but prosperous as well, and everything connected with them seemed to make them richer and more famous. The money positively poured in. It was so unexpected that the brothers hardly knew what to spend it on. They encouraged their wives to splurge on designer clothes and take up charitable work. They themselves embraced that most expensive sport, polo. Joined by some of their better-paid animators and by Gunther Lessing, the lawyer, who had now joined Disney as head of the legal department, they took lessons from a professional in the San Fernando Valley and then sallied forth to do battle against the film colony's best players.

Walt built up his stable to twelve crack ponies. He was a daredevil if

---

*Other voices were also found among the studio staff. For example an animator named Fred Spencer could talk with a gargle that sounded like a fish speaking under water, and Ollie Johnston did a marvelous imitation of a talking sheep for a *Silly Symphony*.

†He died in February 1985, aged 80.

not exactly a skillful horseman and pitted himself against such dedicated and ruthless players as Darryl Zanuck, Big Boy Williams, and Will Rogers, at whose hands he took some nasty tumbles. In one such spill, he broke a collarbone and wrenched his neck, which caused him a lot of pain later.

Delighted with his baby daughter, Diane, Walt still dreamed of having a son and tried hard with Lilly to produce one. But nothing happened. Breeding a second baby was one thing, it seemed, all this newfound prosperity couldn't buy. This time the doctors blamed Walt's physical condition alone and decided that though he seemed fit enough to play in the toughest polo matches, his sperm count was too low for easy fatherhood. They began pumping his thyroid full of liver extract and other injections. It did no good. Lilly showed no sign of becoming pregnant again.

Walt, who had first taken up cigarettes while still in school, was now consuming at least two packs a day. Curiously enough, none of the doctors suggested that he might improve his health and nervous system if he cut down his consumption. He had developed a persistent smoker's cough, and it soon became an alarm signal around the Walt Disney Studio; the animators always knew he was on his way to see them when they heard him hacking his way along the corridors.

Walt's sudden prosperity certainly didn't seem to bring him satisfaction or peace of mind. In many ways, he was as racked with self-doubt and angst as he had been in the days before his breakdown.

Roy and Edna worried about him and about the state of his marriage. And when Lilly showed signs of catching Walt's nervous twitches, too, Roy intervened to suggest that both their families should take a vacation trip to Europe. The excuse was the decision by the League of Nations in 1935 to award Walt a medal for the creation of Mickey Mouse.

Before the League meeting, which took place in Paris, the sponsors of the ceremony forgot to inform the brothers that the proceedings would be informal. While the delegates turned up in casual dress, Walt and Roy appeared in formal wear, specially tailored for the occasion—the only time in their lives when they dressed in top hats and morning suits. In one passage of his acceptance speech, Walt couldn't resist the temptation and dropped into the famous mouse's high-pitched squeak and said he was "taking the Mickey" out of himself and Roy for "getting above themselves."

It was the first time Walt had been in France since the Red Cross days at the end of World War I; and he took his wife, Roy, and Edna for a tour of the old battlefields. Afterward there was a trip to Holland, England, and Italy.

Everywhere they went, crowds assembled to greet the creator of Mickey Mouse. In Rome they were given a private audience with the Pope and then had a long interview with the Italian dictator, Benito Mussolini, who said he was a Donald Duck fan. The trip did them all good, and Walt seemed fully recovered by the time they got back to California. But it still made no difference to his domestic situation. Diane remained their only child and Lilly resigned herself to the fact that she would never become pregnant again. But she wanted another child badly and began to think about adoption.

Still the money rolled in from all over the world. In several movie theaters in Europe during their trip they had run across exhibitors who made a prosperous living showing nothing but Disney cartoons, six or seven of them in one program. It was an idea that shortly afterward caught on in America, too.

NOW, ANYTHING CONNECTED with Disney could be turned into gold. One day, Walt got a call from a man called Kay Kamen. He said he had a scheme for guaranteeing the Walt Disney Studio an extra income of fifty thousand dollars a year, for which Walt wouldn't have to lift a finger. Could he come to Hollywood and talk about it?

There was something in the approach that Walt couldn't resist, and he told Kamen that if he wanted to make the journey—at his own expense, of course—he would set up a meeting. And so Kay Kamen entered Walt's life, and more money flowed into the Disney coffers. And much more besides.

In a nation that has produced some remarkable entrepreneurs in its time, Kay Kamen was something special. "He was a fantastic salesman," said De Witt Jones, one of the men who worked for him at Disney later.

> You meet a certain number of people in your lifetime who make a great impact on you, and Kamen certainly did on me. He was an incredible-looking man. He had a wide nose and wore thick glasses, was six feet tall and very strong physically. And he was proud of the fact that he wasn't exactly pretty. He maintained his appearance was a great advantage in his profession. Any good salesman will tell you that if you want to be remembered, you're either completely bald, you have flaming red hair, or something else is striking about you. Guys who wear Brooks Brothers suits just get forgotten, but not extraordinary-looking guys like Kay Kamen.*

Later on, after he had been put in charge of his own department at Disney, Kay Kamen and Roy Disney were walking together down Fifth Avenue in New York, and everywhere, people were stopping or waving and shouting "Hi, Kay" or "Hello, Kay," or "Nice to see you, Kay."

Finally, Roy, who liked to be recognized, too, became annoyed at the

---

*De Witt Jones, in a conversation with the author.

popularity of his companion, and said, "Jesus, Kay, my brother Walt and I run one of the best-known organizations in the world, and yet everyone around here knows you and doesn't know me at all."

"Well, Roy," Kay said, "if you were as ugly as I am, everybody would know you. In fact, they would find it impossible to forget you. How would you like to change places with me and take on this fizzog?"

Kamen had been watching the progress of Disney's cartoons with particular interest. He was always seeing Disney souvenirs in shop windows and drug stores; Mickey Mouse badges, ties and scarves with the images of Pluto and Goofy and Minnie Mouse imprinted on them. And when he made inquiries about how much the manufacturers were paying the Disneys for these popular images, he was surprised to discover that they were getting them free. They paid no royalties. Most of them didn't even ask the Disney studio for permission to use Mickey or Pluto or Goofy on their products.

It was this discovery that had moved Kay Kamen to call up Walt Disney, after which he decided the big moment in his life had arrived, and it was time to gamble. "So Kay got together all the money he possessed in the world," said his future Disney associate. "He turned in all his life insurance and took a mortgage on his house; it came to about sixty-five thousand dollars. This he changed into one thousand-dollar and hundred-dollar bills. He sewed them into his coat, and then, he took the train from Chicago. He had no money for a Pullman; and besides, he was so scared because of all that money on him that he didn't dare sleep. He sat up and clutched himself for four whole days, and as soon as he got to California, he went straight to see Walt Disney—and what did he do but fall fast asleep right there in his office while Walt was talking to him!"

But what he offered the Disneys was money for no effort on their part. He put fifty thousand dollars in cash on Walt's desk as an earnest of his intentions and said he would guarantee a minimum of another fifty thousand dollars a year for the right to handle the use of their name on national merchandise.

"The first fifty thousand dollars will be yours," he said, "and after that, we will split everything down the middle. I will charge manufacturers 5 percent of their wholesale price for the use of your name or logo on their product, and from every dollar they pay me, half will be yours."

Both Walt and Roy were well aware that they could have handled the royalty business themselves, and there was really no reason to pay an outsider for exploiting their name on other people's products. On the other hand, they had no organization for doing it, and Roy showed no inclination to set up an appropriate department. Moreover, they were incapable of resisting Kamen's proposal to increase their annual income with absolutely no effort on their part.

As a result, Kay Kamen took over the merchandising of Disney's name on every kind of product from watches to running shoes to ice-cream cones. He was soon putting $2,500,000 into Disney's account every year and, of course, earning a similar amount for himself.

It was not until Kamen's untimely death in 1949—he was killed in an airplane accident—that Roy Disney realized that they had been making him rich and cheating themselves. And they had barely tapped the potential magic of the Disney name.

Meanwhile, what were they to do with all their money? Roy was all for spending it on improvements on the studio. Realizing that Hyperion Avenue was already cramped and would soon be too small an area to cater to their future needs, he had begun looking around for a plan for a new studio and had his eye on a site in Burbank.

Walt had other ideas. The moment he returned from his European trip and settled back at his desk, he felt a surge of euphoria. He was later to say it was one of the most exhilarating periods of his creative life, and he was bursting with ambition. He had loved being hailed in Geneva as the pioneer of new discoveries in cartoon films, and he had basked unabashedly in the praise the statesmen had heaped upon him. Now he came back to find that the critics were acclaiming the first Mickey Mouse cartoon in color, *Band Concert*.

WHAT NEXT? WHAT new challenges could he meet and overcome now?

The trip to Europe had spawned an idea. It has already been mentioned that in Paris the Disneys had discovered one happy exhibitor who was making a handsome profit from showing nothing but Disney cartoon films—not one but six in succession, one after the other. What if, instead of six short films, Walt Disney provided exhibitors with one feature-length cartoon lasting the same amount of time? There had never been a full-length cartoon film before, and all the professionals were confident movie audiences would never pay at the box office to see one, not even if it came from Disney.

But since when had the professional movie pundits ever been right? Had they not prophesied doom for the industry when sound came to films, and look what had happened to Hollywood since *The Jazz Singer* and *Steamboat Willie*.

An indication of the way in which his mind was working was given in a memorandum Walt wrote to his animators just about this time:

"The animation has made a very definite advance forward which, in my estimation, is close to 100% over what it was a year and a half ago. I know that eventually we are going to attain a degree of perfection never before thought possible. It proves to me that the time we have spent studying, trying to analyze our problems, and systematizing ourselves, is bearing fruit. The hit-and-miss is going."

Could there be a more effective way to show off the enormous strides Disney had made in technique than through a feature film? As Walt pointed out to Roy—scared, as usual, of changing the formula—making a feature-length cartoon would increase profits rather than threaten them.

"If we put 10 of these 700-foot shorts together, we've got us a feature— 7,000 feet," he said. "Now they won't pay us but $15,000 for a short, but for 10 of these, that would be $150,000, and surely we can get more than this for a feature!" It was clumsy financial logic, but Walt was convinced that not only would a feature cartoon bring glory to the Disney name, not only would it entertain the multitudes, it would be a great financial success as well.

The more he brooded on the idea, the more Walt became convinced that the movie world was waiting for something new from Disney; not a new character (Donald Duck, already in the works, would take care of that), not a new kind of *Silly Symphony*, but a cinematic breakthrough. And what better way to satisfy all their expectations than with a full-length feature cartoon—with a hero, a heroine, music, a theme, plus a solid story. But what story?

NO ONE IS quite sure how Walt Disney finally came up with the decision to make *Snow White and the Seven Dwarfs*. The only plausible explanation is that many years earlier, during his boyhood in Kansas City, he had seen a silent movie called *Snow White* and had been enraptured by the fairy tale. Whatever the reason, the heroine of his dreams was Snow White; a fairy-tale heroine who seemed to him to provide the perfect opportunity to portray his ideal of young womanhood on the screen.

So one night in the fall of 1934, he called a group of his animators together after office hours and told them he had decided to make a cartoon feature. It would be called *Snow White and the Seven Dwarfs*. He then proceeded to give them a sixty-minute preview of how he thought the story should work out, and it was evident to most of his audience that he had already roughed out the scenario.

He swashbuckled across the stage in the role of Prince Charming and fell to the floor to simulate the innocent Snow White after she had been put into a trance by the Wicked Witch. As the witch herself, he cackled and hideously grimaced, wobbling his mobile eyebrows in a graphic simulation of malevolence. Finally, one by one, he demonstrated the different characters of the seven dwarfs.

It was a virtuoso performance, and he won them over. They found themselves highly excited at the prospect of the new project. But then he suddenly stopped his clowning and told them that this was a film that would be made or ruined by the portrayal of Snow White. The heart-aching appeal of her kindness and innocence meant everything to the film and he needed inspiration from his artists as never before to capture her qualities on the screen.

As some of his senior animators remembered it later:

> Walt was all fired up. The great problem, he said, would be finding the right Snow White. She wouldn't just need to have talent but also be able to inject sincere moments, tender moments—which would need to be an integral part of the film. It would be a great challenge for the artists, too, because they would be called on to provide not just gags and comic tricks but the impression of fantasy combined with a real world full of real people doing believable things. Walt stressed that this would not be simply a cartoon film but drama, theater, with characters coming alive on the screen as never before in an animated film.*

If the animators were galvanized by the possibilities of their boss's latest idea, his brother certainly was not. Roy groaned with dismay when Walt outlined the Snow White project for him. "But it's a terrible gamble," he said. "How much is it going to cost?"

Walt said he had already drawn up a preliminary budget. The production would cost around half a million dollars. (It would in fact, eventually cost very much more.)

"Half a million dollars?" Roy cried, in dismay. "Christ, it's almost as much as we have saved up in the bank."

"Of course it is!" Walt said. "But we don't need to touch it. We'll borrow it from United Artists. Or the banks. Any bank will lend us the money."

"And how are we going to pay it back?" Roy asked.

---

*In conversations with the author.

"From the box office receipts, of course," Walt said.

"And what if there aren't any? What if the movie's a bust?"

Walt laughed. "The trouble with you, Roy," he said, "is that you have no faith. Now stop worrying. *You* get the money, and *we'll* make the film."

"You're going to ruin us," Roy said. "Half a million dollars for a single film! Why can't we just stay with Mickey Mouse?"

13
Snow Ball

BY LATE 1934 Walt Disney had worked out the scenario of Snow White and knew roughly what kind of cartoon feature he was proposing to make. But his plans were not made without some heavy opposition.

Roy still quailed at the thought of all the money and the risk involved and was convinced Walt was heading for disaster. He looked around for allies who might bring his brother to his senses and found one in Walt's wife, Lillian. By this time, Lilly was one of the most comfortably established and prosperous of the Hollywood wives, and Roy played on that fact to convince her that her husband was about to embark on an extremely questionable venture. Couldn't she persuade Walt to think again? Was this the time, just when both she and Edna had started families, to risk Disney's reputation and standing on an expensive, and very self-centered, gamble that was almost certain to lose them all their money?

Lilly made her apprehensions clear to Walt in one of the sharpest quarrels of their marriage. She did not persuade him to change his mind, but she did give him some sleepless nights and did make him realize that he could not afford to fail. Consequently, he began to regard Snow White as the most testing ordeal of his career whose failure could not only cost him his fortune but his marital happiness as well. It had to succeed and be the most acclaimed and entertaining movie he had ever made.

Walt was sure of one thing: In order to be a box office success, *Snow White and the Seven Dwarfs* had to be highly romantic, funny, and frightening by turns, and it had to be full of the sound of both lively music and sentimental songs. He spent his nights reviewing the day's work and his days exhorting his animators to give of their best, and at first he was not by any means satisfied by their efforts.

Fred Moore, who had a flair for conveying the zest and vivaciousness of young womanhood, had already done some sketches of the heroine, but the results were unsatisfactory. In the end he became the directing animator for the dwarfs. Meanwhile, Walt decided to begin a search for a real girl who might act as both the heroine's voice and the physical inspiration for the animators of his movie.

There would be songs for Snow White, of course, and for most of the principal characters. He had already alerted Frank Churchill, the composer of "Who's Afraid of the Big Bad Wolf?" to go to work on a compelling theme song, and the first chords of what would subsequently become the popular hit of the movie, "Whistle While You Work," were already beginning to be heard around the music department.

For Snow White's own voice he sought a special quality of sheer vitality, bell-like musical clarity, and vibrant youthfulness. When an agent turned up one day with a young Canadian singer named Deanna Durbin, he was enchanted with her at the audition; but when he heard her voice on records, he decided she would not do. Despite her refreshingly girlish appearance, her voice sounded too mature and professional when heard alone and would not, he felt, fit into Snow White's little girl persona. He turned her down, and Miss Durbin, who was only thirteen at the time, went on to become a famous singing film star in her own right.

Instead, he picked an untrained twenty-year-old amateur named Adriana Caselotti to dub the singing voice of Snow White, feeling her thin soprano had the requisite childish timbre. He also hired a slim and supple Los Angeles dancer named Margie Belcher to walk, pirouette, and dance before Fred Moore so that he could inculcate the rhythm of her movements into his Snow White sketches. She too went on to a more lasting fame and, later, became the female half of a famous dancing team, Marge and Gower Champion.

By this time he had four of his most talented and experienced animators working full time on *Snow White and the Seven Dwarfs*. (Although, of course, hundreds of other artists and inkers would be needed to complete the more than two million drawings required for a ninety-minute feature film.) Norm Ferguson was put in charge of setting the scenes and coordinating the action, and he was also doing his preliminary sketches for what would later be hailed as one of the most effective (and frightening) characters in the movie, the Wicked Witch. Hamilton (Ham) Luske was concentrating on sketching out the character and idiosyncracies of Snow White, and Vladimir (T-bone) Tytla was thinking up situations in which the dwarfs would become involved as the plot unfolded.

Overall Walt Disney was testy, wary, and watchful, fully conscious now that his reputation and the studio's future were at stake and

doggedly determined that none of his animators stray a hair's breadth
from his conceptions of his characters and the way they would act and
behave. He had already written down each scene for his animators to
follow and had meticulously emphasized the atmosphere that they must
seek to create. He constantly reminded them—particularly the rebellious
Norm Ferguson—that this was his film and nobody else's and that it
would stand or fall by the way he saw it.

He could be extremely short-tempered and rough-tongued with them
when he felt things were going wrong. Only dedicated artists, with
complete loyalty to him and absolute faith in the quality of his inspiration, could have swallowed the harsh insults he sometimes hurled at
them. (And not all of them did, as will be seen.)

Walt's rough outline script for Snow White is in the Disney archives in
Burbank. He had no doubt that one of the big moments of the movie
would be the first encounter between the innocent Snow White and the
jealous and malevolent Queen in her disguise as the Wicked Witch.

"At the time the menace comes in," he wrote, "Snow White should be
doing something that shows she is happy and that she is trying to do
something nice for these little men [the seven dwarfs]. That's the time
the menace should strike. It's most powerful when people are most
happy. . . . She's taken aback when she first sees the Queen. She doesn't
suspect the Queen, but there's a lunatic around somewhere and he
approaches you. You have that funny feeling. It's nothing you can put
your finger on. You wouldn't have the police come, but you'd be on your
guard."

He urged his animators to bring out the instinctive feelings of appre-
hension in the animals of the forest at the menacing aura of the Queen as
she passes by them. "They are dumb but they have a certain sense," he
wrote, "like a dog who knows that somebody is not a friend. When the
birds see that old witch they know that everything is not right, and
they're alarmed and back out of the way."

For the illustrators he had mimed the scene as the rabbits and deer and
birds cringed and scuttered for cover because of the fear suddenly blan-
keting the forest. Crouching down, he pulled his jacket over his head and
mimed the slouch of the evil witch, chuckling horribly as a cloud of
attendant vultures wheeled and squawked over her head.

"Vultures!" he cried. "An entourage of vultures! That tells the birds
and animals what this hideous crone is like!"

The top pay of the four chief animators of *Snow White and the Seven
Dwarfs* was one hundred dollars a week, which, even in those days,
seems a meager reward for such talented labor. It is true they also earned
bonuses for doing the extra drawings to link up sequences and give

guides to their assistants and the inkers, and these sometimes doubled their weekly take-home pay. But obviously, even when a dollar meant something and living was cheap, none of these artists—and they were the best in the world in their field—was getting rich on his Disney salary.

Walt and Roy, who were now paying themselves $250 a week and managing quite well on it (though they and their wives could draw extra when they needed it), did not feel any guilt about the wages their employees were receiving. It did not occur to them. They felt the work was so inspirational and the studio conditions so congenial that no one could possibly feel discontented, either with their pay or their jobs. After all, where else in Hollywood could they find such fascinating work in such challenging surroundings? Despite the fact that an assistant animator often had to get by on thirty-five dollars a week, and an inker—whose work was meticulous, highly-skilled, and full of stress—was lucky if he (or usually she) made more than twenty dollars a week, both Walt and Roy would have been shocked if it had been suggested that they were underpaid.

Roy would have pointed out that for all the modest salaries the Disney staff received, producing animated cartoon films was an increasingly expensive operation. In his constant search for "flow" and "realism," Walt was now insisting that more and more individual drawings had to be made to illustrate every single movement. Instant dismissal was the punishment for any animator who attempted shortcuts or who inserted repeats.

As a result, the labor force grew and grew. New technical methods of achieving three-dimensional effects, of heightening the reality of each character and each scene, were constantly being introduced, and they were expensive. To keep ahead of rivals, the Walt Disney Studio had financed, tested, and adopted new kinds of cameras and pioneered revolutionary new techniques in animation.

It all cost money.

ROY FOUND THAT, in financial circles, the reaction to the project, was not good. All over Hollywood, the big studios were filling their quotas of first-feature films, sometimes with well-known stars, for around $250,000 apiece. It was true that the Walt Disney Studio was regarded as a bankable organization, and no one would have hesitated to lend money for a new Mickey Mouse series or for half a dozen *Silly Symphonies*. But a full-length cartoon feature budgeted at five hundred thousand dollars? The bankers shared the opinion of Roy and Lilly and doubted the success of such an innovation. Roy was always, when it came to the crunch, his brother's loyal supporter, but he was dismayed when he found himself—

in the absence of help from the banks—dipping into the company's own monetary reserves to finance the production of Snow White; and he was profoundly depressed when Walt's weekly demands inexorably mounted.

"We'll be ruined!" he groaned to Lilly.

Eventually, Joseph Rosenberg, a director of the Bank of America, bailed out the Disneys when their own money began to run out. But skepticism over the venture was such that Rosenberg was called a reckless fool, and as he later confessed, he suffered from sleepless nights for a time.

> I was green in the picture business. I wondered if my judgment was sound. I called up some Hollywood people and asked their advice [about Snow White], and one of them said, "I wouldn't put a dime in it if I were you."

When he consulted Louis B. Mayer, Jack Warner, and Harry Cohn, they scoffed at the idea that a ninety-minute cartoon film could be expected to draw the same audiences as a movie containing "real live people," and prophesied disaster. "Who'd pay to see a drawing of a fairy princess," hooted Louie Mayer, "when they can watch Joan Crawford's boobs for the same price at the box office?"

Months later though still not finished, *Snow White and the Seven Dwarfs* had already cost more money than MGM spent on the big musical hit *Broadway Melody of 1936* (with Robert Taylor, June Knight, and a cast of hundreds). Roy was in despair. His brother needed another $500,000 to finish the film, and the Bank of America was balking at his repeated requests to increase their loan. Joseph Rosenberg was not only being called a sucker by the heads of the Hollywood majors, but he was now running into trouble with his superiors, who kept asking him what Snow White looked like and would it make a profit. Rosenberg was forced to reply that Walt didn't like showing outsiders his productions until they were finished, and he had so far not had even a glimpse of Snow White. His embarrassment was such that in the end Roy pleaded with his brother to give him a showing, "so he can at least report back to his bosses."

Walt's reluctance was such that it took a threat to stop all work on his film before he consented to piece together a rough cut of the production and to give Rosenberg a private showing. There were still big gaps in the story line, and Fred Moore, who was the only animator to be asked to sit in on the showing, later remembered it as one of Walt's most glorious feats of spontaneous ad-libbing.

He kept up a running commentary throughout the screening, filling in the dialogue and some of the songs that had not yet been dubbed onto the film. But it was his performance during the gaps in the action that won the laughter and appreciation of Roy and Moore. Neither had ever seen him perform more brilliantly.

"He leaped to his feet and pantomimed the missing action," Moore said later, "including all the different antics of the seven dwarfs, the palpitating scene where the Wicked Witch tempts Snow White into biting into the poisoned apple, and the penultimate drama of Snow White being awakened in her glass coffin by Prince Charming's kiss."

Moore described how Walt stood beside the screen. "It's so terribly sad," Walt cried, "because Snow White looks so beautiful lying there. The birds fly around and drop flowers on her. The dwarfs are sneakily wiping tears from their eyes. The whole forest is in mourning. Then you hear the prince arriving through the forest. He is singing the theme song. As he approaches the coffin, everyone sort of steps back and lets him through. He finishes the song as he lifts the lid of the coffin, and maybe there's a moment's hesitation as he looks down at his loved one. Then he kisses her, kisses that beloved face, those beloved lips, so still, so cold! His heart is breaking. He droops and buries his head in his hands. The dwarfs see it and look sadly down at the ground. Everyone is sad, for everyone loved her and now she is dead! But then . . . ," he pauses dramatically, "then Snow White, roused by her beloved's kiss, begins to wake up! The music swells and picks up, the birds go crazy, the dwarfs go crazy and hug each other! The prince picks her up as the music crescendoes. All the forest goes mad with joy as he carries her back to his horse, and they ride away together. And we fade out. . ."

Moore said later, "It was just too brilliant for words! Walt had never been so good, so eloquent. He played every single role in the movie, and each one was worth an Oscar! Even Roy, who was a tough nut to crack, had tears running down his cheeks."*

Not Rosenberg, however. Hard-eyed, seemingly unaffected, he said not a word until he had shaken Walt by the hand and allowed Roy to lead him back to his car. Only then did he say, "It should be quite a film. I'm going to recommend that my board advance you the money to finish it."

And he added, with a hint of a smile, "Pity we won't be seeing Walt up there on the screen. It's the best performance I've seen since Lillian Gish in *Way Down East*."

Among the exhibitors who kept a close (and sympathetic) watch on the production woes of *Snow White and the Seven Dwarfs* was a dedicated admirer of Walt Disney named Willy van Schmus, who managed and booked films for Radio City Music Hall in New York. Van Schmus had always done well with his showings of Walt's shorts, especially *Three Little Pigs*, and he not only paid bonuses to the studio when his programs

---

*Disney Archives, Burbank.

(left) The house on Tripp Avenue, Chicago, where Walt Disney was born on December 5, 1901. (© *Walt Disney Productions*)

(below left) Roy Disney as a young man. (© *Walt Disney Productions*)

(below right) Walt's parents, Flora and Elias Disney, photographed in 1913. (© *Walt Disney Productions*)

(left) Walt Disney, age 17, pictured before he left for France with the Red Cross in 1918. (© *Walt Disney Productions*)

(below) Walt Disney sends home a photograph of himself and his truck while serving with the Red Cross in France. (© *Walt Disney Productions*)

doing something I very seldom do I "Work"

once every once and a while I make trips with this truck.

Walt Disney went to France as a Red Cross ambulance driver in the last days of World War I. He had already determined to make his future living as a cartoonist and drew avidly in his spare time. This is one of his illustrated letters home, written in 1919 from Red Cross headquarters at Neufchateau to former classmates in Chicago. (© Walt Disney Productions)

(right) Ub Iwerks's poster for one of Walt Disney's original Alice Comedies

(facing page) Walt Disney, age 20, in Kansas City. Photo taken before he grew a mustache. *(© Walt Disney Productions)*

Walt Disney does a sketch for the Alice Comedies in Kansas City, before his move to Hollywood in the 1920s. *(© Walt Disney Productions)*

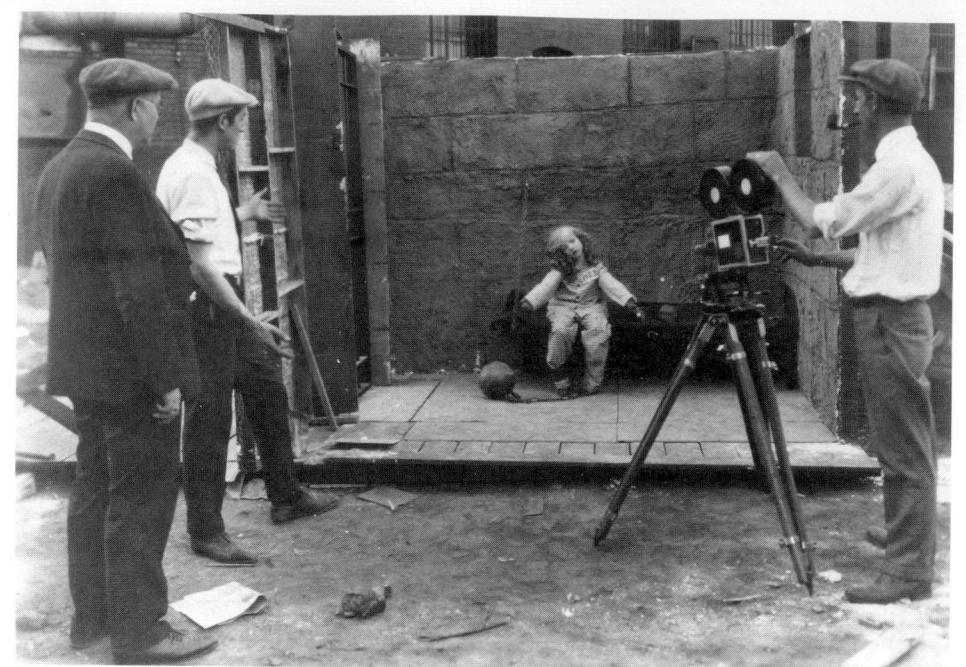

(above) In both Kansas City and Hollywood, Walt made a series of short live-action/cartoons with a child actress, Virginia Davis (shown here). But she dropped out and was replaced by Margie Gay. (© *Walt Disney Productions*)

(left) Walt Disney, Margie Gay, and Roy Disney during the shooting of an Alice Comedy live-action/cartoon in Hollywood. (© *Walt Disney Productions*)

Original poster by Hugh Harman and Carmen Maxwell for
Oswald, the Lucky Rabbit cartoon

(left) Walt Disney and his wife, Lillian, outside the studio in the 1920s. (© *Walt Disney Productions*)

(below) Roy's wife Edna and Walt's wife Lillian, photographed in the 1920s. They remained close friends and confidants even when the Disney brothers were quarreling (usually over money). (© *Walt Disney Productions*)

Roy Disney (left) and Walt pose in an orange grove. (© *Walt Disney Productions*)

(above) Drawn by Walt, an illustrated birthday greeting for Elias Disney from his two sons in Hollywood. It was sent in the 1920s before they built the new Hyperion studio. (© *Walt Disney Productions*)

(facing page) In the late twenties and early thirties, Ub Iwerks drew Mickey Mouse with button eyes and "hosepipe" limbs. Seven years later, Fred Moore gave him a rounded body and eyes that moved. (© *Walt Disney Productions*)

Mickey in the 20s - drawn by
Walt Disney.

"Doodles" by Fred Moore

(above) Animator Fred Moore, a self-taught artist, first gave Mickey Mouse eyes that moved. He liked to doodle drawings of lightly clad young ladies between studio chores, and the results were widely sought after by his colleagues. (© *Walt Disney Productions*)

(facing page top) A sound-syncing session for a new Mickey Mouse short in the 1930s. Walt Disney is second from left. To the right of Mickey is his long-time associate, Ub Iwerks. (© *Walt Disney Productions*)

(facing page bottom) Leopold Stokowski (with baton) at the Burbank studio during the making of the animated feature *Fantasia* (1940). Walt Disney is next to him, on Stokowski's left. (© *Walt Disney Productions*)

Walt Disney talks to two "inkers" on his staff in Burbank. Most of the members of the "Ink and Paint Department," as it was officially known, were young women who painstakingly transferred the animators' drawings onto the "cels." *(© Walt Disney Productions)*

(above) Walt Disney holds a conference with his storymen before starting the production of a new animated feature. Note the "story-board" on the wall. All sequences were illustrated before shooting began. (© *Walt Disney Productions*)

(below) Walt Disney (left) watches as two of his artists mime an effect they were seeking for a new animated feature. (© *Walt Disney Productions*)

(facing page top) Animator Ward Kimball and Walt Disney shared an enthusiasm for railroads. Here they are aboard one of Kimball's locomotives in the yard of his house in the San Gabriel Valley, California. *(Ward Kimball Collection)*

(facing page bottom) Walt Disney looks on as Ward Kimball, one of his top animators, mimes an expression in a mirror. *(© Walt Disney Productions)*

(above) Vince Jefferds took over the handling of merchandise for Walt Disney after the premiere of *Peter Pan* (1953), and subsequently his department made the company $50 million a year from Disney spin-offs. Here he is seen just before the *Peter Pan* opening with Walt Disney. *(© Walt Disney Productions, photo from Vince Jefferds Collection)*

Walt Disney poses with his two most popular cartoon creations, Mickey Mouse and Donald Duck. (© *Walt Disney Productions*)

(above) The orange groves in Anaheim, California, which were transformed into Disneyland by landscaper Morgan "Bill" Evans (© Walt Disney Productions, Morgan Evans Collection)

(below) The ornate landscaping at both Disneyland and Walt Disney World was done by a California landscape gardener, Morgan "Bill" Evans, who transformed the orange groves of California and the swamps of Florida in order to bring Walt Disney's dream of a new kind of leisure park system to fruition. Here he is seen with Walt Disney making a tour of Disneyland, Anaheim, shortly after its opening in 1965. (© Walt Disney Productions, Morgan Evans Collection)

(above) Walt Disney shows the Indian leader Pandit Jawaharlal Nehru Nehru around Disneyland in Anaheim, California, in 1961. (© *Walt Disney Productions*)

(facing page top) Hayley Mills (center) with her mother, Mary Hayley Bell, and Walt Disney during a break from shooting at the Disney Studio in Burbank. (© *Walt Disney Productions, Hayley Mills Collection*)

(facing page bottom) Matte-shot artist Peter Ellenshaw, who created effects for *Treasure Island, Mary Poppins,* and other films, talks to Walt Disney. (© *Walt Disney Productions, Peter Ellenshaw Collection*)

(left) Julie Andrews poses for a scene in *Mary Poppins* against a matte-shot drawn by Peter Ellenshaw (below, center). (© *Walt Disney Productions, Peter Ellenshaw Collection*)

(below) Peter Ellenshaw sketch for a scene with Julie Andrews and Dick Van Dyke and the children in *Mary Poppins*. (© *Walt Disney Productions*)

(left) Walt Disney studies plans for Walt Disney World and EPCOT in Florida. (© Walt Disney Productions)

(below) The countryside landscape gardener Morgan "Bill" Evans had to transform to help build Walt Disney World in Florida. (© Walt Disney Productions, Morgan Evans Collection)

(left) Roy Disney (left) and Morgan "Bill" Evans, landscaper (third from left), during the building of Walt Disney World in Florida. (© Walt Disney Productions, Morgan Evans Collection)

All Aboard . . . Mickey Mouse celebrates his golden anniversary. As part of the festivities, Mickey and animator Ward Kimball embark on an Amtrak whistle-stop tour covering 18 states and 57 cities. Mickey retraces his roots with stops including Kansas City (where Walt Disney had his first studio), Chicago, the White House, and New York, where he first appeared on screen 50 years before. (© *Walt Disney Productions*)

were a hit but he also let the movie world know how well he had done with them, by taking out full-page ads in the trade papers. He knew Walt Disney well enough to know it would boost his morale if he publicly demonstrated his support of his controversial artistic endeavor; so he not only telegraphed the Walt Disney Studio to say that he was booking *Snow White and the Seven Dwarfs* in advance, but he also made a public announcement about it in *Variety*. He was the first exhibitor to take an option on the film, and soon the whole country followed.

Work went on steadily all through 1936, and often the studio was open seven days a week as the animators and inkers struggled to complete the quotas Walt was now demanding of them. Sometimes it seemed to Ward Kimball, who was working as an assistant animator on the movie at the time, that the number of drawings needed to complete it would, if laid out lengthwise, stretch from Burbank to Minneapolis, where he had been born. "Just think, there were more than two million of them!" he said later. "Everyone who could draw on paper or do brushwork on the cels was called in to help. There were a lot of newcomers around, but Walt just laid them over an anvil and beat the Disney style into them."

So far, there were no female animators in the studio since Walt did not believe that they had the flair or the artistic ambition for the job, but there were plenty of women in the inking department, where they did work that was not only highly skilled but also full of tension, causing the worst kinds of headaches. These dedicated young women struggled uncomplainingly and with touching good humor to meet Walt Disney's increasingly strident demands on their time, their meticulousness, and their expertise.

Their enthusiasm was such that absenteeism in the largely female inkers' department, even on Saturdays and Sundays, dropped dramatically. It became so noticeable that even Roy was persuaded to recognize the tremendous efforts they were making, and he announced that he was giving all the women working on *Snow White* a weekly ten-dollar bonus. Moreover, he said that he and his brother would show their gratitude in an even more spectacular way when *Snow White* was finally finished.

SNOW WHITE AND *the Seven Dwarfs* had its world premiere at the Carthay Circle Theater in Hollywood on December 21, 1937. It would be the Christmas attraction that year at Radio City Music Hall, but Walt wanted his professional colleagues in Hollywood to see it first, especially since they had been so skeptical about its chances. Besides, a Los Angeles opening gave Roy a chance to invite Joseph Rosenberg and the board of directors of the Bank of America to join in the celebration; even if Walt did not realize it, Roy was acutely aware that without their financial support, the film could never have been completed. Word had already spread through Hollywood that *Snow White* was going to be a hit, and the glittering first-night audience—which included most of the top stars and moviemakers in the film colony—left no doubt about it when they rose to their feet at the end and cheered.

Walt was up on the stage to receive their acclamation, and he confessed it was music to his ears. "I always dreamed that one day I would attend a gala premiere in Hollywood of one of my cartoons," he told them. "Tonight you've made it come true. You make me feel like one of you." Until that moment, he said later, Hollywood had seemed to regard cartoon filmmakers as people they looked down on, like garbage collectors. Now they were not just welcoming him into their club, they were saluting him.

"They no longer think I smell bad," he told Lilly. "It's wonderful!"

She had stood beside him on the stage of the Carthay Circle Theater, her eyes shining. No one would have guessed that she had once had doubts about the film.

Snow White became one of the most successful films of all time. It earned over eight million dollars in its first release, and has made a profit of forty-one million dollars for the Walt Disney Studio (so far). Its songs became the most popular radio and record sellers of the day. Kay Kamen rushed out millions of replicas of the seven dwarfs, and they were soon to be found on mantels and nursery niches around the world. Royalties on the model of Dopey alone made nearly a hundred thousand dollars for Disney (and, according to the terms of his contract, for Kamen, too).

One day in 1938, after the Bank of America loan was paid off and the profits began to pour in, Roy Disney remembered he had promised to reward the studio staff for its unremitting efforts to finish *Snow White* on time. He went to Walt and told him about his pledge; he suggested that it might be appropriate to give the workers a generous Easter bonus. But to Walt, for whom money would always be unimportant, this seemed a poor way of rewarding the staff for its magnificent efforts. "Let's give them a real celebration instead, a kind of thank-you party they'll always remember," he said.

A few days later, he announced to the studio staff that he and his brother were going to throw a monster thank-you party for everyone who worked for them and added that their wives, husbands, and children (or a nominated friend or relative) were included in the invitation. All of them would be welcome to spend the weekend at a desert resort near Palm Springs, the Narconian Hotel on Lake Narco, as the guests of Walt and Roy, and he went on to emphasize that charges for everything, accommodation, food, drink, whatever they might wish to order, would be taken care of by the Disneys.

IN A PERIOD when many of Hollywood's major studios were notorious for the uninhibited and unbuttoned behavior of some of their stars—and tycoons like Louis B. Mayer, Darryl Zanuck and Harry Cohn were legendary for the wear and tear they were said to inflict on their casting-office couches—Walt Disney Studios had acquired a very different reputation. It was sometimes known among cynical acting types as Mickey Mouse's Monastery, and players given a contract to work there, usually dubbing voices for the cartoons, knew that anything less than circumspect behavior while appearing on the lot would result in instant dismissal. You did not carouse, raise your voice off the set, look lecherously at a member of the opposite sex, or, in fact, indulge in any kind of hanky-panky at Disney. It was a rock-ribbed island of rectitude and middle-American morality in a southern California sea of Bohemian shamelessness. In the 1930s, it even had a dress code for its employees. Men came to work in jackets and ties though, like Walt himself, they were allowed to take them off when they settled down to their drawing boards. Pants for female employees were taboo, and sober-colored skirts and blouses were a kind of accepted uniform for the demure army of inkers.

Ward Kimball, who later became one of Disney's more distinguished animators, remembers that in those early days he used to change into shorts during the lunchtime break and play volleyball with his fellow artists on the chalk-marked court behind the old Hyperion Avenue sound stage.

"These shorts were not very secure," he said later. "They kept precariously dropping down with all that jumping around. A pretty blond girl who worked in the studio paint department named Betty Lawyer (later, Mrs. Kimball) and her friend, Dorothy Disney (Walt's niece, daughter of his brother, Herbert), used to come and watch the games and giggle a lot over the errant tendencies of my shorts, which many times I had to hold up with one hand while trying to spike the volleyball with the other. I guess the news of the girls' hilarity about the falling shorts situation finally reached Walt's office, because someone soon hinted that maybe I had better buy myself some better-fitting athletic equipment or give up the lunchtime game. (There was the Disney "image" to uphold.) After Betty and I were married she answered the often-asked question of how she first met me by usually replying: 'When I first met Ward, his pants were falling down.'"

Only once had a real scandal been connected with the Disney studio, and that had been quickly hushed up. One of the animators who had thrown away his glasses as a result of a new therapy involving eye exercises began approaching girls around the studio who wore spectacles. By the use of almost hypnotic powers of persuasion, he enticed a number of the girls to do the eye exercises with him and explained that a prerequisite of the routine was that they must first relax by taking off their clothes. Quite a few of them did so and gained experience in certain male behavior if not a restoration of 20/20 vision.

But then one girl panicked when asked to disrobe and rushed home to tell her parents; they demanded the immediate arrest of the shameless pervert who had tried to seduce their daughter. Walt was shocked and angry when he heard about it. Gunther Lessing, the studio lawyer, was called in and, on Walt's instructions, compensated the girl for her embarrassment and the parents for their righteous indignation. As for the animator, he was summarily dismissed and told never to darken the gates of the Mickey Mouse Monastery again.

Few people ever heard about this unfortunate incident. Walt told Lessing to keep it a secret, pointing out that the wives of his animators and the parents of his inkers—not to mention the staff, decent, respectable people all of them—would be stunned and shocked to learn that the Disney studio could be just like the rest of Hollywood, with lechers and libertines lurking on the lots.

But after that there were no more incidents. Walt walked the corridors and looked over his male and female staff with approval, knowing that in a movieland full of vice and permissiveness, his moral, well-behaved, and decent young people were safe from temptation.

That, at least, is what he thought—until the weekend of the thank-you party.

WHAT WALT DISNEY did not seem to realize was something several of his employees could have told him had they dared—that it had been a tense two years at the Disney studio and most of his staff had been working under a terrible strain.

"When I arrived at the studio [in 1934], I was the youngest person there. I was twenty," Ward Kimball said later. "Of course, there were some middle-aged guys there, but most of the artists, including the girls, were in their twenties. Walt was thirty. And he was our father figure and the boss."

Everyone looked up to Walt and admired him, but they were afraid of him, too. If they saw him as a father figure, he also seemed a very stern father figure to most of them. For one thing, he had such a terrible temper; and he was so demanding and unforgiving. Though he did not always appreciate it, he had the most dedicated staff in the history of the movies—mostly because they were so proud to be working for such a remarkable man. Despite the modest amount of money he paid them, his animators and inkers had worked night and day on *Snow White* because they appreciated what he was trying to do for the art of cartoon films and were willing to give all they had, to the limit of their talents, to help him achieve his goals.

But had their exertions really been appreciated by him? Quite often, they had reason to doubt it. One of Walt Disney's quirks was that he never praised anyone to his or her face. A worker who had sweated blood to do a good job only learned that his or her efforts had succeeded through other people, to whom Walt might casually mention it. He almost never said "thank you," and took efforts beyond the call of duty as a given.

On the other hand, he did not hesitate to criticize his employees in front of others, and he could be rough. His language was abrasive, and the dressing-downs he often gave to those who he felt had failed him were often public and could be bruising, brutal, and humiliating.

By the time *Snow White* was finished, the atmosphere around Hyperion Avenue was tense. It could only have been relaxed by a mass meeting at which Walt expressed his heartfelt gratitude to his staff for the superhuman work they had performed for him. But he did not do it.

So when he did eventually get around to inviting them to a thank-you weekend, it was almost an anticlimax. Nerves were still taut as the young staff and their friends climbed into the buses and set off for Lake Narco one weekend in the late spring of 1938, and no one seemed able or willing—with the exception of some of the wives and children and boyfriends—to relax and enjoy themselves.

But then they arrived at the Narconian Hotel and suddenly everything was wonderful. Very few of the animators and their families, and certainly none of the young female inkers, had ever seen or experienced such luxury as now confronted them. No expense had been spared to give the staff everything they could possibly wish. There were pools to swim in, a lake to sail on, tennis courts, putting greens, music, a nursery for the children, a smiling and willing staff—and loads of food and champagne. It started slowly at first. Then the first "whoopee!" was heard from around the pool, followed by a female scream, laughter, and a splash.

"And," one of the animators who was there said, "by the end of the first evening, something snapped. All the animators and assistant animators and inkers, who had always been so staid and contained at the studio, suddenly let go. Nobody worried here whether your shorts fit or not, because everybody's were suddenly slipping. Playsuits flew out of the windows. There were naked swim parties in the pool. Inhibitions, respectability, and tensions vanished with each new bottle of champagne, and all those circumspect characters who had damped down their lecherous instincts around the studio for years were suddenly reaching out and grabbing someone. Everybody got drunk. It developed into what was practically an orgy, with animators reeling around tipsily and staggering off to sleep with whomsoever took their fancy, which was more likely to be that demure little inker from desk number 17 rather than the mother of their children. You'd be surprised who woke up with whom next morning."

Walt, who had come down with Lilly to share in the fun, was horrified.

He was so shocked, in fact, that he did not stay for the rest of the weekend but drove his wife home the following morning. Nor did he ever refer to the party again.

As for the Disney staff, they did not talk about it much either. They turned up at the studio on Monday and looked sheepishly at each other, inkers dimpling and animators glancing hastily the other way when they passed in the corridors. It was years before anyone dared make any reference to what subsequently became known as the "Snow White Orgy."

Even if Walt Disney never really forgave his staff for demonstrating that they could be so weak and fallible, it certainly cleared the air around the studio. It had been a most therapeutic weekend, and it gave his staff the relief from tension they needed to face the new challenges with which Walt and Roy were about to confront them.

14
The Hollow Sound of Music

IN 1936 LILLIAN Disney decided she and Walt would never have a second child. She told her husband that she wanted him to cosign formal papers adopting a little girl as a companion to their three-year-old daughter, Diane.

It was only with great reluctance that he agreed. He said that he still hoped that one day they would have more children, maybe even a son. Lillian doubted it. By this stage in their marriage she realized he wasn't really interested in producing children—except those of the cartoon kind—and guessed the only reason he spoke about the possibility of a son was because he was constantly having his brother's boy, Roy Edward Disney, thrust under his nose. She suspected that there was envy, maybe even jealousy, there but certainly no real urge to increase the size of his own family. Perhaps it was just that he wished Diane were a boy?

Lilly continued to thrust the papers at him until he signed them, and shortly afterward Sharon Mae Disney came to join the family. She had been chosen as a playmate for Diane. Originally, neither Walt nor Lilly bothered to conceal the fact that she had been found through an adoption agency. But soon Lilly let it be assumed Sharon was her own flesh and blood and was upset if she was treated any differently than Diane was.*

In fact, there have been moments when friends have suggested that Lilly came to favor her adopted daughter over her own, and these hints were revived in 1984 when she backed Sharon's election to the board of Walt Disney Productions at a critical moment—after her son-in-law, Ron Miller, Diane's husband, was summarily dismissed as president of the

---

*After Walt's death, when Bob Thomas was writing his semiofficial biography, Lilly asked him not to reveal in his narrative that Sharon is not Diane's natural sister, and there are no indications in the book that she was adopted.

company. When the official announcement was about to be made of Sharon's election, Lilly requested that she be referred to as "Walt Disney's daughter," with no hint that she was an adopted child.

But if she brought a warm light into Lilly's life, Sharon's arrival in his household made little or no impact on Walt, who, in any case, saw little of her. She was still asleep when he left for the studio in the morning and had gone to bed by the time he got home. He sometimes saw her on Sunday morning when he accompanied his family to church but often, whether deliberately or not, professed not to recognize her or remember her name. "Who's that?" he once loudly asked Lilly during the service, indicating Sharon singing hymns in the middle of the pew.

"Sharon! Your daughter!" she indignantly whispered back.

The Disney blood relations were coming back into the family circle, "like bees to the honeypot," as Roy once cynically put it. Raymond, the unmarried brother, moved from Kansas City to California, where he opened a new branch of his insurance company. The oldest brother, Herbert, still working for the post office and sharing a house with the Disney parents, Elias and Flora, in Portland, Oregon, got himself and his family transferred to Los Angeles, where he announced he proposed to live permanently when he retired. Meanwhile, he asked Roy to find a job at the studio for his daughter, Dorothy, and she was hired as an inker.

So Walt and Roy began to have pangs of conscience about their parents, left stranded in Oregon. Roy went to see them and reported back that Elias was doing odd jobs as a carpenter but finding the work an increasing strain, especially as he was now suffering from a bad rupture. Flora looked frail, and he suspected she was sick and in pain though she refused to talk about it. He discussed the situation with Walt and they decided that they would try to persuade the old folks to move to Los Angeles, where they could keep an eye on them.

They bought a house for them for eight thousand dollars in North Hollywood, just around the corner from Roy, and planned to move them into it in the fall of 1938. In the meantime, the Disneys came south to stay with Roy and his family, and it was in their home that they celebrated their golden wedding anniversary. It proved to be a somewhat lugubrious occasion.

Flora Disney was now sixty-nine but looked much older than her husband, Elias, who was nearly eighty. Fifty years of marriage to this god-fearing man, who continued to lecture her daily about the virtues of piety, puritanism, and socialism, seemed to have squeezed her dry. She had lost her sense of humor and her interest in life. She never even visited the site of the new studio Walt and Roy were building on Buena Vista Street. And though she was sometimes taken to see new Mickey Mouse or Donald Duck cartoons, she did not seem to find them entertaining. Walt was unhappy about Flora. He sensed that she was hugging some private sorrow to herself, that she not only hated Los Angeles but seemed to have grown weary of life itself and could not wait for death to arrive.

He had always loved, admired, and respected his mother, and he was distressed by her mental and physical condition. He found himself hoping that she would not have to endure for too long a life she so obviously found so trying—and then felt guilty with himself for wishing her dead.

About a month after the Disney parents had moved into their new home, Roy Edward Disney, who had grown fond of Flora, came to see his grandmother after school and was told she had been found inert on the kitchen floor. He learned later that she was dead—from inhaling the fumes from a defective boiler. Walt was deeply upset by his mother's death but took comfort by persuading himself she probably found it a profound relief.

ON ONE OF the infrequent occasions he had persuaded Flora to see some of his latest cartoons, she had stayed particularly stony-faced over what he thought was a very successful new Mickey Mouse short. He had always had a special sentimental feeling for Mickey, and he was hurt by her reaction. When he asked her why she found it so unfunny, she had told him she didn't like Mickey's voice.

"But that's my voice," he had pointed out.

"I know it belongs to you," she had replied. "But it's put on, girlish, unnatural. I just don't think it fits."

He was stunned by her comment, especially since he had always shared everyone else's opinion that his simulation of Mickey's voice was the secret of the mouse's success. On the other hand, he put great store in Flora's reactions, and her comment worried him. Could that be the reason why Mickey Mouse cartoons weren't doing so well anymore? Had audiences grown sick of the sound of Mickey's voice?

Even before he had started production of *Snow White*, he had mentally begun to phase out cartoon shorts from the Disney menu of films and was sometimes tempted to abandon them altogether. With the exception of Mickey Mouse, he had grown bored with them. He didn't like Donald Duck. He had only a mild affection for Pluto and Goofy and the Three Little Pigs. In particular he regretted he had "wasted" the characters of the Three Little Pigs and the Big Bad Wolf on a short when they could have been put into a real story and won him acclaim—and vast profits— as stars of a full-length feature.

Even Roy Disney was now antipathetic to the short-film program. He had changed his mind about full-length features once he had seen *Snow White* and decided (even before its premiere) that it would be a moneymaker. Soon afterward, he began pointing out to his brother that their short cartoons were no longer economically worthwhile. In the old days they had made enough money to pay the rent, but they didn't even do that anymore. The Donald Ducks and Goofys and the like were sold in batches for not much more than their basic costs, and though the public loved them, the profits were disappointing.

As for Mickey Mouse, "He's passé," Roy said. "Nobody cares about Mickey anymore. There are whole batches of Mickeys we just can't give away. I think we should phase him out."

The idea of killing off Mickey Mouse was a painful thought to Walt. Only his money-grubbing brother could have mentioned it so casually, and the callousness of his remark wounded him. Had Roy forgotten what Mickey Mouse meant to both of them and to the success of their enterprise? He obviously had. But Walt would never forget how he had conjured him up in his mind after the debacle of Oswald the Lucky Rabbit and how Mickey had saved them from ruin at a critical moment in their lives.

Mickey Mouse was his talisman and always would be. Walt had a feeling in his bones that when Mickey died, he would die, too. For that reason, whatever happened to his other cartoon stars, he was determined to keep Mickey alive.

IN THE SUMMER of 1937, in between cutting *Snow White* and planning the production of *Pinocchio* (which would be his second full-length cartoon feature) Walt Disney went back to his drawing board and began working on a program to resuscitate Mickey Mouse. Taking Flora Disney's comment seriously, he planned to make a cartoon in which Mickey would not speak at all. Music would be the substitute for the mouse's (or, rather, Walt's) falsetto tones. Not a word would be heard from Mickey.

It was Carl Stalling who had originally given him the idea, recommending Paul Dukas's *The Sorcerer's Apprentice* for a follow-up to the first Walt Disney *Silly Symphony, Skeleton Dance*. Somehow, Walt had never got around to it. But now he revived the idea—not as a *Silly Symphony* but as a comic vehicle for a Mickey Mouse comeback, with Mickey playing the part of the magician's overambitious assistant.

When he put the idea to the story department, first reactions were mixed. Ben Sharpsteen, the studio manager, pointed out that *The Sorcerer's Apprentice* was highbrow music and over the public's head. He suggested that only by using Dopey out of *Snow White* could the project be popularized. But Jim Algar, who had made several Mickey Mouse cartoons, had already dug out an Arturo Toscanini recording of the Dukas piece and declared he could see Mickey's persona in every musical phrase. He was told by Walt to start developing a script and was given the job of directing it. It was at this point that the famous conductor,

Leopold Stokowski, came into the picture. Stokowski was already well-known to movie audiences, having recently had a big success conducting his orchestra in Paramount's *100 Men and a Girl,* starring Deanna Durbin. Walt saw him dining in the Beverly Hills Hotel one night and asked whether he could join him.

"He began to tell me that he was interested in Dukas's *The Sorcerer's Apprentice* as a possible short," Stokowski recalled later, "and did I like the music? I said I liked it very much and would be happy to cooperate with him."

He was invited to the studio to discuss the project with the Disney animators. Since Stokowski loved seeing his name in the newspapers and knew a good publicity stunt when one was handed him on a platter, he turned up at the studio the very next day, before Walt Disney could change his mind. Jim Algar remembers racing around hiding all traces of the Toscanini recordings before inviting him into the music department. On November 15, 1937, a confidential memorandum was sent to all members of the Disney story department:

> We are preparing a special short subject in collaboration with Leopold Stokowski, who will conduct his renowned [Philadelphia] symphony orchestra, one hundred men strong, in his own interpretation of the world-famous descriptive score of *The Sorcerer's Apprentice. The Sorcerer's Apprentice* will be released as a "special," so we are naturally hopeful of a special response to the attached outline. It offers a challenge to the best imaginations on the lot. Please *give.*

Almost immediately the ideas came flowing in, for the imaginations of the animation department suddenly caught fire. Everyone agreed that casting Mickey Mouse as the cocky, overconfident sorcerer's apprentice was an inspiration on Walt's part, and two of the staff artists, Dick Huemer and Joe Grant, came up with some vivid sequences to match it. They were immediately assigned to work on the film. Shortly afterward, they were joined by, among others, Fred Moore, who was given the task of redrawing Mickey Mouse and designing the broomstick that would play a vital role in the action. Moore's first action was to give Mickey pupils in his eyes to increase the range of his expression, "because he will really be acting in this one."

ROY DISNEY WAS appalled when he heard the news. All he knew about music was that Stokowski was paid a thousand dollars a night as a guest conductor and his musicians made fifty dollars an hour. He told his staff to work out a provisional budget, and it was worse than he feared. He figured *The Sorcerer's Apprentice,* as his brother visualized it, would cost three or four times as much as a normal *Silly Symphony* and, at the rate paid by renters for cartoon shorts in those days, could not possibly make money.

"I know that," Walt said. "How can we merchandise it so that it *will* make money?"

"No way," Roy said. "What with those overpaid fiddlers and the way audiences feel about Mickey these days, it's going to be a financial disaster." He added, "Look, Walt, why don't we abandon the whole Mickey idea and do it with Goofy? That means we can forget the music and send that show-off Stokowski and his long-haired musicians back to Philadelphia?"

"Not a chance," Walt said. "This cartoon is going to be made my way. If we don't use Mickey, we're not going to make it at all."

Ironically enough, Roy Disney might have found an ally in Stokowski in his opposition to Mickey Mouse. Though he would never had said so out loud, Stokowski did not by any means share Walt's sentimental enthusiasm for the mouse. In fact, during the first stages of the collaboration, he was so ignorant of Walt Disney's feelings that he suggested abandoning Mickey altogether.

On November 29, 1927, he wrote Walt Disney from New York tentatively suggesting the creation of an entirely new character instead of Mickey Mouse as star of the film. He envisioned a "personality that could represent *you and me*" and possibly be built up as a character in future films that Stokowski was already envisioning. It would create a brand-new personality representing "every one of us," and "it might be a valuable factor in the years to come and enlarge the scope," he wrote.

He counseled Walt to discard his suggestion immediately if it didn't interest him. In fact, Walt was furious at the conductor's insensitivity and strongly tempted to tell him so. But mindful of Stokowski's reputation, he never answered the letter.

Could Stokowski really have been serious in asking him to abandon Mickey Mouse? To do so at this stage of Walt's preparations would have been tantamount to abandoning himself. For Walt, overseeing the daily work on *The Sorcerer's Apprentice*, rehearsing Mickey's step-by-step actions in the role, the mouse had come back to life and taken over all his waking thoughts, even his dreams. He was not Mickey Mouse just when he acted out scenes before his animators at the daily story-board conferences; his staff noticed that he looked and moved like Mickey when he walked around the studio, rolled his eyes like Mickey, grinned like Mickey, ate like Mickey. Once, when he walked past a group of animators, they noticed that Walt suddenly glanced behind him as he scampered out of the way of a passing truck.

"What's with the boss?" someone asked.

"Don't you get it?" Dick Huemer asked. "He's looking to see if that truck has run over his tail."

As one writer later remarked, Walt Disney's identity was entwined with Mickey's. He theorized in *The Sorcerer's Apprentice* that he dreamed Mickey's dream of being given "complete control of the earth and the elements"—a dream that later resulted in Disneyland, Walt Disney World and EPCOT Center.*

In the end, of course, the Mickey Mouse project never did make it into the movie theaters as a separate short. *The Sorcerer's Apprentice* became one segment of the full-length cartoon, *Fantasia*. Stokowski gave Walt Disney credit for deciding to abandon his plan for a Mickey Mouse "special" and to slip him, instead, into a full-length musical film, but in truth it was he who put the idea into Walt's head. He confessed many years later† that having no wish to be remembered as the conductor of a Mickey Mouse cartoon, he persuaded Walt to add other pieces from the classical repertoire which he would conduct and the Disney staff would illustrate.

The film was given the provisional title of *The Concert Feature*, and only later known as *Fantasia*. Suddenly Walt Disney, whose interest in music had hitherto been minimal, spent his time listening to concert recordings of the great masters and gravely discussing the tonal phraseology and decibel content of Bach and Mozart with his sound experts. The Disney studio swarmed with stars from the musical world brought in by Stokowski and the publicity department. Deems Taylor was hired as a commentator. Stravinsky arrived to hear the playback of his *Sacre du Printemps* and see a preview of its cartoon accompaniment. Stokowski posed happily for publicity pictures with the composer and the great Swedish soprano, Kirsten Flagstad, who was disappointed when she was told *Fantasia* would not include any Wagner.

Stokowski was in his element. He even began to relax about the linking of his name with Mickey Mouse and finally consented to a shot of Mickey shaking his hand at the conclusion of a musical number. But only in silhouette. "A fabulous little fellow," he was quoted as saying about Mickey later. But he was glad the mouse had been squeezed out of the limelight, in favor of Stravinsky, Bach, Beethoven, Tchaikovsky, Mussorgsky, Ponchielli—and, of course, Stokowski.

ROY DISNEY WAS shaken when the bills for *Fantasia* began to come in. By the time the film was finished, it had cost $2,280,000, Disney's most

---

*See *Walt Disney's Fantasia* by John Culhane, New York, Walt Disney Productions, 1983.
†In conversations in the south of France with the author.

expensive production so far. Expenses for recording and playing the music alone had come to half a million dollars, of which Stokowski received $80,000 plus royalties. Since he would only have been paid five thousand dollars had the project stayed as a Mickey Mouse cartoon, he was well content.

And, to be truthful, so was Walt. He was enthusiastic about the finished cartoon, convinced that he had discovered a formula for popularizing classical music. For a time, there was a danger that Walt would become a musical bore. He began to sound like an echo of Stokowski and the more erudite musical critics. He would buttonhole animators around the studio, many of whom had been enjoying Bach and Beethoven for most of their lives, and talk about them as if they had just been discovered, expatiating learnedly on the special significance of the pizzicato arpeggios in the harp quartets, which they suspected he had never even listened to. Ward Kimball used to upset him deliberately by listening intently to his disquisitions and then remarking, "Personally, I hate that pretentious crap. Prefer Gershwin myself."

Not that Walt tried any of this musical snob talk on his brother, who would have hooted in derision. With Roy he confined his remarks about *Fantasia* to its box office potential. He assured him that *Fantasia* was the most brilliant film he had ever made and that it would top *Snow White* (receipts for which were now beginning to roll in) and more than double their fortune. Roy agreed with him. He was impressed with *Fantasia* and though the public would "lap it up."

"People are saying that anyone who can make a box office smash out of a long-haired musical has to be a miracle worker," he told his brother after the triumphant premiere of *Fantasia* in New York. He was particularly pleased with *The Sorcerer's Apprentice* segment. "You've even put that dumb bastard Mickey Mouse—and dumb is right!—back on the map! I take back all I said about this project, Walt."

He couldn't help adding, "Though I still think we didn't need to spend half a million on that crappy music, and I'll never understand why we couldn't have sneaked a little Tommy Dorsey in there."

He grinned and slapped Walt's back. "Never mind, all we need to do now is sit back and wait for the money."

They had to wait a long time as *Fantasia* turned out to be one of three major Disney box office flops, the other two being *Pinocchio* and *Bambi*. By 1939, not only had all the profits from *Snow White* been dissipated, but the Walt Disney Studio was in debt to the banks for nearly five million dollars. But not because the studio had made poor or unentertaining films. In the opinion of most critics, Walt's cartoon conceptions were now better than ever before. *Pinocchio,* for instance, was Walt's most brilliantly executed, as well as the most watchable, cartoon he had made so far in his career.

NO ONE IS quite sure nowadays who first suggested *Pinocchio* as a major Disney animated feature. Some years before he died, Norm Ferguson told the author it was he who first gave Walt a copy of Carlo Collodi's last-century classic to read, suggesting it might make a good full-length cartoon. Others, including Walt himself, claimed it was they who first discovered the book. Whoever deserves the credit, it was Walt, in 1937, who called a studio conference of his principal animators, Fred Moore, Bill Tytla, Milt Kahl, Norm Ferguson, and Ham Luske, and told them he had found a marvelous subject, and they were about to help him make the most remarkable animated feature of his (or their) career.

"He was just busting his guts with enthusiasm," Ferguson said.

This would be a breakthrough film for all of them, he said, in which all the lessons and new techniques they had learned from *Snow White* would be implemented and perfected, and all the mistakes they had made in earlier films would be rectified. "What I will be looking for in this production will be color and dimension and wonderful effects of a kind that have never been seen in animated movies before," he said. "It will be the costliest cartoon film ever made, but we've got money in the bank [which was true at that moment]—and damn the expense. Because *Pinocchio* is going to be the biggest challenge in the history of animation."

He added: "You've all been sent a copy of the outline, so you know the story. We start off with the puppet Pinocchio—and what will that mean? Even when we bring him to life, folks are going to say, 'Who cares about this little freak? He's still just nothing but string and sticks,' and what we have to persuade them is that though he still looks and moves like a puppet, now if you prick him he'll bleed, if he falls over he'll hurt himself, if his nose starts to grow or his ears sprout it's because they're growing from inside and not because someone's pinned a new schnozzle or earflaps on the kid. And," he went on, "if something really awful happens to him, you'll weep for him. Because he's no longer a puppet. He's real. And that is our challenge. It means we're going to have to surround him with characters who look so alive and treat him so much like one of themselves, that their genuineness rubs off on the kid. And because of that, we're gonna have to do a special job on all the surrounding characters in the story. They've gotta look rounder, softer, *realer* than any we've ever put into a cartoon before. So real audiences will imagine at any moment they might walk right out of the screen and sit down beside them."

He paused and then went on, "As for backgrounds, they have to come specially alive, too. Mountains have gotta look as if you could climb 'em, houses as if you could walk through the front door and find something cooking on the stove in the kitchen, and when we get to the whale sequence, the seas must look real wet and cold and deep and salty. As for backgrounds, they've gotta jolt the audience as never before. It's essential they look and feel genuine. Like this."

He turned to the studio wall behind him, over which a curtain had been drawn, and dramatically ripped it aside. On the wall, where roughly drawn storyboards usually hung for a conference like this, they saw displayed a series of huge canvases painted in bold and startling colors —mostly dramatically backlighted undersea scenes of wrecks lying on the ocean bed, one with a particularly menacing octopus swimming through Stygian, purple depths, and the terrified figure of Pinocchio cringing in the wreck below, away from the probing tentacles.

Even the jaded professional animators were impressed by the boldness of the concept. These were meant to be scenes from the sequence in which Pinocchio is swallowed by a whale, and the paintings had been done by a talented newcomer to the studio, Gustaf Tenggren. They almost literally hit you in the eyeballs and provided a vivid impression of the way Walt saw the film's settings. One by one the little group listening to him realized they were being exhorted to pioneer an entirely new kind of animated cartoon, and they would be using shock tactics all the way through.

Not all of them approved, but they responded to the challenge. In the next few months the animators added a new panache to their usually painstaking craft and, with great mastery, brought to life the colorful characters in the story. By the middle of 1938 the film had taken on life and shape. The new color techniques and the skilled brushwork of the women in the ink department brought a remarkable glow to the figures in Collodi's story. All the animators understood that this time, more than ever, Walt knew exactly what he wanted. He had continual conferences with his Color Model advisers to make sure they developed new techniques that would, for instance, change a flat area into a rounded form.

They pioneered a startling effect that softened the harsh areas of color on the screen. The twenty women in the airbrush department worked out a method of blending color so that when it was rubbed on and then touched up with drybrush and airbrush, it gave the characters a magical, soft, furry look that was particularly effective with, for example, the figure of Figaro, the cuddly kitten in the cartoon.

Everything, as Walt had hoped, looked "realer" than it had ever done before in his cartoons. But though most people who saw them thought the scenes fairly pulsated with life, Walt Disney was not satisfied. For him, something—a vital element—was missing from the action. What else did he need? It took him some time to realize that Pinocchio had still not come alive, still looked like a puppet, that he needed another side to his character to complete his personality and transform him from a wooden, if mobile, puppet into a living being about whom you could laugh or cry.

And then one day, Ham Luske came into the studio and looked over the storyboards on the wall, showing a sequence in which Pinocchio is teasing—almost cruelly teasing—Figaro, the kitten. Figaro is howling with fear and desperately trying to get away. Walt Disney, watching Luske closely, noticed that he grinned at the drawings and, then, winced a little.

"You know," Luske said, "I think he goes a little too far in this one, and the audience ain't gonna like him for it. Oh, I know it's in the script and it's right in character. But the trouble is, he just doesn't seem to know it's cruel to put the fear of God in a tiny creature like that kitten. He just doesn't know what he's doing. Nobody's ever told him—told Pinocchio— the difference between right and wrong. That's what's the matter with this script. We've made him into an unfeeling little monster instead of a human being. Walt, what this kid needs is a conscience."

That was it! Walt was suddenly inspired. Why hadn't he thought of it? Instead of fleshing out Pinocchio, what he had to do was find him an alter ego—a sidekick who would act as the voice of his conscience whenever he was troubled by what was right and what was wrong. But which character? How could he find one without going beyond the parameters of Collodi's story?

He was so sure Luske had found the fault in the film that he called a temporary, and very expensive, break in production, while he went back to Collodi and read the book through again and again. There was one character in the story who impressed him, though his appearance in the story was so temporary that they hadn't even used him in the script. This was a grasshopper, who briefly appears in the narrative to admonish Pinocchio for his waywardness and is, finally, casually crushed to death under the puppet's foot.

How about a grasshopper as Pinocchio's voice of conscience? He got out his scratchboard in the middle of the night and began to put his idea down on paper. And bells began to ring in his mind. He would resurrect the unfortunate grasshopper and make him a running character in his film. But what the hell was he going to call him? And how would he look? It was at this moment that memories of his dearly beloved Uncle Elf began to swim back into his mind.

At the next story conference he outlined his idea and got an enthusiastic response. Someone produced a name for him. "After all," Bill Tytla said, "what else do we call a grasshopper but a cicada or a cricket. How about Mr. Cricket?"

"Too formal," Fred Moore said. "What about Jimmy Cricket?"

"What about a first name that's a little more eccentric," Ham Luske suggested. "How about Elbert....or Jiminy ... yes, that's it! Does that grab you—Jiminy Cricket?"

Everyone knew at once that they had their character and their name, and Jiminy Cricket was born. Walt had his scriptwriters write him up as Pinocchio's sage and salty conscience, always on hand when needed, and a new quality came into the cartoon.

But not all of Walt's troubles were over. To his intense frustration, no one else saw Jiminy as he did. In his imagination, this perky little grasshopper could be no one but a personification of his long-regretted Uncle Elf, and he couldn't picture him any other way than as that beloved leprechaun. But try as he might, he could not seem to draw on paper the exact concept of the darling little man he so fondly remembered. Typically, he never mentioned Uncle Elf when he spoke of his conception, so repeated attempts by his top animators to create a believable, memorable, and comically endearing Jiminy Cricket failed— to Walt's sentimental eye, anyway.

IT WAS HAM Luske once more who solved the problem for him. He suggested that they solicit the help of his young assistant animator, Ward Kimball, a bright kid who he knew was brimming with ideas and the talent to draw them. He was convinced the kid could produce a fresh view of the elusive Jiminy. And he had another reason for making the suggestion to Walt. Luske knew Kimball was in a rebellious mood and was about to quit Disney, and he didn't want that to happen because he felt it would be damaging both to Kimball and the Disney organization if he departed.

Kimball was disgusted because he had been encouraged to draw several sequences for *Snow White,* and though at least one of them—a bed-making scene in the home of the seven dwarfs—had turned out to be brilliantly funny, it had, like his other drawings, ended up on the cutting room floor. Kimball felt badly about it. Never one to underestimate the worth of his own work, he felt his drawings had deserved a better fate and was prepared to try some other studio where his talents might be better appreciated.

Encouraged by Luske, Kimball marched into Walt Disney's office to express his disgust and hand in his notice. Walt, primed by Luske, and equally appreciative of Kimball's potential, put on one of his best and most charming performances. He did not even give Kimball a chance to

air his grievances. Instead, he began to talk about the wonderful possibilities of *Pinocchio*, his hopes and dreams of creating a revolutionary new
cartoon, and the reasons why he had stopped work on it. He showed
Kimball the sketches his animators had done of Jiminy Cricket and
expatiated on the kind of character he was looking for but despaired of
getting. "These certainly ain't what I need," he said, contemptuously
indicating the sketches. "Frankly, they're dull—they stink! If only I
could find someone who could see Jiminy the way he should be. If we can
just get him right, he'll become as immortal as Mickey Mouse."

He rambled on, and then suddenly, it all came out. As Kimball listened,
he began to talk about Uncle Elf down on the farm, and how this little
Peter Pan of a man had changed Walt's boyhood. "How about letting me
see what I can do about getting him right?" Kimball finally asked.

Simulating reluctance, Walt sent him off to try his hand. The young
man, fired by his boss's enthusiasm, forgot all about resigning and went
back to labor at making Jiminy Cricket into a "character" as well as a
conscience. Walt had fired him up, and he had a vivid picture of a
grasshopper like Uncle Elf in his mind. He felt he knew exactly how
Jiminy Cricket appeared in his boss's imagination, and he was determined to drag him out and create a cartoon character everyone would
remember as well as Walt did.

He more than succeeded. A few hours later, he came back with four
sketches that, to judge from Walt's reaction, might have been plucked
right out of his mind.

"I saw tears come into his eyes as he studied my sketches," Kimball
said later.

This was Jiminy Cricket just as he had envisioned him but somehow
failed to draw him—in a funny hat and formal suit, and carrying an
umbrella; with a deprecating look on his crumpled face, a finger raised to
chide, and a hand held up to counsel, "Stop! Think! Don't do it!"

It was Uncle Elf back again with him. He was so taken by the character
Kimball had brought to life that he ordered the script completely rewrit-
ten to bring in all the lines and scenes he needed to make Jiminy a star of
the film. Shortly afterward his scriptwriters suggested that he add a
couple of sequences in which the chirpy cricket sings two songs, and he
agreed. They became the hits of the movie.*

WORK RESUMED ON *Pinocchio* with new verve and enthusiasm, and it
was finished and ready to be shown by 1939. Everyone was vastly

---

*"When you Wish Upon a Star" and "Give a Little Whistle" by Leigh Harline and Ned
Washington, sung on the sound track by Cliff Edwards.

pleased and impressed with it, and Walt knew it was the best animated feature he had made so far.

There was only one problem. All the doubts and delays had driven up the cost, and when the studio accountants came to review it, the figure came to nearly three million dollars, which was a daunting sum in those days, even for an epic with a cast of thousands. Added to the monies expended on *Fantasia* and the production of *Bambi*, which was now in the works, it more than wiped out the studio's surplus and put Disney heavily in debt to the banks.

Not that Walt, who never cared about money, worried too much about that. Nor did Roy. Not at first, anyway. Roy was convinced that the studio would get it all back once *Pinocchio* began its worldwide distribution, along with *Fantasia* and, later, *Bambi*. The Disney company had always relied for much of its success on box office receipts from overseas, and Roy was sold enough on the films to be convinced this latest trio of productions would recoup all their extraordinary expenditures and make them a profit, too.

But then disaster struck. Something happened to the international box office that not even the Disney sales office could control. World War II started in Europe in 1939, not long before the *Pinocchio* and *Fantasia* features were to open in London, Paris, and Berlin.

The war destroyed the market overnight. Movie receipts from Britain, Germany, France, and the Low Countries had always paid Disney's bills, and this time they had expected handsome profits as well. But now with currencies blocked, movie houses closed, blackouts, troop movements, and other restrictions, everything dried up completely.

To make matters worse, the three new films—undoubtedly the finest Walt Disney ever made—proved to be before their time as far as American audiences were concerned. Those American critics who still considered Walt Disney an entertainer for children found them somewhat pretentious. The public, willing to line up by the millions to see Mickey, Donald, and Pluto, was disconcerted when it got illustrated classical music in *Fantasia*, graphic reality and subtleties they did not appreciate in *Pinocchio*, and sentimentalities over a deer in *Bambi*. *Pinocchio* had a modest success, and its two Jiminy Cricket songs made all the charts, but the public decided the latest Disney films—particularly *Fantasia*—lacked the simple humor and slapstick they had come to prefer in Walt's cartoons, and receipts were disappointing.

Hollywood blamed Walt for the studio's misfortunes that year and said it was because he had "gone highbrow," trying to foist classical music, a wooden puppet, and a "dumb deer" on an unwilling public. But that was unfair. The films were all brilliant, if somewhat ahead of their time as far as America was concerned.

As for the disaster abroad, Walt was certainly not to blame for the outbreak of war in Europe. In subsequent showings, under normal peacetime conditions, all three films have made a handsome profit for the Disney studio. In the United States they have proved big, enduring box office hits, appreciated for their superb effects and production values as well as for the inspirational quality of their characters.*

Moreover, three million dollars of the money now owed to the banks had not been lost by the failure of Walt's films but by Roy's overoptimism. He had borrowed that huge sum to pay for the new Walt Disney Studio on Buena Vista Street in Burbank. Roy had been confident profits from the three new features would soon cover the loans.

It was the drying up of income from overseas that hurt them the most. Suddenly, heavy debts and the horrid prospect of bankruptcy plagued Roy Disney again. He came moaning to Walt with dire prophecies of disaster.

Though Walt didn't worry over money, he agonized when it wasn't around to be spent. When he realized the grimness of the situation, he was in despair. Lillian was concerned about him all over again and thought he might have another breakdown.

She was right to be worried because that was only the start of his troubles. Suddenly, *everything* seemed to go wrong at the studio. For the first time in his life, he came up against labor problems—workers at Disney suddenly went out on strike. It proved to be a strike that changed his outlook and his nature.

---

*A revival of *Pinocchio* in the spring of 1985 was again highly profitable for Disney.

15
Rebellion in Burbank

FROM THE STANDPOINT of labor relations, Hollywood had been a cockpit of bitter battles between studio workers and their bosses all through the turbulent 1930s. But somehow, the Walt Disney Studio escaped the turmoil.

The election of Franklin D. Roosevelt to the presidency and the implementation of the New Deal had given union agents the opportunity they had been seeking to move in on the big studios and organize their employees, most of whom were restless, insecure, unhappy, and did not belong to unions. The result was a series of savage strikes as writers and technicians clashed with the studio heads, the majority of whom were not just ignorant and fearful men but ruthless, too. The Great Depression was still sweeping the United States, and they had used the pervasive fear of unemployment to scare their employees into accepting longer hours and lower wage scales. Those who dared protest were told to swallow the new conditions—or else.

But then some of the studio bosses went too far and imposed such pressure that even the most craven workers were provoked into rebellion. When the studio chiefs were informed that their workers were listening to the recruiters and lining up to join the unions, it was decided to tighten the screw. Such industry leaders as Louis B. Mayer of MGM, Jack Warner of Warner Brothers, and Harry Cohn of Columbia equated union membership with communism and reached for every weapon at their disposal—from instant dismissal to boycott—to keep their employees in line and "these Commie agitators out of our industry." The result was a series of bitterly painful work stoppages.

No member of the Walt Disney Studio staff belonged to a union at the time, and these wounding disturbances left the company unscathed and the work force uninvolved. If there were pro-union sympathizers among the Disney staff, none was motivated strongly enough to appear on the picket lines with his striking colleagues. Work went on normally even when the remainder of Hollywood's studios were closed down.

This was not necessarily because Disney workers were better paid nor because the conditions under which they worked were more enlightened. When Ward Kimball, a talented young art student, first arrived at the studio in 1934, he had been offered a job as an assistant animator at fifteen dollars a week, the first two weeks' pay to be withheld in case he should prove unsatisfactory. He discovered there were other eager young men around the studio, cleaning, carrying messages, inking cels, who had been hired under the same conditions and were let go at the end of their probationary period, simply to save Disney two weeks' wages.

Nor did Disney stay unscathed because it was an oasis of liberal benevolence in the right-wing Hollywood desert. "When I first went to work for Disney in the spring of 1934," Ward Kimball said, "California was in the middle of a hot political race for governor. The Republican candidate, Merriam, was running against the socialist author, Upton Sinclair, representing the Democratic ticket. As a teenager, I had read all of Sinclair's books, and he was one of my literary heroes. We were in the depths of the Great Depression, and on weekends, even though I was too young to vote, I went door-to-door, handing out literature, extolling Sinclair's EPIC plan ("End Poverty in California"). While at work, during the week, I would park my 1929 Chevy in the Disney lot with my large Sinclair window sticker for all to see. This was sheer heresy. I was told by my friends it was a gesture sure to get my ass kicked out of the studio."

Gunther Lessing was by this time firmly established at Disney as its political adviser, and with Walt's blessing he had taken it upon himself to be the arbiter of the studio's politics.

"You would have thought he would be a liberal-minded guy, having once worked for Pancho Villa," Kimball said. "Not Lessing! He called the whole studio to a meeting on the Hyperion Avenue sound stage and proceeded to give us a fatherly lecture on the danger of a Commie revolution rolling through California if Sinclair got elected. He warned us that if we did not vote for Merriam, the state would turn into an Okie dust bowl, that Sinclair was a radical Marxist, that he would bring in a flood of alcoholics, layabouts, and bomb-throwers from the East who would ruin the film industry, doing us all out of our jobs. Punctuating his tirade against Sinclair, he would quote generously from the Los Angeles Times editorial page [it was ultra-right-wing in those days] that dire things would happen to each of us if we did not vote for Merriam."

After Lessing's harangue was finished, he asked for questions. There was a stony silence.

"Even though many of us were politically mature enough to see how corny Lessing's doomsday rantings were," Kimball said, "there were those who were genuinely frightened by his implied threat that if we did not see things his way we would not have our job at Disney.

"I guess I was naive about the political situation at the studio. Ham Luske, who was one of the 'older' animators, took me aside to counsel me that I had a promising future at the studio, and he thought it would be advisable for me to remove the Sinclair sticker from my car before Gunther Lessing saw it. But I had heard that Lessing had already seen the sticker and was reported to have complained about my heresy to Walt. Nothing happened though. Sinclair lost the election, and I removed the sticker. Many years later, Walt laughingly recalled this episode and revealed that he had brushed aside Lessing's objections by pointing out that Kimball really meant no harm. 'And besides, he's too young to vote.'"

But Kimball had learned a lesson.

"During the many presidential elections that followed, my politics took an outwardly conservative appearance, and I would prominently display on my car an old 'Keep Cool with Coolidge' sign."

Walt had seen Kimball's specimen drawings and decided he had too much talent not to be encouraged and kept on the staff.

"When I started work doing in-between drawings, my salary was fifteen dollars a week," Kimball said later. "After a few months it went up to eighteen dollars a week. By the end of the year, I was making twenty-two dollars and fifty cents a week, and I had a chance to be an apprentice assistant to one of Walt's highly respected animators, Ham Luske. Walt's top animators during the nineteen thirties were getting around one hundred dollars a week, which was a lot of money, especially in those Depression days. Disney artists were paid bonuses to finish their sequences under the allotted time at so much a foot. I helped Ham make generous bonuses because he gave me the responsibility of making all of his time-consuming animation corrections, and this allowed me to learn much faster. My only reward was a set of golf clubs that Ham once gave me, but I didn't mind a bit. It was a great learning experience, and in little less than a year I was animating on my own, full time, making forty-five dollars a week and saving money at that."

Kimball recalls that his routine was to animate a group of scenes in pencil and then send his drawings to the Camera Department where a negative loop of film would be made of his work. This he would view on the moviola.

"After making any corrections needed, the drawings were rephotographed," he said, "and the looped scenes cut into the main picture reel for Walt's viewing. In what we called a 'Sweat Box' (a no-ventilation projection room), we animators would sit behind Walt and the director of the picture, nervously waiting for Walt's critique. Walt was very harsh and direct if he did not like what he saw. He knew what he wanted and we respected his judgment. But we did not like his habit of balling us out in front of our coworkers. On the other hand, if our efforts pleased him, he merely said, 'OK, let's go ahead with it,' and walked out of the room. He never complimented us to our face. If he liked our efforts, we would usually hear about it second hand from someone else."

Walt seemed to need a "whipping boy," someone to take his abuse when he was in a bad mood. It was usually a director or someone he obviously did not respect.

"Ben Sharpsteen had to be Walt's favorite target," Kimball recalled. "Ben was an older guy who started out as an animator and later became supervisor of the studio animation department. Finally, he had the title of producer, but it was in name only. If Walt thought things were going wrong on a picture, he would give Ben Sharpsteen hell. Ben would then turn around and ball out the directors under him, who in turn would pass on the abuse to the animators. They kept the chain of harassment going by giving their assistants a rough going over. We figured that the assistants, or in-betweeners, would then take it out on their wives—if they could afford one, that is, on eighteen dollars a week!"

BY 1940, IN fact, Walt Disney's staff was the most brilliant and the most overworked and underpaid in Hollywood. Yet unlike the other studios, they stayed out of strikes and remained un-unionized. That was almost wholly due to Walt Disney's influence.

"Walt was our father figure," Kimball said. "We both respected and feared him. He ran the studio as a sort of benevolent and paternal dictatorship. He was the total boss. You learned early on never to argue with him or to cross him. Walt might be harsh or egocentric, but we all knew he was a genius whose tough demeanor seemed to stimulate and bring out the best in all of us. Even though he was prone to badger and bully us at one time or another, we knew that Walt had revolutionized the animated cartoon, and we were inwardly proud to be part of this process."

But they did have their grievances. Perhaps even more than the meager wages he paid them, what many of the animators objected to was Walt Disney's attitude toward credits. Like most Hollywood studio technicians, what they wanted more than anything was professional recognition, in particular the prestige of seeing their names as part of the credits up on the screen. But Walt Disney insisted on complete anonymity except for himself. No matter how modest his own contribution had been to a film, it was mandatory that his name, and his name only, should appear on it. Time and again, members of his staff came up with new characters who would soon win international fame—Donald Duck, Pluto, the Big Bad Wolf, the Wicked Witch, Jiminy Cricket, Dopey the Dwarf—but he aggressively refused to allow them to take credit for their inventions. Nor would he share it with them. *Everything* was the work of Walt Disney.

One of his youngest and brightest animators, Ken Anderson, remembers that when he first joined the studio, Walt was so struck by his brilliance that he did something most unusual for him: he sought out the newcomer to tell him that he liked his work. But then, according to Anderson, he added, "You're new here, and I want you to understand just one thing. What we're selling here is the name *Walt Disney*. If you can swallow that and always remember it, you'll be happy here. But if you've got any ideas about seeing the name *Ken Anderson* up there, it's best for you to leave right away."

It was rough going, sometimes, but the staff put up with it. Walt was the great galvanizer, and they knew it. "They thought it magnificent the way he had changed the nature of animated cartoons and given them the chance to be part of the revolution," Kimball said. "Some of them were so devoted to his regime that, rather than leave, they would have worked for nothing, so long as he was around to badger and bully—and stimulate them, too."

They had stayed particularly loyal during the fraught but exciting early years before the big profits began to come in. Their instinct then had been to say,

Okay, so he underpays us. How can he do otherwise without going bankrupt? He'll make it up to us when he gets rich. And yes, it's selfish the way he wants to hog all the credit for everything. But why not? Isn't he the catalyst? Hasn't he earned the right to sole recognition?

But then things happened at the Walt Disney Studio that changed everything. First, the profits from the showing of *Snow White* began to come in, and they were larger than anyone had anticipated. In 1939 there was even a moment when Walt and Roy Disney, after paying off all their debts, found that they had $1,500,000 in their joint bank account. In those days it was an enormous sum, and neither brother could think of anything but how to spend it. Strangely enough, it seemed to occur to neither of them that now that affluence was knocking at Disney's door, the time had come to share the rewards with those who had helped earn them—and in a more substantial way than the occasional bonus or a splashy desert weekend.

Roy, ever the practical manager, completed the plans that he had already made to move the company to a brand-new studio on Buena Vista

Street in Burbank. The expanding staff of animators, inkers, and clerical workers now numbered more than a thousand, and the studios on Hyperion Avenue were bursting at the seams. The move, he knew, would cost much more than their reserves, but he was confident that because of their new financial prestige, the banks would lend him all the money he needed.

Meanwhile, Walt had plunged into the production of three new feature-length cartoons which, though they would each cost more than *Snow White,* would have no trouble getting support from the banks since they seemed bound to be even more successful. It was just a question of sitting back and waiting for the money to come in.

BY THE TIME they moved into the new studio on Buena Vista in late 1939, the atmosphere among the employees was expectant. Every animator and inker on the staff believed that now, at long last, things were going to be better. The lean days were over. Walt was about to reward them, with higher wages and professional recognition, for all they had done for him during the time of struggle.

Kimball remembers how, shortly after they moved into their new quarters, the rumor spread like wildfire among the staff that the Disney policy on screen credits was about to change. All of them had been to see *Snow White* and had noticed something special about it. Not just Walt Disney's name was up there on the screen, but also those of the many artists, animators, composers, and "voices" who had worked on the production.

And this innovation produced startling results. Suddenly, from all over Hollywood, telegrams began to arrive at the studio congratulating Fred Moore, Ham Luske, and Frank Churchill, among many others, for the parts they had played in the success of *Snow White.* For years they had been unknown workers in the Disney vineyard, and no one had been able to accurately assess what talents they possessed. Now, thanks to *Snow White*'s screen credits, their fellow craftsmen had a yardstick by which their work could be measured. They were suddenly acclaimed, and it made all the difference to their pride and reputation. "Did this mean that things would be different in the future?" Kimball asked. "Would the workers in the cartoon shorts also get screen credit from now on? Would I soon be seeing *my* name up there, and those of Norm Ferguson and Art Babbitt, to name a trio of us working on the short cartoons?" Alas, no.

When the rumors reached the new executive offices at Disney, George Drake, the studio manager, was deputed to address a meeting of the animators, and he explained that because of the sheer number of technicians involved in *Snow White,* Walt had felt it necessary to share some credits. Manifestly, he could hardly have done a whole feature film himself. So he had allowed certain other participants to be recognized, and the studio would continue to follow a similar policy with future feature-length cartoons.

But, Drake added, where ordinary cartoon shorts were concerned, there would be absolutely no change in the rules. Walt would continue to get sole credit. Drake looked at the discontented faces and shrugged his shoulders. Yes, it was tough. But that was the way Walt wanted it.

One of the animators spoke up. His name was Arthur (Art) Babbitt. Among the memorable cartoon characters he had invented was the foolish, feckless hound, Goofy. He had also been responsible for the oriental dance of the mushrooms in the Nutcracker Suite segment of *Fantasia*, and many other lively cartoon inventions.

Now Babbitt asked why Walt himself had not come to explain his attitude to the animators? Since they had moved into the new studio, they hardly ever saw him. Everything was done through go-betweens like Drake or Sharpsteen or (grimace) Gunther Lessing. Was Walt avoiding them?

"No way," Drake said. "He's too busy. He's got more important things on his mind."

"Such as?" Babbitt asked.

"Money," Drake said. He hesitated and then added, "We may be in trouble. And it's serious this time."

AS MENTIONED IN the previous chapter, the outbreak of World War II in Europe had blighted the prospects of Walt's latest feature films, *Fantasia, Pinocchio,* and *Bambi,* and turned potential profits into heavy losses. And it had happened at a particularly unfortunate moment. Roy Disney had borrowed heavily from the banks to complete the move to the new studios on Buena Vista, hoping profits from the three new features would take care of it. But now the repayment was due, and there was no money. He had called in Walt to tell him that the $1,500,000 in their joint bank account was already spoken for, and they were $4,500,000 in debt to their creditors. Walt had once thought the world was coming to an end a few years ago when the studio was in hock for a mere twenty thousand. Now he was really in despair. They couldn't possibly find such a massive sum. The specter of bankruptcy stared them in the face, and he could hardly bear to think about what it could mean to Lilly, his two children, and his thousand loyal employees.

"What the hell are we going to do?" he asked.

If he hadn't felt so desperate, he might have noticed that his brother seemed much more cheerful about the situation than he did. In fact, from Roy Disney's point of view the situation had its advantages—as well as its solutions. Over the years, being a practical moneyman, he had been trying to persuade his brother to turn Walt Disney Productions into a public company and offer shares on the open market. Walt had always turned him down because he maintained the change would mean that outsiders would have a say in future decisions, which he had always reserved for himself.

Now Roy told Walt they would have to go public. It was the only way out. In fact, he had already talked over the situation with Gunther Lessing, who prophesied hard times ahead for Disney as the war situation worsened in Europe. Lessing was all for cutting back on staff and production and for an immediate reduction in the wages of the staff who were retained. But Roy knew it wasn't going to be as easy as that. Walt, as the paternal head of the studio, concerned for the welfare of his staff, would never stand for wholesale firing and salary cuts. Not so long as he was in charge.

But could he continue to object once Walt Disney Productions was a public company, responsible to its shareholders for its balance sheet? Especially if, once the public company was established, the staff could be persuaded that Disney was in a much worse financial situation than was actually the case and that wholesale firings and wage reductions were the only way out?

Walt was reluctantly persuaded to accept what seemed the only solution to their financial problems, and Walt Disney Productions offered 755,000 units of common stock and preferred shares to the public in April 1940, at prices ranging from five dollars to twenty-five dollars a share. They were quickly sold out, enabling Walt Disney Productions to pay off its outstanding loans of $4,500,000 and build up a working capital of $3,500,000.*

The studio was saved. The pump had been primed with public money. Once more they had credit at the bank. It was obvious that though they would have to be careful in the future, there was now no reason to ordain savage reductions in staff and wages. But did Walt realize this?

This is where the upholders of Walt Disney's image bring an element of conspiracy into the affair. They suggest that Roy Disney deliberately led Walt to believe that the public launching of the company had by no means solved the studio's financial problems, that wholesale staff dismissals and wage cuts would still be necessary.

Knowing Walt would accept widespread firing only to save the studio, Roy (according to these stories) concealed the real facts of the situation from both his brother and from the studio employees. He encouraged rumors of disaster and provoked panic among those who feared for their

---

*Walt, Roy, Lilly, and Edna retained large blocks of shares for themselves.

jobs. It was necessary to prepare them for the worst, Roy decided. They would go more willingly that way.

IF HE REALLY believed that, it was a gross misjudgment of their reactions. Instead of inducing a mood of fatalism around the studio, it sounded a clarion call to the unions. Hitherto, they had regarded the Walt Disney Studio as the Rock of Gibraltar, impregnable to assault mainly because of the work force's faith in the integrity of Walt Disney himself. They knew that if things were really as bad as studio rumors had it, one thing was certain: the employees would stand by Walt and accept any cuts he decided to make, no matter how Draconian.

But then someone inside the office leaked the true state of Disney's financial status to the union leaders: the company wasn't broke at all! Walt Disney, the trusted boss, was pulling a fast one on his work force, deliberately deceiving them. Word quickly spread through the Buena Vista headquarters that Walt had tricked them and that if personnel wanted to save their jobs, they had better sign up with the union right away. A sense of betrayal consumed many Disney workers, made worse by the sneers of the union organizers and their fellow workers at other studios.

"What about your Great White Father now that he's turned out to be a phony?" they gibed. "That's one thing you have to learn in this business: never trust the boss, trust the union instead."

At the beginning of 1941, Walt Disney and his brother received a visit from Herbert Sorrell, who presented them with an ultimatum. Sorrell was the tough-talking head of the Screen Cartoonists Guild, which was part of the Painters and Paperhangers Union, a powerful Hollywood affiliate of the AFL. He said he had signed up enough Disney employees to turn the studio into a union shop and needed the signed agreement of Walt and Roy Disney. Otherwise, he would declare an immediate strike.

"You can't do that," Roy protested. "Our employees don't want to sign up with you. All you do is bring them trouble. Anyway," he added, "what about the other union?"*

Walt refused to believe Sorrell had signed up the majority of his members. "They'd never do that to me," he said.

He called a meeting of all the studio personnel and pleaded with them not to strike. "He tried to play down the seriousness of the situation and made a joking sort of speech," said David Swift, a junior animator who was there at the time. "He put on his more-in-sorrow-than-in-anger act as the benevolent and understanding father of them all, and he treated them as

---

*There was indeed a rival union, called the Federation of Screen Cartoonists, but it was an industry-sponsored association and lacked both independence and muscle.

if they were wayward sons. To his astonishment, a large section of the crowd booed him, and he took that very badly. He had never been booed before."*

Next day when he met with Sorrell again, Walt insisted the question of a closed shop should be decided by a secret vote. "Don't talk to me about secret votes," Sorrell retorted, nettled. "It's taken me two years to get this place lined up. It's about time your workers learned what kind of a boss you really are. Now get this straight, Walt If you don't do a deal with me now, I'm going to strike you."

"Not till I've called the Labor Relations Board in Washington," Walt said, "and asked them to superintend a secret ballot."

"You just try that and see what happens," Sorrell said. "I can make a dust bowl out of your place here, Walt. I can pick up that telephone on your desk and make just one call and you'll be on unfair lists all over the country. I have connections." Indeed he had.

There was a picket line around the Buena Vista studio when Walt arrived one morning in May 1941, and he was catcalled as he drove through the gate. Posters and pickets proclaimed that the Walt Disney Studio was "unfair" and its workers were on strike. In fact, 60 percent of the studio staff crossed the lines that day, but 40 percent —some 400 plus workers—obeyed Sorrell's call, and Walt Disney recognized some of his most talented animators among them. One of them was Art Babbitt, the inventor of Goofy, but there was nothing goofy about his activities that, or any other, day. He had a megaphone in his hand, and he was organizing the concerted calls of the pickets.

One day, as he drove through the lines, Walt thought he heard Art Babbitt scream through his megaphone, "There he is—the man who believes in brotherhood for everybody but himself. Altogether now—booooooooo!"

Walt was annoyed at the raucous cries and deeply wounded by the charge and by the man who, he believed, screamed it at him. He even stopped his car and took off his jacket, intending to beat up the heckler but was restrained by a studio guard. Still fuming, he got back in his car. But he decided there and then that however the strike came out, of one thing he would make certain: Art Babbitt would never be forgiven, and he would never work for Walt Disney again.

---

*Later on, David Swift was booed, too, by his fellow workers and also found it a painful experience. He joined the strikers as their publicity man and stayed out with them until he became disenchanted by some of the labor racketeers behind the strike. So he told a public meeting of his fellow strikers that he was returning to work—which was when they catcalled him and vowed that, once the strike was over, they would see to it that he never worked in Hollywood again. In fact, when he came back from World War II, he made some of Walt Disney's most successful live-action films and is still directing in Hollywood.

"YES, IT WAS a deep wound that Walt suffered over the strike," Ward Kimball said. "It hurt him because guys he had trusted were letting him down. He always felt like the benign father who was giving us things, looking after us. Because this was the Depression and people didn't have jobs, and he had kept them all working. And he sort of felt that after all he had done, it was plain ingratitude to call a strike just because he wanted them to vote before joining a union.

"What he didn't know was what was going on in his own studio, he was shielded from the truth by the executives in between. For instance, he didn't know that there were guys making eighteen dollars a week and they couldn't even buy enough food for their families, and then George Drake would go to New York and hire a bunch of guys who'd come back with him—guys who hadn't even learned the cartoon business yet. Drake put them in the big room and ordered the eighteen-dollars-a-week guys to show these new guys how it was done. And the new guys were being paid fifty dollars a week. That sort of crap."

As strikes always do, this one began with jokes and cheerful give-and-take between the opposing parties; and at first, no one was prevented from crossing the picket lines. But Sorrell and Babbitt were effective organizers, and soon they were exerting pressure on Technicolor not to deliver or process film for Disney.

There were other boycotts spawning around the country. The insults got louder and nastier. There were scuffles and heated arguments around the picket lines. The strike took an ugly turn when a gang of pro-Disney workers drove up in trucks, carrying baseball bats and cans of gasoline. They sprinkled the gasoline in a circle around the pickets and threatened to set it afire if the strikers didn't move on. The strikers moved but came back the next day with police protection.

When the negotiators met, Sorrell packed the most militant of the Disney strikers around the table and goaded them into making increasingly strident demands. Walt was so appalled at the tone of hate and resentment in their voices that he came back to Lilly one evening in despair and said that he was resolved to pack it all in—he would close the Walt Disney Studio down and go into some other occupation.

News of his pessimistic mood soon reached Washington. Since it was no part of the New Deal's intentions to kill off Mickey Mouse and Donald Duck for the sake of humbling the popular Walt Disney, the administration decided that it was time to find a face-saver—but for him, not for the union. First, came an invitation to Walt Disney to go on a tour of South America as a goodwill ambassador of the United States. That solid capitalist, Nelson Rockefeller, Coordinator of Inter-American Affairs, was recruited to persuade Walt to undertake the mission as a patriotic American duty and to take animators and technicians with him so that he could make a cartoon down there with a Latin American theme—as a counter to pro-Nazi and anti-American propaganda in Brazil and other south American states.

"But what about this terrible strike?" Walt asked.

Rockefeller said he had been assured by the president that if Walt would leave it to the administration, they would arrange a settlement agreeable to all concerned.

"You mean the unions will get what they want?" Walt asked.

"It's the climate of the times," Rockefeller agreed. "This is a battle you can't win."

Walt finally agreed to go, grimly resigned to what government conciliation would achieve during his absence. He was now sure that he would be defeated, that things would never again be the same between him and his technicians. In an open letter, which he wrote just before taking off for Brazil, he said bitterly:

> To me, the entire situation is a catastrophe. The spirit that played such an important part in the building of the cartoon medium has been destroyed. . . . The Union refused to use the ballot to give people here the right to determine their choice. In turning down the ballot, they said, to use their own words, "We might lose that way. If we strike, we know we will win."

He added:

> The cards were all stacked against me, so for the time being I have capitulated, but, believe me, I'm not licked—I'm incensed. The lies, the twisted half-truths that were placed in the public prints cannot be easily forgotten. I was called a rat, a yellow-dog employer and an exploiter of labor. . . . My plant and my methods were compared to a sweat-shop, and above all, I was accused of rolling in wealth. That hurt me most, when the fact is that every damned thing I have is tied up in this business.

Then he revealed what the strike had done to his political outlook, and how it was going to affect his attitude toward his workers in future.

> I am convinced that this entire mess was Communistically inspired and led. The People's World, the League of Women Shoppers, the American Peace Mobilization and every Communistic outfit in the country were the first to put me on their unfair list. The legitimate American Federation of Labor unions were the last and they were reluctant to move.
>
> I am thoroughly disgusted and would gladly quit and establish myself in another business if it were not for the loyal guys who believe in me—so I guess I'm stuck with it. . . . I have a case of the D.D.s—disillusionment and discouragement.

He flew to South America in the summer of 1941 with Lilly, and his mood was black. It was while he was still filming in Brazil that a cable arrived to tell him that the strike had been settled. As part of the terms, the Walt Disney Studio would not only become an AFL union shop but wages and the work force would be maintained. Moreover, Walt Disney would no longer have the monopoly of credits on the short cartoons. His animators and artists would also get their due recognition.

"Ironically enough," Walt said later, "the union never even bothered to ratify the agreement. But I insisted on swallowing the terms whole. I told Roy he must never employ a nonunion man in the studio again. I even insisted that the gardeners join the union, and saw to it that it was one that would pay them the top rate. I accepted every single thing they forced on me." With one exception.

When the strike leader, Art Babbitt, came back to the studio after the strike to resume his old job, he was stopped at the gate and told he could not come in. He would have to sue the studio before he was allowed to work there again. "Okay, so we'll sue," Babbitt said.

16
Bad War

ONE DAY IN 1940, some months before the traumatic Disney strike, Walt's secretary, Dolores Voght, broke into a busy afternoon to say there was a man to see him. "Didn't I tell you not to interrupt me?" Walt asked, irritably. "I haven't time for anyone. Get him to state his name, business and make an appointment."

"His name is Ub Iwerks," Dolores said. "And I have an idea he is looking for a job."

Walt Disney bounded to his feet and opened the door of the outer office. "Ubbe!" he exclaimed, then grinned, adding, "My God, I never thought I'd be pleased to see you, you bastard! Come on in." Ten years had passed since his erstwhile partner had quit the Disney company. In the intervening decade they had gone their separate ways, Ub Iwerks to open his own small cartoon studio as a rival to Walt Disney Productions. Their operations were only a few miles apart, but they had rarely encountered each other, and when they did, at Oscar ceremonies and official movie occasions, they had nodded distantly across crowded rooms.

But, in fact, both had kept in touch with the other's doings. When Ub, by then head of Ub Iwerks Studio, had signed up with MGM to distribute his *Flip the Frog* series, Walt had sneaked into a downtown Los Angeles movie house to see the first showing but sent no telegram himself.

That was perhaps because he had liked it but couldn't bear to say so—it will be remembered he never praised anyone's work but his own. In any case, he had no interest in Ub's successes but did seem to get a kind of sadistic satisfaction out of hearing of his setbacks. According to rumors in the industry, they had been increasing lately, and a story was going around that Ub's whole operation was in trouble. Since Walt always swore he would never forgive his friend for the disloyalty he had shown him, he had hardly appeared downcast by the reports of Ub's difficulties. "Serve the bastard right," he told Roy when he heard the bad news.

Though he would never have admitted it, however, he missed Ub and felt for him in his misfortune. From the days of their first encounter in Kansas City, the shy, gentle, talented Dutchman had filled some sort of gap in his life, and it had not been closed by the passage of time.

It was a gap for both of them; regret over the breach between the two men was mutual. But because of the dependent nature of his character, Ub Iwerks had probably missed Walt the most and was like a dish lacking a vital ingredient without him. He had always needed Walt; and at the same time had always resented him for his brash, flashy, thoughtlessly self-confident and self-contained ways. But the years of estrangement from Walt had made Ub fatalistically aware that he was not a full man without him. Now they faced each other across Walt Disney's office like two old lovers who had bitterly quarreled and parted years ago over something that they could hardly remember and wondered now why it had been so wounding at the time.

"I suppose you've heard the news," Ub said. "It's happened again. I just don't seem to be able to manage on my own. I'm closing down the studio, and you were the only one I could think of to come to for help. I have debts to pay off and I have to find a job."

"How much do you need?" Walt asked, reaching for his checkbook. "And when can you start? You know we can always find you a job here. I'll fix up an office for you."

"Thank you, but that won't be necessary," Ub said. "But I would like to use your workshops. I have some new ideas about optics and animation that might be helpful, and I'm sure I can improve the quality of present-day cartoons. Maybe even yours," he added, apologetically.

He neither asked for, nor was he given, the say he had once had in the running of the Walt Disney Studio. He rarely went near the animators' rooms, where once he had been the busiest and best of them all. Roy Disney viewed his return with a mixture of scorn, contempt, and dismay. Roy carefully refrained from reminding his brother that if Ub Iwerks had held on to the block of shares Walt had once given him, he could have sold them in the market, now that Disney was a public company, and made himself millions. And he made no comment when, out of company funds, Walt paid off Ub's outstanding debts and provided him with a fully equipped workshop where he could experiment with cameras and animation techniques.

When Ub moved back into the Disney organization, no word was ever mentioned of the situation that had caused the rift with Walt. It was as if it had never happened. He stayed quietly loyal and supportive during the strike, walking casually through the picket lines as if they were not there. During the following years he produced some invaluable technical improvements in lenses and coloring methods for cels and pioneered other ways of making Disney cartoons more lifelike and simpler to produce. None of the strikers catcalled Ub when he crossed the picket lines. They probably did not even notice him.

As the years passed, he came to be accepted as a popular, good-humored, gentle, patient member of the staff, and his younger associates would have been astonished to learn that he had once been so consumed with jealousy of Walt Disney that he would like to have killed him—and had once nearly broken Walt's heart by deserting him.

They would also have found it hard to believe that Ub and Walt had once been such bosom friends, for much of the intimacy had now gone out of their relationship. But so had the tension and animosity. They had become like an old married couple, aware of the weaknesses and faults in each other that had once driven them to distraction but now willing for the sake of peace to put up with them and do it with comradeship and good humor.

One day, Walt was walking through the grounds with an acquaintance and passed the studio garage, where Ub had his head under the hood of his car. "Look at that guy," Walt said, with mock indignation. "Working hours yet, and instead of calling in a mechanic, he wastes the company's time tinkering with his auto. That's what you get when you employ Ub Iwerks, the greatest animator in the world!" At that moment, Ub's head came up for air, and his oil-streaked face broke into a delighted grin as he recognized his boss.

"Hi, Walt!" he called out happily. "Just tuning up the old jalopy!"

"When you've finished, have a look at mine!" Walt replied. "It's falling to pieces."

This was during the embittered years, when Walt Disney was rarely amiable with anyone around the studio. Yet the acquaintance doing the rounds with him said the tone of Walt's voice and the expression on his face as he spoke to Ub Iwerks was one of unalloyed affection. "He obviously loved that guy," he said.

ONE OF THE cartoons on which Walt was working when the studio went on strike was a sentimental story about a baby elephant named Dumbo. Originally, Walt had planned it as a half-hour long/short, but the chief animators who labored on it and drew the original storyline, including Norm Ferguson, filled it with such effective and touching incidents that it eventually came in at sixty-four minutes—at a cost of $800,000.

When they saw it, the RKO salesmen were dismayed and asked Walt to cut it. He refused. They then took their complaints to Roy. In their view it was not a salable production, being too long to sell as a short and not long enough to sell as a feature. Roy called Walt into his office and gravely reminded him that they were in hock to the banks and badly needed every penny they could lay their hands on.

"And here you are," he complained, "spending nearly a million dollars on a cartoon no one can sell. I'm talking about *Dumbo*. It may be about a baby elephant, kid, but as far as the box office is concerned, it's neither fish, fowl, nor red herring. It's not going to fly unless you make it a salable size—when at least we'll get something back."

"Have you seen it?" Walt asked.

"I don't need to see it," Roy said. "I only know the exhibitors won't buy it unless you stretch it to feature length."

"No way," Walt said, firmly. "It's a little gem just as it is. Adding anything more would ruin it."

"Then cut it, for Christ's sake," Roy said. "You know what the renters are like—anything less than eighty minutes is box office poison. All you can sell it as is a B-film—and how much are we gonna earn from that? We need cash, Walt—every penny we can grab . . . and fast. I want you to stretch that cartoon or cut it down to a fifteen-minute short—and please hurry!"

"Not until after you've seen it, Roy," Walt said. "Let's go and screen it now. I'd like your reaction."

"Okay," Roy said, reluctantly. Then he added, "But I'll tell you this. Even if it's the classiest movie you ever made, it's not gonna change my mind. The renters just won't buy a first feature that's less than eighty minutes."

But they did.

After Walt had screened him a run-through of *Dumbo* in the studio sweatbox, even Roy had to admit that this one was special. It had three touching scenes that have since become classics so far as animation films are concerned. There was the so-called "trunk touching" scene, after Dumbo's mother has been chained up as a mad elephant after trying to protect her flap-eared offspring. Dumbo makes a secret night visit to his mother and fondles her trunk through the cage. The sequence was drawn by Bill Tytla and executed with such tenderness that it probably evoked more tears in the movie theater than anything since Mary Pickford in *Daddy Longlegs*. Fred Moore drew an ingenious sequence between Dumbo and Timothy Mouse, when the clowns spill liquor into a bath full of water, and Dumbo drinks some and begins to hiccup. Then the mouse falls into the bath. And there was the Pink Elephant sequence in the film, conceived with a glow of real fantasy by animator Howard Swift.

Roy Disney said nothing to his brother after he had seen the run-through of *Dumbo*. But he went straight back to his office and told the RKO salesmen to sell the new cartoon exactly as it was. "And," he added,

"I want the same fees for it as you get for a special feature—and to hell with its length. This one is special."

In 1941, Walt Disney and his party flew back from Panama, the last leg of their South American trip, by way of New York and attended the world premiere of *Dumbo* there. It was an immediate hit and became so popular that it subsequently made the Disney studio a profit of over a million dollars.

IF WALT DISNEY had made it up with Ub Iwerks and resumed a warm and special relationship with him, that could hardly be said about his attitude toward the studio employees who had struck him. Them he would never forgive. The strike, in fact, had soured him and turned him mean.

Back from South America came a changed man. He was rough with nearly everybody around him at the studio. He discovered the girls in the inking department had a preference for cookies with their morning coffee, so he ordered the catering department to cut down on the supply. During the midmorning break, a lot of the animators had been in the habit of playing volleyball. He had the nets taken out. And time clocks were installed. Despite the agreement with the union to freeze wages and staff, he instituted a 10 percent cut in salaries and let scores of workers go. The union sued to get Art Babbitt's job back, and Walt assigned Gunther Lessing to fight the case.

Lessing felt as malevolent toward the strikers as Walt did. He had not forgiven them for hanging his effigy on a telephone pole outside the studio and setting fire to it. When Art Babbitt's case came up, his shrewder colleagues advised him to read the rules of the National Labor Relations Board, pointing out that under the terms of the settlement, the union could insist that every striker, no matter who, be given his job back.

"Okay, if they have to have their pound of flesh," Lessing said, "then let them spill some blood in getting it."

It was Walt Disney's blood they spilled. After a messy case in which a slew of young lawyers from Washington ran rings around Lessing, Babbitt was ordered reinstated. But Walt saw to it that things were never the same for him. His days as a creative cartoonist (at least as far as Disney was concerned) were over, and the other animators, fearful of Walt's wrath, carefully avoided him. It was a lonely time.

When the war came, Babbitt joined up. His qualifications were sufficient for him to be made an officer, but each time he was considered for officer status, he was refused a commission. It was not until the war was over that Babbitt found out why. Someone (whether Walt or Lessing he never did discover) had informed the War Department that he was a dangerous Marxist and likely to spread unrest among the troops if he was given any authority. So he stayed in the ranks for the duration of the conflict.

When he came home, he applied once more for reinstatement at Disney and was reluctantly given his job back. But conditions had not changed in the slightest, and he could feel the waves of unfriendliness all around him. The air froze when Walt came anywhere near.

Out of touch and out of sympathy with the laws of the new regime in Washington, Lessing had long since been demoted, and his only opportunity to show off his former power was to make life impossible for the reinstated rebels.

"It was kind of pitiful," Ward Kimball said. "Gunther had become a shadow. He'd come to the office every day with an umbrella, like it was going to rain at any moment. He always wore his hat to conceal the fact he'd lost most of his hair—and when he took it off, the timberline separating what hair he had left from the bald part was way down here. He had a fringe but it wasn't long enough to grow over the top—and he was always combing it when he thought you weren't looking, in the vain hope he could cover up the gaping dome. Pathetic. But God, even when he was hairless, he could still be just as vindictive!"

Babbitt found his life made so miserable and so involved in unnecessary litigation that, in the end, he left Disney and went to work elsewhere. But the damaging report about his supposed political affiliations dogged him until his retirement. It was almost certainly Lessing who had put the FBI on to him and ruined his career, but Babbitt placed the blame squarely on the shoulders of Walt Disney. Like Walt, the strike had soured a hitherto amiable character and warped his sense of judgment. The irony in Babbitt's case was that he even developed a contempt for Walt's achievements as a cartoonist—in the creation of which he had once played so important a part—and professed to despise the standards of both the movies and those who flocked to see them. "Walt Disney had the innate bad taste of the American public," he liked to say.

IF THE IMPACT of the strike had left Walt Disney bruised and resentful, what happened once the United States became involved in World War II exacerbated his feeling that the administration was singling him out for persecution. On December 7, 1941, a few hours after the announcement of the bombing of Pearl Harbor, a security guard telephoned Walt at home to inform him that units of the U.S. Army had occupied the Buena Vista studio.* Overriding all protests, they drove straight to the main sound stage, threw out the camera and audio equipment, and set up the

---

*His was the only Hollywood studio to be singled out in this way, and it is still not clear why.

space as a repair shop for trucks and guns. The parking lot became an ammo dump, and other buildings were annexed as dorms for the troops. The explanation given was the need to have a headquarters from which they could protect southern California from an invasion by the Japanese.

In vain did Walt and Roy protest that they were already, for all intents and purposes, working for the government and, therefore, deserved some consideration. Walt had paid all the expenses for himself and his crew during the government goodwill mission he had led to South America.* He had since been producing instruction films for the Lockheed Aircraft Corporation and the Canadian government. And within hours of the Pearl Harbor disaster, the U.S. Navy was on the phone from Washington asking him to make a series of films training personnel in enemy aircraft identification.

But the army stayed in full occupation at Buena Vista for nearly a year and left skeleton units behind when they finally left. Space was also preempted by the government for outside companies working on service contracts. In cramped quarters, hemmed in on one side by troops and the other by Lockheed assembly shops, the animators practically abandoned commercial moviemaking for the duration and concentrated on producing instructional and propaganda cartoons. Walt complained, after a trip to Washington, that his efforts were not appreciated by the administration.,

"They can't seem to recognize what sacrifices I'm making to help the war effort," he said. "I pointed out we have abandoned three major cartoon features [*Peter Pan, Alice in Wonderland,* and *Wind in the Willows*] to make propaganda shorts for them, and some snooty secretary had the sauce to say other Americans were making sacrifices, too—some with their lives. As if all of us aren't willing to die for our country if they ask us to! Then I showed the cans of film I'd made of Donald Duck persuading citizens to pay their taxes and that Jew, Henry Morgenthau [he was secretary of the Treasury], had the nerve to complain it had run over budget and he didn't think Donald Duck was a typical taxpayer anyway.† I had to tell him what it meant to be given Donald's services for free and what it was going to cost us in ordinary commercial cartoon rentals. I had to tell him Donald Duck was worth more at the box office than Greta Garbo. Do you think Louie Mayer would have lent him Garbo—for nothing?"

The most costly fun Walt had during the war was producing a cartoon

---

*It was true that he more than recouped these expenses by exploiting two cartoon films he had made on the trip, *Saludos Amigos!* and *The Three Caballeros.*

†Called *The New Spirit,* the cartoon was so much in demand that hundreds of extra copies had to be made by Technicolor, whose charges inflated the original budget. Far from turning off tardy and reluctant taxpayers, the fact that Donald Duck dutifully paid his taxes made millions of potential dodgers reach for their checkbooks.

feature called *Victory Through Air Power*, based on Alexander de Seversky's 1942 book of the same name. Seversky was an ex-Russian pilot from World War I, who passionately believed the bomber plane was the secret weapon for winning future wars, and Walt Disney became his most fervent disciple. He asked the government in Washington to let him make a cartoon version of Seversky's book (with the administration financing the project, of course), but he was turned down—chiefly because navy officers were irked by Seversky's obvious contempt for the role of the navy in general and battleships in particular in winning wars. They strenuously lobbied against any government financing for such an antinavy project. So Walt decided to make it as a private Disney movie. Ward Kimball was called in to animate the flying sequences and later said that he "had a ball animating the early history of flight."

Victory Through Air Power was put out as a Disney entertainment feature but was never accepted as such by the moviegoing public, who were inclined to swallow the suggestion of navy publicists that it was "just air force propaganda."* It lost the studio nearly half a million dollars at a moment when they could ill afford it. Forced to cancel all plans for feature-length cartoons for the duration, pinned down to prewar rental rates for commercial cartoon shorts, and out of pocket on most of the government-sponsored propaganda films they had made, the Walt Disney Studio finished World War II badly in the red.

UNLIKE THE REST of Hollywood, which had made millions pouring out entertainment features (and any old trash made money in those days), they owed close to five million dollars by the time the war ended. Only Joseph Rosenberg of the Bank of America had saved them from going out of business. He had won praise for his shrewdness in backing *Snow White* at a time when its prospects seemed shaky, and its subsequent worldwide success had turned him into an overnight expert on the animated cartoon industry.

Now he went to his boss, A. P. Giannini, and persuaded him to keep the credit flowing. That did not mean, however, that there was now enough money available to finance feature-length cartoons of *Peter Pan* and *Alice in Wonderland*. They would need a budget of nearly two million dollars each, and even the Bank of America was not prepared to take the risk of advancing that much. It was true that *Fantasia, Bambi, Snow White*, and *Pinocchio* had begun to get the showings in Europe that had been interrupted by the war; but the big box office receipts from them, particularly

---

*Though Winston Churchill, who was given a private showing, thought it was "a superb film" and boosted it to Roosevelt.

in Britain, were blocked by postwar regulations forbidding currency exports. There was only enough money available to the Disney studio for the most modest postwar ventures.

And modest they were. Mediocre too, many of them. Walt finished the war deflated, downhearted, and short-tempered. He was depressed to find himself surrounded in Hollywood by smug film men from all the other studios who had grown fat and prosperous turning out pap for the undiscriminating multitudes, while he, who had striven so hard to keep up his standards, had emerged from the war on the verge of penury.

He was particularly downcast one day when a studio chief, whose capabilities he particularly despised, called him up and offered him the millions he needed to make *Peter Pan* and *Alice*—but only if he agreed to sell out his operation to him. "Can you imagine that?" Walt stormed. "Letting that fat Jew rescue me from bankruptcy . . . just because he made all those crooked millions out of the war!"

Disappointment and resentment seemed to bring out his latent anti-Semitism. He was often heard making snide comments about the Jews, whose success seemed to infuriate him. When David Swift, the young animator who had returned to work during the strike, announced that he had been offered a better job at Columbia Pictures, Walt was annoyed at his departure but seemingly too proud to offer him rewards for staying on.

"He called me in, finally," Swift said later, "and putting on a phony Jewish accent he said, 'Okay, Davy Boy, off you go to work with those Jews. It's where you belong, with those Jews.' And when I came back to him later after the war, he was still resentful. 'Well, Bud,' he said, at the first studio meeting I went to, 'you can see we didn't come to any harm while you were away with those Jews. We got on quite well without you. We don't need you—and it looks as if those Jews don't need you, either.'"

The bleak situation over money drained him of his dynamic. Misery and worry brought out the worst in him, and he was apt to blame everybody—Jews, blacks, Commies, union workers—for his misfortunes. He was brusque at home and rough with Lilly. He punished his two daughters with painful spankings for disobedience. He even began to have violent quarrels (usually over money) with Roy, and though they always made up later, some sediment of bitterness remained behind.

He was surrounded by a good deal of subbrilliant talent at the studio, since many of his best artists were still in the armed forces, and after repeatedly excoriating the worst of his animators for incompetence, he seemed to lose interest, and to lapse into a kind of apathy. He became so apathetic, in fact, that he even gave up on Mickey Mouse and abandoned him as his talisman of good luck. In the modest program of cartoon shorts that he now agreed to inaugurate, he did make one more attempt to revive the appeal of the Mighty Mouse, but it is an indication of his mental state that he allowed Donald Duck and Goofy to play roles in the production, which meant that though it was called *Mickey and the Beanstalk,* the two more outrageous cartoon characters inevitably stole the movie away from the mouse.

What unmistakably revealed Walt's low state of mind was his decision not to dub Mickey's voice himself, as he had always done in the past. He said his smoker's cough had lowered the tone of his voice and made it difficult to achieve Mickey's high falsetto, and he turned the dubbing over to Jim Macdonald. It wasn't the same, and Mickey Mouse began to die from that moment on.*

AMONG OTHER THINGS troubling Walt was guilt over his father, Elias, who had died at the age of eighty-two while Walt was away on his South American trip. Why hadn't he rushed back to be with the old man in his final hours? It was true that he had never loved his father, had always preferred his mother, but his failure to return for Elias's death and funeral nagged at him and was an affront to his sense of filial propriety.

Walt was bored and disenchanted with everybody and everything, particularly cartooning. One of the films on which he had begun work when the studio strike hit him was a cartoon version of the Felix Salten book about a baby deer, *Bambi.* It was an all-animal film, and Walt wanted to try some new experiments in animation—and it did not go well to begin with. He had picked a quartet of his youngest and newest animators, Frank Thomas, Ollie Johnston, Milt Kahl, and Eric Larson, to give him the fantasy qualities he wanted; and they failed to satisfy him.

Although *Bambi* was started before *Fantasia, Pinocchio,* and *Dumbo* it was not until 1942 that it was publicly shown. Walt later thought *Bambi* was one of the most beautiful films he had ever made and would openly cry whenever he saw it. But at first, the public did not agree, and it took some time for the film to become profitable.

One of his great ambitions had been to make a sequel to his classical musical feature, *Fantasia;* but the war in Europe and public apathy at home, resulting in the failure of the first release at the box office, had put paid to that. Now, Roy, irritated and alarmed at his brother's lack of energy and enthusiasm, tried to pump Walt up by stimulating him into reviving the plan for a *Fantasia* sequel.

Unfortunately, having piqued his brother's interest, he then spoiled

---

*In 1968, in Paris, the British artist, Ronald Searle, did a drawing of Mickey Mouse for his fortieth birthday. He drew him with a considerable paunch, a distinct stoop, and no teeth. When they saw it, many of his old animators said that was how Walt himself regarded Mickey during those gray postwar days.

everything by revealing it was not a real sequel that he was proposing. He visualized a cut-rate series of "musical" shorts—which was all they could afford at the time. His idea was "popular" music numbers with singers like Dinah Shore, Nelson Eddy, and the Andrews Sisters. As a sop to Walt's musical pretensions, Roy went on to propose that the series include a single cartoon with a "serious" classical theme.

In the early days of the war, one of the visitors to Burbank had been the Russian composer Sergei Prokofiev, who told Walt that he had been so impressed with the qualities of *Fantasia* that he hoped to see a subsequent edition including a composition of his own. To that end, he said, he had composed a special piece of music and was entrusting it to Walt Disney's care for him to use whenever he was able to make his sequel.

At which point he had handed over the manuscript of *Peter and the Wolf*, which had never been performed in public at that time. Walt was extremely touched by the gesture and had taken it to the music department to be played over, something which both stimulated and depressed him. *Peter and the Wolf* was a natural for the cartoon screen, and he was downcast because he already knew that there would be no new edition of *Fantasia* in which he could include it.

Nevertheless, he promised the composer that he would make it one of these days and extracted a pledge from Prokofiev that he would come back for the first performance, when they would settle his contract (Prokofiev had refused to discuss it at the time) and pay him handsomely for the privilege of using his music.

Now, with Roy's offer, the opportunity had arrived, and it was such a temptation that Walt was persuaded to produce the other cartoons, which he rightly suspected would be dull and tasteless, in order to make it. He put Ward Kimball to work on the Prokofiev, and Kimball came up with some lively barnyard inventions, in particular a mischievous duck and a feisty and temperamental cat as well as a highly eccentric wolf. But the "popular" musical items in the series were extremely dreary, lacking all sense of fun or liveliness. In the end they were all combined into a cartoon feature called *Make Mine Music** and released to the movie theaters in 1946. The film had a success that was less than modest. Neither the nonmusical hoi polloi nor the addicts of classical works found it palatable.

Except for the *Peter and the Wolf* segment, Walt thought it was execrable and was tempted to fire the animators on the spot. One consolation was that Prokofiev failed to turn up for the premiere of the movie. Nor did he appear (though Walt was present) at the first public performance of

---

*Later known as the 3Ms movie: Messy, Maudlin, and Miserable

Peter and the Wolf by Koussevitsky and the Boston Symphony Orchestra.

The composer never did come back, in fact, and all Disney attempts to communicate with him or pay him fees and royalties went unanswered. But after his death, someone—it has never been revealed who—turned up with the necessary authorization and collected the money.

In 1946, Walt Disney finally managed to borrow enough money from the banks to make another feature film, and it indicated the way he would soon be going. It was his version of a book from his childhood reading, *Uncle Remus,* which he called *Song of the South,* and the special ingredient in it was that he reverted to his earliest days as a moviemaker and made it a production combining both cartoon figures and live-action characters. *Song of the South* had a lavish world premiere in Atlanta, Georgia, and subsequently scored a big success throughout the United States. One of its songs, "Zip-a-dee-doo-dah," won the Oscar for the best movie song of 1946.

But the film had been extremely expensive to make and despite big box office returns from everywhere it was shown, Roy sourly pointed out profits were modest in the extreme. Still, bored as he was with cartoon films, *Song of the South* had given Walt Disney a renewed taste for films with real people. The trouble was, real-people movies cost a lot of money. How was he to get around that?

What about *real animals*? You didn't have to pay *real animals*.

17
Brotherly Breach

GROUCHY AND MEAN with his wife and children at home, contemptuous and insulting to his brother Roy, ill-tempered and spiteful with his staff at the office, Walt Disney was in such a state by 1947 that Lilly, convinced that he was at the cusp of a second nervous breakdown and fearful that he might overdose himself with sleeping pills more thoroughly this time, persuaded him to consult a doctor about his condition. All the doctor could suggest was that he try to forget his problems at the studio and go away for a "change of air."

Walt decided to take a trip to Alaska, where he had already commissioned nature photographers Elma and Alfred Milotte to make a travelogue. It would give him a chance to look over their work. He asked his wife to come with him and bring their daughters along, but in the end Lilly, whose own nerves were becoming frayed from the unhappy atmosphere around the house, arranged to send Diane off to summer camp and dropped out of the trip herself at the last minute, glad to be rid of Walt and his troubles for a time.

He flew north to Nome with Sharon, and they ran into some hazardous flying conditions, including a heavy landing that bruised his neck and gave Sharon nightmares. But they did see Mount McKinley and some other dramatic scenery and came back with interesting photographs that he had taken of the Alaskan fauna, particularly the seals.

It was his delight with his own seal pictures that made him look with special interest at the seal sequences included in the enormous footage the Milottes had shot in Alaska. After a series of showings to selected groups in California, he began to describe these sequences, which were both spectacular and diverting, as "really a true-life adventure." He was sharp enough to sense that the moviegoing public was becoming interested in the world around it, of which it had still seen too little, and knew that if he found a new cinematic angle on nature films and a good selling title for a movie series to go with it, he might well be able to mine a productive seam. He took the Milottes' footage and threw away the bulk of it, retaining only the seal segments.

These he assembled as a short nature film, which he entitled *Seal Island*, and announced it as the first in Walt Disney's *True-Life Adventure* series. For the moment he had no idea what kind of *True-Life Adventure* he would follow it with, except that the films would have to be longer than *Seal Island*, which the RKO salesmen said they would have difficulty in peddling to movie managers because it fitted into no recognized rental category, neither program short nor special feature.

Not for the first time they were mistaken. He was sufficiently encouraged by audience response to begin sending out cameramen to remote spots all over the globe to shoot spectacular nature and animal sequences for him. Walt's problem with nature filmmakers, to begin with, according to his daughter Diane, was that they were all free lances, and they were inclined to be stingy with film because they had to pay for it themselves. Walt persuaded them to "shoot, shoot, and keep on shooting," guaranteeing that he would pay their bills for everything.*

One of the cameramen came despondently back from Canada with millions of feet of backwoods material but doubted if there was anything interesting there at all. But when Walt ran it through, he found the sequence that eventually became *Beaver Valley*. It showed a beaver trying to get a tree through a hole in the ice. He had to chew the tree into small bits, enlarge the hole, and push the bits through. It became a classic moment in films.

In fact, when *Beaver Valley* was shown, audiences clapped and cheered the segment when the beaver pushed the last bit of tree down the hole, and the film became a smash hit. Walt eventually followed it with a series of full-length *True-Life Adventures*, including *The Living Desert, the African Lion, The Vanishing Prairie,* and *The Secrets of Life*. No one had ever seen such vivid plant and animal photography before, and their popular success would make enough profit, eventually, to help pay for producing the two cartoon features that had been hanging around the studio for years, *Peter Pan* and *Alice*. (He still felt cartoons were vital to the financial well-being of the studio.) There also appeared to be enough money to finance a third, *Cinderella*. *Peter Pan* eventually made a modest profit and *Cinderella* did well both at the box office and with the critics, but *Alice*—which was started before but presented after *rella*—was a was a costly flop.

---

*Later, he equipped Alfred Milotte with a mobile, dustproof studio, which he used in Africa.

DESPITE ITS FAILURE at the box office, *Alice in Wonderland* was probably the most ingeniously experimental of all Walt's animated features. But it was probably ahead of its time—a conclusion that seems to be confirmed by the nice success it has had with audiences whenever it has been revived in recent years. It had been a promising project in Walt's mind ever since his earliest days, when, it will be remembered, he made the *Alice Comedies*, a series of live-action cartoons with Virginia Davis and, later, Margie Gay and cartoon figures. He had even considered making a live *Alice* film when he first came to Hollywood, with Mary Pickford in the title role, but she was preempted by another studio. Even so, he registered with the Academy his intention to make an animated version one day, but it was not until World War II was over that he had adequate funds to contemplate actually doing it.

The project ran into trouble practically from the start. For one thing, Walt did not grasp the subtle Englishness of the book and the fact that it was not one of those stories to which he could add his brilliant but quintessentially American touches of Disney imagination. *Alice* was vulnerable and would be ruined by the introduction of false notes or false characters.

Walt thought Alice herself was a bit dull and suggested that she be "livened up" by giving her a companion with whom she could get into comic situations and gag routines. His idea was to bring in the March Hare for this purpose, as a running character who would keep popping up at unexpected moments all through the film, lifting his top hat to Alice and saying, "Who ho!" and getting her out of scrapes. He was crushed when it was explained that he would be attacked for tampering with a classic.

His advisers were equally condemnatory of his attempts to subordinate Alice to other Carroll characters, and he took it badly. Thereafter, he edged away from the project altogether and gave his animators unexpected latitude and freedom to draw the characters as they saw them. They respectfully took a good deal of their inspiration from the original Tenniel drawings—with some brilliant variations. Frank Thomas, for instance, invented the famous doorknob sequence during which the comically animated doorknob remarks, "You did give me quite a turn!" when Alice opens a door into Wonderland. Jim Macdonald achieved miraculous effects in creating the menacing but gossamer quality in the cobweb sequence, and Josh Meador drew what was possibly the most difficult sequence of all: Alice floating in the bottle, skilfully calculated to suggest her tiny size (she has shrunk), and the consequent ocean vastness of the water in the bottle.

But difficulties supervened and production was interrupted several times. And when Walt did decide to examine the rushes he was dissatisfied. After four years' work and nearly three million drawings, he still had his doubts.

He decided to risk the wrath of the British critics and premiere the film in London. He wrote a note to his London office beforehand that hints at some of the apprehensions he was feeling about *Alice*'s prospects.

"Alice is just about wrapped up and I think it is about as good as can be done with it," he wrote. "I think it is going to be an exciting show. While it does have the tempo of a three-ring circus, it still has plenty of entertainment, and it should satisfy everyone except a certain handful who can never be satisfied."

He was hinting that he might be mauled by the critics. But when *Alice* opened at the Leicester Square Theatre on July 26, 1951, it was, on the whole, tolerantly received by the press, though one critic did suggest that it lacked "any sense of summer peace, the comfortable drowsy Victorian quietude that used to brood over these magic stories."

Moreover, the reaction of the public was cool; and when it subsequently opened in New York a few days later, it did not exactly click at the box office.

Roy Disney was appalled at the amount Walt was spending—and eventually losing—on *Alice* and one of the increasingly rancorous quarrels broke out between the brothers. Roy centered his grievances on the folly of trying to make *Alice* at all, a project he had been against from the beginning. He accused Walt of deliberately trying to ruin the company for the sake of indulging his extravagant whims.

"You just don't care about anything any longer," Roy exploded. "I kept telling you *Alice* would never catch on. You only made it to puff up your goddamned ego. Intellectual crap, that's all it is—and that's why you made it, to go over big with the eggheads and the critics."

To give him his due, Walt Disney had never made a film for an egghead or a critic in his life. His gift had been the unique one of sensing instinctively what would appeal to the common moviegoer of all ages. He did not need to be told that he had made a mistake in trying to tackle *Alice in Wonderland*. He said later that he really should have stopped production of *Alice* completely once he realized its pitfalls. But at the time, he didn't care enough to call a halt, and he allowed himself to be stuck with it, even if he knew it was a mistake.

So he found Roy's accusations particularly hurtful and insensitive. Financially speaking, they had more than a grain of truth in them, it was true. He didn't give a damn about making a moneyloser. Or, the way he was feeling lately, about anyone or anything anymore. Not even whether he lived or died.

The grim news of *Alice*'s failure, however, plunged him even deeper into depression, and Lilly worried about him. Soon *Alice*'s losses were estimated at more than two million dollars. They more than wiped out the profits that *Cinderella*'s success was beginning to bring into the studio and bit into the receipts being built up by the triumph of *Seal Island*.

Nor did the release of *Peter Pan* in 1953 do anything to relieve the financial crisis. Once more, Roy objected to the cost and even the idea of the production of *Peter Pan*. In any case, Walt's heart was no longer in it. Back before World War II, when he had first bought the rights to Barrie's play, he had thought the magic of this soaring boy who never grew up could be conveyed through the medium of the animated cartoon. But as he studied the story line and the animated sketches accompanying it, his original enthusiasm ebbed away; he decided that the title character never came to life or seemed believable to a modern audience. Nor could he seem to find the vigor and determination to make the concept work.

Therefore, he was neither surprised nor too downcast when the premiere of *Peter Pan* failed to galvanize the critics or bring lines to the theaters where it was shown. His wife, his brother, and his colleagues had never seen him so apathetic.

The therapy that snapped him out of his dangerous depression this time was all but anticlimactic. He found himself a hobby, and it was to stimulate, absorb, and soothe his nerves for the rest of his life.

WAY BACK IN 1938, Ward Kimball had bought himself a full-sized railroad train. "Those were the days," he said later, "when small Western railroads were innocently scrapping their historical equipment and selling the scrap iron to Japan for its secret munitions build-up. Since I was already a train buff, I decided to buy an 1881 locomotive and passenger car for around five hundred dollars, and have it shipped down from Nevada to our two-acre backyard in San Gabriel (our place had once been part of an orange grove). With the help of friends, I restored the train to its original Victorian splendor. Walt came to one of our early steam-ups and when I invited him to take a turn at the locomotive throttle I noticed his expression was like a kid in a candy store. Walt, as it turned out, was secretly a railroad buff himself, having sold papers on trains in Missouri when he was a boy."

Ollie Johnston, the animator, was another train buff around the studio. Now, while moiling in the depths of his latest depression, Walt recovered some of his spirit when Kimball and Johnston told him about the latest craze among railroad hobbists. Model makers had begun building half-sized steam locomotives, and Walt was intrigued enough to decide to construct one of his own. It eventually became a scale model for his estate in Holmby Hills.

"It was here that he started throwing his own railroad-type parties, inviting a few close friends to ride on his miniature train," Kimball said. "Sometimes he would ask me to come out and take care of running the train while he was busy making ice-cream sodas in his own full-sized soda fountain by the pool. I remember one party in particular because it had a rather bizarre guest list headed by actress Una Merkel, the agent Jules Stine (whom Walt kept calling "The Octopus") and Salvador Dali, the surrealist."*

So great did Walt's fascination with trains become that when he began planning the building of Disneyland in California, he was determined it should have its own railroad. But what kind? Kimball recalled a trip he made to Los Gatos with Walt and Eddie Sargent to inspect some small-sized trains that had hauled people around the 1916 Panama-Pacific Exposition in San Francisco. "Later, we all went to Trader Vic's in Oakland for an early dinner. This was before Walt began hosting his weekly Disneyland TV show, and most people had no idea what he looked like. The maitre d' at Trader Vic's didn't know Walt from Adam and wouldn't let him in because he wasn't wearing a tie. I kept saying, 'Tell him who you are, Walt, tell him you're Walt Disney!'

"'No, no, no!' Walt protested, 'to hell with it—they just serve South Seas crap anyway.'

"So we all drove to Jack's, a posh restaurant in San Francisco, where Walt, believe it or not, ordered his favorite dish, a plain old hamburger."

But he was still seriously run-down, and his doctor kept warning him he was badly in need of a real vacation. To begin with, one thing the doctor advised to him do was stop coming into the studio on Saturday and Sunday when, Kimball recalled, "he would snoop around to check up on how the work was coming along in the different story departments."

He was strongly urged to relax and spend more time with his family, get really enthusiastic over his hobbies.

"Walt had developed a lot of muscle tension in his neck, and it was becoming chronic," Kimball said. "Every evening at 5 p.m. the studio nurse, Hazel George, would go up to Walt's office and massage his neck muscles, after which he would take a couple of belts of booze and head for home. When Walt related to the nurse his doctor's advice about getting away from work, she told him about the big Chicago Railroad Fair she had read about in the papers. 'Why not take a week off and go see it?' she suggested. 'It would do you the world of good. Take Ward Kimball with you. He likes railroads too.'"

So Walt called Kimball that evening and suggested that they make the trip together. By the following Sunday, Walt and Kimball were saying goodbye to their wives at Pasadena station and boarding the Santa Fe Super Chief for Chicago.

---

*He came to the studio and worked on storyboards for *Destino,* which was never produced.

"After we had got settled in our rooms on the train," Kimball said later, "Walt rapped on my door. 'How about a drink?' he asked and motioned me to a chair in his room. He then brings out this special cut-glass liquor decanter and glasses from his special traveling case and pours out three fingers in each glass.

"Now I never could stand whiskey, in fact I hate it. I like 'pretty' drinks like grasshoppers and stingers (Walt called them 'diluted toothpaste'). He kept pouring more whiskey, and I kept politely protesting. He would say, 'Drink up, for Chrissakes, relax!' (This evening drinking bout was to be a regular occurrence for the whole trip, I soon found out.) By the time Walt had his fourth shot, I was still struggling with my second, and when he decided it was time to eat, the swaying train made my unsteady trip to the dining car a nightmare to remember."

Kimball was hungry, nevertheless, and had been looking forward to a famous speciality of the Super Chief's kitchen, the pot roast. "We were going over the Cajon Pass," he remembered, "when the steward handed us the menus. Walt ordered the most expensive thing on the list, the big thick filet mignon steak. When I made it known I was looking forward to the pot roast, he couldn't believe it. 'Pot roast!' he roared. 'Why in the hell do you want pot roast?' He then turned to the steward and said, 'He really doesn't want pot roast, tell the waiter to bring him the filet mignon.' And that was that. Since he was footing the bill for the trip, I didn't complain."

Things looked up the next day when the Super Chief stopped at Winslow, Arizona, and the conductor asked Walt if he and Kimball would like to ride in the cab of the locomotive. "The invitation was courtesy of Mr. Ripley, president of the Santa Fe Railroad, and Walt could hardly control himself. 'Let's go, Kimball! Bring the camera!' What an experience! The engineer told Walt he could blow the whistle every time he saw a small sign with a 'W' on it. Those were genuine moments of happiness for Walt as, grinning from ear to ear, he pulled the cord for the longest, most-drawn-out locomotive whistling I've ever heard. After we returned to our car at Gallup, New Mexico, Walt just sat there, staring into space, smiling and smiling. I had never, ever seen him look so happy."

Equally fulfilling was their stay in Chicago. "We had the time of our lives," Kimball said. "The Chicago Railroad Fair was in full steam, a world's fair with trains. The highlight was a presentation of a three-times-daily pageant, 'Wheels A-Rolling,' which told the history of America through the progress of the country's railroads. Dozens of historic steam locomotives were taken out of museums, refurbished, and put under steam for the show. Major Lenox Lohr, the director of the Chicago Museum of Science and Industry, gave Walt and me VIP treatment. Every morning after breakfast we would taxi down to the fair grounds on

Lake Michigan, and the engineer in charge would let me and Walt try our hands (under supervision, of course) at running such famous locomotives as the Tom Thumb, De Witt Clinton, John Bull, and the New York Central's 999. Then we would have lunch and stay around for the afternoon show. Sometimes Walt would be invited to don period costume and take part in some of the historical episodes. I remember one in particular where he was part of the Santa Fe's Harvey House bit. Walt would watch the other actors and play it accordingly, all in pantomime. In the meantime, I was busy filming the whole show and Walt's cameo appearance from the orchestra pit. We were both acting like a couple of kids."

The stage was gigantic, 200 feet wide with the lake as a background. Once, when Walt and Kimball were both in costume for another crowd scene, they found themselves on the wrong side of the stage and had to get to the other side by going through the many subterranean dressing rooms for the huge cast.

"It was August and very hot," Kimball recalled. "In the large crowded dressing rooms the female ballet dancers solved the sweat problem by stripping down to just their panties. I will never forget the crazy scene as Walt, in top hat and long coat, nonchalantly elbowed his way through a sea of bosomy female pulchritude with me tagging along, shouting, 'Not so fast, Walt, what's the hurry?' Looking at me over his shoulder, he yelled back, 'If you've seen one, Kimball, you've seen 'em all!'

"I thought about Walt's comment later, when I recalled the long discussion we animators had with Walt during the making of *Fantasia* about what size the breasts of the Centaurettes should be, and when, and when not, to indicate the pink nipples."

Tired and content, Walt talked most of the way back from Chicago about the future amusement park he thought he might now build "to give visitors from all over the world something to see when they come to Hollywood."

"Disneyland was forming in his mind," Kimball said. "Of course, he thought such a showplace should have an almost-full-sized steam train to carry the sightseers through the attraction, a train that he could have fun operating himself on days when the park was closed."

A FEW WEEKS after their return from the railroad fair, Walt's wife, Lilly, met Betty Kimball at a party, and said: "You know, Walt told me the trip he took with Ward was the most fun he ever had in his life."

Kimball added, wryly: "Unfortunately, his euphoria soon wore off, and he was back to his own unpredictable, grouchy self, shouldering all the studio's troubles and facing the return of his neck problem—which he hadn't mentioned once during our trip to Chicago."

But his depression was gone. For the time being, anyway.

WALT HAD BEEN building a new house for his family for several months. It was in Holmby Hills, and by the time it was finished, so was the miniature railroad system that Walt had been helping to build at the studio. Lilly had been horrified when she realized he proposed to run it through her new garden; so as a joking way of overcoming her apprehensions, he called in his lawyer, told him to draw up a formal agreement, and had his wife and daughters sign it, giving him the legal right to put a railroad around the house. In the end, to save some of his wife's shrubs, Walt made a tunnel under one part of the garden, at great expense, and every weekend he invited guests to come over and ride in his new train.

Lilly hated it and never got used to the noisy contraption, filled with shrieking grownups, chugging around her beloved new garden and plunging into the tunnel below the lawn. She could hardly contain her delight when, one weekend, the locomotive turned over and Walt and his guests narrowly missed serious injury. *That's the end of that particular caper,* she thought, and decided her husband would soon forget his obsession with nasty, smelly trains. Even the damage suffered by her plants was worth it if it meant the end of that.

But then she realized the spill had stimulated Walt rather than turned him off his hobby. It took some time, but slowly she came to accept the importance of the railroad as therapy, and became resigned—if never reconciled—to its brazen presence.

As for Walt: "It saved my sanity," he said later.

When Walt Disney celebrated his 52nd birthday on December 5, 1953, the studio on Buena Vista had fully recovered from its postwar slump, and the organization was thriving again. *Cinderella* was still coining money at the box office. *Seal Island, Beaver Valley,* and the other *True-Life Adventure* movies were making surprising profits as public interest in wildlife—and Disney's startling close-ups of it—grew and grew.

BY THIS TIME, the Walt Disney Studio had become an international operation and not simply because its products were now booming in all parts of the world. Studio accountants, worrying over the accumulating amounts of money in Europe, had stumbled at last upon the obvious way to utilize them. In Britain, particularly, there were enormous sums lying idle. So why not use them by transferring some Disney productions to England, where there were plenty of actors, actresses, and studios available? Taking Lilly, his daughters, and a skeleton crew with him, Walt left for London and used the D&P Studios to make a film of Stevenson's *Treasure Island.*

The change of scene and the fascination of being back in the production of movies containing real people instead of cartoon characters was almost as magical a therapy as the discovery of railroads. *Treasure Island* was a big success, and both Walt and his family found the atmosphere in England congenial. He was extremely happy there. The first film was followed by *The Story of Robin Hood, The Sword and the Rose*, and *Rob Roy*, and they all made money.

To begin with, one of the inhibiting factors in making *Treasure Island* was the difficulty of finding a suitable tropical location as well as the great expense of transporting cast and crew overseas. But Walt had a stroke of luck. He encountered a talented young Englishman named Peter Ellenshaw, a skilled painter of detailed landscapes, who had learned from his mentor, Percy Day, a well-known English portraitist, how to be a studio matte painter. This was a highly respected form of artistic deception that persuaded movie audiences that they were being carried away to exotic locations when, in truth, what they were watching was being shot inside a studio.

First for Alexander Korda and then for other movie producers in Britain, Ellenshaw had developed superb expertise in painting realistic landscapes and seascapes so that, when combined with real photographs, they fooled audiences into thinking that they had been transported to where they were not. He painted such a convincing series of tropical desert island scenes for *Treasure Island* that the company never had to travel overseas. He did the same for the other three live-action films, bringing the glades of Sherwood Forest and the glens of Scotland to suburban Hertfordshire with such success that he saved Walt hundreds of thousands of pounds in location costs. Nor did he seem downhearted at the fact that Walt never thanked him for the miracles he wrought.

For the length of their association, Ellenshaw was continually bullied or teased by Walt, who often made his life at Disney uncomfortable by telling false and unlikely tales about him. In some ways it resembled the relationship with Ub Iwerks all over again. But with this difference: Ellenshaw never resented Walt's patronizing attitude toward him, and his admiration for him never dimmed. He always continued to worship his boss and thought he was one of the greatest geniuses who ever lived.

ADMIRERS LIKE ELLENSHAW may not have noticed it, but with middle-age, Walt had lost his boyish charm and had become something of a bully and a know-it-all. There were plenty of people in Hollywood by now who were convinced that he had developed an overweening ego and delusions of grandeur. He was increasingly hard to talk to and took criticism, or even mild suggestions, badly.

He would brook no opposition of any kind to his ideas. In story conferences, if somebody argued with his line, he would shoot them down. "Do it my way—or else," he would say. Even the veterans whom he liked had to be careful how they approached him.

"There was a little bit of reverse psychology we had to use at times," Ward Kimball said. "If you praised something too much in front of him, he would automatically build up a negative attitude toward it. For instance, there was a guy called Kemp Niver, who had spent his life patiently making copies of varied-size paper negatives of early films, right from the days when the first filmmakers had to deposit a paper negative for copyright reasons. Niver spent years building a new machine and turning all these into 16mm negatives. Since we often used clips from these old movies in our films—and paid for them by the foot—Niver offered us the whole caboodle for thirty thousand dollars. It was worth ten times that. There were treasures there, like the complete version of *Boadicea,* shots of the Russo-Japanese War, all transferred to acetate so it would never crumble."

Kimball went to Walt and told him, stressing what a trove it was.

"You like it, huh?" Walt asked.

"I think it's great—the biggest bargain ever," Kimball said. He added, "But word came later Walt had turned it down and the Library of Congress and some museum got it. And I realized it was because I had praised it too much, and that had turned him off."

Walt tolerated union members inside the studio—he would have had another strike on his hands otherwise—but he was always surly and suspicious of any of their leaders and could sometimes be heard muttering "Goddamn Commies!" as he came away from policy meetings that he was forced to attend with AFL leaders.

He had become close to John Wayne and other right-wing actors and would have made alliances with Harry Cohn, Jack Warner, Louie Mayer, and all the other pillars of the Republican party in Hollywood if they hadn't all been Jews. He didn't trust Jews, no matter what their proclaimed political affiliations, nor did he ever employ blacks as studio technicians. For reasons of his own, which he was reluctant to discuss, he equated the two ethnic groups with communism and did his best to cut them out of his personal and professional life. He was a firm supporter and contributor for all kinds of extreme right causes, particularly cliques of conservatives like members of the Motion Picture Alliance for the Preservation of American Ideals.

"Roosevelt called this the Century of the Common Man," he once said. "Balls! It's the century of the Communist cutthroat, the fag, and the whore! And FDR and his NLRB made it so!"

Yet, despite this bitterness and malevolence, this fear and resentment of the workers who had once been his friends ("They were my responsibility, but they let me down!") he could still occasionally be humble and charming, and nothing brought out these qualities more than children.

"If all the world thought and acted like children," he once said, "we'd never have any trouble. The only pity is even kids have to grow up."

One day at a movie show a small boy came up and asked him if he drew Mickey Mouse. Walt had to admit he didn't draw Mickey anymore. At which the boy asked him if he thought up all the jokes and ideas in his movies, and he confessed that he no longer did that either. "Then just what do you do, Mr. Disney?" the small boy asked.

"Well," Walt said, "sometimes I think of myself as a little bee. I go from one area of the studio to another and gather pollen and sort of stimulate everybody. I guess that's the job I do."

Now he had another flower he wanted to pollinate. He had been paying consultants for several months out of his own pocket to help him draw up plans for his fun park, and now he was ready to go. It would be so different from all the other fairgrounds he had ever visited that he would not even use the word to describe it. He would call it Disneyland instead, the first and only park devoted to thrills, fun, edification, and leisure. He already had the area picked out where Disneyland would be built: a great tract of orange groves near Anaheim, California, where the growers were ready to sell.

He bustled into Roy's office and spread his architect's drawings across his desk, the plans and projections of a fantastic collection of exhibits and experiences, all of them based on the worlds he had built up in peoples' imaginations with his fabulous collection of films—Sleeping Beauty's Castle; Never Land; the African jungle complete with crocodiles, hippos, and lions; the Pirate's Lair from Peter Pan. And a railroad.

His eyes were shining with excitement. "Isn't it marvelous?" he said to Roy.

As Walt recalled it later, his brother grunted. "How much?" he asked.

"Only a million dollars," Walt said.

"And then some!" Roy said.

"We'll see, we'll see. But will you let me have the money?" Walt asked.

"You should know better than to ask that, Walt," he remembered Roy saying. "I'll have to consult the bank and the shareholders. Have you forgotten this is a public company now?" The next day he came into Walt's office, threw the plans down on his table, and said, grimly, that neither the banks nor the shareholders were ever going to let him do it. They would turn him down because it would cost too much, it was too risky an undertaking. Roy added that the bank had asked him whether he thought it would ever make money, and he had been skeptical.

"Knowing what some of your crazy ideas have cost us, I think I was right, too," he had said. Then he added, "We could do with a good box office smash."

It was at this point that Walt angrily accused his brother of deliberately letting him down. He could easily have persuaded the bank to let him have the money, Walt said. But he hadn't really tried.

Roy admitted it. He hadn't tried because he was convinced it wouldn't work. He took some of the plans and riffled through them contemptuously. What kind of crazy crap was this, anyway? Pirates? Red Indians? Walkways? Jungle adventures? Space ride? What was Walt trying to build—a Barnum and Bailey sideshow? For a moment it looked as if Walt Disney would do something he had never done before and punch his brother in the nose. Instead, he snatched the plans off the table, pointed at the door, and told his brother to get out.

Roy came nearer and made as if to put his arm around his brother's shoulders, but Walt moved swiftly away. "Don't be like that, Walt," Roy said and urged him to put it out of his mind. It was just a fantasy. It wouldn't work. He should get back to doing what he did best and make them another movie.

Walt still pointed at the door, and Roy, shrugging his shoulders, walked toward it. Just before he went through it, Walt said, "You know I'm going through with this, Roy, don't you . . . even if I have to use my own money!"

"That'll be the day!" Roy said. "Anyway, how are you going to raise a million dollars?"

He had already seen his lawyer, Walt told him. He was cashing in all his assets and would somehow find the money to make a down payment on the land purchase. And he had already signed an option. He paused and took a deep breath. "Roy, you'd better realize I'm serious," he said. He made it plain he was going through with this Disneyland project if it took every last cent he had.

"What did you call it?" Roy asked.

"Disneyland," Walt said.

"What makes you think you can use the Disney name if the shareholders don't approve?" Roy asked. "They'll never let you get away with it. Walt Disney Productions doesn't belong to us anymore—the shareholders own it. And that includes our name."

PART 3

Theme Parks

18
Disneyland

LATER ON, AFTER Walt's death, Roy Disney tried to persuade people that he hadn't really been against his brother creating Disneyland and that the real opposition had come from the banks and the shareholders. It wasn't true, of course. Walt was quite right in accusing Roy of letting him down. With a modicum of eloquent insistence, he could easily have convinced Disney's creditors and shareholders that Disneyland was a bold and promising enterprise and one that well deserved to be financially supported.

He failed to back his brother because he lacked vision and had lost his courage. He was terrified of losing more money, of putting the studio in jeopardy. So long as the company was still in debt to the banks, he was desperately anxious for Walt to play safe—something that, over the years, he should have learned was impossible for his brother to do.

"That was the trouble with Roy," one of his former employees said later. "He wasn't like Walt at all. When he took over after Walt died, everybody tried to foster the impression he was a genius just like his brother. He wasn't. He would like to have been, but he wasn't. Make no mistake, everybody liked Roy, much more than they liked Walt. They weren't afraid of him as they often were of Walt. He was amiable and outgoing and sympathetic. But fundamentally he was just a shrewd country boy who sometimes made a smart deal and was always worried afterward whether he had done the right thing. When it came to big, bold projects, in fact, he wasn't even as good a businessman as Walt was. Right through their association together, he would take up schemes only after Walt had carefully thought them through—and he would still go on being hesitant, worried, and reluctant even then, especially if there was a risk involved. And of course there always was. I don't mean to suggest Walt's schemes were always successful financially. Making money was never important to him, just grease to keep his wheels turning. But he was always challenging, original. On the other hand, Roy's instinct was to turn down any idea, no matter how fresh, that couldn't guarantee a profit from the start. He was against Disneyland, against Disney World, and against EPCOT, all of them. It was Walt who finally drummed up the money for them—and he got it from outsiders."

But not at first. There were plenty of outside investors willing to listen to Walt talking about Disneyland, but they proved reluctant when it came to giving him money. To a certain degree, that was because Roy, still opposing his brother, anxious to justify his opposition, had begun circulating stories that the banks were against Disneyland and the shareholders were not even going to allow him to use the company name. "We're a film studio, not an amusement park company," was what Roy reported them as saying. "What have we got to do with coconut shies and bearded ladies? Walt should get back to making films."

ONE OF THE members of Disney's promotional staff at this time was a remarkable character named Vince Jefferds. The former executive vice president of a chain of New York stores, he had recently joined Disney to handle merchandising and exploitation. Operating through the New York office, Jefferds had put together one of the most successful marketing programs in the history of the movies on Walt's feature cartoon, *Peter Pan*. Now Walt called him in to help him drum up the money to finance Disneyland. In 1953, he asked Jefferds to join him at a meeting with a venerable insurance company in Philadelphia from which he hoped to promote a sizeable investment.

Jefferds had come from New York and had dressed for the meeting in a conservative charcoal suit and dark tie. Walt had arrived in a Hollywood uniform of sport jacket and slacks.

"We went into the boardroom, which was a mile along, with huge portraits of all the directors from 1750 or something on the walls," Jefferds said. "The chairman of the board was, I would say, around seventy or seventy-five, ruddy cheeked, short, robust, cheerful, eager, looking just like Edmund Gwenn. I had a feeling he liked Walt and genuinely wanted to do something for him if he could figure out a way. He was replete with goodwill and guffawed when Walt introduced me in my Wall Street clothes and said, 'This is my representative from Forest Lawn.' But wild rumors had reached the chairman, too, and he obviously believed Walt had lost his senses and was trying to drum up money to get into the honky-tonk business—like Palisades Park or Coney Island when the fleet came in. And *his* shareholders would never have stood for that. So eventually, but with obvious regret, he turned us down."

Roy had spread the word in other places, too, and in other company boardrooms Walt was warmly welcomed and then sorrowfully rejected. So where and how was he going to get the money?

He now knew exactly how much he was going to need. He had refined his figures, and he calculated that, to carry out all his plans, he would have to collect two million dollars. He had already spent most of his savings hiring architects and planners; he had traveled thousands of miles with them making surveys of amusement parks around the country, studying the rides and attractions and audience reactions to them. He went overseas, too, taking Lilly with him on a trip to the Tivoli Gardens in Copenhagen. The Danish amusement park impressed him, and he immediately decided Disneyland should try to emulate its happy and unbuttoned air of relaxed fun.

But as his savings were drained by fees and expenses, he picked up no really wealthy backers. In desperation, he went to his lawyer and told him to cash in his life insurance policy (from which he got one hundred thousand dollars). Determined to beef up his resources to give himself more negotiating power, he briefly considered mortgaging his new house in Holmby Hills but finally resisted the temptation and signed over the property to Lilly instead.

Meanwhile, to circumvent Roy and the threatened interference from the shareholders of Walt Disney Productions (and, quite frankly, to keep them from sharing in any of the profits if and when his leisure park succeeded), he had formed a new company in 1952 to take control of Disneyland's affairs. He called it Walt Disney Incorporated, with himself as president and one of his planners as the sole vice president. Since Roy was hostile and Lilly was scared, he asked neither of them to come in with him.

The moment Roy heard about the new company, he threatened legal action on behalf of the shareholders over the use of the Disney name. Walt was advised by his lawyers to change the title of the new company to WED Enterprises.

The breach with Roy was now so serious that they were no longer speaking but communicating only through each other's secretaries or wives. His brother's son, Roy Edward Disney, who had developed into a cocky and self-confident young man, had recently come to work in the studio. One day, according to a story that eventually went the rounds in Hollywood, he approached Walt and said, "Uncle Walt, is it true what my father says—that you're going to become a ringmaster for Barnum & Bailey's Circus?"

He giggled at his own joke, while his uncle struggled for an answer and got red in the face. Finally, Walt said, "It isn't true, Junior. But I'll certainly see about it if you and your father will join me . . . as the company clowns."

He was later to forgive Roy for his behavior during this critical phase in his life, but he never did forget his nephew's insufferable attempts to be funny.

Disneyland was now no longer a joking matter where he was concerned. It had become a grim obsession, and he swore he would never do another thing at the studio until he had enough financing to get the project going. It had become the only thing in life that mattered to him, and animated cartoons—any kind of films, in fact—had totally, if temporarily, lost their savor for him.

In an interview that he gave to the Hollywood *Citizen-News* at this time, he said, "The park means a lot to me. It's something that will never be finished, something I can keep developing, keep 'plussing,' and adding to. It's alive. It will be a live, breathing thing that will need changes. When you wrap up a picture and turn it over to Technicolor, you're through. *Snow White* is a dead issue with me. I just finished a live-action picture, wrapped it up a few weeks ago. It's gone. I can't touch it. There are things in it I don't like, but I can't do anything about it. I want something live, something that would grow. The park is that. Not only can I add things to it, but even the trees will keep growing. The thing will get more beautiful year after year. And it will get better as I find out what the public likes. I can't do that with a picture. It's finished and unchangeable before I find out if the public likes it or not."

In the end, he had to look outside normal business channels for backing. But the idea of approaching television, which was what he eventually decided to do, was not something that came to him in a flash.

LIKE MANY ANOTHER Hollywood film man, Walt Disney both feared, and was fascinated by, the burgeoning TV industry in the United States. He shared with all the other movie chiefs lively apprehensions over what TV would eventually do to the film industry; and he believed that the longer Hollywood stayed away from it, refused to feed it with material and competitive ammunition, the more likely it was to collapse beneath the weight of its own mediocrity.

At the same time, he knew that both of the main TV networks—there were only two in those days, NBC and CBS, with ABC a small upstart struggling to keep going—would give their right arms and lots of money to get their hands on some of the Disney cartoons and *True-Life Adventure* movies. They were desperately short of movie entertainment and, several times, had offered substantial fees for the right to project Walt Disney productions, but all of the approaches had been curtly turned down.

Not only was it general Hollywood policy not to sell movies to TV, but

Walt had long since decided that airing his cartoons through what he regarded an amateurish outlet would do nothing but demean them. However, now he was desperate—not desperate enough to break the Hollywood taboo on selling theatrical products to TV but prepared to look for a way of circumventing the ban. For instance, what if he made a series of films especially for TV, and not for theatrical exhibition—and then offered them as a quid pro quo to the networks in return for backing for Disneyland? Ignoring any conflict of interest, he proposed:

> *You back my leisure park and I'll give you a TV series you can announce as a "Walt Disney Presents," with all the prestige and public interest that name will stimulate for you.*

Even Roy was taken with the scheme when he heard about it and, immediately, made overtures to his brother and offered his help in pushing it with the networks. Walt suspected Roy was more interested in getting a lucrative new source of revenue for the studio than in procuring financing for his brother's Disneyland scheme, which he still opposed. Nevertheless, he welcomed the offer as a gesture of reconciliation and took him up on it, whereupon Roy offered to go to New York and sell the proposition to the networks himself.

To make sure that he would keep "money for Disneyland" as the paramount priority in his mind, Walt called in one of his staff to write a pamphlet about the leisure park so that Roy could show it to the prospective backers. Meanwhile, he had bought the rights to the *Zorro* stories* and told his script department to run up a series of draft scripts, which he would agree to make and deliver for TV showing as part of the quid pro quo.

The pamphlet was written by Bill Walsh, a pear-shaped, cigar-smoking, former gag writer for the ventriloquist, Edgar Bergen, who had since joined Walt Disney Productions to do Mickey Mouse scripts and promotion films for Disney's British operations. He loathed television and when he heard Walt was contemplating making a deal with the networks, hastily scribbled him a note pleading with him not to do it.

Typically, Walt promptly commissioned him to do the text of the pamphlet explaining to the TV moguls how he proposed to organize Disneyland. Herbert Ryman, a former animator, was hired to do the drawings.

---

*About a masked bandit. Both Douglas Fairbanks and Tyrone Power had played the character in full-length movie versions.

It was obvious Walsh's heart was not in it. "The idea of Disneyland is a simple one," he wrote.

> It will be a place for people to find happiness and knowledge. It will be a place for parents and children to share pleasant times in one another's company: a place for teachers and pupils to discover greater ways of understanding and education. Here the older generation can recapture the nostalgia of days gone by, and the younger generation can savor the challenge of the future. Here will be the wonders of Nature and Man for all to see and understand. Disneyland will be based upon and dedicated to the ideals, the dreams, and the hard facts that have created America. And it will be uniquely equipped to dramatize these dreams and facts and send them forth as a source of courage and inspiration to all the world.
>
> Disneyland will be something of a fair, an exhibition, a playground, a community center, a museum of living facts, and a showplace of beauty and magic. It will be filled with the accomplishments, the joys, and hopes of the world we live in. And it will remind us and show us how to make those wonders part of our lives.

Except for the last paragraph, it was a low-keyed, not terribly impressive presentation of Walt Disney's intentions; and the details that followed—setting out such Disneyland attractions as a True-Life Adventureland, Rivers of Romance, World of Tomorrow, Lilliputian Land, Spaceship to the Moon—hardly gave a convincing picture, even with the illustrations, of the thrills to come. True, it also stated that there would be a Tom Sawyer River Ride and a trip through Fantasyland, a moving walkway for the tired-of-foot, and of course, a railroad from which the antipedestrians could see everything without walking a step.

But neither Walsh nor Ryman conveyed the vividness of the concept bubbling in Walt Disney's mind, and it made no impact whatsoever on the head of CBS when Roy pressed the pamphlet into his hand. One of CBS's main sponsors, the drug firm Johnson and Johnson, did agree to consider making an investment provided they were satisfied with what TV entertainment Walt was willing to give them in return. They asked to see a pilot film of the *Zorro* series.

Roy uncomfortably shook his head. "Walt doesn't do pilots," he said. "Never has. Says he never will. You know our track record. You'll have to judge us on that and the draft scripts."

"TV doesn't work that way," the Johnson and Johnson people replied. "No pilot, no sponsorship."

David Sarnoff, the head of NBC and RCA, was rather more receptive; but each time his negotiators took over, the discussions became bogged down on conditions. They too wanted to see a pilot of *Zorro*. Roy came back from New York convinced more than ever that Disneyland was never going to get off the ground.

Then, one morning in the spring of 1953, the telephone rang and a voice said, "Walt, I hear you need money to build your fairground. If you will agree to let us put Mickey Mouse on our network, my directors are ready to advance you $250,000 for it. Furthermore, we're willing to come in on a joint venture with you and guarantee loans up to three million dollars."

"For God's sake, how many times do I have to tell people it's a leisure park, not a fairground! Who is this anyway?" Walt asked.

"My name's Kintner," the voice said, "and I'm an executive vice president of the American Broadcasting Corporation, otherwise known as ABC."

"The peanuts network!" Walt said. "What the hell good would it do me to work with you? You're the Little Orphan Annie of the TV airways, with hardly a station to call your own."

"Give us Mickey Mouse, Walt, plus the Disney name," the voice said, "and I guarantee that within two years we'll be one of the big three." A pause. "I hear you need the money real bad. A quarter of a million and a three million guarantee could be a great help, I figure. Is it a deal?"

"Make it half a million in cash and a $4,500,000 guarantee and Mickey is yours," Walt said.

"Done," Kintner said. Then, in a mock announcer's voice, "And welcome to the TV airways, Walt Disney!"*

IN THE SUMMER of 1954, the first orange trees were torn out of the ground in Anaheim, and work began on the building of Disneyland. Mickey Mouse was seen for the first time on television later that fall. A revolution had begun in the nature of TV and leisure entertainment in the United States, and soon, for Walt Disney and for the American public, things would never be the same again. Nor for ABC either. As Kintner had foreseen, Walt Disney turned ABC into a major network in the space of a few months.

Walt got a hint of what he had wrought during the opening ceremonies of Disneyland that August when, after the first sod had been turned and the first bulldozer had butted its nose against a tree, his brother Roy came over to talk to him. His son, Roy Edward Disney, was with him, looking, to Walt's admittedly jaundiced eye, even cockier than usual.

"I just wanted you to know," Roy was later reported to have said, "that I've been talking to the board of directors, and they want in."

Walt knew exactly what had been going on during recent days but

---

*Roy Disney later clinched the deal with ABC president Goldenson.

pretended to be obtuse. "In?" he queried. "What do you mean by in? In where?"

"In here," Roy said. "Disneyland. They like the concept. They like the way you've handled the deal. I've talked it over with them, and they're prepared to buy you and your share out for $500,000. Sign over Disneyland, Incorporated* to Walt Disney Productions and the half million bucks is yours."

According to onlookers, Walt pretended to give it deep thought. Finally, he said, "I'll tell you what I'll do, Roy. You just go back to the board of directors and say I'll give them exactly 50 percent of Disneyland, Incorporated for that half a million bucks." Then he is said to have added, "Or I'll cut that figure down to 25 percent for me—on one condition."

"What's that?" Roy asked.

Walt indicated his son, smirking away in the sunlight. "On the condition that your son, Junior, here, signs up to work at Disneyland once the park is finished."

"That might be interesting," Roy said. "As what?" He put a fond arm around his son.

"As a clown," Walt said. "Did I tell you we plan to set up a circus sideshow in the park? Junior would do a real good job whooping it up as the back end of a horse." He is said to have added that he might even agree to give an occasional performance as ringmaster if Junior would consent to perform.

They finally settled for Walt keeping 17.25 percent of the Disneyland holdings. He sold out the rest to Walt Disney Productions, which henceforth shared the investment equally with ABC and Western Printing and Lithographing (with 13.79 percent). As for Roy Edward Disney, Jr., he continued to work at the Buena Vista studio and never did make an appearance at Disneyland. But neither did his relationship with his uncle improve in the years to come.

---

*During the negotiations with ABC, Walt Disney had formed an additional company to handle his Disneyland interests under this name.

19
Acolytes

PETER ELLENSHAW'S WORK on four Disney live-action films made with frozen sterling funds in Britain had proved to be the most formative experience of his life simply because it brought him within the orbit and influence of Walt Disney.

Thirty years old in 1950, Ellenshaw had already worked with at least two giants of the film world (one recognized, the other comparatively unknown) during his short career in the movies. He had done the artwork for some of Alexander Korda's most memorable epics, including *The Shape of Things to Come, Rembrandt, The Four Feathers, The Drum,* and *The Thief of Bagdad.* And he had learned the art of matte painting, at which he now excelled, from the pioneer and master of the craft, Percy (Pop) Day, whose immeasurable contributions to the refinement of aesthetic movie technics would save the industry millions of dollars.*

But for Ellenshaw even these two remarkable movie men diminished in size when measured against Walt Disney, who left such an indelible impression upon him that even today he is apt to remark: "What a wonderful thing to be able to say, 'I once knew Walt Disney.'"

When Walt was bitten by the Disneyland bug and returned to California in the early 1950s, temporarily halting his filmmaking activities in England, Ellenshaw felt like an adoring son whose father has suddenly been wrenched away from him. It moved him to desperate measures.

Walt Disney used to tell an apocryphal story to the animators in the "sweatbox" at Buena Vista about how Ellenshaw came to work for him

---

*It is to be hoped some cinema buff will eventually write a biography of Percy Day. His experiments with matte painting began in France in 1910 and flowered in 1927 when he provided the simulated battlefield backgrounds for Abel Gance's classic epic, *Napoleon*. The career of this often irascible perfectionist is full of rewarding incidents and discoveries.

in America. "I was in London, in Trafalgar Square, watching these pavement artists,' he would say, 'and there was a young man and he obviously had talent. So I asked him whether he would like to work for me, and he looked up from the sidewalk and said, 'Oh, yes, Guv!' And that was Peter."

It was a completely untrue story. Because Ellenshaw had never been a pavement artist in his life, it made him squirm each time he heard it—which was probably why Walt was always repeating it. And since his staff never quite knew whether Walt was joking or not, they believed it. Ellenshaw would always be the ex-pavement artist to them.

In fact, he came into Walt Disney's orbit through quite legitimate movie channels. Tom Morahan, an Irish art director well known in movie circles in London, was aware of Peter's work for Korda and of his reputation as both a serious artist and a talented pupil of Pop Day. He called Peter and said he wanted matte shots for a movie of Robert Louis Stevenson's *Treasure Island* that Disney was about to make. The budget didn't allow for location trips, so Ellenshaw was required to simulate the real thing—and do it quickly.

"Painting matte shots is a most tricky and meticulous art," Ellenshaw said later. "Let us suppose we are on location and need a castle on a hill. We have the hill but no castle. On a large glass, about six feet in front of the camera, we paint the castle. Through the clear part of the glass, the characters in the scene (or boats, or other objects) go into action and are photographed—at the same time as the background scene with castle is recorded. This is matte-painting in its simplest form."

In this case, Ellenshaw had to visualize the sultry atmosphere of a tropical island as Stevenson had described it in his book and painstakingly reproduce in exquisite detail matte shots of every cove, cave, beach, and forest glade specified in the script. Moreover, Walt Disney, who liked to follow through every stage in production, wanted to see his rough sketches. "I took them along to his office every morning and there would be dozens of them," Ellenshaw said. "I soon discovered Walt liked drawings with dramatic backlighting. It happens that I like backlighting, too, so that started us off with something in common. Subsequently, I had as many failures with him as I had successes, but in the main, he liked what I did."

He did more Disney films after *Treasure Island,* and his two principal producers in Britain, Fred Leahy and Perce Pearce, admired his work so much that they were always saying to him, "Would you consider going to America?"

"Wouldn't I just!" Ellenshaw said, describing his reactions later. "You know what it was like in England in those days, just after the war. I had my young American wife, Bobbie, there with our three-month-old baby, whom she had brought over from America in a troopship.* We were living in one room because there was no accommodation available. Food was scarce. There was rationing. It was really a desperate time for Bobbie, and I couldn't wait to get out of the country."

But Walt never personally invited him, nor did his producers ever offer him a specific job. In fact, whenever he tried to talk to them seriously about the prospects of working at Buena Vista, Leahy would always say, uncertainly, "I can't say Walt thinks it would be a good idea. He's going to take a bit of persuading."

And then abruptly Walt departed for America to get Disneyland organized, and Ellenshaw was bereft. Disney's film operation in Britain came to a halt, and Ellenshaw felt like a clipper ship that for months has been running before a strong and steady wind and is suddenly becalmed. For weeks on end, he wallowed in miserable uncertainty, not knowing what to do, hoping against hope he would get a call from California to rejoin his boss. But from the man he had tried so desperately to please, whom he had come to admire so much, whose influence on him had been so inspiring, came no word at all. And the prospect of working with anyone else now seemed so bleak and unpromising that he could not bring himself to seek another job.

In the end, he decided there was only one thing to do. If Walt Disney did not send for him, he would go, unsummoned. "We sold up everything we had in England, the tiny flat, the furniture, everything," Ellenshaw said. "And we came across the Atlantic by boat and across America by train, and since we were paying our own way and didn't have much money, it was dreadful. I had found out from Leahy we would probably be given a job once we reached Burbank, but it had nothing to do with Walt, and the wage I was offered when we got there was very low. I took it. I'd have taken anything to get back into Disney." He was back in Walt's orbit again, and life was suddenly full of hope again.

"WHEN WALT HEARD I was there on the lot, he called me into his office," Ellenshaw said. "He was sitting at this low desk. For anyone else it would have been chichi to have a desk that low. Instead of being perched up high, as the other movie moguls were, he was hunched down and looking up at you and smoking. He looked at me kind of half-pleased and said, 'Well, Peter.' Of course, I had got to know him quite well in England, and when he was away from the studio he had been quite free and open with me. But here he obviously had to be Walt Disney. The big guy. Chain smoking. 'Sit down,' he says. 'Now I'll tell you about the people

---

*Ellenshaw met and married his wife while training as a navigator in the United States during World War II. He then returned to Europe and served for four years in the RAF.

you'll be working with. But I must say, I don't understand why you came. There aren't many mattes to work on, and I don't think you're going to find enough work to merit your being here.' God, I'd sold up everything, burned my bridges, and he sounded as if he was about to send me back!"

Later on, he concluded it was Walt Disney's way of putting him down in case he began to think: *I've been brought specially from England and I'm the big cheese and if anyone wants to know anything, he should come to me.* "He was making sure I didn't get an inflated idea of my own worth and start getting above myself. I think for the same reason, I was kept hanging around the studio for days on end, with no one telling me anything about what I was supposed to do. It was disconcerting, chilling, humbling."

Despite the fact that Disney didn't mention a word about it, Ellenshaw could hardly have arrived at a more propitious moment. The Disneyland negotiations had gone into high gear and seemed certain to be successful. Walt had turned his attention back to moviemaking again and was fizzing with enthusiasm over his biggest and most expensive picture so far: a version of Jules Verne's *20,000 Leagues Under the Sea*. As if to celebrate his reconciliation with his brother, he was pressing Roy to okay a budget on the movie that had long since passed two and a half million dollars and was rising every week as Walt strove for effects that were more and more authentic, effective—and expensive.

They were shooting underwater miniatures for *20,000 Leagues* on the back lot at Buena Vista under the direction of an old-time effects man named Ralph Hammeras, an eccentric character who sported a beard and wore a cloak. Like everybody else in the studio, Walt knew the special effects would make or break the movie.

With nothing better to do, Ellenshaw would go to the "sweatbox" every evening to see the "rushes" of Hammeras's work for the day, and he was appalled. "When I saw what was supposed to be a submarine, I thought, 'My God, it doesn't have the scale! This looks like a little tin something going through the water. They're not lighting it from the back. It should loom up very big.'"

He realized not only that this was his opportunity, but that he had to do something to improve these phony effects for the sake of the film, for Walt's sake too. But how?

Like everybody else, he had learned that Walt was an inveterate snooper. He had developed the habit of wandering around the studio at night after everybody had left, riffling through papers on desks, opening drawers, reading letters, or going through the contents of cubbyholes to find out what his staff was up to. Ellenshaw was not the first Disney employee to realize that his boss's nosiness provided an ideal opportunity to plant things deliberately for his boss to see.

He was working on the top floor of the animators' building at this time, and he did a series of drawings—highly dramatized with heavy back light—of how he thought Captain Nemo's submarine should look as it cruised the murky waters in *20,000 Leagues Under the Sea*. These he left spread carelessly over his desk.

A couple of weeks later, Walt called everybody into the "sweatbox" and said, "We're going to run the rushes on how the underwater sequences have gone over the last two weeks."

After the "rushes" had been showing for a time, Walt suddenly pressed the button and brought the screening to a halt. The lights went up and he said, "Guys, this isn't working. We've gotta start again."

Everybody was looking at Ralph Hammeras. Whenever he was nervous, he had his script on his knee, and he would shuffle through the pages, trying to appear busy. Suddenly, Walt turned. "Ralph," he said, "I've seen some sketches of how these scenes should be lit, and these have been done by Peter Ellenshaw, and he's sitting right behind you."

Hammeras glared malevolently at the blushing Englishman.

"You and Peter have to get together," Walt went on. "And you, Peter, have to stay with Ralph and make sure these scenes are going to be shot like your drawings from now on." He looked at Hammeras's stony face and went on, "You boys know this is the way we work here. We work together." And then, clapping Hammeras on the back, "I know you're in charge, Ralph, but I want Peter here to be with you there to help."

HAMMERAS TOOK THE change very well, on the whole. "He had been in the business since before the first war, but he was a sweetie really," Ellenshaw said. "He would ask me where I wanted the lights, and we worked as a team. We had to. Walt had his eye on us. But I did come in one day and I sensed Hammeras's attitude toward me had changed. We'd been shooting Captain Nemo's submarine hitting the hull of the pirate ship, the one that was carrying the munitions. I had kept it very low-keyed, and all you could see was the blackness of the hull. I saw the warning signals on Ralph's face. He said, 'I'm sorry, Peter, but I'm not going to be able to listen to you any longer. I just got the clips back from Technicolor, and they say there's nothing on the film. You've got me to light it too low key and there's nothing on it, and I've got my reputation to consider . . .'"

Ellenshaw asked him to put the clips on the screen. "I'd known what I wanted from the start," he said, "and when the scene came on it was just gray. Then out of the grayness comes this black shape and then the other black shape appears and then—bam—it hits. True, there was only a feeble spark and it wasn't strong enough, and we had to build it up later. But the scene did have a tremendous, uncanny, convulsive power. And it certainly caught the mood. I turned to Ralph and I saw he was sold on the scene, and to hell with what Technicolor said. But for me it had been a close one. From then on we worked harmoniously together, and you know the result. Those underwater sequences made all the difference to the impact of *20,000 Leagues.*"*

But so far as his relationship with Walt was concerned, Ellenshaw was still feeling for some sort of rapport. One day he heard Walt coughing his way along a corridor to a staff meeting he had called, and he came out of his cubicle and asked him whether he could end his collaboration with Hammeras and get back to matte painting.

"I didn't have time to finish," Ellenshaw said. "He got mad at once. 'For Christ's sake, Peter,' he said, 'what the hell's the matter with you? Don't you understand plain English? I told you to stay with old Hammeras, and I meant it. I'm not going to tell you any more times.' I started to say something and he said, 'I'm talking. You shut up.' He cut me down as if he had a scythe in his hand. We swept on to the meeting with me trailing behind, and I suppose the expression on my face betrayed just how miserable I was feeling because he came across to me afterward and said, 'Don't take it to heart. But you see, you have to learn to work with the others.' God, he could be rough with you!

"We had a writer and sketch artist called Don DaGradi, a wonderful fellow with a great feeling for the way scenes should be played, and one day, Walt came up to him and said, 'Have you been on the back lot today?' and Don said he hadn't. So then Walt said, 'Look, I go down there every day to see how things are going. So how come you can't go down there? Get out and find out what's happening. For Christ's sake, don't hang around your office all day. Get your butt out of there.' No matter how important you were, he'd rough you up."

But slowly, painfully, surviving many an insult and wounding practical joke, Ellenshaw felt himself getting closer to his boss. Like everyone else who ever knew or worked for Walt, he never did achieve intimacy with him. But he did win back some of the friendliness and appreciation he had had from him in England. He was soon working on matte paintings for such successful films as *Darby O'Gill, In Search of the Castaways,* and *Mary Poppins.*

The occasion when Walt seemed to relax and come closest to him, he decided later, was during the making of the last-named film. He went to London with the company for research on *Mary Poppins* and not only did matte paintings for many London scenes but also hundreds of sketches for the cartoon sequences.

Shortly after the company returned to California to shoot the film at

---

*So did reworking the scene with a giant underwater squid, which looked artificial until Walt okayed its remodeling and reshooting at a cost of $250,000.

the studio, they were shooting a number with the chimney sweep on the back lot, and when they saw it in the rushes, it seemed to sag. Ellenshaw suggested to Bill Walsh, the director, that it might be lightened up if the chimney sweep and all the Cockney characters around him did a singing and dancing number to the tune of "Knees Up, Mother Brown," explaining to him that it was a Cockney classic.

"I said it was a number that would get you thrown out of any pub in England," Ellenshaw said, "because the moment you started dancing it, everybody always stopped drinking and joined in. It was a wonderfully vulgar dance and Bill asked me to demonstrate it, and after seeing it said, 'Great! Let's bring in Walt and get his approval to put it in.'" So Walt was summoned, and he watched a demonstration of the song and dance and agreed that it should go into the sequence.

"And of course, it was infectious," Ellenshaw said. "Everybody joined in, Walt included. We linked arms and went charging across the room, roaring out 'Knees Up, Mother Brown!' The only trouble was, the dancers didn't realize this was the kind of dance you don't do in polite places, you have to get your knees really high up, and you're not elegant at all. In fact, you show so much of what you've got underneath that you're downright rude. I had to keep telling everybody, Walt included, to 'get those knees up!' until we all collapsed, out of breath from laughter and exhaustion. But it made, oh, such a wonderful clip in the film! And I suppose the whole episode excited me so much I didn't worry that when we finished singing and dancing, Walt, although he was laughing with the rest of us at the end of it—well, he didn't look too good. As if it had all been too much for him." But it certainly improved his relationship with Ellenshaw.

SHORTLY AFTER THIS incident, the telephone rang, and Walt's secretary was on the line. Some time back, Disney had made a film about the U.S. training ship *Eagle,* and Ellenshaw had painted pictures of her for the movie. Now the *Eagle* had arrived in San Diego on an official visit, and Walt had been invited to take a trip in her. Walt wanted to know if Peter would accompany him on the trip. It was a royal command, and Ellenshaw knew better than to refuse to go.

All the same, he was somewhat disconcerted when he learned that there was only one guest cabin aboard the *Eagle* and that he and Walt would be sharing quarters. (The press would be covering the trip, but they would be accommodated on another ship.) "I knew that Walt, being such a very private person, wouldn't really want anyone sharing with him overnight," Ellenshaw said. "But what was I to do? Walt wouldn't have accepted an excuse." So they flew down to San Diego and went aboard and had an interesting day exploring the ship and then had a slap-up dinner in the wardroom.

"Now as evening draws on, Walt's getting restless," Ellenshaw said, "and I'm getting restless, too—both of us thinking that we have to share this extremely small cabin, which was a little room for dwarfs. Almost immediately after dinner he said he was feeling very tired and he wanted to turn in. That was a signal for me to get lost while he got himself ready for bed, and he suggested I take a turn around the deck. I took several turns. When I calculated he should be tucked up in bed and sound asleep, I went down to the cabin."

It had two bunks, one on top of the other, and Walt was far from sleeping. He was sitting on the lower bunk in pajamas, and he looked tired and drawn. Fixing Ellenshaw with his gimlet eyes, he said, "Now Peter, I'm here on this bed. But there's no reason why I should have it. I can sleep in the one up above."

"No, Walt," Ellenshaw said. "I'll be quite comfortable in the upper bunk."

He said, "I can sleep up there."

"No, Walt, really."

"Well," he said, "I'd *rather*." He began to crawl into the lower bunk, and then he said, after a long pause, "Peter, if you are going up there— you don't pee the bed, do you?"

Ellenshaw said, primly, "I can assure you, Walt, I've never peed the bed yet, and I'm certainly not going to do it tonight."

"Well, I was just wondering." Another pause as he settled down. "Some people do, you know." Then he launched into a long rigmarole about bed wetters he had known. "Meanwhile, I had been hesitantly taking off my clothes," Ellenshaw said. "I was not going to bother much with washing tonight. I was trying to get up into that damned bunk and get out of the eyeline because Walt had eyes that penetrated rather." Finally, in his pajamas and stretched out on his bunk, Ellenshaw tried to settle down.

"After what seemed hours—it was probably about forty-five minutes, really—he seemed to drop off to sleep, and I lay there thinking: *If I miss a night's sleep it won't be a big problem, I'll catch up when I get home tomorrow.* Because I certainly didn't feel like sleeping with this precious man beneath me.

"Then just as I was beginning to get a bit drowsy, there was a great bump below me. The head of my idol had hit the bottom of my bunk, solidly. I jumped a mile. I could hear him muttering below me, 'Goddamn this bunk!' He climbs out with what he considers very great care, but he seemed to make a hell of a lot of noise as far as I was concerned. I was lying on my back with my eyes barely open, like when your mother comes to tuck you in, and he peers up. His great head comes over the edge of my bunk and he checks to see if my breathing's regular. Then he tiptoes across this tiny cabin, which had a tiny bowl in which you were supposed to wash yourself, and he gets a wet washcloth."

By this time Ellenshaw was watching carefully and slowly realized that Walt was in pain. He took the washcloth, quietly ran hot water on it, and then held it against his face and neck. "And from then on, every half hour or so, all through the night, he would bang his head against the bunk, climb out of bed, and wearily, groaning, swearing, he would go across to the washbowl and try to do something about his pain. I knew better than to show I was awake and aware of what he was doing, but it was agony to watch the poor man."

When morning came, bright and early, Walt was awake and dressed. "Well, Peter," he said. "How did you sleep?"

"I slept like a top," Ellenshaw said. "How about you?"

"Not bad," he said, grinning. "Not bad at all."

"I didn't have the courage to tell him I hadn't slept a wink and I knew he hadn't either," Ellenshaw said. "That was the trouble with Walt. People were so scared. Walt was such a private person you dare not show you knew he was ill and in pain. Even the doctors were scared of him. Examining him must have been quite a strain for his medical advisers because he hated it and them so much. His illness probably progressed faster because he didn't have himself examined in time. He didn't think doctors were any good—not for him, anyway."

Ellenshaw added, "Of course, people, doctors, should have told him much earlier on to stop smoking those dreadful black cigarettes. He never for a moment thought they would do him any harm. They just made him cough, and he didn't worry about his cough. You could recognize him at Burbank by his cough. He coughed 'Woof, woof!' and you'd hear it as he came down the corridor. And you'd think, 'Oh, here's Walt coming to see me. Good.'"

THE OPENING OF Disneyland on July 17, 1955, was disastrous because nothing was ready in time. Some of the rides didn't work, and others weren't finished. Cement and blacktop hadn't dried, smearing clothes, wrenching heels off shoes, tempting small boys to leave footprints and rude finger messages. The gardens looked bare and ragged because too many orange trees had been bulldozed out of the ground.

Press complaints about the theme park's facilities were strident and unfriendly, concentrating particularly on a shortage of drinking fountains, which, they grumbled, forced customers to buy expensive soft drinks when all they wanted to do was quench an honest thirst. Walt had his publicity department explain that a plumbers' strike had forced him to choose between free fountains and toilets, and he had chosen the toilets since he didn't want the customers to "have to pee in the streets."

Meanwhile, he spent hours snooping around the park to watch how the visitors were treated by the staff, and he had no hesitation in ordering an attendant fired on the spot for surliness or lack of patience. "Always smile," he ordered. "Turn the other cheek to everybody, even the nasty ones. And above everything, always give them full value for their money. If a boat ride is supposed to last twelve minutes and they only get eleven minutes thirty seconds, they've a right to feel cheated. Thirty seconds shy, and they hate us for selling them short. Thirty seconds extra, and they feel they've gotten away with something. That's the way we want them to feel. Contented, even smug."

He did not relax until everything was in order and even his beloved railroad was running smoothly. The millionth visitor was clocked in before the end of the second month of operation, and twelve months later Walt Disney Productions was able to pay off nine million dollars in outstanding loans to the banks and inform the shareholders that the company was in a profit position. It was not entirely due to the success of the theme park, of course. The TV program (also called "Disneyland") was consistently at the top of the national ratings, ahead of NBC and CBS, and had, by the end of the first year, transformed ABC, its sponsor, into a major network.

"The ugly duckling has turned into a swan, thanks to Mickey Mouse and Walt Disney," a newspaper article said about the rise of ABC.

Through his deal to put his products on TV, Walt demonstrated both his inherent contempt for the medium and his shrewd knowledge of its capacity for propaganda and exploitation. So far as he was concerned, TV was not an entertainment outlet but just another means of selling Disney to a wider public. His first two programs were devoted, for example, to a guided tour of Disneyland and a movie about the making of *20,000 Leagues Under the Sea,* which was due for release soon. Though expertly made, both had no other purpose but to act as come-ons for potential customers for other Disney products.

To handle the making of them and other programs in the "Disneyland" series, he assigned Bill Walsh, who was, like Peter Ellenshaw, one of his most fervent disciples, in his own sphere just as talented and perhaps even more admiring. In fact, so completely did Walsh regard Walt Disney as an all-knowing father figure that when he met and fell in love with a beautiful ballet dancer, he first took her to Walt for his approval before proposing marriage to her.

In spite of the fact that Walsh loathed television and all it stood for, regarding it as fundamentally meretricious, appealing to the shallowest of public emotions, he had a natural instinct for knowing what would make the most effective impact, what images on the small screen would grab most public interest and keep multitudinous eyes glued on the abysmal but magic box. When Walt called him in and told him that he had been given the job of writing the stories and producing the weekly TV program, he said, "Why me? I don't know how to produce a TV show."

"Who does?" Walt said, with a shrug.

So Walsh began "by using a combination of glue and chicken wire" to piece together clips incorporating scenes from Disney films past, present, or in the making; all for the purpose of promoting them for future paying audiences at the movie theaters. "We promoted anything that moved in the studio," he said. "Walt felt that nothing we ever made should be left to stand by itself, so we always had to do something to help it along at the box office. We did a review of the year's product at Disney, and it boosted the receipts when we put out the old films in revival.

"The amazing thing is that nobody complained that we were doing publicity movies. Far from it. Our '20,000 League' documentary even won us an Emmy. *And* it brought in sponsorship for our programs, including Coca-Cola and Johnson and Johnson."*

IT WAS SHEER boredom with old Disney products, plus the ambition to do something a little more original, that persuaded Walsh to branch out into productions of his own. "I thought it might be a good thing to do a series on vaunted American heroes," he said, "and we mulled over subjects like Johnny Appleseed, Daniel Boone, Wind Wagon Smith, Big Foot Wallace, and Davy Crockett. The first one we picked, by dumb luck, was Davy Crockett, who was someone at that time nobody had ever heard of."

Walsh and a writer named Tom Blackburn researched their subject and produced a script, and because Walt would have to approve it first and understood pictures rather than words, they illustrated most of the action on storyboards, which they hung around the walls of the office, showing Davy Crockett's progress from the Tennessee wilderness through his election to Congress and then to his death at the Alamo. Davy Crockett was drawn wearing a coonskin cap and fringed leather jerkin and breeches, and his huge body and facial features bore an uncanny resemblance to one of the Western film heroes of the day, James Arness.

But Walt wanted the budget to be kept low, and Arness cost too much money. In any case, when he ran one of Arness's movies, his eye was caught by one of the minor players in the background, and he pointed to him and said to Walsh, "What about using that guy?"

The actor turned out to bear the name of Fess Parker, and he was by no means flattered when Bill Walsh approached him for the part of Davy Crockett. Parker hated Wild West roles. As in the case of most minor Hollywood actors, hunger had sometimes forced him to play in Western

---

*They were sponsors of the Christmas shows in 1950 and 1951. From the Oral History in the Disney Archives.

films, and he found he was allergic to horses and loathed the clothing cowboys wore. His ambition was to appear in drawing room comedies, wearing smartly tailored suits; and his lip curled in derision and distaste when he saw the drawings of Davy Crockett's outfit.

"You trying to make a Gene Autry out of me?" he asked, contemptuously.

"That'll be the day," Walsh said.

But eventually hunger won out, and Parker signed up for the film. They had to teach him how to ride a horse, first, and do it without having him come down with a case of hives. His leather breeches were specially sprayed before he wore them, and when he was out of camera range he shied away from them as if they were a bunch of poison ivy, swearing they would give him "crotch rot."

By the time Walsh had finished the three segments of Davy Crockett's adventures, he had a sinking feeling that he might have given birth to a turkey. Not only was the film long-winded but it was choppy, and the drawings were unsatisfactory in bridging the disjointed gaps in the narrative. Moreover, it ended with Davy Crockett dying at the Alamo. As one of the studio executives said after seeing the first rough cut, "Who the hell wants a hero who gets killed in the final reel?"

Walsh gives credit to Walt for insisting on keeping the tragic ending. "We'd have every academic in the nation down on our necks if we tamper with history," he said. "It's a pity, but we'll just have to let him die."

But he agreed that the segments needed some connecting link to cure the disjointedness, and eventually came up with the suggestion of a theme song. Tom Blackburn, the scriptwriter, provided the subject matter ("Born on a Mountaintop in Tennessee"), and George Bruns, in the music department, came up with a tuneful and rollicking number. When Disneyland put the first installment of "Davy Crockett, Indian Fighter" on the ABC network just before Christmas in 1954, it was "The Ballad of Davy Crockett" that caught the nation's ear and gave the opener of the series instant popularity. In a matter of days, the song was at the top of the hit parade, and the program soared in the network ratings. At which point, those viewers who also read newspapers learned the historical facts about Davy Crockett and were reminded that he died fighting for his country at the Alamo. Avalanches of letters descended upon Buena Vista from children of all ages pleading with Walt Disney to give history a twist and keep the hero alive at the end.

There were so many thousands of them that Walsh went to Walt and asked what he was going to do. "You'll keep your word and let him die, won't you Walt?" he anxiously asked.

"Hell, I suppose we'll just have to," Walt said, glumly. However, two more episodes of Davy Crockett were made and shown after the episode in which he died.

IF EVER THERE was an opportunity for exploitation by the Disney rights department, Davy Crockett was it, and Kay Kamen would have gloried at the chance presented him to sell Frontierland logos and replicas of everything in the series. But Kamen had recently been killed in a plane crash, and his widow had sold back his share of royalties to Walt and Roy. Meanwhile, Roy had appointed O. D. Johnston, an accountant, to take Kamen's place.

Totally failing to appreciate the spinoff potential in the Davy Crockett series, which he didn't much like anyway, Johnson signed away merchandising rights to a manufacturing firm, which was soon quietly making a brisk profit from reproductions. Belatedly, one member of the marketing staff at Disney did realize the possibilities in pushing replicas of Davy's coonskin cap, but enthusiasm waned when it was discovered American fur dealers had lost their expertise in manufacturing fur hats, and cheap and adaptable fur—or fake fur—was not easily available.

But then the department had a stroke of luck. Someone came up with information that there had once been a brisk trade in coonskins between the United States and China, but that since China had now gone Communist, with the resulting imposition of a trade embargo by the United States, the commerce in coonskins had come to an abrupt halt. But what about the American suppliers and their coonskins? Had they found an alternative market, or did they have a lot of surplus coonskins lying around?

They did indeed. It was shortly revealed that a small exporter in California had a whole warehouse full of the skins and was so resigned to seeing them lie there until they rotted that he was willing to let them go cheap. A deal was made. A merchandise company dug out from retirement a veteran fur-hat maker, and a roaring trade began in Davy Crockett coonskin caps. Soon the warehouse was empty and still the demand for Davy Crockett hats mounted, until every amateur hunter in the country was shooting raccoons and shipping them to the manufacturer for a price that had climbed ten and twenty times in six months. For the first time, the future of America's most fecund wild animal was threatened as housewives banged away at the nightly pack gathered around their garbage cans.

Meanwhile, Walt had told Bill Walsh to put the TV series together and cut and shape it into a full-length feature film, and although industry experts were skeptical about its chances after such widespread free coverage over the airwaves, *Davy Crockett, King of the Wild Frontier* became a smash hit. Its success stimulated a renewed demand for Crockett memorabilia, and this time it was international. So desperate were the cries of small boys everywhere for coonskin hats that they had to be made out of rabbit and squirrel skins.*

BY 1960 CARD Walker, who ran promotion and exploitation at the Disney studio, had been appointed to the Executive Committee and named by both Walt and Roy as the man who would eventually become president of the company. Walt would retire first (though he left it vague when that would be), then Roy would take over for an interim period and soon afterward hand the reins on to Walker.

In the meantime, Walker wanted someone to run his promotion department, and he asked Vince Jefferds, whose talents he admired, to work with him and to move from New York to California, where it was planned he would eventually take over the entire character-merchandising operation from its then controller, O. B. Johnston. Jefferds accepted the invitation with mixed feelings, partly because his strikingly attractive wife, Jean, was a successful model in New York and did not want to move to California. But Walker insisted and eventually persuaded him the move was in his own best interests. (Eventually Johnson, with whom Jefferds worked at first, was kicked upstairs, and Walker made Jefferds vice president of merchandising, then vice president of the consumer products division, and finally vice president of marketing.)

Appalled at Johnson's mishandling of the Davy Crockett spinoffs, both Walt and Walker decided Jefferds should be given a free hand to remedy the situation, and he soon lined up stores throughout the nation to handle Crockett posters, hats, jerkins, and wooden rifles, all carrying the official Walt Disney logo and all paying royalties to Walt Disney Productions.

It was the beginning of a new source of massive income for the studio. At his peak, Kay Kamen had made Walt Disney Productions three million dollars a year in royalties. Jefferds increased that within two years to twelve million dollars, and when he resigned in 1983 he was bringing in a profit of fifty million dollars a year, after paying all his department's expenses.

No possible source of income escaped his ingenious instinct and sales technique. Exploiting *Peter Pan,* he had thousands of children all over the nation sleeping in nurseries—purchased from local furniture stores —exactly modeled after the one used by the Darling family in the Disney

---

*And not just small boys. One fur manufacturer in New York even produced a sable version for women with a price tag of around $750.00, and it sold well.

film. The furniture manufacturers and the stores both, of course, paid royalties to the studio.

Inspired by Davy Crockett's coonskin cap, he invented the first Donald Duck hat, a simple skull cap with a beak grafted onto it and plastic eyes, and it squawked when you squeezed it. There were 8,500,000 copies of it sold in the first year. "I could make a good case," Jefferds once said, "that licensing of an article is more profitable than manufacturing it. I often made money out of movies that were a loss at the box office."

One thing was certain. Davy Crockett was as much a turning point in Walt Disney's history as Mickey Mouse or Donald Duck. It made the Disneyland TV program one of the most popular in the nation. It brought a flood of national advertisers to ABC, the network on which it was shown, and it changed the nature of their operation. Its signature tune stayed at the top of the charts for months and persuaded Walt to go into the record business to cash in on the demand for recorded versions of the ballad. And the movie's success at the box office proved that a prior showing on the home screen enhances rather than diminishes its chances before a paying audience in the theater.

Incidentally, it not only made Fess Parker into a big star but cured his allergy to leather. And if he never did learn to prefer fringed jerkins to business suits, there is no record that they ever gave him a case of the hives again.

AT THE END of a hectic year during which "Davy Crockett" became the most popular TV series in America, Walt Disney called Bill Walsh into his office and told him that he was taking him off the weekly program. "Thank God," Walsh said. "I'm exhausted."

Walt grinned mischievously. "I've signed with ABC for a new program," he said. "It will be called 'The Mickey Mouse Club,' and it will play for an hour every day. I want you to run it."

"Oh, no!" Walsh fell to the floor in a simulated dead faint and lay there, puffing furiously on his cigar. Finally, he climbed to his feet again and said, "Look Walt, if I do that, two things will happen. First, I'll be dead. Second, it will ruin my marriage."

You had only to look at him to know he was serious. It was well known around the studio that Walsh was a serious diabetic who did not take care of himself. From a health point of view, he was already a living time bomb. Furthermore, his wife, Nolie, was becoming increasingly resentful of her husband's utter devotion to Walt Disney and of the way he allowed himself to be overworked by his boss. She hated, in particular, Bill's uncomplaining willingness to let Walt take all the credit for his achievements, even when Walt's contributions to them had been nil.

Nolie Walsh was young, beautiful, sensitive, talented, and devoted, and she knew Bill was deeply in love with her. But even at this stage in their marriage, a troubling question often nagged at her: *What would her husband's decision be if it ever came to the crunch and he had to choose between the wife he loved and the boss he worshiped?* She had a feeling in her bones that the choice would have to be made one day.

For the moment, however, that prospect was still over the horizon. Walt assured Bill Walsh that he would only be expected to work on "The Mickey Mouse Club" for ABC for a maximum of two years and then would be allowed to transfer to something he had always wanted to do, producing real films for movie theaters. Under Walt Disney's name, of course.

20
Tempus Fugit

DIANE DISNEY WAS twenty years old in 1953 and considered by her professors at the University of Southern California to be a bit of a rebel. High-spirited and tomboyish, she looked like a typical sunburned California blond, but she was more sensitive and intelligent than her general behavior would indicate.

Earlier, life at the Marlborough School, an academy near the Wilshire Country Club in Los Angeles, had had its difficult moments for her. As the daughter of one of the nation's richest and most famous men, she had spent her formative years in a kind of familial cocoon. This was the time when celebrities feared for the safety of their offspring and—with the tragedy of the Lindbergh baby still vivid in their minds—had them closely guarded against the omnipresent fear of kidnap and murder. In consequence, enrollment in school had been for Diane like release from a luxurious prison, and like any high-spirited girl, she savored the sudden freedom from the silken ties with which her parents had perforce bound her to them. It was hardly surprising that she instinctively rebelled somewhat—not against her new environment, where she anxiously tried to appear just like the other students—but against the establishment, against her parents and the respectable and conformist rules her famous father stood for.

Particularly at fashionable schools it was chic to consider Walt Disney's movies corny and the sentiments he expressed in them sugary, blatantly commercial, and out-of-date. Student comments about the character of Disney himself, whose conservative attitudes were well-known, tended to be patronizing or insulting; and Diane, who loved her father, often felt desperately unhappy to hear these condescending opinions expressed. But she refrained from springing to his defense not simply out of fear of being jeered at as a carbon copy of her parent but because she guiltily agreed that many of his movies were indeed oversentimental and could only have been made by a man with the old-fashioned outlook young people despised. In any case, as a rich man's daughter, deeply anxious to be accepted by her fellow students as neither spoiled nor overprivileged but just like one of them, she felt she had to demonstrate beyond doubt that she shared their lofty contempt for the older generation and all it stood for.

These were the days before American women students began publicly burning their bras and espousing feminist causes, but the clarion call of sexual freedom was already being heard. Diane knew her father would have been shocked at the thought of a daughter of his indulging in such shameless extracurricular activities. He believed unmarried females should always behave like well-brought-up young ladies and never act "cheaply" with men. He was of the opinion that no decent girl should ever marry before the age of twenty-five—and then not before consulting her parents. Nor should she ever, no matter what her age, surrender her virginity to anyone out of wedlock, even if she had fallen in love.

So when Diane went with a party of her fellow students to a football game at Stanford University and fell head over heels in love with a handsome player named Ron Miller, she determined not to hurt her father unnecessarily. She brought the young man back home to Holmby Hills, introduced him to her parents, and made it clear that she was going to marry him, no matter what. Lilly was pleased and Walt, although initially shocked—after all, Diane was still only twenty—reluctantly welcomed Miller, an amiable young giant, into the family.

The couple was married at an Episcopalian church in Santa Barbara in 1954. Diane's adopted sister, Sharon, came in from the University of Arizona, where she was a student, to be her bridesmaid, and tears streamed down Walt's cheeks as Miller slipped the wedding ring on his daughter's finger. It was normal behavior for the father of the bride, but Walt seemed to feel it necessary to explain his overwrought state. "I'm an easy weeper," he whispered apologetically to those around him. Which was indeed the truth. But what was more natural than an open display of emotion over a daughter's wedding?

It had not escaped notice, however, that practically anything seemed to bring Walt Disney to the verge of tears these days. If a strange mother thrust her child at him—which often seemed to happen whenever, for instance, he got out of his car—he would feel the telltale moisture welling in his eyes the moment he felt the weight of the infant in his arms. He rarely went to the theater anymore because moments of tension on the stage made him audibly gasp or sob and often drew titters from other members of the audience.

Yet there were certain events that left him surprisingly dry eyed. The year following Diane's wedding, before its official opening, Walt and

Lilly took over Disneyland, on July 13, 1955, to celebrate the thirtieth anniversary of their wedding. Hundreds of guests were invited. A high point of the evening was the maiden voyage of the paddle steamer *Mark Twain* sailing down the Mississippi in the great Frontierland exhibit, with Dixieland bands playing, drinks circulating, and everyone enjoying themselves.

Except Walt. He was good and mad because, earlier in the evening, he had found the decks of the *Mark Twain* not clean enough for his satisfaction, and just before the first guests came aboard he and Lilly had taken brushes and tidied up the decks themselves.

By 1955, Diane's husband, Ron Miller, was doing his military service at a camp in northern California (they still had the draft in those days), but Diane had come down for the celebration as had his adopted daughter, Sharon. Diane had already given birth to a son, making Walt a grandfather for the first time, and he knew he should be pleased and proud about it. Back in his youthful days, a fortune-teller had once forecast that he would die before he was thirty-five years old, and here he was, still alive and kicking, fifty-four years old and a grandfather! He should be happy, but he wasn't.

After the trip on the *Mark Twain* was over, the guests adjourned to the Golden Horseshoe Restaurant for dinner and a cabaret, and soon all of them were on their feet acclaiming Walt and Lilly, with Diane at their side holding on to Walt's hand. Under the circumstances, everybody would have forgiven him for becoming highly emotional. But no tears glistened on his cheeks on this occasion. The unsanitary state of the *Mark Twain* had soured his mood. Furthermore, he hated this kind of thing—anniversaries, birthdays, commemorations, and the passing of time such milestones recorded only depressed him.

Normally, he rarely took more than one drink in Lilly's presence and certainly never allowed himself to get drunk. But on this occasion, it was noticed that he was continually holding out his glass for refills. Once he gloomily speculated out loud whether the fortune-teller might have made a mistake. Could she have meant he was going to die at fifty-five and not thirty-five—next year, in fact?

In any case, each time that he looked at his smiling daughter and remembered that she had made him a grandfather, he wondered why she had named her first son Christopher—*Christopher!* for Christ's sake—instead of Walter Elias, after his grandad. He had been deeply disappointed when he was told about it.* Altogether, it was an unhappy

---

*It was not until 1961 that Diane got around to giving one of her sons her father's name. Walter Elias Disney Miller was born in that year, the fifth of her seven children. "At last," murmured Walt, at the christening ceremony, "you've named one after me." And, of course, promptly burst into tears.

evening, and Walt, who usually preferred to drive himself, ended up, dry eyed and drunk, being driven home to Holmby Hills by his daughter.

Even though he had put no opposition in Diane's way, it could hardly be said that his daughter's marriage had overjoyed him. Since Ronald Miller's only talents seemed to lie in his speed and capacity to take punishment on the football field, he fully expected to have to put him on the Disney payroll when he came back from doing his military service.

It subsequently became clear, however, that Miller neither looked for nor needed a meal ticket from his father-in-law. After his release from the army, he was recruited by the Los Angeles Rams and did well for them. Walt accompanied his daughter to several games, and in the end, it was the agonized expression on her face each time her husband was roughed up on the field below, rather than the bruises on his son-in-law's body, that moved him to offer him a job. Miller worked on various TV and movie units around the studio as an assistant director, and Bill Walsh took him in hand for a time. Then he was moved, on his father-in-law's orders, into the only sphere that promised real promotion at Disney so long as Walt was in charge—that of a producer. For the first time, Miller came in close contact with Roy Disney's son, Roy Edward, who was working on television shorts. It was antipathy at first sight.

THIS WAS THE period when Walt Disney was not only troubled by morbid thoughts but also by almost constant pain from an old polo injury. On the recommendation of his friend Floyd Odlum, he had been to see a specialist and had been told that he had better learn to live with it. Rectifying the condition would necessitate a major operation on the spinal cord, and the risk was greater than the probability of the cure. Since the specialist, however, assured him that he was otherwise in good physical condition, he was persuaded to go and try to make the best of his aches and pains. Even his most faithful employees now often found him, as David Swift put it, "at times tyrannical, dyspeptic, and outright obstinate."

Swift added, "But later, when I became a producer, I found myself reacting the same way with writers and directors I'd hired, when they irritated me by not comprehending immediately what I had in mind. I was in a hurry to communicate, like Walt. He had a studio to run, many projects, and when an employee like me didn't catch on immediately, he grew testy—it was that simple."

Not quite that simple, for he was rarely without the nagging and almost continuous agony of the pain in his neck. To help cope, in the early 1950s he gave a permanent job at the Burbank studio of Walt Disney Productions to a remarkable woman named Hazel George, a trained nurse and a qualified masseuse. Hazel was by no means a Florence Nightingale in her attitude toward her job, and most of the studio staff feared her salty tongue and rough ministrations and wondered how Walt could possibly put up with her.

"A hardened pock-mark-faced bit of infelicity she was, indeed," David Swift wrote of her. "Of course, she had to function in a man's world there [at the studio]. The inkers and painters [girls] were segregated in another building. Only Hazel and a few secretaries with huge rumps were the exceptions in the male animation buildings.

"Last time I saw Hazel, my God! Ward Kimball, whose assistant I was at the time, had offered to buy all the chocolate ice cream sodas I could drink, but I had to do it consecutively (in those days there was a little coffee shop on the first floor of the animation building, and they made deliveries). The first eight sodas went down without a hitch, the next three put a pallor on my complexion, and the twelfth put me on the floor moaning and groaning. Ward, Walt Kelly, and Fred Moore stopped laughing and called Hazel, the medical world's answer to Eva Braun, who stormed in on the emergency call, saw me thrashing and moaning on the floor, and was ready to administer to a dying artist . . . when Ward informed her I had drunk twelve chocolate sodas on a bet. She stood up, kicked me with her size 14 Enna Jettick, and slammed out, cursing all animators!"*

However, Walt Disney had great faith in the soothing powers of Hazel George, and every evening, after the day's work was over, he would go to the clinic he had had installed for her. While he was stripping off his shirt, she would pour him some scotch and let him take a couple of gulps before she motioned him onto the rubbing table. Then, with magical fingers, she massaged away the physical pains and the nervous tensions that had built up during the day.

At the end of thirty minutes he would finish the remains of his drink, and, while he made another for himself and one for her, they would talk. It was usually going on seven o'clock by the time he climbed into his car to drive home to Holmby Hills, above Bel Air. Walt Disney confided in Hazel as he did in no one else, including his wife, his daughter, and his brother. It was as if he sensed that, unlike anyone else around him, this rough, tough, down-to-earth, and practical woman not only liked and admired him but was never afraid to tell him the truth, especially about himself.

He took remarks from her that he would never have accepted from anyone else, even allowing her to mock him about what she called his "ostrich-egg-size ego." One night, when a thunderstorm was raging over Burbank and he expressed doubts about what it was going to be like

---

*In a letter to the author.

driving home through it, she asked, "Well, why don't you just go out and tell it to stop?" When he laughed over the way some of his employees hero-worshiped him, and added, "Peter Ellenshaw, for instance, thinks I can walk on water," she looked him straight in the eye and asked, "Well, can you?"

Most of his employees were afraid of him, and she was constantly counseling him to be kinder and less irascible with them, adding that he must learn to live with them and accept the fact that "most of us are just ordinary people, not geniuses like you." She urged him to be more understanding, especially with Ron Miller and Roy E. Disney, Jr., who were always getting the rough edge of his tongue.

"But *they're* not ordinary people!" he would protest. "They're..." he struggled for a word and then blurted out "mediocrities!" However, he did try to watch his tongue and stopped abusing them for incompetence—at least in public.

DAVID SWIFT HAD been working mostly in the animation department ever since he came back from war service. But he was eager to change his status and get into directing. One of the schemes he had cooked up for getting Walt to let him direct a movie was to do a draft script of Pollyanna. He had always thought that Eleanor Porter's American classic (about a maddeningly perfect child) would make a splendid Disney film, and in his spare time he worked on the treatment, hoping Walt would let him make it.

"I couldn't get it right, and I hated it," Swift said later. "Still, I sent it over to Walt, and a few days later I got a phone call from him. 'I read it, Bud [he always called me Bud],' he said, 'and I got a little tear there.' I was surprised because I knew from the way he said it I was to go ahead and finish the script—with him looking over my shoulder, of course. Until the final script was finished, he sat in on everything, and always had a concept of how the movie was going to be, the music, the photography, the casting, the look of it."

The only trouble was that with *Pollyanna* casting was where they ran into a problem. Who was going to play the title role? Pollyanna not only had to be perfect in appearance, in speech and behavior, but she had to be sympathetic, too, "or she would just make everybody who saw and heard her puke in their seats," Swift said.

He auditioned scores of little girls—and there were hundreds of them in Hollywood, where mothers with would-be child stars are as common as oranges in citrus groves—but couldn't find anyone totally satisfactory. He finally narrowed down the choice to three girls, none of whom really satisfied Walt. "They don't hit me in the heart," he kept saying.

It so happened that Bill Anderson, one of Walt's senior producers was heading for London to meet with British director Ken Annakin to finalize their production plans for the movie *Swiss Family Robinson*. As usual Anderson was called into Walt's office for a final review before he left. During the meeting Walt mentioned his dissatisfaction with the progress being made in finding a girl to play the title role in *Pollyanna*. In fact, he was so disturbed he said to Anderson: "This girl is so important to the success of the film that if I can't find the right one, I will cancel the picture."

Anderson had no immediate suggestion but promised to keep his eyes open.

"We don't have much time," Walt said. "Two to three weeks at most."

In London, Anderson and Annakin got to work on their preparations for *Swiss Family Robinson*. For their final sessions, they took over Anderson's hotel suite, forcing Ginny Anderson and Pauline Annakin out for the day in London. They returned in the early evening, praising a new British movie they had just seen, *Tiger Bay*, starring Horst Buchholz and John Mills. The movie also included a young girl who, they said, was simply fabulous.

Anderson was interested. "Young girl?" he asked, remembering his conversation with Walt about *Pollyanna*. "How young? Who is she?"

Their estimates of her age ran from 8 to 14, but they were certain about her name, Hayley Mills, and the fact that she was the daughter of the film's star, John Mills, and his playwright wife, Mary Hayley Bell.

Later that evening, as the Andersons were leaving the hotel to join the Annakins and friends for dinner, Anderson instructed the driver to drop them off first at the West End theater where *Tiger Bay* was being shown. He wanted to take a look at Hayley Mills. He was so enthusiastic about her performance that he couldn't wait for the film to end, but tapped Ginny on the shoulder and indicated that they should go back to the hotel.

"How about dinner?" Ginny asked.

"We'll dine at the hotel," Anderson said. "I'm going to call Walt."

The time was nine hours earlier in California, and Anderson caught Walt in an early morning *Pollyanna* production meeting. "I tried to keep my great enthusiasm out of my voice," Anderson said later, "because I knew Walt always resisted a sales pitch. But the attempt failed because my glowing recommendation was interrupted by Walt stating that they were in the middle of a final casting meeting for the picture. He said the boys at the studio had found a new girl and were about to sign her up."

Anderson pleaded with him not to sign up anyone until he had seen Hayley Mills.

"How *can* I see her?" Walt asked.

Anderson promised to obtain a print of the film by the following day, even if he had to buy it, and to ship it back to Burbank as soon as he got his hands on it.

"But Bill," Walt protested, "don't you understand that we're ready to go here? It will cost a lot of money to hold up the entire company for another two or three weeks. And what if she isn't right?"

"But she *is* right, I know it," Anderson insisted. "Please, just give me one week."

He decided to take a chance and fly back to California himself, and the first people he saw when he reached his office were the producer and associate producer of *Pollyanna*. They were furious with him. What the hell did the casting of their picture have to do with him? They had the girl, and his interference was creating tremendous problems for them. Further, they had already screened *Tiger Bay* the previous afternoon, and as soon as they could get in to see Walt they were recommending the signing of their choice—in spite of Hayley Mills.

"At that moment, the phone rang," Anderson said. "It was Walt. He had just seen *Tiger Bay*. Hayley Mills was terrific, perfect for *Pollyanna*. Not only should she be signed for the picture but for a long-term contract. I asked if I could do anything more, and he told me to get back to the *Swiss Family* preparations. The studio would take over from here on. He then told me to send in the *Pollyanna* producers."

About a week later, Anderson was working in his office when Walt telephoned. "He was in the hospital with a bad case of laryngitis," Anderson said. "Through the raucous cough and hoarse voice, it finally became clear that he was having difficulty signing Hayley to a contract. Only a few things really irritated Walt: one was personal illness, and another was making a decision and then being unable to act on it. I asked if I could help."

"Hell, yes," Walt croaked. "Don't you realize we have to get *Pollyanna* started, and we can't do that until Hayley Mills is signed?"

Anderson thought for a moment. "I have an idea what might be causing the problem," he said. "Ken Annakin and I recently had a talk with John Mills regarding playing the father in *Swiss Family*. John likes the idea and agreed to read the script. Probably the two deals are linked together."

"Well, what's wrong with Johnny as the father?" Walt asked. "Anderson, you're holding up the entire studio. For God's sake, sign him."

The next morning, Mill's agent was in Anderson's office, and two days later Walt had Hayley Mills for *Pollyanna* and her agreement to a seven-year contract. As for John Mills, Anderson had pinned him down to a firm contract to play the father in *Swiss Family Robinson*.

THE MORE HE looked at the *Tiger Bay* film, the more fascinated Walt became with Hayley Mills. While the negotiations were still in progress, he had flown with Lilly to London and stayed, as he usually did, in a suite at the Dorchester Hotel. And from there he asked that Hayley be brought to see him.

"I seem to remember I was taken out of school in order to meet him," Hayley Mills recalled. "I was well aware of who he was of course, and I was thrilled at the idea, although I only knew vaguely at the time he was interested in me for a film. It happened that we had recently been given a very small and sleazy Pekingese called Suky by Vivien Leigh. She had given it to Mummy because it peed all over her carpets, and it peed all over our carpets, too. In our case, it just joined a lot of other dogs that were doing the same thing, so it really didn't matter.

"So I took this dog along with us and I met Walt Disney, who was lovely, very kind and very calm, and we spent most of the time on the carpet playing with the dog. My parents must have been terrified that he would start peeing there, too, but fortunately on this occasion he didn't. Then he showed us the sights of London from his balcony, served some champagne, and began talking to my parents. I didn't take much notice of that because, I suppose, it was all above my head. But shortly afterward, I learned I was going to Hollywood to play in *Pollyanna*."

She remembers it as the most eventful period of her life and still savors her arrival in Hollywood, where ("of course") they stayed at the Beverly Hills Hotel. "I had a suite, my brother had a suite, and my mother had a suite," she said, "and there were televisions in every room, and the tables were piled high with mountains of fruits and candies and all sorts of goodies. And flowers! I mean you couldn't get into the room for all these things. I remember there was a great bowl of sweets [candies] from David Swift, and of course he went up in my estimation right away."

For both Hayley Mills and David Swift, the making of *Pollyanna* was probably one of the happiest experiences of their professional lives. Swift doesn't recall a moment during the production when there was any friction. The crew was completely cooperative, and Jane Wyman and Adolphe Menjou, who were also starring in the movie, took great pains to be helpful and friendly with the child actress from Britain.

Under normal circumstances, once he was satisfied with the script and the director seemed competent and capable, Walt did not interfere with movies in progress on the studio lot (except to check up on the day's rushes). But in this case, he not only came onto the set frequently but regularly invited Hayley and her mother back to the Disney house in Holmby Hills.

"He had a small movie theater in his home," Hayley said, "and he used to show us films. He had this soda bar in the theater and all through the film you could hear the squirts and hisses as he would make those wonderful ice cream sodas while we were watching. Then he had this big model train in his garden and he would take us for rides in it, driving it himself. And of course, we had this most sensational launch into Disneyland—with him personally conducting us around everything, for two whole days. That was fun. He even took us to his private apartment at Disneyland over the fire station, and I believe that was a special privilege. My father was there then, and my mother and my brother, Jonathan, who was nine. And we stayed at Disneyland overnight and it was absolutely wonderful. I've never done it since, but I've been saving up the experience so next time I'm in Hollywood I can take my children there and let them realize what it's like, too."*

Hayley Mills has strange but affectionate memories of Walt Disney. "He was so mild and nice and so eager to anticipate what would be pleasant for a young girl to see or experience," she said. "But then, of course, he could be a very tough person, too. Once while I was there he fired somebody on the set, and it shocked me because it was so sudden. He was wandering around in such a relaxed way, and he knew everybody there, Dick, Chuck, Wally, Fred, everybody. Then someone came up to him, and said, 'Hi, Walt,' and he replied, 'Hi, Jim, you're fired.' I never did find out what the man had done, or why he sacked him. It was done so abruptly and so casually. But I felt sure Walt had done it for the right reasons. I never felt he could be unjust. I always felt you could trust him."

Her feelings toward him were warmly reciprocated, and more. For Walt, this shy, smiling, affectionate English child became his ideal of the perfect young lady, and for the rest of his life he was inclined to measure all other girls against her, to their detriment. Certainly in his eyes neither his daughter, Diane, nor his adopted daughter, Sharon, possessed her modesty and charm.

"*Pollyanna* was Walt's favorite film," David Swift said later. "Because watching it made him cry. Of course, he would cry at the drop of a chord. I remember I showed him the rough cut of *Pollyanna,* which ran two hours and twenty minutes, and I was surprised to see him crying, right there in the sweatbox. I hated it. But he had his handkerchief out and he was crying. I said, 'Walt, we've got to take twenty minutes out of this,' and he said, 'No, no, no, don't *touch* it!'"

HAYLEY WON A special Oscar for her performance in *Pollyanna,* but it was nearly two years before she made her second film, *The Parent Trap.* It too was directed by David Swift and was a greater success at the box office than *Pollyanna* had been. But Walt was seen less frequently on the set during the shooting of this one, and Hayley did not meet him as often. Swift remembers it as a time when he often found her curled up in

---

*They visited it together in the summer of 1984.

a corner of the studio or hidden in her dressing room, sobbing her heart out, and her mother would ask the director to treat her gently "because she's going through a bad time just now." Swift put her distress down to the fact that Hayley was now fourteen years old and was struggling with the problems of puberty. Hayley herself remembers it as the time when she had a revulsion against herself and decided that she was growing up into an ugly duckling; she resented her body because she thought she had "no bosom" and hated her face so much that she covered it up with a cloth when she cleaned her teeth in front of her bathroom mirror in the morning. Gradually, she passed out of Walt's immediate ken, although she made several more films for Disney.

David Swift quarreled with his boss and left the studio to work for "those Jews" at Columbia.

"I was sorry about that," Hayley said, "because I think David Swift had a nice abrasiveness and a lovely quirky sense of humor. But like all other directors who worked for Walt, he had difficulty expressing his individualism. You had to direct exactly as Walt wanted the film directed. The usual Disney approach, where every movement and camera angle is mapped out on the storyboard, is all right for cartoon films. David Swift was very cleverly able to adapt it in such a way he didn't allow it to suffocate his own originality.

"But other Disney directors found it manacled them. I remember I was on Crete for ten weeks on location doing *The Moon Spinners* and we had terrible difficulty getting authority from Walt to change anything. Jimmy Neilson was the director, and he had a lot of theater actors in his cast, and theater actors work in their own way. They get together and discuss things, and they often come up with something quite different from the script—or, in this case, the storyboard. We had Joan Greenwood and Irene Papas and Eli Wallach, and they wanted to change things, and we would literally stop shooting for days on end while we waited for permission to make changes—and we rarely got it."

But her memories of Walt's fond attitude toward her stayed with her long after her contract with Disney came to an end, and she will always think of him as one of the nicest and most sympathetic of men. As for Walt, he never forgot her impact on him, either. "Hayley—what a lovely young English lady!" he would often remark, and then add, nostalgically, "What a pity they don't make nice girls like *her* anymore!"

"Oh, Daddy!" his daughter Diane would say when she heard him voicing such sentiments, "don't be so terribly old-fashioned!"

21
Twilight

BY THE 1960s, Walt Disney Productions had paid off all its debts and had assets worth nearly eighty million dollars in the bank. It was now one of the most prosperous entertainment organizations in the United States. Yet unless you counted Mickey Mouse and Donald Duck and the rest of the cartoon characters, it had no famous stars in its stable and picked up its name players as and when the scripts demanded them. But then, it did not need to keep stars on its payroll, just as it did not need to boast of the glamour of those who, temporarily, joined them, or make headlines by publicizing the far-out nature of their life-styles.

Disney's policy remained unchanged; it frowned on scandal and was still the sternest and most respectable studio in Hollywood. But, uninhibited by its strict moral stance, it was quietly becoming the most profitable studio. Nowadays, every activity in which it engaged turned into money. As vice president in charge of marketing, Vince Jefferds squeezed tens of millions of dollars out of the artifacts of its movie and TV productions: Mickey Mouse and Donald Duck books and T-shirts, hats worn by Davy Crockett and absent-minded professors, "magic" rubber (or flubber) playsets, squawking birds, snorting pigs, barking dogs, mouse costumes, duck costumes, dog costumes, Snow White wedding gowns, Peter Pan pipes, Tinker Bell chimes, and a horde of other outrageous and often wildly eccentric memorabilia, all stamped with the Disney logo, all earning vast profits in royalties for the company every year.

The crowds were so thick at Disneyland that Anaheim had become the entertainment Mecca of southern California, and all the citrus groves for miles around had been bought up by outsiders and besmirched with flashy motels, restaurants, bars, cabarets, and junky fairgrounds cashing in on the theme park's popularity. Walt cursed the poverty of a few years back that had prevented him from buying up more land and controlling the honky-tonk instincts of his rivals.

"Over there," he was already saying, pointing east, "is the rest of America, yearning for theme parks, too. And some day I'll build them. But I'll not make the same mistake next time, because next time I'm going to buy up a whole state, not just a few orange groves. And no one is going to be allowed to cash in on me." Although animated cartoon films were what had made Walt Disney famous and unique, it was not only because he was becoming bored with them that they now ceased to be the *raison d'être* of the Buena Vista studio. They had quite simply become too expensive to make by the 1960s.

The budget for *Sleeping Beauty*, completed in 1959, rose to six million dollars and lost the studio one million dollars. *101 Dalmatians* cost nearly four million dollars. It fared better at the box office, however, and did make a profit.

The studio no longer made many short cartoon subjects, and there were no more Mickey Mouse or Donald Duck series; the *Silly Symphonies* were long since forgotten. True, Ward Kimball still went on making his own short subjects, but then Kimball had a special relationship with Walt and was always the exception. In any case, he had already made an important breakthrough so far as animated cartoons were concerned. In 1951, Walt had assigned Kimball to direct the first Cinemascope animated film, *Toot, Whistle, Plunk and Boom*. Kimball had decided to gamble with a new graphic style that would lend itself better to the short's subject matter, the history of musical instruments.

"I got a lot of flack from old-timers at Disney when they saw some of the drawing techniques we were using in the picture," Kimball said later.

They were, in fact, so revolutionary that many of the animators and directors were convinced Walt would fire Kimball when he came back from a European trip.

"We had the picture about half animated when Walt finally screened our efforts," Kimball said. "I guess he surprised everybody by liking it. In fact, he even told some of the others to look at the picture because it had a lot of good ideas in it."

Kimball's next departure was a direct result of the success of *Toot, Whistle, Plunk and Boom*. "Around this time," Kimball said, "Walt was being interviewed on tape by Pete Martin for a series of articles dealing with Walt's life which appeared in the *Saturday Evening Post* [and subsequently as a book]. Called 'My Dad, Walt Disney,' it was supposedly dictated by Walt's daughter, Diane. By using this ploy, Walt avoided sounding too egotistical in the interview."

When the articles appeared, one whole segment (and later a chapter in the book) was devoted to Ward Kimball. In the course of it, Walt stated: "Ward is the one man who works for me I am willing to call a genius."

Reading those words by his boss in a national magazine left Kimball in a state of mixed emotions. "At first I was flattered, then alarmed at what might happen to the harmonious relationships I had with the people I worked with at the studio," Kimball said. "Fortunately, the good-natured heckling subsided, but the real problem developed from Walt. I began to realize there was method in his bestowing on me the genius title because whenever I would protest being given too big a workload or an impossible deadline, Walt would interrupt, lower that famous eyebrow, and with a half-diabolic smile remind me, 'What do you mean, not enough time? You're supposed to be a genius, aren't you?'"

But Walt saw to it that Kimball's life was never made impossible, and it was a time of happy collaboration for both of them. "I had won the Academy Oscar for best animated short, *Toot, Whistle, Plunk and Boom,* and in 1954 Walt asked me if I would like to direct some space shows for the Tomorrowland segment of Disney's new weekly TV show. With a crew of young creative talent we did an impressive story board on all phases of space travel. Walt was very excited about the idea of our working with such famous rocket scientists as Wernher von Braun. He insisted the shows had to be not science fiction but 'science factual' and believable. I remember especially our first meeting with von Braun and Walt together. When von Braun outlined just how some day we would travel to the moon and the planets and even outer space, Walt listened wide-eyed, his mouth open in pure rapture at what he was hearing. I realized then how fascinated he was with things scientific and with the scientists themselves. After being around von Braun for only two hours, Walt became an instant 'expert,' his elephantlike memory quoting all the facts and figures he'd picked up in those brief conversational encounters with the wonders of space travel."

The first of the Kimball shows, *Man in Space*, was aired on ABC on March 9, 1955, and the next day President Eisenhower called Walt to tell him how great the show had been. He asked for a print of the film "to show all those stuffy generals in the Pentagon" how they should start planning for space travel. "The second of our Tomorrowland shows," *Man and the Moon,* Kimball recalled, "was aired later the same year."

A few years later, when NASA's Apollo 8 actually made the successful flight to the moon, von Braun phoned Kimball and said: "Well, Ward, it looks as though they are following our script."

In December, 1957, at a studio press conference at Disney after the preview of the third space show, *Wars and Beyond*, the critics told Walt they had loved the show. "Walt put his arm around me and, in his joking style, started calling me 'My son.' This, I decided later, was as close as he ever got to complimenting me on my work."

But otherwise, animated cartoons no longer kept Walt Disney Productions going. Some of the most talented of Disney's animators had already left the studio, not always under the happiest circumstances. Norm Ferguson, still dissatisfied with the share of the credit Walt had given him for his felicitous invention of Pluto and other cartoon characters, had gone to another studio but had shortly afterward died of diabetes, alcoholism, and, it was said, an acute case of Disney-deprivation. Fred Moore, once the bubbling, uninhibited portrayer of nubile, unclothed nymphets, had been killed in an auto accident.

Partly to relieve the atmosphere of gloom in which the animation department was wrapped these days, Walt had assigned several of its luminaries to the designing of new features for Disneyland. Kimball (and von Braun) had provided most of the inspiration for the Tomorrowland exhibit. Woolie Reitherman and others first designed the tree house for the *Swiss Family Robinson* movie, and then reproduced it again in the theme park. From another film directed by Ken Annakin, *Third Man on a Mountain*, which had been made in Switzerland, the animation department produced a scale model of the Matterhorn for Disneyland, with a hair-raising ride down its steep slopes. This was officially opened at Disneyland by Walt's much-admired friend, Richard Nixon, who rode in the first car down the mountain with Walt, Lilly, Diane, and Sharon. Annakin, traveling in the car behind, sustained an injury to his back when it swerved too violently around a curve.

"Thank God it wasn't Dickie!" was Walt's reaction, when he heard about it. He ordered the ride halted and the public barred until the defect was found and cured.

HAVING LIFTED THE ABC TV network to national status, the Disney Channel ran into the inevitable resentment felt by a beneficiary toward its benefactor. Once it was no longer dependent upon Disney for its continued existence as a major network, ABC began complaining about the impact and ratings of some of its programs. It then tried to impose onerous production conditions, which persuaded Walt to look elsewhere for a TV outlet.

Thanks largely to the benison of the Disney Channel, the man who had originally given it a TV platform, Robert Kintner, had since left ABC for better things at NBC, where he was now president. Having brought him good luck and prosperity once, he was convinced Disney would do it for him again. The moment he heard the rumors, he indicated he would welcome Walt's TV productions on his channel. ABC, however, though willing to agree to a divorce from Disney, wanted alimony for the separation and, eventually, after some litigation, had to be compensated to the tune of $7,500,000 for their shares in Disneyland.

But the moment the papers were signed, Walt announced a tie-up with NBC and with it a significant step forward in the character of his TV presentation. Though most of the programs the Disney studio had filmed for ABC had been in color, they had, in fact, been shown on the small screen in black and white. But new technical developments were becoming possible on American television, and by the beginning of the decade, network engineers had made sufficient strides to begin national color presentations. What competing networks now needed was the requisite material. With his usual foresight, Walt was ready to provide it in abundance for his new sponsors.

"Walt Disney's Wonderful World of Color" began its first transmissions over NBC on September 21, 1961, and a profitable new era in television began for both of them.

BILL WALSH HAD, by that time, already quit working as the principal programmer of the Disney TV Channel, and, true to his promise, Walt had switched him to a new career as a producer of live-action theatrical films. Walsh more than made his impact from the beginning and revolutionized the character of Disney's new generation of live-action movies.

One of the reasons for Disney's break with ABC had been the network's refusal to let Walt make a series out of a story called *The Hound of Florence,* written by Felix Salten, about a magic ring that changes a small boy into a dog. ABC thought the TV public would never swallow such a far-fetched premise, so when Disney quit for another channel, Walsh took the script with him, and with his boss's agreement, made a theatrical movie out of it called *The Shaggy Dog.*

"It brought Fred MacMurray back into films," Walsh said later. "It cost next to nothing and made an enormous amount of money, as well as making Fred MacMurray a bigger star than he had ever been before—especially when the movie was later turned into a TV series [for NBC, of course] as 'My Three Sons.'"*

He followed that with several other money-making films, culminating in one called *The Absent-Minded Professor,* also with MacMurray, which proved to be one of the most profitable movies Disney had ever made. "Somebody had written some short stories for the old *Liberty Magazine,* and Walt bought them" Walsh said. "One was about rubber and one about flying cars and one about milk, and we combined them. A Professor Sumner Miller from El Camino College was brought in to supervise the laboratory sequences, and he helped to develop the idea of flubber, a sort of substance with the resilience of rubber and the malleability of plasticine." *The Absent-Minded Professor* made $2,500,000 in profits for Disney and subsequently exacerbated a growing crisis between Bill Walsh and his wife, Nolie.

Other Hollywood studios had been impressed by Walsh's skill and

---

*From the Oral History, Disney Archives.

monetary success as a producer, and several attempts were made to woo him away from Disney. One of the most tempting was an approach from Darryl Zanuck at 20th Century-Fox who invited him to join that studio and start his own production division, with ample budgets, his own choice of subjects, stars, and directors; plus, of course, the credit he was not allowed to have on the films he was making for Walt.

Walsh turned down this offer as well as all the others, and his wife was both irritated and depressed because it confirmed a growing realization of the relationship her husband had with Walt Disney and how secure were the bonds that bound him to his boss.

NOLIE WALSH WAS a dancer who had appeared on the show when Walsh wrote and produced a TV program for Edgar Bergen in New York and she had subsequently married Walsh when she came to Hollywood. A long, lean, beautiful, and ambitious young woman, she agreed with most of his admiring colleagues that her new husband was a highly talented showman, who would one day be a powerful force in the film world. It was not, of course, simply his professional promise that had drawn her to him. Like everybody else, she found Bill Walsh to be a charming giant of a man ("a cross between Clark Gable and Ernest Hemingway" was how she subsequently described him), and she loved being his wife.

But one of the shocks of their life together was her discovery of how closely his life was tied up with Walt Disney's. Gradually she became aware of the constantly increasing demands made upon Bill and their lifestyle by Walt Disney, and the realization was a disagreeable one for her.

"He thought Walt was a genius," she said later. "He totally worshiped him. When I first met Bill I had the impression he could be like a Neil Simon. He had a wonderful sense of humor, a very sophisticated sense of humor, and I never realized that his whole career would be with Walt, that he absolutely adored him. Walt was only ten years older than he was, but it was like a father and son relationship.

"Maybe that was because Bill was an orphan, and he was looking for a father figure. His mother had died of tuberculosis when he was ten years old, and he had been shipped off to live with a sister, and I don't think they ever told him when his father died. So he was the outsider, looking for acceptance—and for a father. And there he was when Walt found him, ready to play apprentice to the master, even though Bill already had a highly successful career in writing and public relations and was greatly respected in the industry. It was a shock for me to discover that his whole career hinged on Walt's approval and Walt's wishes. Obviously, Walt had great power over him—as he did over all the vastly talented people in the studio's inner circle. The brilliant artist, Peter Ellenshaw, a close friend of Bill, was in a similar situation. I'm sure that if someone had offered either of them six million dollars to leave Walt and go some place else, they wouldn't have done it. Walt had that charisma. He had very talented people who devoted their entire lives to him."

Like most women Nolie Walsh was never as impressed with Walt Disney as so many brilliant men, particularly his acolytes at the studio, seemed to be. "Walt surrounded himself with men who were better than they, themselves, realized. Men whose tremendous talents in writing, producing, and graphic arts were sublimated, repressed—sometimes totally lost as far as public recognition was concerned because of the dominance of Walt himself," she maintained. "He was a master of playing people off against each other. He never praised, never made anyone feel secure. And he got people around him who obviously, psychologically, had that need to feel obligated to him"

Ironically, though she increasingly resented his hold over her husband, Nolie Walsh felt no strain in her own relations with her husband's boss. It was obvious, however, that he left her cold. "Walt did not like women," she said, "particularly women with minds of their own. But I met him when I was nineteen, and I was very shy, and I never made any pronouncements that would offend him. Even before we were married, Bill took me along to Walt's house to get his approval. Having looked me over, he said fine, so we got married. Subsequently, I went on location and Walt was there, and we talked about the weather, and that was about it.

"But I must say," she added, " he was crazy about Diane and her children. We spent about three weeks in Paris and three weeks at the Hotel du Cap, in Antibes, and Diane had brought her three eldest children with her and was pregnant with her fifth [the one she subsequently named after her father], and on a day off we all went for a cruise on Fritz Loew's yacht, with Ron and Diane. And watching Walt I could see he was crazy about his grandchildren."*

But his enthusiasm did not extend to attractive young women, particularly the wives of his favored producers. "Later, when I must have been twenty," Nolie said, "we were shooting in Mexico, and every morning I used to ride down to the location with Walt, and there was never a word spoken, and that was obviously fine with him because he didn't want women talking to him. And I didn't bother him. So we sat there, each of us in our silence." Though neither of them ever said a word to the other about it, the battle for possession of Bill Walsh between Walt Disney and Nolie Walsh was already beginning and would increase in bitterness over the years.

Almost all the films Walsh produced for his boss won acclaim and

---

*Bill Walsh was producing a film called *Bon Voyage*.

financial success. A chain of cinematic triumphs culminated in his production of *Mary Poppins*, which was both a critical and box office smash. And each success resulted in new and better offers to Walsh from outside studios, which Nolie Walsh, with increasing urgency, strongly advised her husband to take. It was no longer simple ambition for her husband's future that motivated her now. She was frightened—frightened of Walt's hold on him, unwilling to share him, afraid of what the relationship might eventually do to their marriage. She became obsessive in her determination to drag him free, but the more she pleaded with her husband to leave, the more determined he became to stay with the man he admired more than anyone else in the world.

She tried every tactic and female wile she knew in her struggle to wrest him away. But she was no match for what she now seemed convinced was Walt's malign hold over her husband. Eventually, realizing the struggle was futile, the bond between the two unbreakable, she gave up the fight and broke up the marriage.

It all ended tragically, of course. There had never been any doubt about Walsh's deep attachment to his young wife, and her decision to leave and subsequently divorce him broke his heart. He was never quite the same again, and most of his zest for life went out of him. After the separation, and after Walt died, Bill Walsh's life and career seemed to go to pieces. So did his health. A chronic diabetic, he not only began to drink heavily but considerably increased his consumption of cigars, which had always been one of his weaknesses. "He became nothing more than a walking ashtray," Ward Kimball said.

There came a time when he began complaining that the injections he was supposed to give himself and the increasing number of pills he had to take interfered with his mental processes. One day, on a trip to London with Vince Jefferds and Ron Miller, he declared it was better to live for a month with a clear and unimpeded mind than for a decade with his brain befogged by the effects of all this medication. In a dramatic (and drunken) gesture, he threw his pills out of the hotel window.

He had his first heart attack shortly afterward. Though she had ended their marriage, Nolie Walsh still felt responsible for him, and she saw him through that first attack. When he became seriously ill, some time later, she brought him into her home and nursed him until he died in 1975.

It cannot have given her much comfort to discover that even death did not break his attachment to Walt Disney. He made only one important stipulation in his will, and that was that he should be buried as close as possible to his beloved Walt. Nolie and his friends did their best to follow his wishes. There was a funeral ceremony and despite the fact that he was a devout Roman Catholic, he was afterward cremated and his ashes placed in a canister on a hillside at Forest Lawn, just below the memorial garden where members of the Disney family are buried. He lies within hailing distance of his old boss.

If his old boss is there, that is.

NO MATTER WHAT the wives of his favored staff thought about Walt Disney, there was no doubt about his ability to bring out the best in the men who worked for him. Would they really have done better elsewhere, free from his selfish but catalyzing influence? In 1964, for instance, before the melancholy events recounted above took place, Walt and his three most faithful disciples—Bill Walsh, Peter Ellenshaw, and Ub Iwerks—came together to work on *Mary Poppins*, and it proved to be one of the most prestigious and financially successful cinematic enterprises of the decade. Afterward, most cinematic experts maintained that only Walt Disney could have brought it off.

Mary Poppins, a fantasy tale about a Victorian nanny who could fly, had long been a favorite book with children and grown-ups. There was always a copy on Diane Disney's bedside table, and she had had it read to her by her mother as a child. It had been written by Mrs. P. L. Travers, an Australian living in England. Both Lilly and Diane read it over and over again and had often urged Walt to buy it and turn it into a movie back in the days when he was still making full-length cartoons. But when he tried to do so he found out that the author had already been approached by practically every studio in Hollywood, all of whom she had turned down. She did not approve of the movies.

In the final months of World War II, someone mentioned to Walt that Mrs. Travers was in New York, having been brought there with her son to escape the ravages of the London Blitz. He sent his brother, Roy, to make yet another attempt to negotiate a film sale with her. She would not change her mind, even though she had heard of, and did not disapprove of, Walt Disney. "Mrs. Travers said she could not conceive of Mary Poppins as a cartoon character," Roy reported back to Walt.

It was not until 1960, fourteen years later, that Walt tried again. He met and talked with Mrs. Travers at her home in Chelsea, in London, and exerted so much persuasive charm that she finally agreed to sell the book to him—on two conditions, which, to everyone's amazement, Walt agreed to accept, so eager was he to make a movie out of Mary Poppins. Not only did he pledge it would not be an animated cartoon but a live-action film with the character of Mary Poppins played by a real human being,* but, most astonishing of all, he gave Mrs. Travers approval of the script—something he had never done before.

The script was co-written by Don DaGradi, a Disney veteran, and Bill

---

*Though he did introduce cartoon characters into some of the sequences.

Walsh, who was also assigned to produce the film. Walt agreed to hire Robert Stevenson, an Englishman who had once had a nanny himself, to direct. And he brought in Peter Ellenshaw to do the matte shots of the London setting and to work closely with Ub Iwerks, who had invented a startlingly effective new matte process of marrying live actors with cartoon characters on the same screen.

But who was to play the crucial role of the flying nanny, Mary Poppins? As Mrs. Travers had portrayed her in her book, she was a matronly old-fashioned Victorian type, of uncertain age, so unprepossessing that when Bette Davis was approached to play the role, she flatly turned it down. It was just as well. Bill Walsh and Walt had already decided the movie should have music, and Mary Poppins would need to sing at least one number; as a singer, Bette Davis sounded like a frog.

Next, Walt became keen on signing up Mary Martin, but she was just about to retire from stage and screen and turned him down. It was some time before they came around to the idea of trying out Julie Andrews, a young Anglo-American actress who had starred in *My Fair Lady* on Broadway and was now playing a leading role in the New York production of *Camelot*. Walt went to hear her in *Camelot* and, stirred by her bell-like voice and the humorously feisty nature of her stage persona, went to her dressing room and asked her to go to Hollywood to do a test for the part. He was sure he had found the star he needed. To his astonishment, Julie hesitated. Though he did not realize it at the time, she had lost her nerve, particularly about starring in the movies. After her triumph on the stage opposite Rex Harrison in *My Fair Lady*, she had done a screen test for Warner Brothers, who proposed to make a film version of the musical, and it had turned out badly. Someone told her that she was unphotogenic. As a result, there was a strong rumor around that Warner would give the Eliza Doolittle role to Audrey Hepburn instead, and a depressed Julie Andrews had become convinced that she was not the cinematic type. Moreover, she was pregnant.

Once Walt realized why she was holding back, he called in Walsh and Stevenson and told them to offer the part to Julie Andrews without giving her a test. "To hell with screen tests," he said. "I just know she'll be good. She bubbles away inside like a stockpot. She has just the presence we need for the role."

To Julie herself, he wrote asking her to come to Hollywood to listen to the music and talk over any problems that she might have about the part. He added, "We definitely feel in our own minds that, with your talent, you would create an unforgettable Mary Poppins, and we hope you will want to portray the wonderful character after you have seen the presentation which we can have ready for you in June."*

---

*Walt Disney to Julie Andrews, February 26, 1962. Disney Archives.

That November, Julie Andrews gave birth to a daughter, and was so euphoric over this happy event that the terrors of filmmaking paled into insignificance. She agreed to make the movie for Walt and arrived in Burbank in February 1964, with her then husband, Tony Walton, to begin work on the film. She made only one stipulation. If Warner Brothers did change their minds and consent to star her in *My Fair Lady*, she would be allowed to drop out of *Mary Poppins*. Walt was so sure Audrey Hepburn had already been signed for the role that he agreed.

At that point, Mrs. Travers arrived on the scene, determined to defend the integrity of her book. "She came over for a month or so," Bill Walsh said later. "I don't think she was too pleased with us, to tell you the truth, because she kept saying things like, 'Well, now, the rustle of Mary Poppins's skirt. There's a certain kind of sound it makes, and there's a drapery shop around the corner in Kensington and we *must* have that fabric.' Walt would interject, 'But Mrs. Travers, we're not going to spend all that time looking up drapers' shops in Kensington Road.' But by this time she would be off on something else. 'And about the letter box,' she would say, 'you haven't got the right kind of red. There's a certain shade of red it has to be.' She was always getting hung up on all these details.

"Meanwhile, what we were trying to do was get a reasonable story out of the book. The original was a series of little fragments with no story, just a sensational character and funny little bits of episodes. We needed a story to bring the whole thing together."*

Mrs. Travers strongly objected to the idea of putting songs into the film. "That was another hang-up," Walsh said. "And when Walt did persuade her to accept the idea that we had to have songs, she wanted us to use something like "Tarara Boom-dee-ay" or "Greensleeves." So there was bumping of noses all the way along the line, until we finally got our way and things got going."

MARY POPPINS HAD its world premiere at Grauman's Chinese Theater in Hollywood on August 27, 1964, and was a huge public and critical success. While the thunderous applause was still roaring through the theater, the severe figure of Mrs. Travers was seen approaching and the smilingly happy Walt Disney felt a premonitory twinge.

Sure enough, she was not pleased. "Julie Andrews is quite satisfactory," she said. "But then *she* is English. But how on earth did you allow the producer to use that Dick van Dyke to play the sweep? He's all wrong—so American! And I just hate that dance number you've put in with those ghastly cartoon figures. You just have to cut them out, Mr. Disney! When do we start the editing?"

---

*Bill Walsh, from the Oral History, Disney Archives.

Walt was too pleased with the reception of the film to be angry with her. "Fortunately, Mrs. Travers," he said smoothly, "you only had approval of the script, not of the finished film. It goes out as it is. Wait till you've seen it again and read the notices. You'll just love it!"

At a celebratory dinner later that evening, Bill Walsh introduced a happy Julie Andrews to Jack Warner, who had just officially announced the casting of Audrey Hepburn in his film of *My Fair Lady*. "Dear Mr. Warner!" Julie gushed. "Did you know I had a clause in my Disney contract allowing me to drop out of *Mary Poppins* if you chose me for Eliza Doolittle? How thoughtful of you not to allow me to do it and picking dear Audrey instead! I'll never forget you for giving me this chance!"

"Jack was absolutely furious," Bill Walsh said.

22

The Wounded Bear

THE RESPONSIBILITIES AND stresses of running the Disney empire were by now beginning to take their toll of Walt. The one-man operation method he had used to run the studio when he was younger and having fun with cartoon-film making was by this time inadequate to handle the added work load of two Disney parks and the building of his future dream metropolis, EPCOT.

"There were so many things going on that even Walt, with his historical attention to all details, however small, couldn't find the time to cope with any more," Ward Kimball said. "Lord knows, he tried. He really was the last of the great rugged individualists. He had always had the final say on every script, every production, every hiring and firing, on the placement of every tree and the color of every building—everything down to the smallest detail. All of this he still wanted to control, including the monumental plans for Florida and EPCOT. One Walt Disney was trying to be *five* Walt Disneys."

Kimball added: "His genius was being spread too thin, and we all knew it. And then came the shocking blow: his lungs were being eaten away with incurable cancer. For half of his life, there had been those awful, hacking coughs from chain smoking. His doctors had continually warned him to give up cigarettes and maybe heavy drinking. During one of those last meetings I had with him, he broke into a long coughing jag that lasted for a whole minute at least. It was terrible. When I timidly asked him why he didn't give up smoking, Walt looked up at me, his face still red from the coughing, and rasped, 'Hell, I gotta have a few vices, don't I?'"

He was always in a bad temper at these times, and in the studio they began calling him The Wounded Bear. Everyone had to watch out, in case you accidentally crossed him. When he got really angry, he would flatten his adversary without a thought, no matter who he was.

For Kimball and those who had worked closely with him over the years, it was obvious that their boss was undergoing some sort of metamorphosis—and even those who respected and feared, rather than loved, him were disturbed and saddened by it, the more so because they realized that he was completely unaware of the changes that were taking place inside him.

One day in the mid-1960s, a story man named Charles Shows was in the hallway at Buena Vista when he realized Walt was just ahead of him. "It was about six in the evening, after a hard day's work," Shows said, "and I guess Walt didn't realize there was someone behind him because the rest of the hallway was absolutely empty. Normally, he moved with a jaunty youthful stride, but as if he realized he didn't have to pose for the time being, he abandoned all pretense. His head dropped onto his chest, his square shoulders slumped, and I saw him age twenty years. As he shuffled down the hallway, his tired feet dragging his exhausted body, I had a dreadful gut feeling that I was looking at a man whose days were numbered." Then Walt heard the footsteps behind him and straightened up and shook himself, and it was as if the years and weariness were being sloughed off like dust from his shoulders.

"I still contend," Ward Kimball said, "that the tension combined with trying to keep control of everything that was going on—even though Disney was at least twenty times bigger than when it started—plus the cigarettes and booze made him like a bomb waiting to go off. He may not have realized a fuse had been lit, but we did."

HE WAS IN pain now for most of his waking hours, and the amazing thing is that he learned to live with it and continued to be so active and look so cheerful. Sometimes the only thing that got him through the day was the thought of the whisky Hazel George would pour out for him when she arrived for the evening therapy session. He no longer went to visit her at the clinic, where she had begun limiting the scotch; she came instead to his office, where the supply of booze was ample, and he could suck at it through a straw while she massaged his neck or treated the aching nerves to some heat.

"You know," Hazel said one night, watching as he refilled his glass, "If you go on like this, you're in danger of becoming a lush. What does Lilly say when you get home smelling of all that booze?"

Walt shrugged, grinned ruefully, and said he kept out of his wife's breathing space. He added that he knew what Hazel thought of his drinking. But he pointed out he didn't touch a drop in the office all day, and didn't drink when he got home. But by the time his working day was over, he went on, he was desperate for a scotch.

Catching the disapproval on her face, he said: "Don't think I'm not aware of what they're saying about me around the studio." He knew he was a grouch, he said, that his fuse was short and growing shorter, that he blazed up and got mad at nice people who hadn't done anything wrong and didn't deserve it. It was all true, and he hated himself for it. He held up one of his specially rolled brown cigarettes—he consumed up to seventy a day—and said that they used to calm him down but added that they didn't seem to do anything for him any longer.

"My nerves are all shot to hell," he admitted, "and nowadays—" he put his hand gingerly on the back of his neck "this fuckin' pain here is driving me nuts!"

"Don't the rubdowns help anymore? Or the heat treatments?" Hazel asked. "Have I lost my magic touch?"

Sadly, he shook his head. The nightly sessions didn't help him any longer, he said. "Frankly, the only reason I come here nowadays is for the booze." He swallowed the last of his scotch and reached for the bottle. Hazel got there first and moved it away, locking it in the closet. Then she began talking to him softly, earnestly, persuasively.

If the pain in his neck was now so bad, he had to go back to the doctors, and do it soon, she told him. He also should try to cut down on all the scotch he drank when he came to see her. There were already rumors around the studio that he was drunk every night when he climbed into his car. She feared he was going to have a nasty accident on the way home, and the highway patrol would pull him in for DWI. He mustn't let it happen. "That's one of the scandals this studio can do without," she said.

But only Hazel George and a few close observers really knew the truth about how he was feeling, and to most of the others around the studio—even many of the veteran employees—he was the same tough and respected Walt Disney of old, full of energy and enthusiasm, ever the perfectionist, harsh and brutally critical of fools and slow learners and those who made errors. The difference was that in the past he had been prepared to forget and forgive when his excesses were pointed out to him.

Nowadays, he was much harsher and relentless, and much more easily aroused to anger by what he thought were attempts to poach on the precious preserves of his authority. When the British director Ken Annakin, for instance, set off for Tobago on location to begin shooting *Swiss Family Robinson*, the company took most of their wild animals with them—forty-eight monkeys, a baby elephant, a tiger, a lion, two anacondas, and eight Great Danes. They were shipped from California to Tobago by plane, and when they left Los Angeles Airport, the Los Angeles *Times* did a story headlined:

ANNAKIN'S ARK LEAVES FOR TOBAGO

Walt was furious when he saw it., The director had already made five successful movies for him; nevertheless, he flung the paper aside after reading the story and shouted: "What the fuck is this? Who the hell is Annakin? It's not his ark—it's Walt Disney's ark!"

Annakin was hurt, but not too much, by Walt's comment. He had always considered that working for Walt Disney was the luckiest thing that had ever happened to his career. He had no doubt at all that Walt was a genius and always knew exactly what the public wanted and how to provide it. But like all geniuses he was apt to be temperamental.

"Of all the studio chiefs I have ever worked with," Annakin said later, "I have never known anyone who operated at conferences so magnificently as Walt. You would go into a story session with him, full of great ideas, and he would scratch his nose and say, 'This is just from the top of my head, but I think we should do this and this....' And it would usually be like listening to a new fairy tale, and we would break up the session happy and amazed that the solution to our story problems should be so simple—and different."

Annakin forgave Walt Disney lots of things.

"Despite his tendency to be a dictator, he had a warm and generous side to his nature," Annakin said. "He once said, 'You and your wife must be at a loose end this weekend. How would you like to use my box at Santa Anita [the race track]?' Pauline and I jumped at the chance, and we had a fabulous afternoon spending the gambling money Walt had secretly given us."

During the first six months of preparation for *Swiss Family Robinson*, Walt had participated in all the production conferences, and when progress on the script was going well he usually invited Annakin and his wife to spend the weekend with him at his house in Palm Springs.

"Sometimes he would cook the meals for us," Annakin recalled, "and afterward we would sit out under the stars discussing his ambition to build an entertainment park or his passion for model railways. Sometimes he would take us down to Smoke Tree Ranch where he would sit at the head of one of the big communal tables and invite discussion on any subject. But even here he could be touchy. Pauline once got into an argument about television. I think she said that British programs were far superior to those in America. She got a thorough earful from Walt for that statement."

At one point during the *Swiss Family* script conferences, Walt had proposed a scene in which a tiger is caught in a trap by the pirates. He liked dramatic confrontations between animals and humans. Annakin remembers saying to Walt at the time, "Does it have to be a tiger? Lions are much easier to work with."

Walt immediately picked up the remark. "Ah ha!" he said. "Ken's afraid of a tiger, is he?"

From that moment, Annakin knew he would not only have to use a tiger in the film but make sure each shot was achieved exactly as sketched out with Walt—which, in one scene, meant that two of the Great Danes would actually have to make bodily contact with the tiger.

"I knew he would have reshot the sequence at great expense and effort to get it exactly as he had conceived it," Annakin said. "And he'd have gotten someone else to do it if I hadn't succeeded."

John Mills was playing the role of Mr. Robinson in the film, so his wife, Mary Hayley Bell, and their daughter, Hayley, flew to the location with Annakin and the producer, Bill Anderson. Hayley Mills remembers the animal sequences with some discomfort because of the way they were treated to get the shots that were needed.

"We had a sequence where a zebra gets caught in quicksand," Annakin recalled. "The vultures are all around it, and the Robinson boys try to save it. It wasn't too easy for me to shoot that. You make quicksand with a lot of bran, and, in this case, instead of struggling, the animal tended to stand still in it. So I had to give it what is technically known as a 'hot shot.' Of course, Pauline [his wife], the continuity girl, and some of the others hated that because they thought it was hurting the animal. It wasn't—not a prolonged hurt, anyway. But I knew perfectly well that unless I got the scene absolutely right, Walt would lose all faith in me. With him, you had to damn well do the impossible. Good training!"

What Hayley found even more disturbing was that for the tiger sequences, the animal had his sharp teeth filed down and his claws removed. Both the director and producer thought Walt might appear at any moment, and they were determined to make every scene with the tiger as graphic as possible. "And we knew Walt would take exactly the same attitude as a circus trainer," Annakin said. "If you wanted to achieve something with a dicey animal, all right, he expected you do what is necessary to get the scene. It was his picture and his conception, and you damn well did what was necessary to get what he wanted."

As it happened, Walt was too busy with other projects to visit the *Swiss Family* location, and the producer and director never saw him from beginning to end. "So perhaps we got the impression that he didn't come because he didn't think it was his film," Annakin said. "And I can remember Bill [Anderson] drawing up the credit cards and putting himself down, correctly, as the producer. Walt was angry, even though he hadn't been near us. And although *Swiss* became a popular success in the cinemas under the banner, "Walt Disney Presents," both Bill and I had a lot of trouble launching the movie because Walt was sulking. The last thing we wanted to do was minimize his creative contribution, but the truth was he hadn't actually done anything to produce the movie after we left for Tobago. There was a certain small-mindedness about him at times—and this was one occasion when it showed."

For Ken Annakin, there was a sad sequel to his disappointment over

Swiss Family Robinson. Some time later, Walt and his wife went on one of their trips to London, and one night the Annakins invited them for dinner at their home in Onslow Square.

"There was a tentative idea I was going to make a film of *Westward Ho!* for Walt," Annakin said, "and we talked about it over dinner while Pauline and Lilly chatted together separately. The time came to leave after a very warm, convivial evening. Six steps had to be negotiated from our apartment into Onslow Square, and Lilly slipped and fell on her butt. I rushed down and picked her up. Fortunately she hadn't broken anything, but rather brusquely Walt took over and hurried her into the waiting limousine."

After they were gone, Pauline Annakin, who has a shrewd insight into character, said to her husband, "I have a strong feeling you're never going to make another film with Walt."

She was right, too.

"I never did make *Westward Ho!*" Annakin said. "And though other projects came up at various times, Walt never came round to offering me another assignment. At one period I brought to Walt's notice the possibility of acquiring Kipling's *The Jungle Book* from the Kordas. I felt it would make a marvelous musical and laid out the sequences as I saw them for Walt. We had some correspondence about it. Then he suddenly decided to make it as a cartoon movie. I've always thought he was swayed into that decision because he didn't want to be embarrassed working with me again. I had been witness to a piece of what he regarded as shameful behavior on the part of a member of his family, and he couldn't face up to the fact that I had been there. Anyway, I never worked for him again."

It was a sad confirmation of how Walt had changed. A year or two back, he would have laughed off the incident and forgotten about it. But this was the way he was—now.

IN THE SUMMER of 1964, mysterious strangers from out of state began buying up large tracts of land on the outskirts of the small central Florida city of Orlando. All efforts to track down the identity of the buyers were unsuccessful. The outsiders, who obviously had plenty of money and were willing to pay cash, made it a condition of the sales that they effected that landowners not divulge the identities of the buyers—who were using phony names, in any case—and swore them to secrecy over the price and other details of the transactions.

Local gossip soon had it that the U.S. Government was behind the purchases, and the wiseacres prophesied that Washington, already beginning operations on its space program at nearby Cape Canaveral, would soon be moving into the Orlando neighborhood and building a vast new complex to manufacture everything from intercontinental missiles to hydrogen bombs.

Then someone let slip the fact that the famous Walt Disney had flown into the area twice recently from Hollywood in his private Beechcraft plane, and that a woman believed to be his wife had even been heard to remark, over a hamburger in a junk-food restaurant in Kissimmee, "But it's just swamp, Walt! How could you possibly want anything here?"

Was it just a coincidence? It seemed so—especially when it was pointed out that Disney's father and mother had been married near Kissimmee, and it was plausible to suppose that their celebrated son was simply making a sentimental pilgrimage. But the mysterious sales went on, and soon thirty thousand acres of central Florida land, citrus groves, forests and swamps, plus some choice farmland, had passed into the hands of the secret buyers.

It was at this moment that Emily Bavar, a reporter who edited the Sunday magazine of the Orlando *Sentinel,* quite fortuitously accepted a promotional trip to California to attend the tenth anniversary celebration of the opening of Disneyland. Mrs. Bavar, intrigued by what was going on in her own state, asked Walt Disney if he was buying up land in Florida to build another Disneyland. He did not bat an eyelid at her question but replied, "Who would ever want to build a theme park in Florida—with the sort of climate, rivers, and landscape you have over there?"

He reeled out a detailed list of reasons why you couldn't possibly open a Disneyland in Florida, and the more he talked, the more Bavar got a crawling feeling up her spine that Walt Disney was trying to bamboozle her. "I just knew he was one of those men who can't tell plausible lies," she said. "He kept pouring the statistics on me, talking about the terrible rainfall, the terrain, the swamplands. And I suddenly found myself asking, If he isn't going to build in Florida, why does he know so much about it? How come he's an expert on all the *drawbacks* of Florida if he hasn't already considered them and decided to go ahead, anyway?"

So she looked Walt Disney firmly in the eye and asked him to confirm or deny if they were his agents who were buying up all the land in Osceola County. Later at lunch she sat next to Walt and repeated her question to him. He nodded across the table toward Roy Disney and said all financial and investment matters were in his hands.

"In essence his reply was, 'I couldn't tell you even if I knew because Roy is in charge.' But," Emily Bavar said, "though I could just as well have been wrong, I just knew Walt was being evasive. But what made me particularly suspicious was the fact that he knew so much about Florida, its problems about rain, humidity, and transportation. I didn't believe him when he denied my instinctive feeling. I decided to take a chance."

That night, on an impulse, she sent a story to the Orlando *Sentinel* tentatively identifying the Disney organization as the secret land grabbers in Florida and predicting they would soon begin work on a new theme park there. The paper's Sunday editor ran the story on an inside page, and that wasn't good enough for the *Sentinel's* strong minded proprietor-publisher, Martin Andersen. Shortly afterward, when his reporter had returned and he had had a chance to talk to her, he ran another story from Bavar and prefaced it with an "Editor's Note:"

> Emily Bavar, editor of *Florida Magazine*, just returning from a visit to Disneyland at Anaheim, Calif., near Los Angeles, where she personally interviewed Walt Disney and was his guest along with other newspaper writers from Birmingham, Montgomery and Ft. Lauderdale, is firmly convinced the so-called "mystery industry" to be located on the $5 million, 30,000-acre tract between Orlando and Kissimmee, is to be a second Disneyland. Or rather a similar attraction to the famous Anaheim attraction, but one, perhaps, with a new name and a new theme. . . . The editors of *The Sentinel* are convinced that her Sunday piece was "underplayed," that it did not have the importance or impact it should have had, and that the new project is really going to be a new type of entertainment built by the world's greatest cartoonist, movie producer, showman and world's fair exhibit-maker.
>
> After talking to Mrs. Bavar, *The Sentinel* is convinced that the mystery industry's author, architect and builder is Walt Disney and that he will spend upwards of $30 million on it.

This time Bavar's story ran on the front page, with a banner headline, and it was confirmed on November 15, 1965, by a statement from Florida's governor, Haydon Burns, that work would soon begin on a new theme park, to be called Disney World, near Orlando, Florida.

From Walt's point of view, all the secrecy was needed because he wished to avoid the mistakes he had made in Anaheim, and he was determined to buy enough land not to be hemmed in by honky-tonk rivals. Once it was known that a vast Disney theme park was in the making, outside hotel, restaurant, and fairground interests would have moved in to snap up adjacent land, sending prices through the roof, as well as ruining the nature of the enterprise.

Not only that. He had sent emissaries from Burbank to Tallahassee, the Florida capital, headed by the shrewd marketing man Card Walker, to make a deal with the local government before signing the final papers. In return for bringing such an enormous tourist attraction into the state, Walker asked for a quid pro quo on behalf of his boss, and the governor gave it to him. For the first time in Florida's history, control over all the territory to be included in the future Disney World was ceded to the owners. The new park would become what amounted to a self-governing community, with its own laws and police services, hospitals, health and all necessary maintenance departments, plus a special tax rate; and no outside authority would be allowed to enter its territory without an invitation from the owners nor would its finances or affairs be subject to control by the state.

WALT HAD AN additional motive for secrecy, but this he was determined not to reveal until he was good and ready.

If anything could have enlivened and inspirited him, Disney World was it. For a time, that is. Nothing in the history of leisure parks had ever been planned on such a scale before. The preparation of the ground at Disneyland in California had been entrusted to Morgan Evans (known to Walt Disney as "Bill"), a landscape gardener from Malibu, and he had prepared every man-made hill and planted all the trees. But the prospect Admiral Joe Fowler, Disney's construction boss, put before Evans when he showed him the site for Disney World in Florida was daunting.

They flew on an inspection tour out of Orlando, and Bill Evans was appalled. The territory stretched practically from horizon to horizon, and all Evans could see were great tracts of bald cypresses and saw grass, gashed every few hundred yards by drainage canals. He had seen the grandiose plans that Walt and his advisers had been working on over the past year, and he knew they included more facilities than there were in Disneyland, and each of them was to be substantially larger.

How, he wondered, could his boss possibly imagine that, out of this endlessly flat prairie wilderness below them, they could build a vast new city of entertainment, with multistoried hotels, fairy castles, river rides, prairie cow towns, boating lakes, lawns and gardens and woodlands, not to speak of a giant monorail intended to whisk visitors from one end of the theme park to the other? Even to his experienced eyes, which could normally see a desert transformed into a garden, this was a really dreary piece of landscape, and he winced at the thought of having to work on it.

"Walt had paid two hundred dollars an acre for the whole thirty thousand acres, and that was all it was worth," Evans said later. "It was no-good land. It wasn't even good as pastureland. After massive earth-moving we probably had the world's worst soil in which to plant. But if I was fazed for a time, my boss certainly wasn't. He had inherited Walt's vision, and could already see the jungle down there blossoming into buildings, roads, hills, golf courses, hotels, and all the paraphernalia of a splendid new community. Plus all the fascinating new entertainment, of course.

"And he wasn't too surprised or downhearted when we had nothing but grief at first. For instance, one of the features Walt had particularly wanted for Disney World was a real live jungle, not one of the kind you have in Florida, nor even like the jungles of Africa and South America, where the same old plants keep repeating themselves for mile after mile. He wanted a really dramatic jungle, full of sensational plants, and we picked elephant ears, ginger lilies, bananas, big ficus from Australia, Africa, and Asia, all telescoped into a few hundred yards and giving more of an exotic jungle vision than you'd get in the real location without traveling hundreds of miles. But the first year, things went wrong with the planting, and a half million dollars worth of exotic plants just died. This was before Disney World was open, and Walt was already dead; and when we confessed to Joe Fowler what had happened and why, he simply said: 'Then you'll have to start all over again, won't you?' There was no question of abandoning what Walt had envisioned."

IN HIS LAST months, Walt had urged everyone transforming the Florida landscape to press on with the project, at top speed, and damn the expense. Later on, some of his associates speculated that he must already have suspected if they took too long about it, he would never live to see Disney World finished—as, of course, he didn't. In that last year, he was impatient for the great new theme park to be opened and operating, so his construction experts could turn their attention to the other project that he planned to build next to Disney World-the one he considered to be much more important. EPCOT.

The secret idea of EPCOT had first been revealed at the press conference of November 15, 1965, when the governor of Florida had announced the plans for Disney World, though its significance was overlooked at the time. Introducing Walt Disney to the reporters, Governor Haydon Burns had described him as "the man of the decade, who will bring a new world of entertainment, pleasure, and economic development to the state of Florida," and all the attention of the press was on the details of the theme park, which Walt described as "the biggest thing we've ever tackled." Most of the questions that followed were about its size, its cost, its potential for profit.

Then, by accident the "Plan beyond the Plan" got its first public mention. Someone asked a question about where the huge working staff of Disney World would be housed once the park was operating, and Walt outlined his plan for building an enormous artificial lake on the grounds, and then using the "fill" from all the dirt they would dig up to make a mountain. "And inside that mountain," he went on, "we will build a small city for our employees, where they can eat, rest, swim, wash, sleep, and breathe fresh, relaxing air that we will pump into the mountain's interior. It will be a sort of model community."

But that was not the only model community he was planning for

Florida, he added. And suddenly the idea began to germinate. "I would like to be part of building something more than that," he said, "a City of Tomorrow, you might say." And he added, "Here, in Florida."

By the time the press conference was over, his enthusiasm for Disney World was already beginning to fade as a new and more exciting project began sputtering in his mind. "I know how to build a theme park," he said. "This new one will be no different from Disneyland, except that it will be bigger and we'll have more water."

But to build a City of Tomorrow—that could be the last great challenge.

BY THIS TIME the bulldozers were churning their way across Osceola County, and the landscape of central Florida was undergoing a vast and convulsive transformation. This was an area that would never be the same again. And if Walt Disney was beginning to be bored with it, the people in the area were certainly not. They already knew what had been wrought in Anaheim by the arrival of Disneyland, and if the ecologists shuddered at the thought of the radical changes that were being made to their environment, the officials of local government, the realtors, the movers and shakers, happily braced themselves for the challenges—and the profits—that they knew were coming. The Orlando *Sentinel* put in an order for extra presses to cope with the increase in circulation that they anticipated from the arrival of Disney World. The editors launched a campaign to construct a community center big enough to handle all those conventioneers who would soon be coming in.*

"They're really excited down there," Card Walker reported when arriving back in Burbank from one of his trips to Orlando. But he and Roy Disney sensed from Walt's apathy that he had somehow been turned off, and from now on, they knew better than to consult him too frequently about details of Disney World landscaping, road making, new canalizations—matters with which, in the past, he had insisted on involving himself. His mind had gone on to other things.

It was not that he had lost his enthusiasm. He was still buzzing with ideas and plans—but for something entirely different. He had a locked room at Buena Vista, behind his office suite, where no one else was allowed to go, except at his invitation. Some of the veteran animators joked about what it contained and called it Walt's "Chamber of Horrors." Ward Kimball even suggested it was the place where "Walt keeps his

---

*They did not underestimate the scale of local development. In little more than a decade, the population of Orlando and its environs, thirty thousand in 1965, would swell to a quarter of a million; and in spite of all the land he had bought to keep the honky-tonks at arm's length, Disney World would still have to accept garish rivals a few miles down the road, even if not upon the immediate doorstep.

dirty pictures." It was, in fact, the repository of his hopes and dreams. No one except his secretary and two members of his immediate staff, who shared his secrets, actually knew that this was the place where he was working out the details of his City of Tomorrow.

As his chief helpmates he brought in two outsiders, General William E. Potter, who was practically a stranger to him, and Marvin Davis. General William E. Potter had retired from the army to become governor of the Canal Zone in Panama and, in 1963, had been appointed chief aide to Robert Moses in the construction of the New York World's Fair. Walt had been asked by Moses to give him some ideas for exhibits, and he had come up with the dramatic model of Abraham Lincoln that moved, appeared to breath, and was so lifelike when it arose and began to make a speech that it had proved to be a sensation. It was in the course of his many visits to New York that Walt had dealt with Potter several times, found him bright and reliable, and eventually invited him to join his staff.

Marvin Davis (not to be confused with Marc Davis, a former animator) had also made his mark with Walt. The original idea had been to put both men to work on Disney World; but they had gradually become Walt's chief consultants, aides, and confidantes on his new preoccupation. As his representatives, they were now scouring the nation and the world, soliciting the aid of experts on future medicine, environment, city planning. They were authorized to pay highly for technical forecasts of what life could and should be like not in some idealized Utopia but in a carefully organized, expertly governed community of tomorrow. And only they really knew what was going on in Walt's mind.

In his secret room in Burbank, he had piled the tables with the documents and surveys Potter and Davis had procured for him. The walls were covered with graphs, architects' drawings, and landscape photographs scrawled with a jumble of heavily underlined comments—all of them concerned with this single project with which he had so suddenly become obsessed. He even had a name for it now, though he would not allow it to be pasted on the office door: EPCOT. He had come up with it during one of the many sleepless nights the pain in his neck now forced him to endure; nights which he passed by studying, reading, and working in the annex of his bedroom in Holmby Hills.

"EPCOT!" he cried out in the early hours of one morning, so loudly that Lilly stirred in her sleep in the next room. It was an acronym, he solemnly explained to his aides the next day, and what it stood for was Experimental Prototype Community of Tomorrow; it had evolved from a phrase used to describe the project in one of the reports they had written.

Even at this strange period in his life, Walt Disney could not keep his enthusiasms under wraps for too long. Soon he was willing to talk about what he was up to, first to Roy, who, as usual, was skeptical; and then to Lilly, who, as usual, was scared.

In the fall of 1966, at the end of a quite painful and miserable summer, he even gave a press conference and spilled out what was going on in his mind. For the first time he used the name EPCOT in public, and tried to explain why he was going to build it, what its significance was, and what it meant to him. Afterwards, one reporter commented that "this famous man, who had looked so pale and lackluster when he first came into the room, suddenly began to glow with enthusiasm as he waxed more and more enthusiastic" and ended by resembling a "born-again Christian at a revival meeting," he wrote.

EPCOT, Walt said, would be "like the city of tomorrow ought to be, a city that caters to the people as a service function." He went on: "It will be a planned, controlled community; a showcase for American industry and research, schools, cultural and educational opportunities. In EPCOT there will be no slum areas because we won't let them develop. There will be no landowners and therefore no voting control. People will rent houses instead of buying them, and at modest rentals. There will be no retirees, because everyone will be employed according to their ability. One of our requirements is that the people who live in EPCOT must help keep it alive."

How on earth, he was asked, had he stumbled into this project, which sounded like one of those idealistic, socialistic communities of the early years of the American nineteenth century. Walt violently shook his head since the mention of the word socialism was anathema to him. "No way, no way!" he said, violently. "It just happens that I am an inquisitive guy, and when I see things I don't like, I start thinking, why do they have to be like this? How can I improve them? City governments, for example. We pay a lot of taxes and still have streets that aren't paved or are full of holes. And city street cleaners and garbage collectors who don't do their jobs. And property owners who let dirt accumulate and help create slums."

EPCOT was to be his final gift to the world: a gloriously self-contained city of the future into whose design he had poured all his hopes, dreams, talents, and know-how. EPCOT would be a metropolis that would control its own climate; recycle its own waste; feed, preserve, and nurture its citizens; and do so in conditions from which disease, hunger, and want would be eliminated forever. Faced by mankind's suicidal impulse to destroy itself by nuclear war or the poison of pollution from toxic wastes, Walt Disney had envisaged EPCOT as the community of the future from which all the blights and blemishes of twentieth-century civilization had been banished. It would demonstrate that if people would only learn how to live properly in an enlightened and sanitized environment, they would be able to avoid not just war and disease but indefinitely postpone death and enjoy life, health, and happiness almost everlasting.

He might have added, as he did to Potter and Davis later, And why do so many people have to die before their time, when advanced medicine and new health techniques could save them? That's what we need most in EPCOT, the latest scientific methods for keeping people alive. And he instructed them to get out a report on the newest medical discoveries in repairing failing human bodies and the prolonging of life.

But even without touching on life preservation, to the listening reporters, his ideas for EPCOT seemed not just socialistic but outlandishly experimental; and one of them wondered how and why he had let himself get involved in it. Was it really any use trying to change the world in such a radical fashion?

"Oh, you sound just like my wife," Walt said, irritated. "When I started on Disneyland, she used to say, 'But why do you want to build an amusement park? They're so dirty!' I told her that was just the point—mine wouldn't be."

Meanwhile, Potter and Davis began their research on medical progress on the prolongation of life.

It was about this time that Walt Disney became acquainted with the experiments into the process known as cryogenesis, or what one newspaper termed "the freeze-drying of the human cadaver after death, for eventual resuscitation." He was shown a report that in California, in the small town of Emeryville, across the bay from San Francisco, a medical laboratory called Trans Time had begun experiments with human cadavers to preserve them for the future. A newly dead body was first treated and operated on to eliminate the diseased organs that had ended normal life. It was then stored away in a refrigerated container until such time as it could be thawed out, organs and blood vessels brought back into action, and life restored.

THIS WAS THE period when he was in such pain that generous libations of whisky and massage and heat treatment from Hazel George failed to give him any comfort whatsoever. When he walked out to his car after one particular evening session, it was noticed that he was staggering—not because he was drunk, but because he had lost most of the feeling in his left leg.

He decided to take Hazel George's advice and consult a doctor. On the recommendation of Vince Jefferds, his marketing expert, Walt Disney went to see Theodore Lynd, a Beverly Hills orthopedic surgeon. Lynd took X-ray pictures of his neck and back and found the reason for the increasing pain. Calcium was clustering so thickly in Walt Disney's neck that it was cutting off the spinal cord and making the slightest movement of the head, neck, or shoulders an agonizing ordeal. It was also affecting the movement of his left leg.

Then he looked at the other areas covered by the X rays and noticed the appearance of the lungs. For years it had been a joke among Disney employees that they always knew when their boss was coming along the corridors, for his continuous cough (which they called Walt's warning signal) would herald his approach. Walt himself believed that he suffered from no more than a mild smoker's cough and thought it the least of his troubles; but Lynd strongly recommended that his patient get himself examined by a lung specialist.

Walt made an appointment to see the surgeons at St. Joseph's Hospital in Burbank, and they tested his heart, his blood pressure, and his lungs. Then they sent him away, telling him that he should try to keep his many engagements, assuring him that they would have a report ready for him in a day or two.

CRYOGENESIS: FROM HIS own research into the process, Walt Disney had no doubts about its feasibility—one day. Since the original studies had been written, it was rumored that at least forty people had already instructed their executors not to allow them to be buried or cremated after death but ordered them instead to deliver their bodies to a clinic for cryogenesis to be performed upon them. There were stories around that at least a score had already "died" and been surgically "cleaned up" for eventual treatment. There were not only sperm banks in the United States now, it was said, but refrigerated body banks in California and plans for others in Wyoming, North Dakota, Texas, and Alaska over the next few years. There was one thing, however, that the researchers had not made clear: How long would the cadaver have to wait before the surgeons had perfected the cryogenic process? And what about the preservation of the organs, especially the brain?

WALT THOUGHT ABOUT cryogenesis a lot on October 29, 1966, as he flew to Williamsburg, the model colonial settlement in Virginia, to accept an award—and even more so on the way back. During the examination at the hospital, the pain in his neck and leg had suddenly ebbed away. But slowly, inexorably, it had come back again; and it was worse now. "This pain is killing me!" he groaned, as the plane took off and headed westward for California. It was indeed, though he didn't yet realize it.

He came home to find the report from the hospital, and though it tried to be reassuring, he did not take any comfort from it. In fact that was when he got the first warning that something was gravely wrong with him. According to the report he had disturbing evidence of "nodules" on the lungs, and treatment for it should be undertaken without further delay.

Walt's confidence in his future collapsed. For the moment, the doctors were not being entirely straightforward. They told him only that if he didn't do something about himself soon, it *could* be fatal. But the more he studied the reports, the more he realized what they were predicting between the lines. He was going to die.

For years Walt Disney had been philosophizing about the inevitability of death. "Like most of us," said one of his associates, "once he reached his sixties, he became vitally concerned about when and how he was going to die. But there was this difference. With him you knew it wasn't just a personal matter. Don't forget that Walt Disney in 1966 was already the most famous man in the world. He truly was a phenomenal guy. He was no longer simply the genius who had created all those famous cartoon characters like Mickey, Donald, Goofy, and the rest. He'd gone beyond that. He was now the most powerful entrepreneur in history. He controlled a multi-million-dollar leisure organization that attracted hordes of people from all parts of the world. And he spent every waking moment thinking up new ideas for them and for this enormous money-making leisure and entertainment complex he controlled. So what Walt Disney worried about was not just how his own death was going to affect him—though he wouldn't have been human if he hadn't been bothered about that, too—but what it was going to do to his future projects and present obligations—to the Disney organization. Millions of people and millions of dollars were tied up in this man and his future, and they all would be drastically affected when he died. What was going to happen to them all *after he was gone?*"

On November 2, 1966, Walt called General Potter and Marv Davis in to see him and went over the plans they were getting together for EPCOT. "Dammit," he said, angrily, "it isn't going fast enough. Why are you dragging your feet? Is it because of the money? Have you been talking to Roy? Roy thinks EPCOT is a loser, but don't take any notice of him. Disney World will make all the profits we need for this operation. EPCOT doesn't need to make any money. Disney World will pay for it."

On November 7, 1966, he drove to the hospital for the operation the medical men were now advising, and shortly afterward the surgeons cut out his cancerous left lung. "I've only got one lung now," he told Lilly, grinning cheerfully, after he had regained consciousness, "but otherwise I'm as good as new."

But Lilly had talked to the doctors and knew it was much grimmer than that. What she did not know—and Walt did—was something he did not intend to reveal to her. The surgeons had taken away his diseased lung to examine it, and then were going to preserve it. Walt was pleased when he heard that. He knew enough about cryogenesis by now to be aware that it was important to hold onto all the organs—just in case the surgeons needed to treat them before putting them back where they belonged.

23
Finis

HE WAS SO bored that, not many days after the operation, the doctors reluctantly let Walt out of the hospital. The first thing he did was cross the road to the studio. He was eager to find out what had been going on.

Everyone winced when they saw him. He had never been overweight, except for a small paunch he had developed lately, but now the flesh seemed to have run off him like melted butter, and he was gaunt and emaciated. What had always been one of his most charming features, his cheerful grin, now had the appearance of a grimace.

He spent some time with his secretary, Tommie Wilck,* regarding his most urgent correspondence; talked with Marv Davis; and then shut himself up in the EPCOT room. More reports were in from the medical experts about possible developments in the World of Tomorrow—projected improvements in disease control, in health and hospital care, organ transplants, and postmortem surgery. It was not until some hours later that he emerged and went down to the main studio.

Bill Walsh was in the process of producing a film called *Blackbeard's Ghost*, directed by Robert Stevenson and starring Peter Ustinov. "Suddenly I came onto the set and saw him sitting on one of those stools, and he was drinking coffee," Walsh remembered later. "I said, 'Jesus Christ, Walt, I thought you were in the hospital.' He said, 'Yeah, well, they cut away my ribs to get at something,' and then added to Peter Ustinov, who had come up, 'It's just some damn thing they're fooling around with.'" Both men were disturbed by his appearance but tried not to show it. Walt was particularly pleased to see Ustinov, whom he greatly admired as both an actor and an amusing and cultivated human being.

He had already earmarked him for the starring role in a film he had assigned Bill Walsh to make called *Khrushchev in Disneyland*. The Soviet leader had come to the United States some time before for an official visit

---

*She had taken over from Dolores Voght, who had retired.

and had been taken on a tour of the big Hollywood studios, but the special wish he had expressed, to visit Disneyland, had been vetoed by the State Department on the grounds of security. Walt had been furious about that; he had planned to put old-fashioned cannons on his jungle and Mississippi River steamers, assemble them with his Jules Verne submarines from the 20,000 Leagues Under the Sea exhibit, together with their replacements, and introduce the Soviet leader to "the Disneyland Navy, the tenth largest battle fleet in the world."

Bill Walsh had written the script of a live-action comedy about Khrushchev defying the State Department's prohibition and secretly visiting Disneyland, wearing some wild disguise as he dodged both U.S. officialdom and anti-Soviet demonstrations. Ustinov, cast in the role of Khrushchev (who, he maintained, strongly resembled his mother) now told Walt he planned to shave his head for the role. "I didn't know your Ma was bald," Walt joked, his face cracking into a ghastly grin.

Both Ustinov and Bill Walsh, shocked as they were by Walt's emaciated appearance, privately concluded that the surgeons had opened him up, found something inside, and hastily sewed him up again. "We decided he was doomed, but thought it would only spread gloom and despondency around the studio if we said anything, so we kept quiet about the visit," Walsh said later.

PETER ELLENSHAW WAS crushed when he heard Walt had been to the studio and that he had missed him. "I think he meant a lot to me because I'd lost my father at a very early age," he said, "and Walt, at a later stage in my life, became a very strong father figure for me. He was always very demanding of me, but he was the sort of person I would appreciate as a parent."

In some ways, Walt had resented the fact that Ellenshaw was leaving matte painting behind and concentrating more and more on working on his own as an artist, and often, when he had asked for leave to go away and paint, Walt had given him homework to do that was calculated to take up most of his "free" time. On the other hand, he liked Ellenshaw's pictures and had taken to inviting him down to Smoke Tree Ranch at Palm Springs, and encouraged him to do desert landscapes, which he found particularly dramatic and suitable to Ellenshaw's style. "The moment I heard he was in hospital, I wanted to go and see him," Ellenshaw said. "I'd run into him in the corridors before he went in and I said, 'I see you're having difficulty in walking,' and he had assured me, 'It's just a polo injury in my back. I'm going to have it straightened.' I thought, *God, if they mess with his back* and I suppose I looked so concerned, he said, 'Christ, Peter, if you go on looking like that, you'll really get me worried.' So when he went in, I waited a bit and then tried to see him. But he wouldn't see anyone. I gathered he had got so thin, he didn't want to be seen."

But Ellenshaw was worried about his boss and longed to talk to him and encourage him so long as he was in the hospital, and he tried to think up a way he could gain access to him. "I finally thought: 'I'll paint him a picture.' I wanted to paint him something special just to show how much we all loved him—loved him like a father, I mean. And I painted him a smoke tree, because it was a smoke tree which had first introduced me to painting in the desert, after he had invited me and my wife down to Smoke Tree Ranch and let us work there. So I did this little picture for him."

He took the painting into Tommie Wilck's office and said he would like to take it to the hospital and give it to Walt. But she said, "But he won't see you, Peter. You'll only feel hurt. Why don't you just leave it with me and let me take it over?"

"So I left it with her, and he sent back word later how much he appreciated the picture." He added, "Sorry I can't see you just now, Peter, but I'd rather you didn't come over. We'll get together just as soon as I'm all right again."

Ellenshaw never saw Walt, or the picture, again. "It was quite a nice little work," he said, years later. "I often wonder what happened to it, but I think Lilly took it away."

IN THE FINAL weeks of his life, particularly between November 6 and December 6, 1966, when he was in and out of the hospital and more convinced than ever that his days were numbered, Walt Disney searched for the answer to the unsolved problems of cryogenesis.

Several of his closest colleagues and advisers* are confident that he eventually became convinced of cryogenesis as a viable medical process and was persuaded that, even in 1966, it was possible for a human being to have himself brought back to life after death.

According to them, the chief problem that troubled Walt was the length of time it might take the doctors to perfect the process. How long would it be before the surgical experts could bring a treated cadaver back to working life? To be brutally practical, could it be guaranteed, in fact, that he could be *brought back in time* to rectify the mistakes his successors would almost certainly start making at EPCOT the moment he was dead?

AFTER WALT CAME out of the hospital in November, everyone assumed, thin and gaunt though he looked, that he would soon be his old self again.

---

*Including his Oscar-winning cartoonist and animator Ward Kimball.

Only Lilly, Diane, Sharon, and Roy—who had had a succession of long consultations with the surgeons—knew the gravity of Walt's condition, and Roy strongly urged them not to say a word about it to anyone. "The effect on the market could be disastrous," he said. "Christ knows what it would do to Disney stock!"

So everyone around the studio was assured Walt was getting better, and no one knew—although some suspected—that his condition was inexorably growing worse. Not that it stopped him from working. Every day he came to the studio and did his round of the lots and labs, keeping tabs on the way work was going. His expression was grim, and he was rude and short with most employees; but he had been like that for a long time now, and they didn't realize it was due to a deterioration in his condition. During each visit, he spent long hours inside his EPCOT room, studying plans for his City of Tomorrow, and no one except General Potter and Marv Davis, perhaps, knew how desperate he had become to make sure that not a single detail of construction had been overlooked. No matter whether he was there or not, EPCOT must go forward exactly as he had envisioned it—if his successors were willing to follow the instructions, that is.

And that was the snag, his aides realized—the worry that dogged him all through November 1966. Would those who came after him *try* to follow his plans? Were they even competent enough to carry them out? Above all else, was there really no way of making sure that if they had made a mess of it, he could come back from the grave and rectify their appalling errors and misjudgments?

NEVER COULD THE approach of death have seemed more monstrously inconvenient. To have this happen now, when there was so much to do, so many things demanding his personal attention! Once upon a time, he had told Ken Annakin that he didn't care what happened to Walt Disney Productions once he was dead. "They won't be able to handle it, anyway," he had said. "So just let it fritter away."

But now he did care about what he was leaving behind, and the thought of what they would almost certainly do to EPCOT bothered, angered, and frustrated him. If only . . .

Since he had never found it easy to talk to his intimates about himself, Hazel George was the only one who heard how he felt about it. He did not conceal from her how devastated he was at the thought of dying; how appalled he was at the prospect that it could happen at any time now. What would happen to EPCOT once he was gone? There wasn't anyone at Disney who could fulfil what he had set out to construct and create. There would be chaos if he disappeared from the scene! The unimaginative characters with whom he was surrounded would be sure to ruin everything!

He scoffed at the suggestion that, if he left precise instructions behind, his heirs and relations might be able to carry through his ideas. Who was there who was capable? He had no son; and he had made it plain, in the studio and out of it, that his son-in-law was no substitute. He was contemptuous of the abilities of his nephew, Roy Disney, whom his brother admired and had appointed his heir. His wife, Lilly, did not have the boldness nor the vision; and his daughter, Diane, did not have the brains. As for his partner and brother, Roy, who had helped found the Disney organization with him, who was the one man he loved and trusted above all others because of the faith and loyalty he had shown him over the years, Walt groaned at the thought of what Roy could do to EPCOT once he got his hands on it. He was good, reliable, dull, unimaginative, and above all, a moneyman. What did he care about the City of Tomorrow? Nothing but its potential profit would interest him.

SO WHAT WAS HE GOING TO DO?

IT WAS ALMOST certainly Hazel George who put the idea into his head that there might be a possible way of cheating death. For a long time she listened to her boss's complaints and then startled him by saying that there was surely no reason why he couldn't "come back later and clean up all the mistakes your relatives might be making with Disney."

This must have been the period when, many of his associates think, he studied and consulted and sought most desperately for any method—transplants while he was still alive, cryogenesis when he had ceased to breathe—by which he might avoid or postpone the dreadful consequences of such a tragically unnecessary and ill-timed death.

At the end of November 1966, he was in such pain he had to be taken to the hospital again, and though a succession of distinguished surgeons concentrated their attention on him, there was little they could do to prevent the rapid worsening of his physical condition. His heart was already failing to pump sufficient blood.

Under the circumstances, it was amazing how cheerful and optimistic he continued to be despite his physical deterioration. It is true that he sometimes burst into tears and was particularly upset when Hazel George came to see him. "Fancy being remembered around the world for the invention of a mouse!" he said to her, mournfully, tears rolling down his cheeks.

"You're better off than Hitler," she told him. "All they remember about him is he killed all those Jews! I don't think you ever killed anyone."

"No, but I wanted to," he said. "Donald Duck, for instance! There were times when I really wanted to wipe out that little monster!" They both laughed.

But when she embraced him to say good bye, the tears were already rolling down his cheeks again.

BY DECEMBER 5 his state was so low that even though Lilly, Diane, and Sharon came by, he was in no condition to celebrate his sixty-fifth birthday. However, on December 14, the last afternoon of his life, after she visited him, Lilly telephoned her daughter Diane and was full of optimism because Walt had seemed so contained and self-confident. "He got out of bed," she said. "I know he's going to get well! I know he's going to be all right!"

In fact, never has a mortally sick man seemed more relaxed and confident on the eve of his death. The last relative to see him alive was his brother, Roy, later that same evening. He came away convinced Walt was going to recover. Like everyone else, he was amazed at his calmness, his equanimity.

They had talked for nearly an hour about EPCOT. Roy faithfully promised to see it through but assured his brother he would be up and about again soon and would look after the project himself—"as you know you always do." But not this time.

In the early hours of the following morning, the doctors were urgently summoned to his bedside and worked on him for many hours to avoid a circulatory collapse. They told his wife at 9:35 A.M. that he was dead.

AND THIS IS where the mystery begins. It was Walt himself who had asked Roy Disney to keep his illness secret, but the manner in which the world was apprised of his death remains surprising.

In fact, it was not until some time after he was declared dead that an announcement was made. First came radio announcements, then a curt official notice informed the press and the public that Walt Disney was no more. It added that there would be no funeral. He had already been cremated, the announcement said, and his ashes interred in the Forest Lawn Memorial Park in Glendale, California. Only immediate members of his family had been present.

Need there have been an interval between his actual death and the official announcement? Did dealers in the New York Stock Exchange need time before they were allowed to learn the news? Was the delay really intended to avoid a panic selling of Disney holdings—especially since, when the news was finally made public, the value of Disney shares did not collapse but went up considerably? Did he have to be rushed into the ground so precipitately and privately—and into a plot already filled with family ashes from which the public would always be barred?

Even today, old Disney veterans still wonder about that. Many of them are convinced the gap between Walt Disney's death and the revelation of his secret cremation and interment had special reasons behind it. "Is old Walt *really* buried out there in Glendale?" one of his old associates asked. "I don't believe so. I think he's someplace else, waiting."

"My information is that he *is* frozen down," Ken Annakin said. "There again, that's Walt, interested in everything. He probably didn't believe in cryogenesis at all, but thought: 'Well, maybe there might be just a chance of coming back, so I'll try it.'" Then Annakin added, "Of course, if he has had himself frozen and he does come back, there's going to be hell to pay at Disney. He wouldn't approve of much that's gone on at the studio, except the animation. He'd like that. He was always great on improvements on technique. But the stories and the way they've been handled, no."

EPCOT, for instance. "He's going to be good and mad at what they have done to his City of Tomorrow," said another old associate. "When he comes back, a lot of heads at Disney are going to roll, that's for sure." Then he added, "*If* he comes back. If he's still around to come back, I mean. Maybe all the rumors are wrong, and he was hurried into the ground in all that secrecy because that's the way he wanted it. Maybe he really is dead. But I don't know. There are too many people who believe otherwise. In any case, how do you *prove* he's dead? Even if you got an order to dig up Walt from the Disney Memorial Park at Forest Lawn, can you be sure what you find is the one and only Walt? How do you tell his ashes from those of any one else?" He prefers to believe Walt is in a strange refrigerated tomb somewhere else, waiting for medical science to deal with him so that he can come back one day and clean up all the mess his successors have made of Disney—and particularly of EPCOT—since he went away on December 15, 1966."

"When Disney fans ask me if it's true that Walt's body is kept frozen for future resurrection," Ward Kimball says, "I answer the question by pointing out that Walt was always intensely interested in things scientific, and he, more than any person I knew, just might have been curious enough to agree to such an experiment."

Epilogue

WHAT DO YOU do when the king is dead and there is no heir worthy of taking his place on the throne? In medieval realms, it is the time of the conspirators, of usurpations and gunpowder plots. In modern America, the greedy financiers emerged armed with takeover bids. In the days following the announcement of Walt Disney's death, the company's shares rose by ten points and more, not because anyone thought Walt Disney Productions and WED would be better without Walt's guiding hand, but because there was money to be made in tearing his creation to pieces. There was a golden backlog of animated cartoons, nature films, live-action movies to be exploited and a fortune to be made from selling off the landholdings in Anaheim and Florida for the rich rewards of mindless expansion.

From the moment they knew he was dead, the money vultures began to hover over Burbank, Anaheim, and central Florida.

"Everybody at the studio started to jockey for position," Ward Kimball said, "to consolidate his own little kingdom in the new pecking order. Name plates were added to the desks. Personal note pads multiplied: 'From the Office of So-and-So.' Framed full color portraits of Walt magically appeared on the office walls of the many self-appointed executives, seemingly to give assurance of Walt's silent blessing to whatever questionable decisions might be made at the desks below. When Walt was alive he was the total boss. No one moved an inch without his final word. Department heads who had never before had to make decisions for themselves now had to strike out on their own. It was tough for some, easy for others."

Kimball watched the organization slowly coagulate into a corporate structure where decisions, good or bad, were now made by committees instead of by the creative father figure upon whom they had all depended so heavily in the past.

"Of course," Kimball said, "there were some rather stupid executives who tried to establish creative niches for themselves by making such asinine remarks as, 'Now I am sure this is the way Walt would do it.' They knew full well it was impossible ever to predict what Walt would have said or done when he was in charge."

Roy Disney seriously tried to take his brother's place. His main achievement was to keep the vultures at bay.

THIN AS A skeleton, his head like a skull with skin stretched over it, he was already a tired, sick old man of seventy-three when control was passed on to him after his brother's death, and his only concern was to see Disney World finished and in operation and Walt Disney Productions out of debt and profitable, and then, he would thankfully retire. A bent and melancholy figure, he spent weeks at a time wandering over the Disney World site in central Florida and hated every moment of it, especially when he and Bill Evans were hauled above the bald cypresses in a builders' scoop to survey the churned-up swamps. He was appalled at the devastation of the landscape and the magnitude of the conception and complained aloud at the "goddamned madness that got into Walt when he decided to make a theme park out of this awful swamp."

As his brother had rightly surmised, he had no enthusiasm whatsoever for EPCOT and ignored the plans for the project Walt had left behind him. "It's a money loser, anyway," he said, contemptuously, tossing Walt's cherished studies aside.

On his money-raising trips to New York to finance the ongoing work for Walt Disney World,* he was careful to keep the subject of EPCOT out of his conversation, deciding the banks would never advance him the money if they thought he would fritter part of it away on his brother's Utopian project. Even so, he paid well beyond the going rate for the money he borrowed, much to the dismay of his associates, who felt it betrayed his basic lack of faith in the legacy Walt had left behind him.

Those were unhappy days at the studio. To help him in his task of running the organization, Roy Disney had appointed a committee to advise him. It consisted, in part, of Bill Anderson, the producer, who was put in charge of filming activities; E. Cardon (Card) Walker, the brilliant visualizer and advertising man; Bill Walsh, Ron Miller, Roy Junior, and others. It was Roy Senior who had the idea that competition between the various members of this group—any one of whom, he surmised,

---

*Roy announced the addition of his brother's first name to the theme park shortly after his death "so people will always know this was Walt's dream."

cherished ambitions to succeed him—would eventually produce a leader whom he could name as his successor when he retired.

But it didn't work out that way. Bill Walsh who was still around at the time of Walt's death, would have seemed the logical man to take over the film division. He might not only have revived Disney's flagging movie production program but also have snapped the veteran members of the animation department out of the sullen and resentful stupor into which they had fallen over the years—ever since Walt had lost his enthusiasm for cartoon films. But Walsh himself had lost his dynamic. Crushed and dispirited by Walt's death and by the failure of his marriage, he was all flab and misery; the ambition drained out of him.

The last thing he wanted was responsibility. He left all decisions about filming to Bill Anderson, who was a reluctant galvanizer. Walsh shared his sorrows with Ub Iwerks, who was also bereft by Walt's death, and both could not resist criticizing Anderson, and this occasionally stirred bad feelings.

Ron Miller, now promoted to executive producer, was tempted to flex his muscles. Long constrained by Walt, he felt unshackled by his father-in-law's demise. Bolstered by the knowledge that he had the backing of his mother-in-law and his wife (they were now the most powerful share-holders in the company), he was free to throw his weight around.

The one he could hustle was his bete noir, Roy E. Disney, Jr. In many ways, particularly in cinematic expertise, Roy, Jr., took after his father, which meant he was good at figures and investments, but as a film-maker, he was short on flair and expertise, and Ron Miller was not displeased when his lapses did not go unnoticed around the studio.

So far as Roy, Jr., was concerned, in fact, life in Burbank was just like old times, only worse. He had always resented being pushed around by his temperamental uncle, genius though he might have been, and he was damned if he was going to take the same treatment from Walt's pip-squeak son-in-law. Relations between the two men became so bitter that if Miller hadn't been such a hulk of a man, they would undoubtedly have come to blows. As it was, there was a heated quarrel (subsequently reported in the *Los Angeles Times*) over Roy Jr.'s right to a permanent parking place on the lot at Burbank. Roy, Jr., stuck it out as long as his father was in charge of the studio, but then quit after the blazing row with Miller.

However, he stayed on the board of Walt Disney Productions and clung to the shares his father had left him. He vowed one day he would come back to the studio—but only after he had got rid of Walt's son-in-law. There were those around Burbank who were convinced that he cherished another ambition too: to eliminate his uncle's name and influence from the Disney organization altogether. So far as he was concerned, it was his father and not Walt who had done all the work of making Disney rich and famous.

ON OCTOBER 1, 1971, Walt Disney World opened at last in Florida although the official dedication ceremonies did not take place until October 23-25. Walt would have made it a gala occasion by inviting famous artists, singers, stage and movie stars to celebrate the occasion with him. Roy hired Arthur Fiedler to conduct the so-called World Symphony, with 145 musicians representing sixty-six countries in a concert of theme tunes from the famous cartoon movies, popular classics, and patriotic music. Julie Andrews and Glenn Campbell hosted the event.

They were all there—Lilly; Roy and Edna; Diane and Ron Miller; Sharon and her husband, William Lund; Roy Edward Disney and his wife, Patricia; plus fourteen grandchildren.

It was a highly sentimental occasion. Down a ramp in front of Cinderella's Castle, to the sounds of "When You Wish Upon a Star," Lilly was led by an employee dressed as Mickey Mouse to join Roy on the platform in front of the tearfully sentimental crowd. Turning to Walt's widow, Roy waved his hands across the trim walks and fairy-tale landscape of this new Disney kingdom and cried, "Lilly, you knew all Walt's ideas and hopes as well as anybody. What would Walt think of it?"

Wiping away her tears, she tremulously replied, "I think Walt would have approved."

Well, maybe.

HE WOULD CERTAINLY have approved of the magnificent, $400 million-dollar job his builders and landscape artists had done in creating the park; they had transformed a hostile, ugly, tangled, and boggy wilderness into a vast, tamed terrain of lakes, beaches, hotels, river rides, and shiningly spotless communities; its flat monotony broken by artificial hills, rivers, and wide roads; all linked by a supermodern monorail system, an overhead chair ride, and an old-fashioned steam-locomotive network.

Walt had always been fond of a sentimental occasion, and he would have enjoyed the moving moments of the opening ceremonies, even if Roy had pinched pennies on the details. But it is also just as likely that he would have had some crisp comments to make about the one unmentioned subject in all the vast number of speeches: EPCOT.

"Well, yes," he might have said, "this is all well and good so far as it goes, and it's big of you to name it after me and call it *Walt* Disney World. As a moneymaker, it should keep the company going for many a year. *But what the hell has happened to all my plans for EPCOT?*"

As he had rightly suspected during those last days in the hospital, the moment he was off the scene, *nothing* had happened about EPCOT.

When Roy had taken over, he had neglected most of his promises to his brother. EPCOT was awaiting what an official statement from his office described as "a practical approach to its complexities," which meant, as far as Roy was concerned, finding some way to make a profit out of it. And he never did get around to solving that problem. Nor did he worry too much about it. As far as he was concerned, he had carried out his brother's wishes by seeing Walt Disney World brought to fruition, and the moment it was opened, he seems to have decided that his obligations had been fulfilled and that his task was over.

ROY DISNEY DIED in 1971, at the age of seventy-eight, shortly after the opening ceremonies of Walt Disney World, and, some time later, Card Walker took over as president. Walker had started working for Walt Disney as a messenger boy back in the days when he had first come to California from Idaho, and he had always been one of Walt's most dedicated admirers.

"Card knew how much Walt wanted to see EPCOT rise in Florida," his associate, Vince Jefferds, said. "He saw a lot of his boss in those last days before his death, and he knew EPCOT was taking up all his ebbing strength and attention. Walt realized EPCOT was going to be monstrously expensive, but he said he didn't care about that. He felt he could get the money from American industry and perhaps even from the U.S. government (for developing a prototype city).

"Walt always felt there was no point trying to reclaim slums. He felt it was better to start anew with perfectly planned cities in fresh locations —cities that would enable the designer to combine urban and suburban advantages in a single plan. That was part of his conception of EPCOT. He died before he completed his blueprint, of course, particularly from a standpoint of economic feasibility. But we all knew he would have gone for broke on this project as he had on all his earlier projects like his first cartoon, his first animated features, Disneyland, etc. In the end, all his ventures paid off. It would probably have been true for EPCOT. Anyway, we all realized that if Walt lived he would have built it, even if it risked bankrupting the company. Risks didn't scare him.

"And I think he would have gotten away with it," Jefferds added. "Walt Disney did things that made other people do things, too, things that didn't seem possible on paper. He had a way of bringing out the best in people, of lifting them to their highest level of performance. I think he could have evolved a plan that worked. But I also believe that in order to get the money from industry to build EPCOT, he would have had to incorporate an exhibit area into it for them—like the present EPCOT."

But would he? Others who knew what Walt Disney had in mind

believe he would have fought savagely and successfully to prevent any such commercialization of his plan.

In any case, Card Walker was dedicated to doing something that, in his opinion, would come somewhere near to Walt's ideas of EPCOT. After Walt's death, he asked his associates to give him their ideas of how EPCOT should be built.

"In 1974," Jefferds said, "the Disney design group [W.E.D.] presented a project costing thirty-five to forty million dollars, which would add some shops and annexes around the Contemporary Hotel [inside Walt Disney world]. Card showed it to me, and I said I thought it stunk. He reacted angrily to that.

"'You're such a smartass, you know about everything,' he said. 'Give constructive ideas instead of criticism.'"

Jefferds, who is also an artist in his spare time, spent a week going over the terrain around Walt Disney World and putting his ideas on paper. The result was an entirely new area that Jefferds called "Interworld." Unlike Walt's original design, which would have been a single, self-contained city, Interworld would combine exhibits of industrial giants and foreign nations inside a new land-and-water complex.

At Card Walker's suggestion, Jefferds presented his plan to the key vice president of Walt Disney World, and the board subsequently voted for it unanimously. It was obviously a commercially viable proposition.

At this point, Card told Jefferds to take it back to the WED design group and have them rework it closer to Walt's original EPCOT concept. WED took Jefferds's plan and separated the industrial exhibits from those of the foreign countries and put them into two concentric circles.

"It would be a showcase for American industry," Jefferds said, "but, of course, not in the context of an operating city complex as Walt envisioned. Still, we lined it up with a monorail at a cost of a million dollars a mile, and Card personally sold most of the three hundred fifty million dollars in contributions from major U.S. corporations. Sale of pavilions to foreign governments was disappointing, but we pressed on."

So the post–Walt Disney EPCOT came into being. It began to make money from the start, and thousands upon thousands of visitors flocked to gape at its wonders.

"DISNEY CONCEIVED EPCOT originally as a single city," Howard Means wrote in the Orlando *Sentinel* (December 10, 1982), "completely climate controlled, on different levels, with deliveries below and a hotel above. In fact, it is few of those things. Certainly it is not a module of a city complex, a community of souls living a quarter of a century into the future, while the rest of us watch. More's the pity, too, because extraordinary things could have been learned from such an idealized laboratory city."

He added, "But more's the shame, too, because if anyone in this century could have pulled off a successful Utopia, it would have been Walt Disney.... Disney's future world wasn't going to be built on the shifting sands of ideology. It would have lifted up the founding rock of future technology. Utopias for all their charm are often the work of misanthropes, people unsuited to their times and place. But Disney, in a way that no other American of this century did, tapped the mainstream of American hopes, desires, and dreams. Whatever flaws he may have had in his private person, the public Walt Disney was loved in a rare and special way.

"To say that EPCOT would have survived and prospered as a Utopian community is not to say that one would have wanted to live in it nor even that those who chose to live there would have been in any way representative of the rest of us. EPCOT would, I think, have been very much like the contemporary city of three million people that Le Corbusier proposed in the Radiant City."

In both cases, it never came to pass.

THE MYSTERY REMAINS whether Walt Disney is still entombed in a deep freeze in a California university hospital, waiting for medical science to thaw him out, clean him up, and deliver him back into life.

But does it matter anymore? It is too late for him to do any good, anyway, to what his successors have wrought with his heritage. All his talented artists are either dead or have disappeared into the obscurity of old age, and even Mickey Mouse and Donald Duck are animated nowadays on computers. The studio has abandoned Davy Crockett, flying autos, magic rubber, and absent-minded professors in favor of "adult" films featuring braless mermaids. The studio is now so "adult" that at any moment now they are likely to show a computer-animated Pluto having intercourse with one of the 101 Dalmatians.

The toughest moneymen in Hollywood have taken over the lot on Buena Vista, and the whole nature of the studio's business is changing. Furthermore, Roy E. Disney's dream is coming true. He has forced the resignation of Walt's son-in-law, Ron Miller, as president of the company, and the wild rumor going around Burbank is that he may soon be getting rid of Walt's name, too.

NOT THAT WALT could care very much about that. The only thing that must really be troubling him now—wherever he is—is what they have done to EPCOT. He certainly wouldn't like to have Walt Disney's name on that.

ASIDE FROM HIS abhorrence of the commercialism surrounding his beloved dream, EPCOT, Walt Disney might well have a different view of how other parts of his empire turned out. Ever practical, Walt Disney realized the importance of making money, often stopping just short of compromising his own visionary goals.

Unquestionably, when EPCOT came aboard it represented an anathema to the spirit and financial well-being of all the other tourist attractions in the area. In the early days with just Walt Disney World in operation, all but the small and financially vulnerable competitors survived; in fact many fed off their geographic proximity. There remained enough tourist dollars to support everyone, and besides WDW only offered up to three day enticements.

With the opening of EPCOT, Disney not only attracted an additional share of the vacationers' money, but managed to keep them and their money around the grounds for another day or two using clever multi-day passes. Now there was less money and time for the others. This dried up all but the most soundly grounded competitor parks.

The subsequent introduction of other Disney attractions—The Living Seas pavilion, Typhoon Lagoon, Pleasure Island, World Swan Resort, Dolphin Hotel, Convention Center, as well as the Disney-MGM Studios—has profoundly changed the flavor and personality of Florida tourism. Openings of new facilities in other cities around the world give further voice to the wealth and power of the Disney empire.

One would suspect, with no proof of certainty, that Walt Disney would not only approve of what has transpired but likely would applaud the courage of those who have been willing to throw the dice in his name. After all, he showed them his mettle when he gambled on that small California amusement park in 1955.

Walt Disney is the mold from which innovative entrepreneurs are cast. He successfully matched ruthless determination and visionary courage. He foresaw a public willing to pay for a good entertainment product even if it turned out to be less human and less personal than those to which consumers had been accustomed. Though his dream of a single city concept did not survive his passing, the standards and visions he left for those who followed surely remain as his most important legacy.

Walt Disney's Film History

NOTE. This section has been checked by Disney archivists who point out that they "try to dignify the animated features by not calling them cartoons, a term usually reserved for the short films." I have decided to adopt the Disney usage below.

1920-23: Kansas City. Animator/director/producer of *Laugh-O-Gram* series. Founder of Laugh-O-Gram Films, Inc. with Ub Iwerks. First of *Alice Comedies* series (live action/animated cartoons featuring 6-year-old Virginia Davis, created and animated by Walt Disney and Ub Iwerks).

1923: Company goes bankrupt. Moves to Hollywood.

1923: Hollywood. New *Alice Comedies* series featuring Virginia Davis (later replaced by Margie Gay plus live dog). Animated by Walt Disney assisted by brother, Roy Disney, until Ub Iwerks rejoins Walt from Kansas City to do principal animation.

1927: *Oswald the Lucky Rabbit* all-cartoon series (created by Walt Disney, animated by Ub Iwerks and others) supersedes *Alice*.

1928: Loses control of Oswald the Rabbit character. Forced to find substitute.

1928: Creates character of Mickey Mouse.

1928: First two Mickey Mouse cartoons—*Plane Crazy* and *Gallopin' Gaucho*, both silent—completed (animated by Ub Iwerks).

1928: *Steamboat Willie*, first Mickey Mouse cartoon with sound completed and shown in New York (principal animation by Ub Iwerks).

1929: *Skeleton Dance*, first of the *Silly Symphony* series, completed (principal animation by Ub Iwerks).

1928-34: Characters of Minnie Mouse, Donald Duck, Goofy, and Pluto added to Disney's cartoon company.

1933: *Silly Symphony, Three Little Pigs* completed and shown. Song from cartoon, "Who's Afraid of the Big Bad Wolf?" becomes a hit.

1934: Work begun on first Disney feature-length animated film *Snow White and the Seven Dwarfs*.
1935: First Mickey Mouse cartoon in color.
1937: Premiere of *Snow White*. Smash hit.

Walt Disney as Producer or Executive Producer, 1940–1966: A Selection

1940: *Pinocchio, Fantasia* (animated features)
1941: *The Reluctant Dragon, Dumbo* (animated features)
1942: *Bambi* (animated feature)
1943: *Saludos Amigos* (animated feature), *Victory Through Airpower* (animated and live action), and other films, made mainly for the armed services and U.S. Government.
1945: *The Three Caballeros* (animated feature)
1946: *Make Mine Music* (animation), *Song of the South* (animation with live action)
1947: *Fun and Fancy Free* (animation and live action)
1948: *Seal Island* (first *True-Life Adventure*)
1949: *Melody Time* (animation), *So Dear to My Heart* (live action with animation), *The Adventures of Ichabod and Mr. Toad* (animated feature)
1950: *Cinderella* (animated feature), *Treasure Island* (live action directed in England by Byron Haskins)
1951: *Alice in Wonderland* (animated feature)
1952: *The Story of Robin Hood* (live action directed in England by Ken Annakin)
1953: *The Sword and the Rose* (live action directed in England by Ken Annakin), *Peter Pan* (animated feature), *The Living Desert (True-Life Adventure)*. *Toot, Whistle, Plunk and Boom* (Oscar-winning cartoon directed by Ward Kimball)
1954: *Rob Roy: The Highland Rogue* (live action with Richard Todd and Glynis Johns), *The Vanishing Prairie (True-Life Adventure), 20,000 Leagues Under the Sea* (live action directed by Richard Fleischer, starring James Mason, Kirk Douglas)
1955: *Davy Crockett—King of the Wild Frontier* (live action produced by Bill Walsh, script by Tom Blackburn, starring Fess Parker), *Lady and the Tramp* (animated feature), *The African Lion (True-Life Adventure), The Littlest Outlaw* (live action)
1956: *The Great Locomotive Chase* (live action), *Davy Crockett and the River Pirates* (live action), *Secrets of Life (True-Life Adventure), Westward Ho the Wagons* (live action)
1957: *Johnny Tremain* (live action directed by Robert Stevenson), *Old*

Yeller (live action produced by Bill Anderson, directed by Robert Stevenson), *Perri (True-Life Fantasy)*

1958: *The Light in the Forest* (live action), *White Wilderness (True-Life Adventure)*, *Tonka* (live action)

1959: *Sleeping Beauty* (animated feature), *The Shaggy Dog* (live action produced by Bill Walsh, directed by Charles Barton, starring Fred Mac-Murray), *Darby O'Gill and the Little People* (live action), *Third Man on the Mountain* (live action directed in Switzerland by Ken Annakin)

1960: *Toby Tyler* (live action), *Kidnapped* (live action), *Pollyanna* (live action directed by David Swift, starring Hayley Mills), *Jungle Cat (True-Life Adventure)*, *Swiss Family Robinson* (live action directed by Ken Annakin, produced by Bill Anderson), *Ten Who Dared* (live action), *The Sign of Zorro* (live action)

1961: *101 Dalmatians* (animation), *The Absent-Minded Professor* (live action directed by Charles Barton, starring Fred MacMurray), *The Parent Trap* (live action directed by David Swift, starring Hayley Mills), *Nikki—Wild Dog of the North* (live action), *Greyfriars Bobby* (live action), *Babes In Toyland* (live action)

1962: *Moon Pilot, Bon Voyage, Big Red, Almost Angels, In Search of the Castaways, The Legend of Lobo* (live action films)

1963: *Son of Flubber* (live action), *Miracle of the White Stallions, Savage Sam* (live action), *Summer Magic, The Incredible Journey, The Sword in the Stone* (animated features)

1964: *A Tiger Walks* (live action), *The Three Lives of Thomasina* (live action), *The Moon Spinners* (live action), *Mary Poppins* (live action and animation, directed by Robert Stevenson, produced by Bill Walsh, songs by Robert and Richard Sherman, starring Julie Andrews and Dick Van Dyke), *The Misadventures of Merlin Jones, Emil and the Detectives* (live action)

1965: *Those Calloways, The Monkey's Uncle* (live action films), *That Darn Cat* (live action)

1966: *The Ugly Dachshund* (live action), *Lt. Robin Crusoe—USN, The Fighting Prince of Donegal, Follow Me Boys!* (live action films)

1967 (appeared after his death in 1966): *The Jungle Book* (last animated feature over which Walt Disney presided), *The Happiest Millionaire* (live action)

The Animators

NOTE. I should point out that the list below is necessarily incomplete and inevitably omits the names of some important animators who did valuable work for Walt Disney. Some Disney archivists feel these omissions are likely to cause ruffled feelings among some of the veteran animators who are unmentioned and feel I should list all or none. Since neither is practicable, all I can do is extend my apologies to those who have been overlooked and stress that I have taken expert advice on those names I have included. Here again, I have run into difficulties. Except in some obvious cases, I have found that opinions differ, even among the experts, over the achievements for which the animators I have named should be particularly saluted. As I mention below, since each animated film was always a joint effort, there is considerable confusion even among the animators themselves over who invented specific characters or was responsible for certain remarkable sequences. It is for this reason that I have had to adopt a general consensus and cite those characters and sequences for which the animators specified are likely to be best remembered.

Even though it is difficult to specify the individual artists on Walt Disney's staff responsible for the characters in his most famous animated films, several of them deserve credit for immortalizing many of the most memorable creations. Which artist invented which character is not so certain, for many were thought up (Jiminy Cricket, for instance) at studio conferences, and though Ward Kimball first drew Jiminy, many of the staff shared in developing him—along with Walt Disney himself, of course. For it should be emphasized that he not only catalyzed the ideas of his staff but sat in on the shaping of every character that appeared in his cartoons.

But, as Frank Thomas and Ollie Johnston remark in their authoritative book, *Disney Animation*:

> Everyone who has worked on a picture will feel that he made the personal contribution that caused the cartoon character to come alive on the screen. The storyman will naturally feel that the character was *his*, because, after all, it was the story work that determined what kind of an individual this figure would be, and the story sketch man will smile because he drew the new character, made the expressions, showed how he would look . . . And the animator nods knowingly, because no one can deny that he set the final model and brought him to life. . . . To all of them he is their character.

It is certain that Walt Disney, for instance, conceived and produced Mickey Mouse, gave him his voice and developed him, but Ub Iwerks drew him first and animated many of the early cartoons, and Mickey's shape, mobility, even character, were taken in hand by many other animators, particularly Fred Moore. Moore considerably altered Mickey's appearance over the years and was the first to give Mickey "eye movement," which made such a difference to the impression he created on the screen. As the earlier part of this book recounts, that brilliant animator. Norm Ferguson insisted he had "invented" Pluto, the lovable but gormless hound, but it has been pointed out that if Walt Disney had not acted him out for Ferguson's and other animators' benefit, mimicked his character and foibles, demonstrated his habits and facial and bodily movements, Pluto could easily have turned out to be too dull a dog to put on the screen. So if Ferguson maintained he was the mother of Pluto, then Walt Disney could plausibly claim fatherhood. (As, indeed, he did; it was Walt's insistence on *sole* parenthood of *all* the famous cartoon characters that particularly disgruntled Ferguson and other Disney animators.)

So all I can do here is append a list of some of Walt Disney's most brilliant and effective artist/animators and indicate in brackets alongside their names what characters, effects or cartoons they played a significant role in making memorable. Though none of them can justifiedly be given sole credit for any particular character, included are those who have surely won a place for their names on the Disney Roll of Honor for particular contributions:

Ed Aardal (Volcanic effects in "Rite of Spring" segment of *Fantasia*)
James N. Algar (Deer in *Snow White*)
Ken Anderson *(Snow White, 101 Dalmatians)*
Art Babbitt ("Nutcracker Suite" segment of *Fantasia*, development of
    Goofy, work on Dopey in *Snow White*)
Mary Blair *(Alice in Wonderland, Three Caballeros, Song of the South)*
*Les Clark (Minnie Mouse, Sugar Plum Fairies in *Fantasia*, dance
    sequences in *Snow White*, animation of Mickey Mouse in "Sor-
    cerer's Apprentice" segment of *Fantasia*)
Claude Coats *(Cinderella)*
Jim Coleman *(The Fox and the Hound)*
Don DaGradi (Tinker Bell in *Peter Pan*)
*Marc F. Davis *(Bambi, Sleeping Beauty*, Cruella in *101 Dalmatians*,
    eagle and octopus scene in *Victory Through Air Power)*
Al Dempster *(The Jungle Book)*
Norm Ferguson (Pluto, Wicked Witch in *Snow White*, animator on
    Dumbo, Pinocchio, Frolicking Fish, Fantasia)
Hugh Fraser *(Mr. Toad)*
Bernard Garbutt *(Bambi)*
Vance Gerry (Sir Hiss in *Robin Hood, The Sword in the Stone)*
Hardie Gramatky (Tugboat sketches and story of *Little Toot)*
Don Griffith *(The Fox and the Hound*, castle scene in *Robin Hood)*
T. Hee *(Victory Through Air Power)*
John Hench *(Cinderella)*
Hugh Hennesy (Lay-out artist on *Snow White)*

Dick Huemer *(Lullaby Land)*
Ralph Hulett *(The Rescuers)*
Albert Hurter ("Dance of the Hours" segment of *Fantasia*, Huntsman sequences in *Snow White*, preliminary sketches of Dwarfs in *Snow White*)
Ub Iwerks (Mickey Mouse animation in *Steamboat Willie*)
Wilfred Jackson *(Song of the South)*
*Ollie Johnston (Work on *Bambi*, Mr. Smee in *Peter Pan*, Dopey in *Snow White*, Mowgli in *The Jungle Book, 101 Dalmatians, Robin Hood*)
*Milton Kahl (Work on *101 Dalmatians, Pinocchio, Robin Hood*, Medusa in *The Rescuers*)
Glen Keane *(The Fox and the Hound)*
Richmond Kelsey *(Trees)*
*Ward Kimball *(The Three Caballeros*, Captain Hook in *Peter Pan*, wins Oscar with original cartoon *Toot, Whistle, Plunk and Boom*, Lucifer the Cat in *Cinderella*, Tweedledum and Tweedledee and Mad Hatter's Tea Party in *Alice in Wonderland*, circus train in *Dumbo*, animation of *It's Tough to Be a Bird, Victory Through Air Power, Man and the Moon*, Dwarfs and other characters in *Snow White)*
*Eric Larson (Figaro in *Pinocchio, Melody Time*, flying horses in Beethoven 6th Symphony in *Fantasia*)
Rico Lebrun *(Bambi)*
J. Gordon Legg (Toccata and Fugue segment of *Fantasia*)
*John Lounsbery (The alligator, Ben Ali, in the "Dance of the Hours" segment of *Fantasia, Bambi, Victory Through Air Power*)
Dick Lundy (Early development of Donald Duck)
Don Lusk (The stag in *Bambi*)
Ham Luske (Animator of *The Tortoise and the Hare*, several characters in *Snow White*)
Josh Meador (Bottle scene in *Alice in Wonderland*)
Fred Moore (Development of Mickey Mouse, character creations and drawings in *Pinocchio, Bambi*, Dwarfs in *Snow White*)
Kay Nielsen ("Night on Bald Mountain" segment of *Fantasia*)
Ken O'Brien *(Bambi)*
William Peet (Mowgli, Bagheera, and the tiger, Shere Khan, in *The Jungle Book, The Sword in the Stone*)
Martin Provensen (Drawings for "Peter and the Wolf" segment of *Fantasia II*)
*Wolfgang (Woolie) Reitherman (Goofy, *Cinderella*, "Rite of Spring" segment of *Fantasia, The Rescuers, Aristocats*)
Art Riley *(Bambi)*
Joe Rinaldi (Ichabod Crane in *Ichabod and Mr. Toad*)

Bill Roberts *(Alpine Climbers)*
Retta Scott *(Bambi)*
John Sewell *(Bambi)*
Mel Shaw *(The Rescuers)*
John Sibley *(Ichagod and Mr. Toad)*
Gustaf Tenggren (Sketches and layouts for *Pinocchio*)
*Frank Thomas *(Bambi, Sword in the Stone)*
Vladimir (Bill) Tytla (Doc, Dopey, Dumbo, Grumpy in *Snow White*, Stromboli in *Pinocchio*, Devil in "Night on Bald Mountain" segment of *Fantasia*, chief animator of *Snow White*)

---

*Veteran studio animators dubbed "The Nine Old Men" by Walt Disney.

Index